Cooperating Rivals

SUNY Series in Global Politics

James N. Rosenau, editor

Cooperating Rivals

The Riparian Politics of the Jordan River Basin

Jeffrey K. Sosland

State University of New York Press

Published by
State University of New York Press, Albany

For information, contact State University of New York Press,
www.sunypress.edu

Production by Michael Haggett
Marketing by Michael Campochiaro

Library of Congress Cataloging-in-Publication Data

Sosland, Jeffrey K.
    Cooperating Rivals : The riparian politics of the Jordan River Basin / Jeffrey K. Sosland.
        p. cm.
    Includes bibliographical references and index.
    ISBN 978-0-7914-7201-1 (hardcover : alk. paper)
    ISBN 978-0-7914-7202-6 (paperback : alk. paper)
1. Water resources development—Jordan River Valley—International cooperation.   2. Water
resources development—Jordan River Valley—History—20th century.   3. Water resources
development—Political aspects—Israel.   4. Water resources development—Political aspects—
Jordan.   5. Water-supply—Political aspects—Israel.   6. Water-supply—Political aspects—Jordan.   7. Israel—Foreigh relations—Jordan.   8. Jordan—Foreign relations—Israel.   I. Title.

HD1698.J58S67   2007
333.910095496—dc22

2006036594

10 9 8 7 6 5 4 3 2 1

For my parents, Neil and Blanche Sosland,

with love and gratitude

Contents

List of Maps, Tables, and Figures

MAPS

TABLES

FIGURES

Preface

The title of this work, *Cooperating Rivals*, has a double meaning. First, rivals as generally understood are competitors who pursue the same object. Second, the word "rival" is derived from the Latin, *rivalis*, one utilizing the same river as another. The title thus reflects the focus of this work: riparian cooperation and conflict in a competitive setting. The book's cover picture is of Israeli Prime Minister Yitzhak Rabin and King Hussein of Jordan having a discussion on the Lake Tiberias shore. The heart of this book is the Jordan-Israel cooperating rival relationship.

I owe a debt of gratitude to Robert Lieber, Miriam Lowi, Aaron Wolf, Adam Garfinkle, Danny Unger, Richard Matthew, and Robert Satloff for providing valuable comments on earlier drafts of this work. Each disagrees with some of what I argue here but all are scholars from whom I have learned much. At different points in the process, others have also aided me—including Ahron Klieman, Eran Feitelson, David Eaton, and Dalia Dassa Kaye. Many individuals gave generously of their time to be interviewed for this book. In particular, I would like to thank Eli Rosenthal, Munther Haddadin, Yacov Vardi, Noah Kinarti, Fred Hof, Thomas Pickering, and Abdul al-Rahman Tamini. In addition, I owe a great deal to many individuals who contributed to the production of the final product: Amy Elfenbaum for her work on the book cover; Josh Sosland, Suzanne Young, and Neil Sosland for editing; Michael Rinella and Laurie Searl for shepherding the manuscript through the various stages of the publication process, Judy Nielsen for the production of the maps; and Janet Kim, Robert Kaminski, and Nadia Awad for research assistance.

Also deserving much gratitude are the staffs of the various archives and libraries in which I worked: the Truman and Eisenhower Presidential libraries, the national archives of the United States and Israel; and the *Jerusalem Post* and *Jordan Times* archives. I also thank the Royal Jordanian Institute, the Truman, Davis, Dayan, and Jaffee centers; and Utah State University Special Collections Department (the Criddle papers). At different points in my research and writing I received funding from Georgetown

University, Hebrew University, University of Missouri-Columbia, and American University for which I am grateful.

While the book is dedicated to my parents, Blanche and Neil Sosland, I would like to recognize, with deepest love, my wife Mindy and our three children, Zachary, Kate, and Henry. This work also honors the memory of Yonaton Barnea.

1

Introduction

In 1979, a group of Israeli water experts secretly crossed the Yarmouk River to enemy territory in Jordan. Their Jordanian counterparts greeted them, and discussions ensued concerning the difficult issue of sharing scarce water resources. These talks and subsequent cooperation continued for a surprisingly long time—the next fifteen years before Jordan and Israel signed a formal peace treaty in 1994. Publicly, during the same period, Jordan rejected all ties with Israel since, according to Amman, that country had failed to address the Palestinian and other issues of its peacemaking concerns. How did these extraordinary arrangements take place and succeed, while other cooperative efforts failed? The water-sharing arrangement that resulted was successful, I would argue, because both riparians were willing to link the mixed preferences of water cooperation with improving secret diplomatic relations. This cooperation came about because the two had water-scarcity related institutions and experts, defined rules for sharing, faced common threats, and finally were both allies of the same superpower, the United States, that promoted this cooperative regime. The difficulties of such cooperation between parties in a protracted conflict and the complexities of sharing scarce water resources are the focus of this book. Overall, the central question is: during a protracted conflict, what is the value of rivals cooperating on functional issues such as water scarcity and what role, if any, should third parties play in facilitating such cooperation?

The United States strongly embraces a policy of facilitating water cooperation among rivals. In 2001, Secretary of State Colin Powell announced an action plan on transboundary water. In part following the lessons learned from the past fifty years, this policy seeks to improve water management, decrease political and economic tension associated with shared water resources, and, as

1

a high-ranking State Department official characterized it, "use water where appropriate as a diplomatic tool to build trust and promote cooperation."[1] While not always pleased with this policy, in the end, Jordanians, such as Water Minister Hazem al-Nasser, concluded in 2004 that "from our experience, water is an element of peace-building and cooperation."[2] This book focuses on the Jordan-Israel case of the past half-century and attempts to analyze how the lessons learned from that experience apply to the other riparians of the Arab-Israeli conflict: the Palestinians, Syria, and Lebanon.

In most cases, states follow international law, such as established norms and water-sharing treaties. However, this book is interested in international cases in which prolonged conflicts have made scarce water resources a key issue and a source of political tension that established norms cannot solve. There are many such examples—the Arab-Israeli conflict, the Indian-Pakistani dispute, and the Syrian-Turkish conflict, to name only a few—that have all, at some point, involved serious disagreements over sharing common water resources.[3] Allocating scarce water may be particularly problematic in arid or semiarid regions. Additionally, when riparians are engaged in an extended cold war, strained political and military relations make cooperation more difficult and outright conflict more probable. Under such conditions, my study suggests, creative statecraft still can be used to facilitate coordination.[4]

Can cooperation on an important functional issue such as water really benefit peacemaking of states in a protracted conflict? This basic question lies at the heart of a host of policy issues. Some argue that third parties such as the United States should concentrate on resolving the protracted conflict while leaving the functional issues for a later resolution. In this view, foreign aid and diplomatic efforts to promote water sharing would be a waste of time until the larger political conflict is resolved. Such an all-or-nothing approach, however, ignores several realities. Political leaders may be under pressure not to be seen as collaborating with the enemy, but they also want to avoid being dragged into an unintended war, making them more open to lower-profile opportunities for cooperation. Moreover, even in times of political conflict, leaders are under pressure to provide daily necessities, such as water, for their citizens. Thus, even when the political environment is not ripe for peace between countries in a protracted conflict, there may still be room for valuable functional cooperation. In a "no peace, no war" situation, interdependent and geographically adjacent states often have common functional interests that exert pressure toward cooperation. The challenge for third party policymakers has been to use this pressure as a tool to encourage cooperation on functional issues such as water resources, while guiding the feuding states toward a larger political settlement.

What place do domestic institutions, economic systems, and political parties have in determining whether a state will move toward cooperation or opt to fight over such scarce resources? In formulating a policy to address water scarcity in the Arab-Israeli arena, some negotiators ignore such local institutions in favor of the international dynamics at play. They first focus on the configuration of military capabilities. So, for example, they might posit that Jordan would not start a violent conflict over water because it would not perceive such a conflict as winnable. On the other hand, diplomats might focus on the configuration of information and institutions and aggressively seek an international agreement, reasoning that similar expectations on water scarcity should help to stabilize political, economic, and military relations. If negotiators feel, though, that the underlying problem is not structural in nature, they first need to understand domestic state preferences or goals, independent of any particular international negotiation. Following this viewpoint, policymakers would, before all else, promote domestic institutions, such as a pool of trained water experts, an independent media, and a free-market economic sector, which could lead states to prefer cooperation and provide states with the capacity to properly address problems of scarcity. Such institutions would help create a stable, ongoing network of practices and professionals that would make cooperation on water resource issues more likely, no matter what the political environment.

In the past decade, scholars and politicians have shown growing interest in the relationship between scarce renewable natural resources and the outbreak of acute conflict and have tried to understand what leadership role the United States or other third parties can play. As part of this new direction in research, this book lies at the confluence of three significant research areas: international security, environmental studies, and American foreign policy. My work uses the tools of international relations—in particular liberalism—to examine an environmental issue, water scarcity. This work will explain why cooperation results in some cases and conflict in others. My detailed examination of the Jordan River basin from 1920 to 2006 uses a case study method. By testing generalizable arguments against particular case studies, I offer a critical framework for understanding how conflict may be mitigated in regions of tension and in developing states around the globe.

This book's thesis is that in protracted conflict in arid or semiarid regions, there is great value to third party efforts that facilitate water cooperation and mitigate violent conflict related to water scarcity. In addition to improved water management and a resulting increased supply for participants, fostering water cooperation produces a limited political benefit by creating rules, building confidence, and reducing tensions among adversaries. While these benefits alone may not resolve the entire conflict, this process does have a positive long-term peacemaking value. In other words, this sort of water cooperation paves the bumpy road to peace.

In exploring how to facilitate cooperation, this work builds on the liberal international relations claim that the configuration of states' preferences matters most in understanding the international politics of resource scarcity. Political scientist Andrew Moravcsik contends that liberal theory explains "what states want and what they do," in contrast to realists such as Hans Morgenthau who argue that "power" shapes a state's "interests."[5] Unlike realists who argue that the relative power of states is paramount or international (regime) institutionalists who maintain that the configuration of information and institutions impacts world politics the most, I, along with other liberals, argue that national preference comes first, followed by interstate bargaining.[6] During the bargaining phase, however, realism and institutionalism, in addition to liberalism, provide understanding for the strategy states use to realize their preferences. This liberal approach has been used to understand cooperation in economically and politically stable regions such as Western Europe and North America, but liberalism has not been used for explaining conflictual cases such as water scarcity in the Arab-Israel conflict. In contrast to the realist and institutionalist approaches, a liberalist approach respects the internal preferences of these supposedly "conflict-ridden" and intractable states. It seeks to understand them from the inside and recognize the variability and specificity of their motivations for acting. The implication, then, is that "low politics"—building expertise and domestic institutions—may influence security concerns or "high politics."

This work looks closely at the precipitating factors in a violent conflict, especially the question of whether increasing the water supply is a likely motivation for a political leader to use force. The lack of sufficient quantities of water has led to the perception among some scholars that water is a potential source of conflict in the Middle East. It has been argued, though most serious analysts are dubious, that the next regional war will be over water rather than oil.[7] In fact, the notion of Middle East water wars, past or future, is faulty. In the last 4,500 years, water scarcity has never precipitated a war.[8] And it is doubtful that this single issue alone will cause war. However, this work makes the case that water scarcity can be a precipitating or intermediate source of political tension and even violent conflict. When a state has a general preference toward violent conflict or even war, as Syria did in the mid-1960s, that preference may be strategically linked to the water scarcity issue in an ideological and nationalistic manner to create international discord. Ultimately, a lack of rules for sharing water leads to misperception, misinformation, and sometimes even violent conflict.

Finally, this work argues, as liberals do, that water cooperation between adversaries in a protracted conflict increases when facilitators pursue an international strategy that clearly defines rules and links mixed issues such as foreign aid and water cooperation. However, for issue linkage to be successful, adversaries need to be on the same side of what may be termed the balancing equation. In other words, this work also argues, as realists do, that states are more apt to have a cooperative strategy on functional issues if they have already improved their relationship by working together to balance a common security threat, or have a common security patron. However, unlike realists and liberals, this work argues that a tactical functional arrangement that facilitates reciprocity and communication will help to maintain coordination.

In the following discussion of water scarcity and international relations literature on cooperation, this work develops a general explanation for state behavior relating to water scarcity. My approach is tested in the case study and the argument's strengths and limitations are discussed in the conclusion. This chapter first discusses the arguments on water scarcity stimulating political and military conflict. The second and third sections explain why and how water scarcity cooperation occurs and defines key concepts, such as preferences, tactical functional cooperation, and hegemonic stability theory. Readers with only minimal interest in international relations theory as it contributes to understanding water scarcity and the Jordan River basin case should proceed to the final section. Methodology, the structure of the book, and my selection of the Jordan River case are discussed in the last section.

WHAT IS A WATER WAR?

This study differentiates between water wars, water-related acute conflict, and tactical attacks on water facilities.[9] Unlike the other two categories of water conflict, tactical attacks on water facilities occur during wars and are a result of military, not political objectives. For example, during World War II, all sides targeted dams, water purification plants, and water-conveyance systems because they had a tactical military value in the war, not because the warring states had a water dispute.[10] In a water war, by definition, mass organized violence is the method for resolving water conflicts among states, and it results in over one thousand civilian and combatant deaths.[11] To date, water wars are a myth. It is true, as geographer Aaron Wolf notes, that in the last 4,500 years, "there has never been a single war fought over water."[12] However, water scarcity certainly has been one of many issues that led to violence, not as a deep, but as an intermediate or precipitating factor. It is important to differentiate precipitating, intermediate, and deep, the three types of stimuli in terms of their proximity in time to the onset of war or acute violence. Those stimuli that occur immediately before the violence are precipitating causes. And the precipitating causes are not always the most important. In many cases, it is the deep or intermediate stimuli that play the most critical role in explaining the onset of violence. Political scientist Joseph Nye gives a couple of useful analogies: "Ask how lights come to be on in your room. The precipitating cause is that you flicked the switch, the intermediate cause is that someone wired the building and the deep cause is that Thomas Edison discovered how to deliver

electricity. Another analogy is building a fire: The logs are the deep cause, the
kindling and paper the intermediate cause, and the actual striking of the match
is the precipitating cause."[13] As discussed in chapters 2 and 3, an acute conflict, unlike war, has limited scope and size but still involves violence.[14]
Although water was a primary reason for the conflict, it was not the only cause
of the fighting, and, unlike a war, the violence was limited.[15] These conflicts
may be a contributing factor to a larger conflict, as illustrated by the events
leading to the 1967 Arab-Israeli War.[16] This book deals primarily with the
political tension that conceivably leads to acute conflict between Israel and
Syria. The challenge is to understand how and why water scarcity leads to
political tension and then how those pressures result in acute conflict.

PREFERENCES

This book utilizes liberal international relations theory, which focuses on the
impact of preferences to better understand water scarcity and violent conflict.
This work challenges the neorealist and neoliberal institutionalist assumption
that the international level of analysis is more important to understanding
world politics than the domestic or second level of analysis. Andrew Moravcsik argues that this liberal "theory elaborates the basic insights that state–
society relations—the relationship between governments and the domestic and
transnational social context in which they are embedded—are the most fundamental determinant of state behavior in world politics."[17] In this view, states
first formulate a "national preference" that is influenced by the state–society
relations and is defined as "a set of underlying national objectives independent
of any particular international negotiation."[18] Next, states pursue strategies to
realize their national preference. To determine state preferences, we must first
examine the sum of individuals in a civil society. There we find different opinions, social commitments, and capabilities. Individuals define their interests
first and then advance those interests through politics and collective action,
such as political parties.[19] Once shaped, state preferences become the basis for
rational, value-maximizing calculations of government leadership in domestic
and international affairs.

These preferences are complex and should not be seen, as neorealist and
institutionalist tend to do, as a fixed, homogeneous conception of security,
autonomy, or welfare. States pursue particular interpretations and combina-
tions of these interests that are preferred by powerful domestic groups or individuals.[20] As a number of liberal thinkers have pointed out, the nature and
intensity of national support for any policy vary decisively with social context.
According to Moravcsik, "it is not uncommon for states knowingly to surren-
der sovereignty, compromise security, or reduce aggregate economic welfare. In

the liberal view, trade-offs among such goals as well as cross-national differences in their definition, are inevitable, highly varied, and causally consequential."[21] Unlike what neorealists argue, a state's relative power to other states does not always determine outcomes where powerful preferences enter into the equation. Vietnam-US and Afghanistan-USSR quagmires are examples of when a strong preference for the issue at stake made up for a country's being less powerful. In fact, between 1950 and 1998 the weak actor or state defeated the strong actor or state more than half the time.[22] In many of these cases, the intensity of state preferences of the weaker side had the greatest impact on the outcome.[23] Alexander George calls this an "asymmetry of motivations" where strong states may be punished if they ignore the "balance of interests" that weaker states sometimes enjoy in disputes with more powerful states. Also, George points out that neorealism fails to differentiate a state's gross capabilities and its usable options.[24] For example, the United States had nuclear weapons during its Vietnam conflict, but use of such a weapon was unacceptable, domestically and internationally.

TACTICAL FUNCTIONAL COOPERATION

Once a state establishes a national preference, a strategy for realizing that preference must follow. Scholars have offered different explanations for how preferences lead states to pursue international cooperation or conflict. Some analysts within the school of functionalism argue that the water issue offers a means for ending the Arab-Israeli protracted conflict. According to Aaron Wolf's functionalist argument, cooperation on purely water issues can spill over into the political realm and lead to increased cooperation in other issue areas. Going a step further, Wolf calls for the interested parties to focus on promoting water cooperation, which may eventually bring a broader settlement of political problems.[25]

How can functionalism help us understand the Arab-Israeli conflict? Wolf argues that Israel, by cooperating on the water issue, would gain politically and hydrologically, albeit slowly and in stages. The benefits derived from negotiating the water issue and from the developing interdependence would encourage the Jordan River basin riparians to continue cooperative efforts and move further from protracted conflict. Wolf supports the view that functional water-related cooperation will not only reduce Israel's water problems, but also move the Middle East peace process forward.[26]

Critics of this view, however, claim that functionalism assumes that ideology and the external world would have little impact on cooperation, when in fact both do.[27] Water relations in the Jordan River basin, as Miriam Lowi argues, have certainly been tied historically to the larger political conflict. As a classical realist, Lowi asserts the primacy of politics over economics, maintaining that "the *sine qua non* of resolving a transboundary water dispute in a protracted conflict setting is the prior resolution of the political conflict." Lowi argues that "states involved in 'high politics' conflicts that provoke wars and engage the visceral issues of territorial sovereignty and the recognition of identities, are not inclined to collaborate in seemingly technical matters that concern economic development and human welfare."[28] Even limited cooperation between Jordan and Israel over a period of many years, Lowi asserts,[29] has had "no implications for the end of the political conflict. . . . These highly delimited, highly specific arrangements have no conflict resolution potential."[30]

Lowi's argument is correct, yet it lacks critical nuance.[31] In fact, states in a protracted conflict that are interdependent on an important functional issue, such as shared water resources, may cooperate tactically. If we revise expectations, we can see that, in cooperating, the immediate objective need not be conflict resolution, as argued by the functionalist approach, but conflict management. The principal motive is to prevent the water issue from provoking an unintended war, and to address the mutual preferences of better water management. In addition to the conflict management benefits of tactical functional cooperation (TFC) over time, such a coordination process builds confidence and trust between adversaries—a critical ingredient for moving toward a resolution of the conflict, at least over a specific pivotal and controversial issue.[32] In other words, if TFC can effectively address the dispute over the water issue, peace will be that much less difficult to realize. Constructivists such as Dalia Dassa Kaye point out, the process matters. A nonmaterial benefit of TFC is that it creates "a process of working together in an effort to achieve common understanding."[33] This notion of cooperation highlights an important value of TFC. Over time, the process of two parties in a protracted conflict meeting and discussing a divisive issue may lead to a change in a state's preferences. A new idea—positive personal relationship among technocrats and elites—and a new sense of trust and confidence may move parties toward a common understanding of a problem and its solution.

Tactical functional cooperation, like informal or formal international institutions, is a set of rules between states that "prescribes roles, constrains activities, and shapes expectations."[34] It also provides critical information, reduces transaction costs, establishes focal points for coordination, and facilitates reciprocity.[35] Tactical functional cooperation is of critical importance to states trying to overcome the difficulties of cooperating in an international environment but lacking the means to enforce agreements. According to the neoliberal institutionalist literature, cheating or noncompliance is the greatest obstacle to cooperation.[36] Tactical functional cooperation, like international institutions, helps to provide states with the necessary information to generate confidence that they are not being cheated. This type of arrangement may reduce transaction costs by providing rules, a sense of continuity, a standard operating procedure, and means to resolve conflicts peacefully. Thus, the time and resources that otherwise would be expended to realize state objectives decreases and expectations become better defined. These by-products are important when political leaders assess whether cooperation is worthwhile. By decreasing the expense of cooperation, TFC increases the probability of its success. In addition, such efforts permit experts in the given area to interact, exchange ideas, and solve difficult issue-specific problems.[37] By the time the overall political problems are resolved, many water-related issues have already been discussed and investigated, allowing difficult negotiations to become faster moving and less competitive because of familiarity with the personalities involved and mutual problems.

Tactical functional cooperation also facilitates the operation of reciprocity by activating a participant's self-interest in not wanting to be exploited and providing the incentive or interest to cooperate. In general, for cooperation to occur, state power does not have to be equal between participants, nor must reciprocal obligations be identical, as in the case of the cold war patron–client relationships. Political leaders determine which values are equivalent. Yet exchange cannot be one-sided; there must be an approximate balance. The exchange should be characterized by the standard "good is returned for good, and bad for bad."[38] The result over the long term is increased trust and fairness between participating states as reciprocity becomes more diffuse.[39]

The means of successful tactical functional cooperation during a protracted conflict depends on diplomacy or statecraft that takes into consideration the involved parties' preferences. Because a formal state of hostilities exists, some political leaders would be unable to rationalize to the public and to allies why they are cooperating with the enemy. However, if only state elites are aware of the cooperation and important policy objectives are achieved, tactical functional cooperation becomes more inviting and more likely to succeed. Secrecy or a low-profile process insulates involved technocrats and elites from public pressure and scrutiny, which makes TFC during protracted conflict possible. However, a major drawback is that secrecy removes the public from experiencing the benefits of TFC, so while Jordanian and Israeli elites and technocrats had fifteen years of a process that built trust and confidence, the public gained no new understanding and, especially for the Jordanians, found the post-1994 peace treaty environment difficult to accept, even with elites defending the new reality. If a secret TFC is exposed, the arrangement could suggest deception to the public and to allies. It could also weaken a government that is more apt to prefer avoiding conflict or a challenge to the overall status quo. By its nature, secret TFC is based on an informal agreement, as opposed to a ratified treaty. A result is that informal TFC rules are, at least at the start of the process, ill defined and apt to lead to disagreement, cheating, and the possibility of violent conflict, as occurred between Israel and Jordan in the 1980s. Once the rules are established and accepted by both sides, conflict over that issue is less likely.

In sum, tactical functional cooperation is an effective means of maintaining cooperation between states in a protracted conflict; it also has long-term conflict resolution value. Given that tactical functional cooperation is an important means for facilitating cooperation, we need to understand how states with a cooperation preference begin TFC and what else is needed to maintain it. International cooperation literature may help to better understand the answers to these questions.

STRATEGY AND INTERNATIONAL BARGAINING

This section investigates what factors shape a state's bargaining strategy to initiate cooperation and what conditions states use to maintain cooperation.[40] In an effort to better explain what strategies states use to initiate cooperation, this work draws on neorealist and neoliberal institutionalist theories. It uses both the neorealist approach that weaker states will form a coalition against a common threat with the neoliberal insight that issue linkage is a powerful motivator for maintaining cooperation. A more complex view that draws from both theoretical points of view may explain how states bargain to initiate cooperation in a protracted conflict.

Hegemonic stability theory, a well-known power-based approach to international cooperation, asserts that cooperation may be facilitated when a single dominant state is willing and able to provide and maintain it.[41] In the water-scarcity literature, Lowi posits as a "malign" variant of hegemonic stability theory that relations among international river riparians depend on which state is strong and located upstream and which riparian is weak and situated downstream. Cooperation is thus best understood and explained primarily by examining the relative power, geographic location, and the "dependency on the basin water" of the participants.[42] The strongest can impose and force the others to alter their policies. The river hegemon may serve as the functional equivalent of a common power or central authority in international politics. However, in some cases a hegemon may not choose to cooperate or perhaps even to participate. Neoliberal institutionalists argue that even here cooperation is still possible—establishing international institutions or regimes, which set the rules, and establishing common expectations by providing information are the best means to cooperation. However, even with the benefits that come with cooperation, some states favor not to cooperate due to national preferences.[43]

Power alone is not the only force at work in the relations between states, as we can see when states form alliances to coordinate security. Stephen Walt argues that states form alliances because they seek to balance against potential threats rather than against power alone. "Although the distribution of power is an extremely important factor, the level of threat is also affected by geographic proximity, offensive capabilities, and perceived intentions."[44] States that balance threats together often have a common patron. The superpower or third party is an important factor in bringing together states that are in the midst of a protracted conflict. The patron serves as a mediator and has credibility because it has or will give assistance to both and is directly concerned with the security of both cooperating states. For instance, in 1970, Israel mobilized its military to deter the Syrian army from invading Jordan during the civil war between King Hussein and the Palestine Liberation Organization (PLO). By doing so, Israel demonstrated its willingness to risk war with Syria to protect its vital interests—preservation of the Hashemite monarchy and opposition to the establishment of a Palestinian state on either bank of the Jordan River. Since 1970, Israel and Jordan have continued to ally, albeit secretly or tacitly, against common threats and for mutual interests. This alliance has been facilitated by both states' close relationship with the United States. As a result of the security relationship, Jordan and Israel were more confident with nonmilitary cooperation.[45] Thus, states may utilize the improved relations from security coordination in order to cooperate more easily on nonsecurity issues. But on which issues will states cooperate?

Neoliberal theory argues that self-interest often motivates cooperation. One such interest-based strategy is issue linkage, a state's policy of making its course of action concerning a given issue contingent on another state's behavior in a different issue area.[46] This translates as giving something on one issue in return for help on another. Under conditions of interdependence, linking or adding issues may increase the likelihood of cooperation. Examples include positive linkage such as side payments in exchange for cooperation or negative linkage such as threats and sanctions for noncompliance. On any single issue, two states may be directly opposed; but on more than one they are most likely to rank preferences differently, which may make possible exchanges across issues. By linking issues, states may accommodate their most basic interests through "conceding on issues of low priority in exchange for reciprocal concessions on more important issues."[47] A state may want to "build up a 'reservoir of good will'" so as to be in a better position in the future when it may seek support or concessions on another issue of greater national interest.[48] Issue linkage does not necessarily require a situation in which states have coincidental or harmonious interests. It may occur, by definition, when states have a conflict of interests but are able to compromise and cooperate nonetheless. A possible constraint on linking issues is the domestic implications for special interest groups. Moravcsik argues that linked concessions often create domestic losers, even though the state perceives a net benefit for itself. If losers have intense preferences and strong political connections, they may be obstacles to cooperation. Losers may be a small fraction of the population, and winners may be a large part of the citizens, but when the benefits are diffuse and those who benefit are unorganized or underrepresented groups—such as taxpayers or utility consumers—then the losers might be able to block the international cooperation.[49] For example, Israel at times limited its cooperation on the water issue because of the criticism of some powerful farmers. The loss of a small quantity of agriculture-sector water was being valued more highly than improved political relations with Jordan, from which all of Israel would benefit.

Tactical functional cooperation initiation is more likely to occur when states in a protracted conflict have already developed a relationship because they are working together to balance a potential threat or when they have a common patron. As a result of improved relations, they are more likely to cooperate on mixed interests that both are willing to link. This work argues that once cooperation is initiated, tactical functional cooperation will be more effective and longer lasting if specific conditions are present. These conditions, drawn from the international relations literature, are: altering the payoff structure, lengthening the shadow of the future, and having a low number of participants. Each has a different impact, but all may help maintain cooperation and all give insight into why TFC may become effective.

Political scientists from various theoretical approaches have utilized game theory to provide insights into why states cooperate in an uncertain international environment.[50] The "cooperation under anarchy" literature argues, first, that mutuality of interests maintains cooperation in an international setting. Mutuality of interests or altering the payoff structure occurs when the gains from cooperation are greater than the benefits for not following the rules—in other words, cheating. An example of this occurs when international financial assistance or political support is only available when the parties follow the rules of the game. Without such incentives, participating states may conclude that cooperation is not in their best interest. In addition, changing the perception of a state's interests with new norms, information, and ideas may also alter a state's understanding of its interests.[51]

Second, lengthening the shadow of the future takes place when the prospect of cooperation improves because states repeat actions designed to spur coordination indefinitely rather than merely a few finite times. Under a competitive and one-time situation, a participant has an overwhelming temptation to cheat. However, if a state knows that the interaction will continue and that others will respond to its cheating with sanctions, it will be less inclined to cheat.[52] This behavior becomes more likely when the states in question are in close geographical proximity and are continually interdependent. For example, Jordan might have been tempted to take more water than it was allotted in a dry year, but it realized that Israel would probably do the same. Jordan recognized that over time it would gain more by cooperating than by cheating for a one-time gain. With both sides understanding the long-term gains, cooperation became more probable. The establishment of a direct connection between a state's present behavior and its anticipated future benefits increases the likelihood of cooperation and decreases the chances that interdependence will lead to conflict.[53]

Third, decreasing the number of participants is a further set of circumstances that favors the continuation of cooperation. The larger the number of states, the harder it becomes for participants to identify and to realize common interests or negotiate agreements.[54] For example, bringing Jordan and Syria or Jordan and Israel together on a water scheme may be possible, but bringing all three states together becomes much more difficult.[55] In fact, Middle East peace negotiations have been much more successful with a bilateral track, such as the Israeli-Egyptian, Israeli-Palestinian, and Israeli-Jordanian agreements, rather than multilateral negotiations, as discussed in chapter 6. Together, these conditions improve the likelihood that states will continue tactical functional cooperation. It must be acknowledged that if a state's preference is conflict, then, as neorealists argue, it will attempt a strategy of building its capabilities through procuring weapons, establishing alliances, and instituting water policies that challenge an opponent, such as building an upstream dam that decreases water to the downstream opponent.[56]

WHY THE JORDAN RIVER BASIN?

As previously noted, this book analyzes the conditions under which states in a protracted conflict cooperate and compete with regards to shared, scarce water resources. Through careful historical analysis, this study focuses on how states behave in such an environment. The variables of state preferences and capabilities are examined to better understand how they lead to cooperation or conflict over water resources. This work takes as its case study the Jordan River basin from 1920 to 2006. Unlike other significant case studies, such as Allison's *Essence of Decision* and Homer-Dixon's *Ecoviolence*, this work does not focus on a single pivotal historical moment, but on a long time horizon. By examining the Jordan River basin over an eighty-five-year period, we also benefit from examining multiple subcases of conflict and cooperation.

This book investigates water scarcity-related conflict and cooperation in the Jordan River basin for several reasons.[57] First, it is a region with an arid to semi-arid climate. In addition, the riparians have been involved in a protracted conflict for over half a century. As a result, the politics of water, which has created a number of subcases for consideration, should reveal more about the factors that determine water-related cooperation and conflict than would an examination of a peaceful region with abundant water. The Jordan River basin is an especially appropriate region within which to assess the issues in question. Second, the Jordan River basin and the Arab-Israeli conflict overall have been and remain an area of considerable political and strategic importance. During the cold war, both superpowers spent much time and resources in the region. And in the post–cold war era, the Arab-Israeli arena is still a central focus of world politics.

Prior to the case study, a brief overview of the riparians' capabilities and preferences will assist in understanding how states behave in relation to the water issue (see Map 1-1). The main hydrological problem in the Jordan River basin is one of rainfall distribution. Precipitation in the region is concentrated in the North—Syria and Lebanon—with the remainder of the region—Israel, Jordan, and the Palestinian Authority controlled areas—dependent on minimal rainfall, the river systems, and underground aquifers for their water supplies. Water is truly scarce in the sense that there is far less available than people would like to consume. For example, water piped to most Gaza Strip homes is not safe to drink and in recent summers in Amman water has been rationed to all consumers.

Prior to June 1967, Syria and Lebanon were upstream Jordan River riparians that had other primary sources of water (i.e., the Litani, Euphrates, and Orontes), while Jordan and Israel were downstream riparians that were dependent on the Jordan. After the 1967 War and its loss of territory, Syria was upstream for only one tributary of the Jordan, the Yarmouk. Throughout this period, Israel has had superior military, political, and economic capabilities. Syria has sought unsuccessfully to gain parity with Israel, while Lebanon and Jordan remain much less powerful states.

Israel is a parliamentary democracy with a Jewish majority. Zionism, a political philosophy promoting the existence of a "Jewish state," has had a significant influence on Israel. Since the early 1950s, that country has been closely aligned with the West. Israel has a relatively small population and geographical size, but has maintained its regional military superiority throughout much of its history. It has continuously sought international recognition and, when it saw this as practical, a peace settlement with its Arab neighbors. Beginning in the early 1950s, Syria experienced successive military coups. By 1963, the Baath party took control of the state and, since 1970, a single ruling family, Hafez al-Asad's, has maintained authoritarian rule. Syria was closely aligned with the Soviet Union. It has been a staunch public supporter of the Palestinian cause, Arab nationalism, and Arab unity. Even so, it has had serious political disagreements at one time or another with all its neighbors (Iraq, Turkey, Israel, Lebanon, and Jordan). Throughout most of its modern history, Syria has rejected cooperation with Israel.

Lebanon has always been militarily weak and ethnically divided. Political stability in the past has depended on dividing the domestic power between

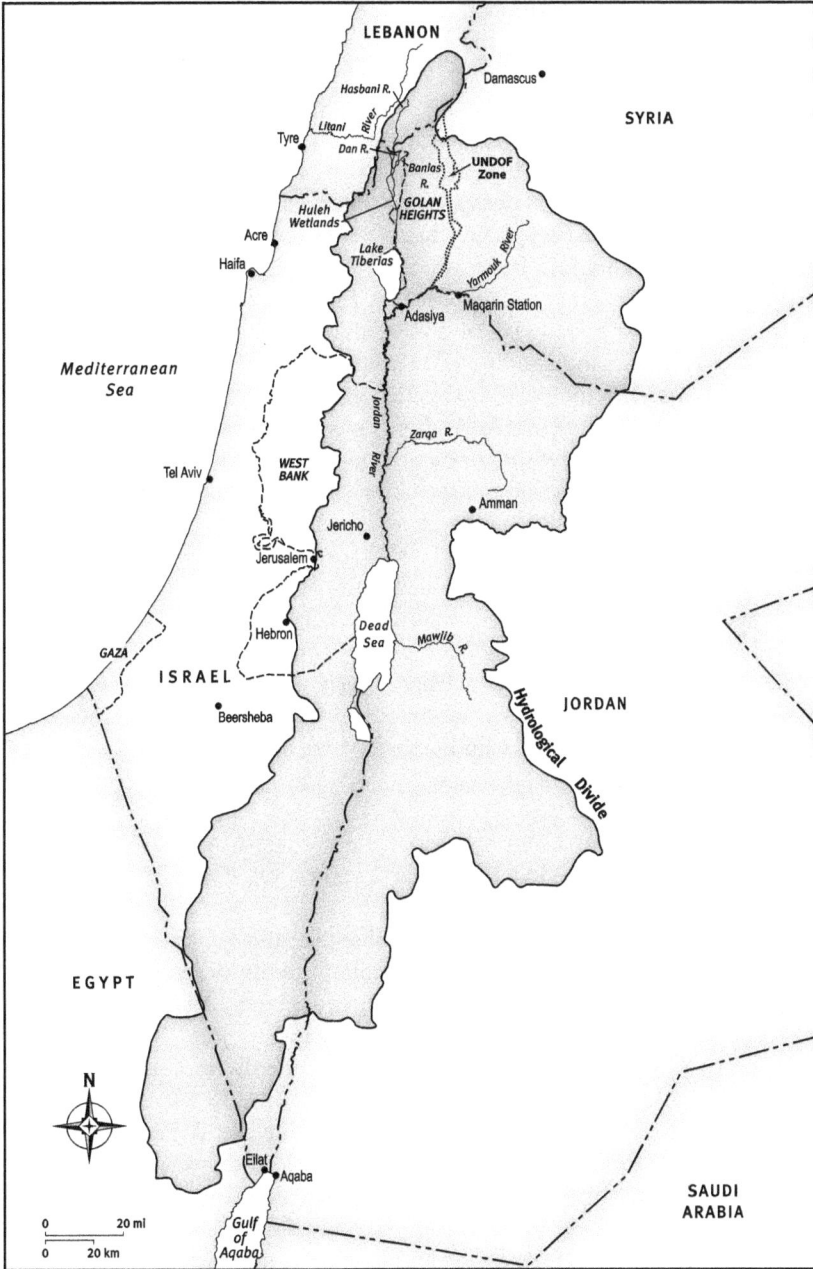

MAP 1-1   Jordan River Watershed, 2004

Muslims and Christians. Throughout the cold war, Lebanon did not ally with the East or the West, and, by the 1970s, civil wars and foreign interventions became an acute problem. It was an active Jordan River riparian prior to June 1967, but not after that date. Jordan's international relations have been influenced by internal challenges—a large Palestinian population—and external threats. Between 1953 and 1999, one man, King Hussein, led the country in a monarchal, sometimes semiconstitutional system. Because of its weakness and vulnerability, Jordan's foreign policy has generally been very cautious. Hussein and his successor, Abdullah II, have had to rely most often on Western support and a policy of appeasing or allying with their neighbors to decrease the threats to their rule. Water scarcity has always been a central problem for Jordan. At present, the Palestinian Authority (PA) is not a recognized Jordan River riparian, but it is an important factor in relation to shared West Bank aquifers with Israel. Politically, the Palestinian Authority's power is still unclear since it has no military, but does have, at times, a large police force. In the past, it has received support from Europe and the United States. Water scarcity is an acute problem especially for the Gaza Strip, which since 2005 is controlled by the Palestinian Authority.

By 1967, Syria was informally allied with the USSR while Israel and Jordan were allied with the United States. The superpowers and their regional clients were united by different but usually compatible goals. The United States and the USSR attempted to balance each other, and their clients sought outside help to counter threats from other regional states.[58] Such alliances are a common occurrence in the Middle East, where unlikely partners join when their interests are threatened.[59]

STRUCTURE OF THE BOOK

This large case study proceeds in five chapters and consists of seventeen smaller subcase analyses with the arguments tested in each (see Table 1-1). Chapters 2 through 4 offer a historical survey of the Jordan and Yarmouk basins' politics relating to the water issue. Chapter 2 discusses the public, multilateral US mediation in the 1950s, which initially succeeded in bringing the Arab (Jordan, Syria, Lebanon, and Egypt) and Israeli sides to agreement on a water-sharing program. However, in the eleventh hour, the parties failed to reach a formal understanding. Even so, the discussed Johnston Plan continued to have an important impact on Jordanian-Israeli tactical functional water cooperation facilitated by the United States over the next forty years, including the 1994 Israel-Jordan treaty negotiations. The plan's strengths and weaknesses along with the limitations of public, multilateral water-related diplomacy in a conflictual environment are assessed here. The

TABLE 1-1
Jordan River Basin Subcases

Cooperation Subcases (Dates)	
Johnston Mission (1953–1955)	Ch. 2
Criddle Mission (1963–1970s)	Ch. 3
Maqarin Dam (1970s)	Ch. 4
Yarmouk Forum Initiation (1979)	Ch. 4
Sandbar Cleaning (1985)	Ch. 4
Bani Hani-Vardi-Rosenthal Regime (1988–1994)	Ch. 4
Unity Dam (Late 1980s)	Ch. 4
West Bank and Gaza (1967–1993)	Ch. 5
West Bank and Gaza (1993–present)	Ch. 6
Jordan-Israel Treaty (1994–present)	Ch. 6
Multilateral Water Working Group (1992–present)	Ch. 6
Unity Dam (Mid 2000s)	Ch. 6
Acute Conflict Subcases (Dates)	
Demilitarized Zone/Hula wetlands (1951)	Ch. 2
Demilitarized Zone/B'not Yacov (1953)	Ch. 2
Upper Jordan Arab Diversion (1965–1966)	Ch. 3
Israeli Bombing of East Ghor Canal (1968–1970)	Ch. 4
Jordan and/or Israel Water-Scarcity-Related Mobilization of Troops on the Yarmouk's Banks (1979, 1986, and 1987)	Ch. 4

plan provides important rules, but the experience highlights to the riparians the limits of public, formal, multilateral water cooperation. It also emphasizes the limits of the United States as a third party facilitator. Chapter 3 traces the readjustment of US policy on water in the region led by the National Security Council and Washington's secret efforts to promote tactical functional cooperation between Israel and Jordan. In other words, the United States was now promoting bilateral, secret cooperation that would follow an informal arrangement. This chapter also examines the events preceding the 1967 Arab-Israeli War and analyzes how water played an intermediate, but not precipitating or long-term role in the advent of war. In other words, the 1967 War was not a water war. By the 1970s, as discussed in chapter 4, the United States, Israel, and Jordan again were attempting to develop a tactical functional cooperative arrangement by linking the water issue to other matters while improving on the already established secret political relationship between the two states. This work examines the failure of the negotiations regarding the Maqarin and Unity dams and the success of the fifteen-year secret Israel-Jordan arrangement on sharing the Yarmouk River water. Also assessed are Israel's bombing of Jordan's canal system in the late 1960s and the water-scarcity-related mobilization of Israeli and Jordanian forces on the banks of Yarmouk, no less than five times between 1979 and

1986. In the end, this chapter explains how the secret water regime developed and why secret, bilateral diplomacy, with the United States as a third party facilitator, was successful.

Chapter 5 looks at the politics of shared West Bank and Gaza water resources between Israel and the Palestinians. In contrast to the other subcases, this example shows no effective potential for reciprocity between Israel and the Palestinians not only because of power asymmetry, but because Israel had physical control over Palestinian areas. This chapter analyzes how the preferences of Israel's two dominant political parties, Labor and Likud, impacted Israel's West Bank and Gaza water policy. It illustrates the important point that, without reciprocity, cooperative efforts are limited. It also debunks the myth that Israel cannot redeploy from the West Bank because of its concern for its water security. Chapter 6 examines the 1990s Madrid Peace Process and the events that followed. By studying the Jordan-Israel treaty, Palestinian-Israeli interim agreement, and the multilateral talks, this work analyzes the past and present value of US-facilitated tactical functional cooperation. It also examines why cooperation has not occurred between Israel and Syria. Chapter 7 summarizes the causes of cooperation and conflict in protracted conflict. The case study provides strong evidence that supports the arguments. Finally, this work proposes policy recommendations that may be culled from this research and used for future international relations regarding water problems.

This study's major finding is that while tactical functional cooperation alone will not end a protracted conflict, it may play an important role in conflict mitigation and confidence-building, both of which have conflict resolution value. As a result, it is worthwhile for policymakers to promote water cooperation initiatives and domestic institution building, even if the states are in a protracted conflict.

2

State-Building and
Water Development, 1920–1956

This chapter examines the formative years (1920–1956) of the Arab-Israeli/Zionist conflict, particularly the water disputes between the players. During this period, the parties developed unilateral and often-competing water development schemes. In response, the United States mediated among Jordan-basin states and negotiated a regional water plan. This well-publicized diplomatic effort came closer to breaking the Arab-Israeli impasse than other initiatives until the 1978 Israel-Egypt Camp David Peace Accords.[1] However, by 1955, the politics of the Arab-Israeli conflict and the cold war combined to halt the US water mission from attaining a formal agreement from all Jordan River riparians.

First to be examined is the importance of water to state-building and why Jordan River riparians perceived water as a vital national preference. The second section analyzes the various water-development programs. These plans were consequential because they established both the basic concepts for state water development and crystallized the contentious water-related issues that would lead to acute conflict between the riparians. Because the United States had vital interests in the region and provided funding for many competing water projects, as detailed in the third section, the United States sent a presidential representative to mediate a unified plan for the development of the Jordan River. Although the mediation failed to lead to a formal agreement between all riparians, it did succeed in producing an important water-development scheme that would continue to influence the water politics of the region for the next half-century. This, in turn, is analyzed in the fourth section.

The final segment explains why water cooperation seemed attainable for the two years of the US mediation but failed in the end to reach an agreement among all riparians and why acute conflict subsequently occurred in two separate instances. Also, as discussed in chapter 1, some scholars have argued that political issues must be addressed first before functional issues, such as water, can be resolved. During this period, there were two major attempts to resolve the political dispute and both failed. The US negotiator was correct that the region was not ripe for a comprehensive peace. He also accurately observed that there was a strong preference to address the Jordan water-scarcity issue. I argue that, in this subcase, the US mediator correctly saw the Arab preference for economic aid, against a political settlement with Israel, and the willingness of elites to cooperate on technical issues as well. However, the US mediator misjudged the Arab public's strong preference to not even tacitly cooperate with Israel. I would argue that, had the United States judged correctly this last preference and used an appropriate strategy such as secretive or low-key diplomacy, limited the number of participants to Israel and Jordan, and concluded the negotiations before 1954, the US mediation for water cooperation might have been a success.

STATE-BUILDING

As the colonial era ended in the Middle East in the first half of the 1900s, newly established states quickly realized that water resources and their development were a critical national preference. Irrigated farming was the means to jumpstart their war-torn, immigrant burdened, struggling economy. Ottoman rule of the Jordan River basin, and the Middle East in general, lasted for more than four hundred years (1516–1918). The Ottoman Empire organized the basin into numerous districts, which were part of larger provinces or administrative units, but they did not adequately develop the Jordan Valley area economically or socially. With the collapse of the empire and its central government in Constantinople, the inhabitants of the Jordan River basin began a long process of nation-state building. At the end of World War I, a compromise was struck between the Wilsonian principle of self-determination and the desire of the colonial powers to control the region and maintain a regional balance of power. The Jordan River area, along with much of the Ottoman Empire, was divided between the colonial powers into new political entities called mandates. The British and French administered these units under supervision of the League of Nations until the inhabitants were ready for independence and self-government. In 1920, the French controlled a mandate incorporating both Syria and Lebanon. Palestine, which included land on both sides of the Jordan River, and Iraq were both under British control. However, in 1921, the British decided to divide the Palestine mandate and create a new entity, Transjordan, on the east bank of the Jordan River. By 1922, the League of Nations had ratified the Middle East mandate arrangement.[2]

Geographically, the Jordan basin is an elongated valley, about 184 kilometers (65 miles) long, that runs from the Golan Heights' Mount Hermon in the north through the Jordan-Israel and Jordan-West Bank border to the Dead Sea in the south. The upper Jordan's three tributaries are the Banias (which rises in Syria), the Hasbani (which originates in Lebanon), and the Dan (which rises in what is now Israel). The Yarmouk rises in Syria and merges with the lower Jordan, below Lake Tiberias (see Map 2-1). Most of the Jordan River's water originates from rain or snow in the northern part of the basin, which is controlled by Syria and Lebanon. The water flows south to what is now Jordan and Israel, the countries most dependent on this water source. Syria and Lebanon, on the other hand, rely on larger water resources—the Euphrates for Syria, the Litani for Lebanon, and the Orontes River, which is utilized by both. Rain falls almost only during the winter in the Jordan basin. Because of the dry summer season, farming—a key economic interest—must depend entirely on irrigation. If there is sufficient water, though, the region can support four harvests a year.

During the mandate period, between 1922 and 1948, nationalism was the primary driving ideology for the establishment of modern states and the motivating force for expelling the colonial powers. During this period, the Zionist movement intensified its efforts to build a Jewish homeland and to ingather Jews from the Diaspora.[3] However, the Arab population of Palestine rejected Zionism, wishing to build their own state. As the administering power, the British found themselves mediating this dispute. The Jewish community in Palestine, or the *yishuv,* aggressively bought land and developed it. As Jewish land purchases and immigration increased in the 1920s, local Arab dissatisfaction boiled over into riots and violent conflicts. To pacify Arab concerns, the British imposed restrictions on Jewish land purchases and immigration as early as 1922. The British also questioned the economic absorptive capacity of Palestine. The availability of land and water for increased Jewish immigration became a focus of debate. To solve the long-term problem, the British investigated partitioning Palestine between Jews and Arabs. This solution to the unrest was continually discussed, but never realized.

During the immediate post–World War I period, the Jewish community pursued an aggressive policy of building institutions and gathering funds to secure its water supply. It established a large, pre-state institutional structure, which included social and economic development organizations such as the Jewish National Fund and the Jewish Agency.[4] In the mid-1920s, the Palestine Electric Corporation, another Zionist-affiliated institution, acquired from the British mandate government a seventy-year concession to develop hydroelectric power using the Jordan and the Yarmouk rivers. The agreement gave the company the right to dam Lake Tiberias and divert its waters by canal to the power station.[5] By 1944, Palestine Electric was producing 173 million

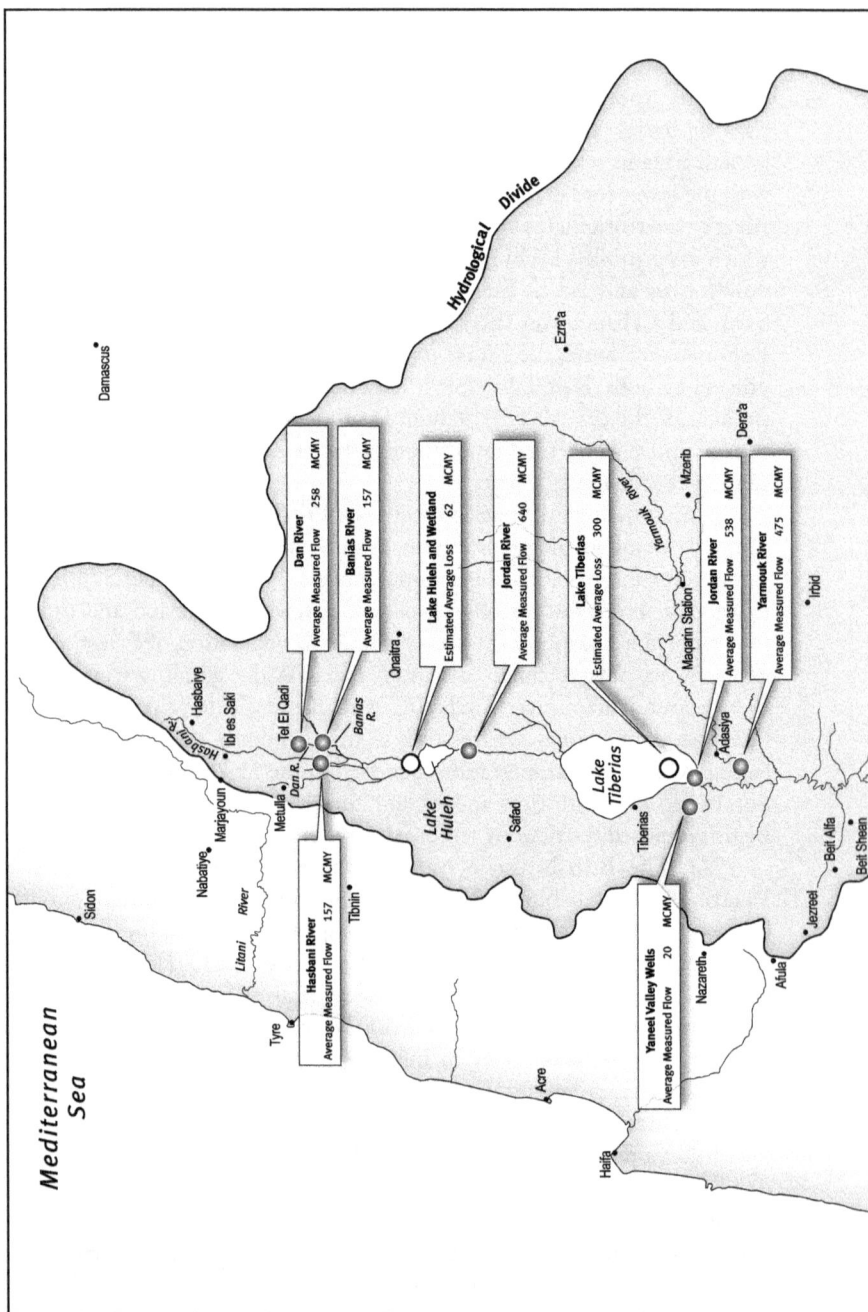

Mafraq

Zerka

Jerash

Ajlun

Zarqa R.

Salt

Amman

Jordan River
Average Measured Flow 1250 MCMY

Madaba

Mewilb R.

Allenby
Bridge

Jordan   River

Jericho

Dead
Sea

Jenin

Nablus

Divide

Ramallah

Hydrographical

Jerusalem

Bethlehem

Hebron

Tel Aviv

Jaffa

Ramle

Lod

Rehovot

Wadis and Wells Below Lake Tiberias East Side of Jordan River Estimated Usable Part only of Water Available		
Perennial Flows of Wadis		
Average	123	MCMY
Flood Flows of Wadis		
Average Recoverable	45	MCMY
Wells		
Average	10	MCMY

Wadis and Wells Below Lake Tiberias West Side of Jordan River Estimated Usable Part only of Water Available		
Perennial Flows of Wadis		
Average	145	MCMY
Flood Flows of Wadis		
Average Recoverable	29	MCMY
Wells		
Average	10	MCMY

N

0 ____ 10 mi
0 ____ 10 km

Note:
Flows are given in millions of cubic meters per year (MCMY)

Legend
● Established gaging station
○ Evaporation loss

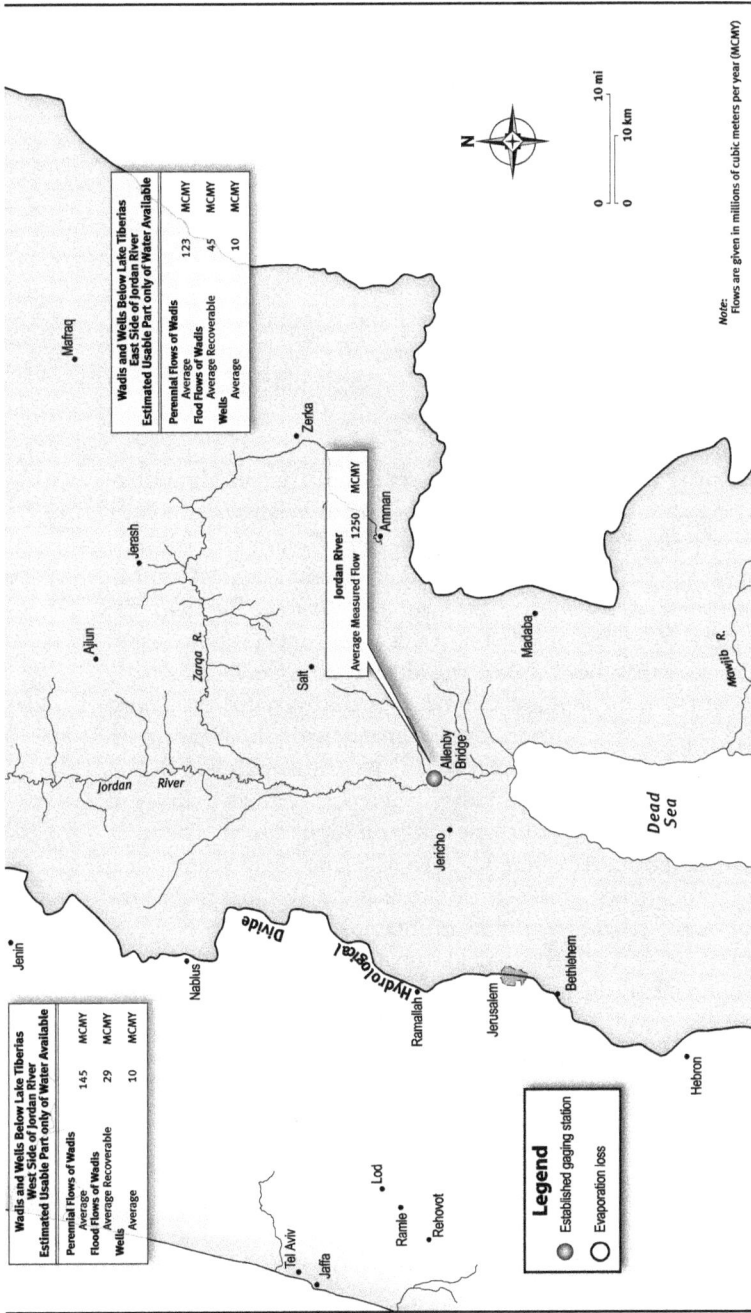

Source: Charles T. Main, Inc.

MAP 2-1   Water Available in the Jordan River Valley, 1953

kilowatt-hours (kWh) of hydroelectric power annually.[6] The Rutenberg concession, named after the president of the electric company, gave the *yishuv* priority usage for some water development by virtue of its control of the supply.[7] Even so, Rutenberg had difficulty financing and completing his Jordan River project.[8] Beyond the Middle East, the Jewish Agency was also active in lobbying the United States for developing Palestine's water resources. The agency asked America in 1943 to send Tennessee Valley Authority (TVA) experts to Palestine to conduct surveys, but President Franklin Roosevelt was advised not to endorse the water plan that the agency advocated because the State Department believed it had technical and political problems.[9] In 1946, the US administration was lobbied unsuccessfully to allow the Export-Import Bank to lend $250 million for a Jordan Valley hydroelectric project.[10] The Zionist movement also was aggressive in raising funds for a Jewish national homeland. In fact, in February 1949, a New York dinner was organized to inaugurate Israeli water projects.[11]

Despite pro-Israel/Zionist lobbying, the Roosevelt and Truman administrations were reluctant to become actively engaged in Jordan Valley water politics because of the perception that their policies were pro-Zionist. In 1945, the United States did accept a British invitation to join a joint Anglo-American Commission Committee of Inquiry on the issue of Palestine. By 1946, the United States and Britain's policy for Palestine water development was one based on a regional perspective that they believed would have more credibility among Arab states. The British and American Cabinet Committee stated that "most substantial Palestinian development should be linked with development in Transjordan and probably in Syria and Lebanon."[12] The Americans and British also recommended that an engineer of international repute conduct a survey of Jordan Valley basin water resources and devise a plan for the best use.[13] The Roosevelt and Truman administrations were highly sensitive to the potential for a negative Arab reaction to policies that seemed pro-Zionist. Without the organization and institutions, Arab leaders simply maintained a maximalist position, refusing any form of cooperation that would signal their acquiescence to the Zionists. This position hampered the Arab community's ability to form a representative body and develop resources such as water. During this period, in fact, there is no record of Arab parties lobbying the United States or even presenting their own water plans before the Anglo-American Committee of Inquiry.[14]

War and Its Aftermath

After much bloodshed and conflict in the late 1940s, the British decided to withdraw from Palestine. Sensing a crisis, the United Nations attempted in

1947 to resolve the Palestine issue by partitioning the territory into Arab and Jewish states with an internationalized status for Jerusalem. However, without neutral armed forces on the ground, a peaceful transition from the British mandate to the partition was unlikely. On May 14, 1948, the British departed from Palestine, and the mandate ended with no peacekeeping forces to fill the vacuum. One day later, Israel proclaimed its independence as a sovereign state. The next day, five Arab armies attacked Israeli forces, beginning the 1948 Arab-Israeli War. By February 1949, the fighting had ended and Israel had signed separate armistice agreements with Egypt, Syria, Lebanon, and Jordan, which was formally Transjordan. Jordan took control of the area known as the West Bank, which it subsequently annexed. Middle East states did not regard the armistice agreements as a permanent border arrangement. Despite constant violations and minor readjustments, though, the boundaries between Israel and its neighbors essentially remained the same until the 1967 Arab-Israeli War.

The end of the 1948 War brought with it great shifts in population and a rearrangement of alliances surrounding water resources. In early 1949, the United Nations estimated that 700,000 Arab refugees—about 70 percent of the Arab population of Palestine—had fled or had been expelled from Israeli-controlled territories. The British estimated that about 320,000 Palestinians moved into, or already resided in, the eastern section of Palestine controlled by Jordan.[15] This influx placed great economic pressures on the already struggling state. From a prewar total of 430,000, Jordan's population swelled to more than a million and a quarter.[16] Even before the 1948 War, Jordan was one of the poorest Middle Eastern states. It lacked industry and infrastructure, and, with the deluge of refugees, was overwhelmed by malnutrition, disease, and unemployment. Given the agrarian background of the refugees and the original Jordanian citizens, agriculture offered the greatest hope for state survival and development. However, Jordan's agricultural system was primitive and lacked a coordinated water delivery system. In the past, Jordan had been dependent on British economic aid, especially for large projects such as irrigation networks. With a weak economy, Jordan looked to the United States for assistance.[17]

After the war, Israel also absorbed many refugees and immigrants, primarily from war-torn Europe and the Arab states. By 1952, about 684,000 new immigrants had arrived in Israel. Like Jordan, the new state also lacked an industrial infrastructure and was highly dependent on agriculture for economic development. Because of the high price of the war and the absorption of many immigrants, Israel's economy was in shambles, and the initiation of an Arab boycott against Israel made matters worse. An austerity program, including food rationing, was initiated during this period.[18] With the country's survival at stake, state planners placed great emphasis on developing water resources for agriculture and immigrant resettlement. This goal meant transporting water from the Jordan River basin to the populated Mediterranean coastal plain and the undeveloped arid northern Negev. To execute such a program, Israel also had to depend on international assistance. In 1949, the Truman administration helped Israel guarantee a $100 million loan from the Export-Import Bank, but the country needed additional assistance to develop its water and irrigation system.

Each Jordan River riparian understood well that economic stability and development were paramount to state survival. A critical ingredient for these agrarian economies was water, which was a scarce item in both Jordan and Israel. Without a reliable flow, a state's economic stability was doubtful. Thus, water for these states was looked on not only as a source of state power but also as an issue of state survival. A sufficient water supply was necessary for developing a strong, independent economy and secure food supply. For example, Israel's first national water program, the seven-year plan, set forth the necessity for irrigation:

> The two most important basic raw materials in the State of Israel are soil and water. The combined utilization of these two raw materials yields the most vital basic product of the country, i.e., food. . . . Food is the only material without which no country can exist. . . . It is, therefore, imperative to give the development of agriculture and irrigation a high priority among the economic activities of the state.[19]

As political analyst Hans Morgenthau notes, "a country that is self-sufficient, or nearly self-sufficient, has a great advantage over a nation that is not and must be able to import the foodstuffs it does not grow, or else starve" during times of war.[20] Self-sufficiency not only meant independence from other food producers but also provided an important source of economic strength for national development. The weak states of the Jordan River basin thus viewed agriculture as the means to accumulate capital that would enable them to participate in the international market. For Jordan River basin riparians during the 1950s, agriculture was the primary consumer of water, accounting for 70 to 95 percent of total use. The expanding population also put pressure on scarce water resources, but not to the same extent as the rapidly growing agriculture sector.

THE WATER PLANS

To realize their water development preferences, riparians of the Jordan River basin formulated an international strategy. Between 1939 and 1953, there were no less than six major water development plans for the Jordan River basin.[21] The schemes fall into two categories: plans centered on Palestine/Israel and on Transjordan/Jordan. The programs sought to survey the amount of available water and proposed means for developing this valuable commodity. In addition to state development, international donors also saw the water plans as critical to Palestinian refugee resettlement. The water schemes are historically significant in that they incorporated basic concepts for Jordan's and Israel's future water systems and crystallized the future political disputes relating to the issue. Because both states engaged in separate planning, it was inevitable that disputes would arise over the development of shared scarce water resources. As a result, the disparate schemes culminated in a "Unified Plan" that was used by the United States as a basis for mediation in the region.

The Jordan Track

The various plans to develop Jordan's water resources included waterworks such as a Jordan Valley north–south delivery canal system, a Yarmouk storage dam, and a diversion weir for the canal inlet. Because this water is shared with Syria and Israel, these projects continue to be politically controversial and hydrologically significant to the present. In 1938, the British established a commission of inquiry under the leadership of Sir John Woodhead to assess the feasibility of partitioning Palestine into three parts: an Arab and a Jewish state as well as a British enclave for Jerusalem and Bethlehem. The commission authorized M. G. Ionides to prepare the *Report on Water Resources of the Transjordan and their Development* to determine how much land could be developed. The report suggested that the only substantial area for development was the Jordan Valley between Lake Tiberias and the Dead Sea. The basic thrust of the Ionides Plan was for Transjordan to irrigate the Jordan Valley's East Bank (the West Bank was not part of Transjordan). Additionally, the report recommended that Transjordan store winter Yarmouk floodwater in the Israeli-controlled Lake Tiberias. Feeder canals from the southern end of the reservoir would supply Transjordan with water during the dry summer.[22] The part of the plan that called for the movement of water from Lake Tiberias was the most sensitive politically, since it recommended cooperation between Jordan and Israel. Shortly after Woodhead issued his general report, the British government rejected any partition of Palestine as impractical. The Ionides water plan thus failed to result in action, but it did establish important water-planning concepts for Transjordan/Jordan.

Two years after the conclusion of the first Arab-Israeli War, the 1951 MacDonald report reexamined the Ionides Plan and adopted its basic concept for moving water through canals and storing it in Lake Tiberias. By the time the report was published, Jordan controlled both sides of the Jordan Valley. Thus, the report took the position that canals should run from north to south on both the east and west banks of the Jordan River. Politically, the report assumed that a Jordan-Israel agreement over Lake Tiberias as a shared reservoir was still possible. While MacDonald formulated the report for Jordan, he also took account of Israeli water utilization. According to the report, the Jordan and Yarmouk water had to be dedicated exclusively to Jordan Valley irrigation. No surplus water would remain if the valley were properly developed. Consequently, the MacDonald report restricted Jordan River water for in-basin use only. This, in turn, began the in-basin versus out-of-basin use debate that became a central political dispute between Arabs and Israelis.[23]

A year later, in 1952, the Jordanian government, in conjunction with the US Technical Cooperation Agency's Point IV program[24] and the United Nations Relief and Works Agency (UNRWA), which had been established in 1949 to provide assistance for Palestinian refugees, drafted a different approach, known as the Bunger Plan, that sidestepped the issue of cooperating with Israel. This scheme, which incorporated the settlement of 100,000 refugees in the Jordan Valley, proposed the storage of Yarmouk River water behind a large upstream dam at Maqarin, which would serve only Jordan and Syria. Unlike the MacDonald or Ionides plans, the Maqarin Dam plan made it possible for Jordan to avoid storing water in the Israeli-controlled Lake Tiberias and avoid cooperating with Israel in any way.[25] The proposed dam would be 140 meters high and store an estimated 500 million cubic meters (mcm) of water.[26] While most of the water would be used for Jordan, 65 million cubic meters per year (mcmy) would be designated for Syria. The dam also would produce 281 million kWh of electricity. The plan specified construction of a small dam downstream at Adasiya, where it would divert water into Jordan's East Ghor Canal for irrigation of the Jordan Valley's east bank. In addition, a siphon would transfer Yarmouk water to the West Ghor Canal for the West Bank.[27]

In March 1953, Jordan and the UNRWA signed a preliminary agreement to implement the Bunger Plan.[28] Soon afterward, on June 4, 1953, Jordan and Syria signed a complementary treaty on "the utilization of the waters of the Yarmouk River" in Damascus that outlined the use of the power produced by the Maqarin Dam. The two riparians agreed to construct a dam, reservoir, and power plant near Maqarin and to the south an Adasiya electric power plant.[29] Syria would receive 75 percent of the electrical power generated from the Maqarin Dam, and Jordan would receive the remaining 25 percent.[30] Jordan would pay 95 percent of the cost of construction and all the costs for the engineering studies.[31] The treaty was unclear as to the allocations of water for the riparians, but it may be inferred from the treaty text and from the Bunger Plan that Jordan would receive the water released from the reservoir and Syria would retain its right to utilize Yarmouk water that originated in its territory.

Although the Maqarin Dam projects were likely to raise objections from Israel, Jordan moved forward with the early stages of implementation. The Jordan government, the UNRWA, and the US government, through the Point IV economic aid program, appropriated funds in July 1953 to begin "noncontroversial" steps, pending an agreement with Israel.[32] Initial expenditures focused on the recruitment of workers to begin construction of the larger Maqarin Dam project, such as canals, roads, and so on. For the sponsors, this project was critical to refugee resettlement and Jordan's economic development.[33] The Israeli government, however, protested to the US government that the Maqarin Dam project did not take into consideration its rights as a Yarmouk riparian.[34] Israel argued that, because of the dam, its Yarmouk Triangle region, formed by the two rivers (Yarmouk and Jordan) and Lake Tiberias, would fail to receive its historical Yarmouk allocation.[35] Although Israel convinced Washington on legal and political grounds to halt the project until this issue was resolved, Israeli officials emphasized that they were eager to discuss water issues with Arab governments.[36] In meetings with Secretary of State Dulles, the prime minister of Jordan was dismayed that the Yarmouk project would be delayed pending an agreement with Israel on riparian rights, since, according to the prime minister, Israel had no Yarmouk water rights.[37] During this stalemate over Jordan's proposed dam project, Israel began construction of its own upper Jordan River water project.

The Israel Track

Israel's focus was a national water carrier that would move water from the north to the populated plain and subsequently help in developing the dry southern region. In the 1940s, prior to the establishment of the State of Israel, the Jewish Agency financed numerous surveys aimed at facilitating a comprehensive development plan for Palestine's water resources. Walter C. Lowdermilk formulated what would become Israel's basic scheme for water development in *Palestine: Land of Promise,* a book that offered an optimistic projection of the region's ability to support more Jewish immigration. His ideas included transporting the waters of northern Palestine through a network of canals and reservoirs to the heavily populated, fertile coastal plain and to the dry, underdeveloped but potentially fertile lands in the southern part of the territory, the northern Negev. In addition to the Jordan and Yarmouk, he also included Lebanon's Litani River's water as an available resource. Lowdermilk outlined a plan for a Jordan Valley Authority, which would be a single centralized agency similar to the TVA. As with the TVA, Lowdermilk wanted to generate electricity and move water to where it was needed. He advocated the idea of transferring Mediterranean Sea water through the Jordan Valley canals to compensate the Dead Sea for water diverted for irrigation. In addition, he argued that, by using the deep incline of the Jordan River valley, needed electricity could be generated.[38] With the proper water management, Lowdermilk believed, Palestine would have the capacity to absorb an additional four million Jewish immigrants beyond the 1.8 million Jews and Arabs who already lived there. Lowdermilk's work was rightly criticized for being overly optimistic regarding the available water, land, and the economic potential of the basin.[39] The *yishuv* development plans, reflecting its collective political objective, sought to show that Palestine had a large absorptive capacity for more Jewish immigration.

Drawing on the optimism of Lowdermilk's work, Israeli water experts began to see their project as a pioneering effort. First, what was needed was a practical blueprint for putting Lowdermilk's idea into practice. This blueprint was provided by James B. Hays, who, in 1948, mapped out the engineering details for Lowdermilk's basic ideas in his book, *TVA on the Jordan: Proposals for Irrigation and Hydro-Electric Development in Palestine*. Hays formulated an eight-stage plan to develop the basin, including greater utilization of the coastal aquifer, building a hydroelectric plant on the Hasbani, dividing the Yarmouk between Israel and Jordan on a fifty–fifty basis, constructing a Mediterranean-Dead Sea hydroelectric project, and reclaiming the Huleh wetlands.[40] Using the basic concepts incorporated in the Lowdermilk/Hays Plan, Israel's first national water blueprint was approved by the government in late 1952. The seven-year plan was formulated by a newly established Water Department within the Ministry of Agriculture.[41] The plan's objective was to "integrate all resources in a single, comprehensive state wide system."[42] Much of the water was to be transferred from the north to the coastal plain and to the arid south. Israeli water experts liked to draw a parallel between their country's economic development to that of the American West, particularly southern California. They pointed out that, in both cases, pioneering farmers reclaimed a desert-like area through irrigated agricultural means. Services, manufacturing, and industry followed later. Like southern California, the capacity of local resources was endangered by water overdraft. Within a short time, a well-established agricultural and industrial economy developed, justifying the import of water from long distances and at relatively great financial cost.

The starting point for the national water system was the area near B'not Yacov Bridge,[43] south of Lake Huleh, from where a 13-kilometer long diversionary canal was to be built near the northwestern corner of Lake Tiberias. A power station at the lake was to utilize the 280-meter drop of the Jordan from the B'not Yacov to the lake to generate electricity. This power then also would be used to begin pumping water through the diversionary system from the lower Galilee to the south.

As the water plans proliferated in the 1950s, the United States, which was paying for much of the work, began to worry that some of the plans might be rendered worthless by others in the region. Originally, Israel was primarily concerned with developing the coastal plain and the northern Negev, while Jordan was interested in developing the Jordan Valley. After 1949 and the first Arab-Israeli War, however, both Jordan and Israel were developing the Jordan water supply separately and racing ahead in order not to be left with less water to develop because of the other riparians' projects. The US State Department funded the study for the UNRWA to ensure that the separate Jordanian and Israeli plans to irrigate the Jordan Valley with Yarmouk and Jordan river water were economical and would not be rendered worthless by the other water projects in the basin.[44]

In 1952, the UNRWA contacted the TVA for review and analysis of past and existing proposals for utilization of the Jordan River. The TVA, in turn, assigned the survey to the Charles T. Main firm of Boston. The result was the *Unified Development of the Water Resources of the Jordan Valley Region* (August 1953), a proposed water project based on all the plans previously described.

The objective of the Main Plan, which was also called the Unified Plan, was to formulate the most economical, efficient, and rapid means for developing the greatest use of the waters from the Jordan River system. The blueprint for using the water resources disregarded political boundaries in establishing a broad program for irrigation and production of hydroelectric power. The basic principle in determining how water should be used was based on moving water by gravity rather than the expensive pumping method. The plan also focused on using natural reservoirs, such as Lake Tiberias, for floodwater storage instead of constructing costly new dams. Thus, canals would bring water to the Huleh area and to the Galilee hills in Israel's north, as well as to the east and west bank of the Jordan Valley, then under Jordan's administration, keeping all the water resources within the basin (see Map 2-1).

In summary, the Main Plan specified that the major sources of water supply should come from the Jordan and the Yarmouk rivers. Jordan would store the Yarmouk's winter floods in Lake Tiberias, using the Maqarin Dam solely for hydroelectric generation and not for storing water for irrigation. Gravity flow canals would move stored water, in basin, to northern Israel and the Jordan Valley. The Main Plan projected the average annual output of hydroelectric power at 210 million kWh. The estimated cost to complete the Main Plan was $121 million, which would be primarily financed by the United States. However, as the director of the UNRWA points out in the document's introduction, "in the interest of sound engineering practices, the Tennessee Valley Authority was invited to disregard political boundaries and efforts to prepare a report indicating the most efficient method of utilizing the whole of the watershed in the best interests of the area."[45] To realize the Main Plan, the United States would have to negotiate a water deal between riparians who had just fought a bloody war.

Before the US Water Mediation

During this period, numerous secret initiatives attempted to resolve the Arab-Israel conflict. However, they all failed. There were also efforts by the riparians to develop water resources and this often led to violent conflict. The United States came to realize that it was in its interest to actively address the Arab-Israeli water dispute. Because the Arab-Israel conflict had not yet become routinized, Israel and the individual Arab states were able to engage in direct but secret negotiations that came close to a permanent settlement. After the 1948 War, the Arab states were not united, and each attempted to initiate talks with Israel. King Abdullah of Jordan conducted extensive negotiations to secure permanent annexation of the West Bank of the Jordan River.[46] Syria's first military dictator, Husni al-Zaim, sought a permanent settlement with Israel to consolidate his power within Syria. Zaim offered to settle 300,000 Palestinian refugees in Syrian territory in exchange for border modifications along the cease-fire line and half of Israel's Lake Tiberias.[47] Egypt also showed a willingness to settle the conflict, but was seeking from Israel territorial concessions including the entire southern Negev desert.[48] This era ended with the assassination of Abdullah, the deposing of Zaim, and, in Egypt, the rise to power of the Free Officers and subsequently Gamal Abdul Nasser. Even so, on the eve of the US mediation on water, many diplomats viewed the end of the Arab-Israeli conflict as a possibility. The divisive politics of the East-West conflict had not yet permeated the Arab-Israeli conflict during the early 1950s. The potential for a settlement of the conflict would disappear by 1956, however, with the advent of the Suez crisis, when the conflict became both routinized and protracted.

Before the 1956 crisis, there were not only negotiations to resolve the conflict, including water, there was also acute conflict over scarce water resources. After the 1948 Arab-Israeli War, armistice talks resulted in the drawing of temporary boundaries between Israel and its neighbors. They did not, however, lead to peace treaties between Israel and Arab states. The armistice agreements called for the establishment of a Mixed Armistice Commission (MAC), which was made up of an equal number of representatives from each state. The chairperson was a UN official from the UN Truce Supervision Organization (UNTSO).[49] Especially between Syria and Israel, there were basic conflicting interpretations of the sovereignty and political status—such as responsibility for civil administration and control—of the demilitarized zone (DMZ). This was an important cause for much of the conflict during this period.[50]

Although most of the water-related violent conflict occurred in the Israel-Syria DMZ, there were post-armistice agreement incidents that show how important mediation boards were for Israel–Jordan Yarmouk riparian relations. For example, in September 1950, 400 Israeli troops crossed the Jordan River into the Yarmouk Triangle, taking control of territory that was formerly owned by the Palestine Electric Company (PEC) and part of the Rutenberg concession. Jordan challenged the Israeli military move to the Americans and to the chairperson of the Israel-Jordan MAC. The chief of staff of the UNTSO ruled that Israel had not violated the Armistice Agreement and that Israeli activity had occurred on the Israeli side of the armistice line. Israeli officials stated that prior to the military action Israelis had been farming and mine clearing the area. When King Abdullah of Jordan saw a map signed by a Jordanian officer that placed an island that was northwest of Naharayim and east of the international boundary in Israel, he asked that this territory be returned. Israel said it would be willing to negotiate, but only as part of a general settlement between Israel and Jordan.[51] After the 1994 Jordan-Israel Treaty, the island was returned to Jordanian sovereignty. Between 1949 and 1955, the MAC served as an important venue for Jordanians and Israelis to meet and discuss numerous issues, including Jordan and Yarmouk water disputes. For example, in an August 1951 MAC meeting at Degania, senior Israeli officials told their Jordanian counterparts that Israel was willing to discuss equitable regulations of the Jordan River.[52] Such meetings continued, and this format would be used in the 1980s and 1990s for secret meetings, which are discussed in chapter 4.

Between 1949 and 1955, efforts by Israel and Syria to go beyond their Armistice Agreement were also facilitated by such mediation committees. Two Syrian leaders during this period made proposals for a peace treaty—Zaim in 1949 and Shishaqli in 1952. In exchange for territorial concessions, Syria agreed to absorb a large number of Palestinian refugees.[53] Unlike the 1960s, during the 1949 to 1955 period both sides attempted to avert violent conflict that could lead to an unintended war.[54] The differences between Israel and Syria on the DMZ issue, however, were too difficult to overcome. Direct negotiations, through the MAC, did take place and agreements on particular issues were successful. Except for the disputes over water and the DMZ, the frontier between the two was "relatively calm" compared to Israel's Jordan and Egypt borders.[55] According to Israeli analyst Aryeh Shalev, "Syria was ready to accept the [DMZ's] undefined status, but Israel initiated activity on the ground to change the status quo in its favor and secure full control of the area."[56]

The military conflict between Israel and Syria between March and May 1951 was triggered by Syrian opposition to Huleh drainage and soon spiraled into a fight for the whole DMZ.[57] In February 1951, Israel had begun draining the Huleh and its wetlands with the initial objective of deepening the bed of the Jordan so more water would flow to Lake Tiberias. Syria objected to the water work and in March the UNTSO requested that Israel cease its work until an agreement could be reached between the parties.[58] An agreement was not reached, and when two weeks later Israel resumed work, the Syrians responded militarily to stop them. In May, there were six days of fighting in the DMZ and a subsequent UN Security Council resolution calling for a cease-fire and resolution of the conflict.[59] The compromise resolution was an Israeli agreement to work only on the western side of the Jordan and not on the Arab-owned land. Syria still objected, but Israel completed the project without Damascus renewing militarily conflict.[60] During this incident, Syrian diplomats indicated to US representatives that the Syrian government favored a division of the DMZ. Under the arrangement, Syria would take control of the "sector along the southeast corner of Lake Tiberias, while Israel got the central sector."[61] In fact, Israel and Syria secretly met to discuss the division of the DMZ, but were unsuccessful at reaching an agreement.[62] Through the MAC, Israel and Syria cooperated. In 1952, the dam gates on the upper Jordan were closed so Israel could repair flood damage to the B'not Yacov Bridge but opened to allow enough water for irrigation of crops on the Syrian Boteiha farm, which was in the DMZ.[63] In the end, the precipitating reason for this violent conflict in the Syrian-Israeli DMZ was water scarcity, the intermediate factor was the dispute over the DMZ, and the long-term reason was the lack of a resolution of the Israel-Arab conflict.

The Dulles Mission

In 1953, anxiety about the instability in the region prompted the Eisenhower administration to send a fact-finding mission to the Middle East led by Secretary of State John Foster Dulles. Afterward, Dulles would formulate the US government's policy on the region. On May 9, 1953, Dulles and his delegation left Washington for a twenty-one-day mission to twelve countries, including Egypt, Israel, Syria, Jordan, and Lebanon. The secretary of state met with state leaders and reviewed the region's many difficult issues, some of which included the Anglo-Egyptian disputes over British military bases in the Suez Canal zone, the Arab-Israeli conflict, and the issues involving the Kurdish minority in Iraq and Iran. During this mission, Dulles observed the signs of poverty and economic collapse, which he believed made the area a prime and easy target for Communist penetration and subversion. The secretary concluded that Middle East policy should be formulated within the context of the East–West struggle and that control over that strategic area of the globe was critical to US interests.[64]

Dulles considered a formal Arab-Israeli peace settlement unrealistic, but thought that reducing the tensions might lay the groundwork for progress. Thus, he initiated an American policy, which this book terms tactical functional cooperation. He explained that the United States would "have to move step by step upon segments of the problem that will reduce tension to where it would be politically possible for Arab leaders to agree to a formal peace settlement."[65] After briefing the president and congressional leaders, Dulles publicly stated the administration's policy of "true impartiality" in the Arab-Israeli conflict during a radio and television address. Dulles spoke of economic and military aid to demonstrate the more balanced US approach to the Arab states and to Israel. He also spoke of a gradual elimination of the refugee problem, as well as resolution of the status of Jerusalem, and gave assurances to the Arabs regarding Israeli aggression. In particular, Dulles described the plight of the Palestinian refugees, adding that an effective irrigation system would allow more land to be farmed and, in turn, provide more refugees with work and hope for the future.[66] A briefing memo prepared for Dulles prior to the trip noted that "development of the Jordan Valley water resources provided the most immediate hope for a partial solution of the Arab refugee problem." The memo concluded that the United States "could not agree to finance conflicting and competing plans on different sides of a political boundary and that water must become one of the outstanding issues in the search for a solution to the Arab-Israeli dispute."[67]

In June 1953, after the Dulles trip, Congress increased its pressure on the Eisenhower administration to solve the Palestinian refugee problem. The United States was paying for most of the UNRWA's budget and by the summer of 1953 America had spent $153 million, with the State Department asking for an additional $30 million for 1954. The administration argued, as it had done in the past, that an economic approach to the Jordan River valley development provided a long-term solution to the refugee problem, but such a solution would cost approximately $110 million. The congressional committee reluctantly appropriated the funds, questioning the State Department as to why it had not already negotiated the development plan between the riparians.[68] During hearings on the matter, the presiding senator pressed a senior State Department official to set a cut-off date for refugee aid within a year.[69] Later, the same senator said Congress wanted to

> liquidate the [refugee] problem as soon as possible so that the refugees may begin to live a normal life, so that this source of friction in the area may be eliminated and so that heavy, nonproductive financial drain of refugee relief on the United States and United Nations may be stopped.[70]

The administration understood well that Congress's patience for refugee assistance was limited and dissipating; thus, immediate action on the issue needed to be taken.

B'not Yacov Conflict

During the fall of 1953, as America was planning to begin formal mediation on water with a mission headed by Eric Johnston, Israel took several actions that strained relations with the United States and heightened tensions with Arab states. The Eisenhower administration was critical of Israel's heavy-handed retaliation policy, especially the attack on the Jordanian village of Kibya. Israel had launched a severe reprisal attack during the night of October 14–15 against Kibya. Israeli artillery first shelled the area, and then Israeli personnel razed the village, leaving at least forty-five men, women, and children dead.[71] The attack was in response to Arab infiltrators from Jordan killing Israelis—in particular, a grenade attack the day before the Kibya raid that killed an Israeli woman and two children.[72] The US government and the UN Security Council harshly condemned Israel for its excessive and disproportionate use of force.

Simultaneously, there was a growing dispute over different water issues between Syria and Israel that involved the demilitarized zone (DMZ). On September 2, 1953, in line with the basic idea of the Lowdermilk/Hays Plan and in reaction to Jordanian water projects, Israel began work on a hydroelectric project as a first stage in the construction of a southbound water conduit near B'not Yacov Bridge.[73] Jordan protested to the UN Security Council, to no avail, when less water and of lower quality was released to the lower Jordan.[74] The construction site was in a DMZ close to the Syrian border, so the Syrians also vehemently objected to the project, arguing that the proposed canals would take water away from Syrian farmers and would give Israel a military advantage. Amid the debate, a number of shootings occurred, raising fears of an escalation of violence.[75] In 1953, the United Nations ruled against Israel on the construction of the water projects near B'not Yacov Bridge. The Syrians, with the United Nations concurring, argued that the armistice agreement had not settled the question of sovereignty and that neither party consequently had a free hand in the area. It was the responsibility of the Mixed Armistice Commission to interpret the provisions of the agreement.[76] On September 23, the chief of staff of UNTSO ordered Israel to suspend work until the parties reached agreement on its continuation.[77] Israel refused to stop construction near B'not Yacov, believing that such a move would give Syria a virtual veto over its water program and economic development. The United States, in turn, supported UNTSO's decision and said it would not tolerate Israel's disregarding UN orders. Thus, the US government informed Israel that, unless it complied, part of its economic aid would be withheld.[78] According to Dulles, "The United States was trying to adopt a fair, evenhanded policy in the Near East. This was difficult to accomplish if the Israeli government appeared to be disrespectful to the UN decisions while we furnish aid which from our point of view was discretionary."[79]

The United States decided that to be truly even-handed and maintain respect for international mediation boards like the UNTSO, and the United Nations in general, it would need to carry out its threat to suspend aid. On October 20, Dulles announced the suspension of Mutual Security Act (MSA) allocations because of Israel's refusal to comply with UNTSO's B'not Yacov decision.[80] At the same time, the United States took the lead on a Security Council resolution condemning Israel for its attack on Kibya. On October 27, Israel stated to the UN Security Council that it would suspend the B'not Yacov project until there was an opportunity to examine the issue more closely.[81] As a result, the next day President Eisenhower announced the resumption of $26 million under MSA to Israel.[82] During the same week, US water mediation began in the region. The pressure to succeed was intense, since, from the outset of the mediation, Israel made its position clear that it would proceed with the diversion project at B'not Yacov if the US mediation did not achieve a regional agreement.

THE JOHNSTON MISSION

The Eisenhower administration's preferences were clear: maintain Middle East political stability by addressing the Palestinian refugee issue and economic development needs of Middle East states. Political stability in the Middle East was critical to the US because of its oil interests and its struggle with the Soviet Union. The US government's international strategy was to focus on the water issues that had led to violent conflict and that, with US foreign aid, could play an important role in the resettlement of the Palestinian refugees and the economic development of all states in the region. The plan was for US mediation to move the parties further away from additional violent conflict and closer to cooperation and the confidence building that comes with it. In a letter dated October 7, 1953, President Eisenhower appointed Eric Johnston to be the personal representative of the president with the rank of ambassador for a mission to the Middle East.[83] At the time of the appointment, Johnston was the chair of the Advisory Board for International Development. He was respected as a talented negotiator in government and business and perceived by the president and secretary of state as unbiased to either side in the Arab-Israeli conflict.[84]

After his mission, an aide wrote:

Johnston set out with no illusions as to the difficulty of the assign-
ment but with a firm conviction that such a plan, if carried out, would
help resolve the urgent refugee problem, establish a pattern for
intraregional development, and perhaps open the way for a general
relaxation of Arab-Israel tensions.

No man ever worked harder at a job than Johnston worked at this
one. On the four separate visits to the Middle East over a span of
three years on which I accompanied him as an advisor, I watched him
argue and cajole his way through hundreds of weary hours of the most
detailed and harassing negotiations it is possible to imagine. He
burned the midnight oil in every US Embassy in the area preparing
argumentation and counterproposals for the next meeting with one
side or the other. American ambassadors winced at his tough talk to
Presidents, Prime Ministers, and Kings, watched him shatter all the
rules of diplomatic exchange, and ended up with a considerable
amount of admiration for what several of them now call the 'Johnston
technique.'

In the end, his persistence and persuasiveness brought the three
Arab states and Israel into agreement on the economic and engineering aspects of a plan for developing the Jordan Valley for the benefit
of all four states. He had accomplished the unprecedented feat of
working out a project that was acceptable to both sides.[85]

Mission's Background

Before the mission, Eisenhower wrote Johnston that he had a personal
interest in his efforts, and that, in his opinion, the trip was of "primary
importance to the United States."[86] The president emphasized the need for
a regional approach that would make economic development possible for
refugees and riparians through needed irrigation systems and hydroelectric
power plants. According to Secretary of State John Foster Dulles, the objective of the mission was "to secure agreement of the states of Lebanon, Syria,
Jordan, and Israel to the division and use of the water of the Jordan River
basin."[87]

At the mediation, the United States enumerated to the riparians its many
reasons for favoring developing the Jordan River basin. Of greatest importance
was the fact that America had actively pursued a policy of economic growth for
struggling states. By supporting economic stability and security, US policymakers believed that weaker states would be less vulnerable to Soviet influence.

The Jordan Valley policy was consistent with the Marshall Plan in Western Europe and the Truman Doctrine for Greece and Turkey.

The Johnston mission grew out of the desire of the US administration and the Congress to reduce the refugee assistance sent to the region since 1949. If the available water for irrigation were increased, refugees would be expected to become self-sufficient in agriculture and related pursuits in the Jordan Valley. The US policymakers saw the Jordan Valley plan as an opportunity to improve Palestinian refugees' "social and economic status without impairing their rights either to repatriation or compensation."[88] The United States wanted to mitigate the political tension arising from water-resource development. Before the Johnston mission, the riparians, particularly Jordan and Israel, had been racing to develop the Jordan and Yarmouk. By establishing the rules of the game, US policymakers believed they could eliminate one source of tension that had the potential for drawing the region into acute conflict.

According to the Eisenhower administration, when the United States provided financial support for water projects, it was "obliged to insist that the plan meet certain conditions necessary to justify the expenditure of United States public funds."[89] First, "the Plan must make full use of all of the available water of the Valley without waste or extravagance." Second, the scheme must be "economically and technically sound." In both cases, the United States was looking for a long-term investment that would provide long-term economic and social returns. Third, "the Plan must be equitable," with no riparian denied fair use of the total water resources. Finally, "the Plan must be accepted by all of the countries having an interest in or now using the waters of the River system." Notably, the administration did not insist that political differences had to be resolved or even that the water agreement had to be formal.[90]

The State Department hoped that Johnston would be able to work out a political understanding that would make possible the implementation of UNRWA's Main Plan, which was released at this time. The State Department believed that this impartial, nonpolitical engineering study established overarching principles, which would serve as a basis for the equitable division of the Jordan-Yarmouk water supply. As previously stated, the major principles set forth in the Main Plan are: (1) water from the Jordan River system should stay in-basin to irrigate the Jordan Valley; (2) the most economical and efficient means to transport water is by gravity, not pumping; and (3) Lake Tiberias is the best site for storage and regulation of Jordan and Yarmouk water. These principles could not be implemented, the State Department knew, "without a political understanding on the part of the riparian states."[91] Dulles expected major concessions from Israel, in the name of refugee resettlement. He argued that Israel must relinquish exclusive territorial control over Lake Tiberias, agree to a fixed allocation of water, and play an active role in refugee resettlement.[92] In addition, the Israeli request to include the Litani River in the program was rejected by the United States because the river lies entirely within Lebanon.[93] Guided by this framework, Dulles gave Johnston the freedom to negotiate in such a manner as he saw fit.[94] For Dulles and the State Department, a Jordan Valley plan "would thus be an important step in removing, over the long run, an important cause of tension between Israel and her neighbors."[95] Johnston agreed with Dulles's notion of tactical functional cooperation, arguing that the negotiations must ameliorate the political tension in the region, "but short of peace, perhaps the sharp edges of antagonism can be dulled by helping the states concerned to eliminate certain critical points of friction."[96]

For Johnston, the water issue was at the center of the Arab-Israeli dispute, which was, according to Johnston, "one of the hottest, bitterest, and seemingly most irreconcilable political disputes going on in the world today."[97] By settling refugees in the Jordan Valley, and getting them out of refugee camps and giving them an economic livelihood like farming, many political problems would disappear.[98] Johnston did not believe a political settlement was possible during his negotiations, but he did think that a Jordan Valley plan was the best means available to break the Arab-Israeli impasse. Johnston wrote Eisenhower that "if we grasp the key firmly and turn it carefully, it may open the way to eventual *rapprochement* between the parties to the Palestine dispute."[99]

Prior to Johnston's first trip to the Middle East, some US diplomats in the region were both critical and pessimistic about the initiative. The chargé d'affaires in Jordan argued in no uncertain terms that the political and psychological obstacles were just too great for the mediation to succeed. He believed that Arab economic interests did not provide the basis for political decision making when it involved any form of cooperation with Israel. According to one US official, Arab "emotion dictates a course of no piecemeal, non-political agreements with Israel until, if ever, a satisfactory over-all political settlement is achieved."[100] Another chargé in Beirut also challenged the initiation of the Johnston mission and quoted the Lebanese speaker of parliament as saying that any Arab government that makes definite moves "toward a *rapprochement* with Israel would fall before sunset" or its leaders would be assassinated, as was Jordan's King Abdullah.[101] The US diplomat in Amman argued that he did "not believe any Jordanian Government would dare give such a scheme serious consideration because of the fact it involves cooperation with Israel."[102] These US diplomats argued that the Johnston mission was doomed unless there was an overall political settlement based on major Israeli territorial concessions.

The Johnston mission used a combination of political savvy and economic pressure to get all parties to negotiate. Johnston well understood the Arabs' position that they could not enter into an agreement or cooperate with Israel. However, the Arabs were willing to sign an agreement with the United States or the United Nations that accepted a US-sponsored Jordan Valley program. From the outset, Johnston assumed that no bilateral or multilateral agreement between Israel and any Arab state would be reached. Instead, the United States would be satisfied with separate assurances of acceptance of a plan by the Arab states and by Israel. This would be sufficient for US funding.[103] In fact, for much of the mission, Johnston successfully convinced many of his Arab negotiating partners that the US was seeking a water solution, not a resolution of the larger conflict.[104] Johnston continuously emphasized to Arab states that a Jordan Valley program would be in their economic and social interest and could be viewed as wholly outside the Arab-Israeli conflict. Johnston clearly stated US policy on this issue in a letter dated August 30, 1955, to the Jordanian prime minister:

> I wish to point out and to reaffirm the distinct delineation between our economic negotiations and the political problems of which [Mr. Dulles] spoke. I have emphasized that my negotiations relate to a program for the economic development of the area, and I insist that they remain in this context and not be linked with the settlement of any political problems.[105]

Since he was the personal representative of the president, Israel and the Arab states took seriously Johnston's position that future US military and economic aid to Middle East states might be contingent on their cooperation in the water negotiations.[106] The riparians were struggling to develop economically, and while the political questions of the Arab-Israeli conflict were considered important, so was US aid for development. Eisenhower, Dulles, and Johnston used US aid as a key incentive and, as a result, all riparians negotiated in good faith for two years. The Eisenhower administration did not want to be seen as advocating any political solutions, but merely as providing useful and impartial recommendations. The United States considered itself a "party" to the Jordan Valley plan in that it was paying a large portion of the expenses. Therefore, Johnston felt the United States had a right to exercise its voice in all decisions related to the plan's financial aspects.[107] In sum, Johnston's game plan for success was simple: distance water negotiations from regional politics, make the plan economical, and emphasize economic and social benefits. The riparians took note of these points because the United States promised to provide most of the financing for the regional water development scheme, then estimated to cost approximately $200 million.

Johnston's Many Trips and Successes

The negotiations lasted for two years and consisted of four separate trips by Johnston to the region, shuttling between state capitals. During the first round, in October 1953, Johnston presented the Main Plan to Jordan, Israel, Syria, and Lebanon. Johnston also visited Egypt, even though it was not a Jordan River riparian. Johnston knew that Cairo could play a pivotal role in influencing the other Arab states, and Egypt understood that its prospects for receiving US aid for its water projects, in particular the Aswan Dam, would be enhanced by its cooperation with Johnston. The president's representative obtained assurances from the Egyptian government that it would "exert the weight of its influence in support of the project as appropriate opportunities arose."[108] In exchange, Egypt also planned for US financial assistance in Nile River development. Initially it was rough going for Johnston; during that first week he was in the region, the Political Committee of the Arab League adopted a "secret resolution" recommending that Syria, Jordan, and Lebanon refuse to negotiate on a joint Jordan Valley plan with "the enemy Israel."[109] American diplomats also reported an increase in the Arab state-sponsored campaign against the Johnston mission. And, in fact, in Johnston's first meeting with leaders from the Arab riparians, they rejected Johnston's proposals. However, by the end of the first round, although both Arab and Israeli negotiators voiced reservations with the Main Plan, they all agreed to study the blueprint and make suggestions for modifications.[110]

In January 1954, the Arab League set up a technical committee with Egyptian, Syrian, Jordanian, and Lebanese representatives, and, two months later, submitted its counterproposal to the Main Plan.[111] Importantly, the Arab plan reaffirmed the basic concept of in-basin use for the Jordan Valley found in the Ionides, MacDonald, and Bunger plans. As such, it opposed Israel's plan to divert water to the Negev or elsewhere outside the Jordan Valley basin. It rejected the use of Lake Tiberias for storage, but it proposed building the Maqarin Dam for water storage, and reiterated Arab opposition to integrating the Litani into the Jordan basin program. The plan also argued that, because most of the water originates in the Arab states, the Arab allocation should be increased and the Israeli allotment should be reduced dramatically. In addition, the plan included Lebanon, which was not originally part of the Main Plan. Despite these significant challenges to the Main Plan, Johnston believed the Arab proposal to be an important tactical functional success and diplomatic breakthrough in that it accepted the cornerstone principle of regional water sharing and gave tacit recognition to Israel's rights as a riparian.[112]

Israel made as a counterproposal to the Main Plan the Cotton Plan, which was similar to its seven-year plan in that it called for a dramatic increase in its water allocation. The Cotton Plan followed the Lowdermilk/Hays basic concepts of including out-of-basin use to irrigate the coastal plain and the northern Negev, development of the Mediterranean-Dead Sea canal, and inclusion of the Litani. Because the plan recommended the inclusion of the Litani, which increased the total amount of available water, Israel felt justified in demanding a greater share.[113]

These counterproposals to the Main Plan became bargaining positions in the second round, which began in June 1954. With both sides recognizing the principle of regional water development, Johnston focused on the issues of: (1) water allocations; (2) out-of-basin use; (3) use of Lake Tiberias as an international reservoir; (4) storage on the Yarmouk for irrigation and power; and (5) method of supervision for the plan.[114]

The United States insisted that Lake Tiberias be included in the plan as the storage area for Yarmouk floodwater. Otherwise, Johnston pointed out, Jordan would lose a substantial share of its water to the Dead Sea. Neither side was enthusiastic about transforming Lake Tiberias into an international reservoir. The Arabs were reluctant to store their water in an Israeli lake because they thought that Israel would withhold water for strategic leverage and blackmail.[115] The Arab parties told Johnston they would accept the lake as a central storage facility if they could have storage on the Yarmouk and neutral controls were provided for the distribution of Lake Tiberias water. For the Israelis, this Arab counterproposal was a pivotal issue.[116] Israel feared that international storage in Lake Tiberias might be used to force future territorial concessions or adjustments against Israel. In addition, the Israelis pointed out to Johnston that Yarmouk water storage in the lake would compel Israel to construct expensive new storage facilities elsewhere in Israel.[117] To allay these fears, Johnston committed to Israel a US guarantee "that Lake Tiberias storage would neither prejudice the status quo nor provide basis for future efforts to do so."[118] He also said that the United States would provide aid for new Israeli water projects.

Both sides also had problems with international supervision. Israel recently had difficulties with the United Nations concerning the DMZ so it preferred that the Arab states build a dam on the Yarmouk rather than store their water in Lake Tiberias, since the latter course would necessitate international supervision.[119] Although unwilling to give up control of its only large freshwater reservoir, Israel was willing in principle to use the lake as an international reservoir if a system could be established that did not impinge on its national sovereignty.[120] Both sides accepted the need for international supervision. The Arabs, however, sought an elaborate system, whereas the Israelis wanted minimum controls.[121] After this round concluded, the State Department was becoming optimistic. In a press release and a memo to Dulles, it was indicated that Syria, Lebanon, and Jordan had accepted the principle of international sharing with Israel and were prepared to cooperate with the United States in achieving a final agreement.[122]

After the successes of the second round, the Johnston mission felt the need to investigate and resolve the problematic technical issues debated during the negotiations. Between June and November 1954, engineer and Johnston technical expert Wayne Criddle shuttled to each of the four Jordan basin riparians, discussed water schemes with local technical experts, and made "field observations in order to provide Johnston with guidance on certain problems" during the negotiations.[123] In particular, Criddle determined that Israel should not be allowed more than 30 mcmy for the Yarmouk Triangle.[124] The achievements of the Criddle mission may have been overshadowed by the Johnston negotiations, but, after the Johnston mission ended, Criddle would return to the region and meet with local technical experts. These meetings established the technical details that formed the basis for a cooperative regime between Israel and Jordan that would last for some forty years, as will be discussed in chapters 3 and 4.

The third round began in January 1955, with Johnston making significant progress toward an agreement, although water allocation continued to be a difficult negotiating point. Israel backed down on integrating the Litani into the Jordan River basin plan, and the Arab negotiators showed flexibility on permitting out-of-basin use for Israel.[125] During this round, both sides focused on allocations and issues such as Lake Tiberias storage and Yarmouk dam capacity.[126] After intense negotiations, allotments were made for Syria and Lebanon, which were identical to the Arab plan. However, Jordan and Israel's allocation continued to be difficult. The breakthrough was the "Gardiner formula" that gave the residual of the Yarmouk to Jordan and the residual of the Jordan to Israel.[127] As will be discussed later, Johnston was, however, unable to reach an agreement on Jordan's allocation from the Jordan and Israel's allotment from the Yarmouk.

Toward the end of the Johnston mission, Johnston received new data on water availability that helped to bring the negotiators closer to an agreement. In February 1955, the American engineering firms of Baker and Harza completed a hydrological survey commissioned by the Jordanian government to determine the amount of water needed to irrigate the Jordan Valley. The study increased the Main Plan estimate of available land to cultivate, but reduced the total amount of water needed to irrigate the Jordan Valley.[128] The new data made it easier for negotiators to agree on a plan. That same month, Johnston secured a nonbinding agreement signed by the Council of Arab Foreign Ministers in Beirut.[129]

At this point, Johnston succeeded in having both sides sign similar memoranda of understanding. On July 5, Israeli and American officials signed a tentative "Draft Memorandum of Understanding" in Washington.[130] Johnston's end game was in sight, and he returned to the region for his fourth and final negotiating round in August 1955. At the end of August, Johnston received from the Jordanian prime minister a commitment that Jordan would fight for the Johnston Plan in the Arab League meeting, if adjustments were made to the plan.[131] In late September, the Arab Technical Committee approved a "US-Arab Memorandum of Understanding" and recommended acceptance to the Arab League Council.[132] While this was Johnston's greatest tactical functional success, there were important conflicting allocations in these memos, and these differences would lead to a great deal of debate and conflict among the United States, Israel, and Jordan, as will be discussed.

In the Political Committee of the Arab League the Johnston Plan ran in to opposition. The political committee, consisting of eight foreign ministers of Arab states, debated the plan for four days and, on October 11, the committee requested "more time" instead of rejecting the proposal outright. In the end, the adopted resolution stated that the plan for the Jordan Valley "still needs further consideration. It was, therefore, decided that the experts be asked to pursue the mission with which they have been entrusted until an agreement safeguarding Arab interests is reached."[133] Some Arab leaders wanted to express to the United States that they were not rejecting the plan outright.[134] However, the Johnston mission, which was now deeply entangled in cold war and Arab-Israeli politics, would not return to the region. On October 26, the Arab Higher Committee condemned the Johnston Plan.[135] The Johnston Plan, however, would continue to have an impact on water politics for the next half-century.[136]

THE POLITICS OF THE MISSION

By the end of his mission, Middle East and global politics had caught up with Johnston and had become too great an obstacle to overcome. The Arab riparian preference was economic development, thus the more political and less economic the Johnston mission was perceived, the more difficult it was for the United States to realize its public and regional water agreement strategy. Initially, Johnston was able to separate the water negotiations from politics, but, by 1955, it became increasingly difficult for Arab leaders to disassociate the Johnston Plan from politics. Numerous global and regional factors led to the cessation of the Johnston mission. Of primary importance was that ministers of the Arab League Council became more interested in the political considerations of the plan than in the technical and functional benefits and US officials became aware of this risk. In a telephone conversation, Dulles told Johnston that "if we don't do something to keep it out of the Arab League, it will sink."[137] Johnston's mission also suffered from a mistaken view of the loyalties of particular Arab states. According to a Johnston aide, Syria vetoed the plan because its premier feared the domestic backlash of accepting the plan.[138] Throughout the mission, Johnston trusted Nasser to be a proponent of his plan and was also convinced that Nasser "remains our best, if not only hope" to put this water plan across.[139] Yet, according to the American account of the Arab League Council meeting, Nasser gave the Syrian premier the "green light" to veto the plan. In the end, neither Syria nor Egypt had much to gain from the acceptance of the Johnston Plan and possessed the political power to veto it.

The Johnston mission was very public and the process itself had the negative effect of overpoliticizing the water issue. From the time the mission began, individuals and states that opposed his efforts attacked Johnston personally. In October 1953, when Johnston first came to the region, a government radio official in Damascus reported that the envoy was a "well known pro-Zionist." In addition, while not having much influence in the region at the time, the Soviets attempted to spread anti-Johnston mission propaganda and labeled the Main Plan "US imperialism."[140] Johnston informed the State Department that during the first two rounds the Arab press bitterly opposed the Johnston mission and foretold its inevitable failure.[141] Dulles believed the anti-Johnston propaganda was having a negative impact. The secretary urged Arab leaders not to give credence to "fabrications regarding Johnston's Zionist sympathies."[142] Dulles went on to point out that Eisenhower would not have appointed Johnston unless he was convinced that he was completely objective.[143] The United States attempted to counter anti-Johnston propaganda in other ways. In December 1953, America took the offensive to influence Arab and Israeli public opinion to support the Johnston mission. The US Information Agency (USIA) conducted an intensive campaign on the benefits of developing the Jordan River basin. Arabic Voice of America radio broadcasts, USIA pamphlets, and motion pictures all focused on the benefits of the proposed water plan.[144]

In the end, the education campaign and the high visibility of the Johnston mission served as a deterrent to its success. The unintended consequence was an even greater politicization of the water issue and the Johnston Plan. By the conclusion of the mission, Nasser went so far as to suggest to the Americans that if the plan were ever to succeed, its name would have to be changed. According to the Egyptian leader, every refugee knew the name of "the Johnston Plan" or "the Jordan Valley Plan." It had been used in domestic politics and for agitation purposes to the point that he felt neither Syria nor Jordan might ever be able to agree to accept the plan under either name. In an effort to depoliticize the plan, Nasser suggested separating the scheme into two separate projects: an Israeli and Arab plan, while quietly maintaining the master plan's basic ideas.[145] For the same reason, he also recommended keeping Johnston out of the region.

By 1955, the events of the Arab-Israeli conflict and the cold war were negatively affecting the Johnston mission. Arab and cold war politics, as well as daily incidents on the ground, were heating up the conflict. Nasser was emphasizing his nationalistic goal of Egypt for Egyptians and favoring the removal of the British from the Nile Valley and the Canal Zone. At the same time, the United States supported the Baghdad Pact that polarized the Middle East between competing Arab leaders in Iraq and Egypt. The United States wanted Egypt to be part of a defensive pact against the Eastern Bloc, but Nasser wanted to maintain Egypt's neutrality. In addition, in 1955, Israel launched a large-scale attack against an Egyptian military post in Gaza in retaliation for numerous terrorist raids from there. Throughout the Johnston mission, tensions on the shared Arab-Israeli border had soured negotiations. All these developments, in turn, brought the cold war to the Arab-Israeli arena and intensified the conflict's instability, making diplomatic initiatives, such as the Johnston mission, that much more difficult.

Nasser played the Soviet Union against the West in order to obtain the best agreement for Egypt.[146] The United States, in an effort to befriend Egypt, provided technical aid through the Point IV program, and augmented this with economic aid as well. Egypt wanted more. Nasser sought to purchase military weapons because of threats from Israel and Iraq, but France, Britain, and the United States were unwilling, at least publicly, to launch a Middle East arms race by selling large amounts of weapons to either side of the Arab-Israeli conflict.[147] In September, Nasser announced an arms purchase from Czechoslovakia, which was financed with Egyptian cotton. The arms were Soviet made, worth approximately $400 million, and included tanks, artillery, and MIG jets, thus bringing cold war politics to the Arab-Israeli conflict.

The final factor in the mission's lack of success was that while Johnston was negotiating, the Eisenhower administration chose to pursue a parallel diplomatic initiative to resolve the whole Arab-Israeli conflict. This effort destroyed Johnston's credibility with Arab leaders, who had been told the water talks were not at all connected to political negotiations. From late 1954 onward, the United States and Britain had been collaborating on a plan aimed at achieving a settlement of the Arab-Israeli conflict. The project, referred to as Alpha, was classified top secret. British and American negotiators toured the region, focusing on an initial peace between Egypt and Israel. The Alpha plan sought an equitable settlement of major issues such as borders, Egyptian right of transit across the Negev to Jordan, Jerusalem's status, and refugee resettlement and compensation. If the negotiations succeeded, the United States and Britain also were willing to increase financial aid to the region substantially from $100 million annually to $1 billion over five years, including $112 million for the Jordan Valley plan.[148] The inducements offered to Egypt to agree to a peace settlement included economic assistance to build the Aswan Dam and military assistance. Israel would receive security guarantees, US economic aid, termination of the Arab boycott, and free passage through the Suez Canal.[149] During the critical last phase of the Johnston mission, British

Foreign Secretary Anthony Eden met with Nasser in Cairo on February 20, 1955, to discuss aspects of the Alpha plan. Nasser did not reject the possibility of a peace settlement with Israel, but insisted that Israel make territorial concessions. In particular, Nasser called for the Negev to be given to Egypt so that it would have territorial continuity with Jordan.[150]

The Eisenhower administration briefed Johnston on the Alpha project in June 1955, and Johnston knew that when Dulles made it public, his water plan would fail.[151] "Johnston thought the Arab-Israeli problem should be approached from an economic standpoint and not a political one, because no Arab leader would feel able to ask their people to accept a political settlement."[152] Once the Alpha plan was known, it would be nearly impossible to convince Arab leaders that Johnston's plan was not political. Johnston feared that the Arabs would feel "double-crossed" and that the Jordan Valley negotiation would be destroyed.[153] The British agreed with Johnston that the United Kingdom and United States should postpone announcing Alpha publicly. Dulles initially went along, but by the end of the summer of 1955, he decided to announce the peace initiative. The secretary of state did not want to wait any longer because the 1956 presidential campaign was near at hand. Neither Dulles nor Eisenhower wanted US domestic politics complicating Middle East diplomacy.[154]

On August 26, 1955, in a speech before the Council on Foreign Relations in New York, Dulles made public a US proposal based on the Alpha project for solving the Arab-Israeli conflict.[155] He mentioned that the Johnston mission was attempting to solve the water conflict, but that "three other issues remained to be solved . . . and if these three principal problems could be dealt with, then the way would be paved for a solution of others."[156] The three principal problems were the Palestinian refugee issue, regional military and economic insecurity, and fixed borders. Dulles suggested that water projects would solve a large part of the refugee problem, thereby implying a link between the two missions. The secretary was less specific on the last two problems. For the first time, Dulles had made public the US intention to resolve the entire conflict, an announcement that served a fatal blow to Johnston's efforts.

In November, just after the fourth and final round of the Johnston mission, the Eisenhower administration tried to revive the Alpha Project Peace Plan as outlined in Dulles's August speech.[157] The administration assigned Robert B. Anderson, the former deputy secretary of defense, as a US envoy for Israel and Egypt. From January to March 1956, Anderson shuttled between Cairo and Tel Aviv. In an effort to recoup influence after the Egyptian-Soviet arms deal, the United States reiterated a willingness to help Egypt build the Aswan Dam.[158] The water project was the centerpiece of Nasser's program to combat poverty and develop Egypt's economy. In the end, the Anderson mission failed because there was little trust between Nasser and Israel's Prime Minister David Ben-Gurion. Egypt wanted Israel to make concessions on territory and refugees before initiating direct peace negotiations. Israel demanded face-to-face negotiations without preconditions, which was a nonnegotiable issue for Egypt. When Dulles and Eisenhower tried to resolve the whole Arab-Israeli conflict, they sacrificed the Johnston tactical functional track. In the end, the Dulles Alpha/Anderson strategy failed because the region had become more confrontational and was not prepared for a resolution of the conflict in its entirety now.

After the failure of the Anderson mission, Dulles increasingly lost patience with Nasser's Arab nationalism, "neutralism," and Egypt's unwillingness to cooperate with the United States. Nasser's recognition of Communist China in May 1956 was the last straw. In July 1956, Dulles abruptly withdrew the loan offer to construct the Aswan Dam. In response, Nasser declared in a public address that Egypt would nationalize the Suez Canal to help pay the costs of building the dam. This set in motion the events that led to the 1956 Suez crisis and war.

ANALYSIS OF THE JOHNSTON PLAN

Because a final agreement was never attained, much controversy has ensued as to what the Johnston Plan specified. The plan was not a formal agreement between the riparians or between the riparians and the United States. However, as will be discussed in chapter 3, riparians who accepted US financial assistance to build their water projects became obligated to follow the guidelines set forth in the Johnston Plan. Additionally, the "plan [was] not one plan but two, Israel's version and the [US version]."[159] Israel's account consisted of a "Draft Memorandum of Understanding," dated July 5, 1955, and other exchanges between Israel and the United States. The American version included all the above and the October 11, 1955, "US-Arab Memorandum of Understanding" that the Arab League Technical Committee approved. Johnston characterized the differences in the two versions as "insignificant,"[160] yet they would cause some noteworthy future problems and are worth reviewing. The first variation involves differences over Israel's allocation from the Yarmouk and Jordan's allocation from the Jordan. Second, the US version of the plan provided for UN involvement in the plan's supervisory mechanism, but Israel rejected any UN association. Even with the different memoranda of understanding, there was still considerable common agreement by both sides. Johnston organized the plan into four parts: storage, division of water, distribution systems, and supervision (see Map 2-2).

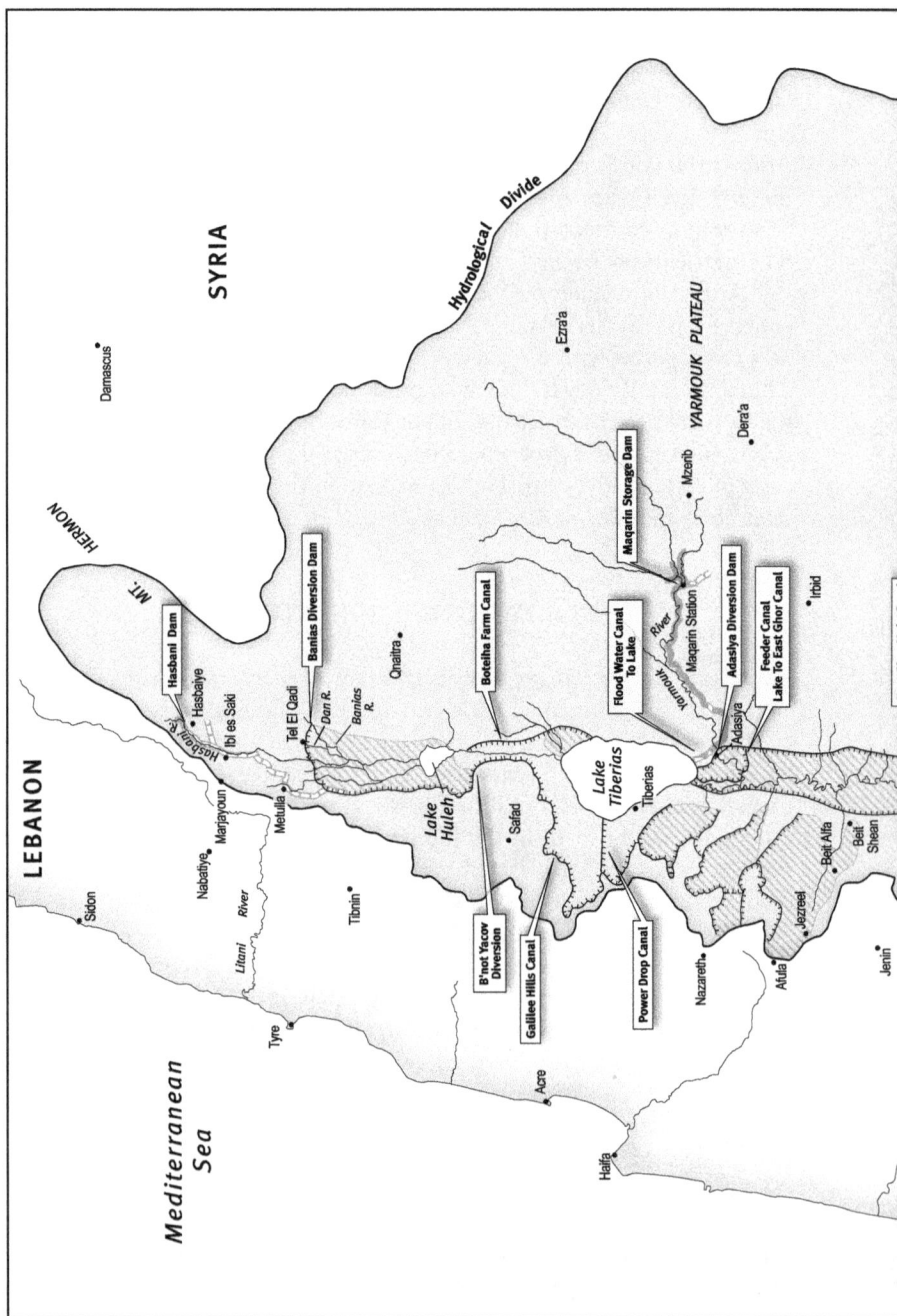

SYRIA

Hydrological Divide

Damascus

Ezra'a

YARMOUK PLATEAU

MT. HERMON

Maqarin Storage Dam

Dera'a

Banias Diversion Dam

Hasbani Dam

Mzerib

Hasbaiye

Boteiha Farm Canal

Flood Water Canal To Lake

Adasiya Diversion Dam

Feeder Canal Lake To East Ghor Canal

Ibl es Saki

Qhaitra

Maqarin Station

Irbid

Tel El Qadi

Dan R.

Banias R.

Yarmouk River

Adasiya

LEBANON

Marjayoun

Hasbani R.

Lake Huleh

Lake Tiberias

Nabatiye

Metulla

Safad

Tiberias

Beit Shean

Sidon

Tibnin

B'net Yacov Diversion

Beit Alfa

Litani River

Galilee Hills Canal

Power Drop Canal

Nazareth

Jezreel

Tyre

Afula

Jenin

Acre

Mediterranean Sea

Haifa

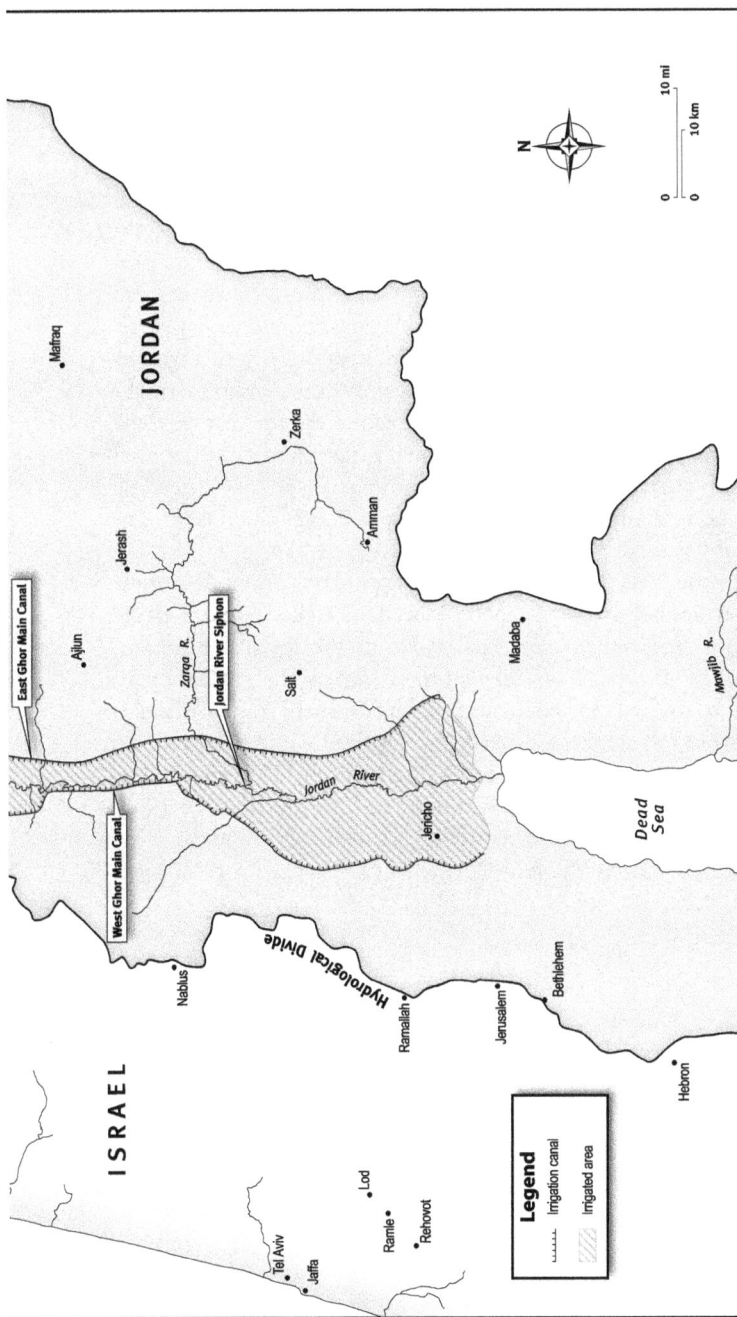

Source: Photocopy "The Jordan Valley Plan" 30 September 1955 and Charles T. Main, Inc.

MAP 2-2   Johnston Plan, 1955

Storage

First, on the Upper Yarmouk, the plan provided for the construction of a dam to store 300 mcm of water for irrigation and generation of 150 million kWh of electricity annually. A 126-meter high dam at Maqarin was deemed justifiable to the United States both on economic and engineering grounds; consequently, the United States was willing to finance the project. However, if Jordan and Syria wanted a larger dam, which would hold 460 mcm, the United States would insist that the riparians pay for it because it did not produce enough additional energy or store enough extra water to make it a worthwhile investment.[161] Since no dam on the Yarmouk could economically store all the floodwaters, which are critical to Jordanian irrigation, Yarmouk water must be stored in Lake Tiberias. The average flood amount to be stored in the lake is approximately 80 million cubic meters per year (mcmy). The Yarmouk water that Jordan deposited and withdrew from Lake Tiberias would be recorded by the watermaster. A total storage space "not exceeding 300 mcm" would be reserved for Jordanian water in Lake Tiberias.[162] The plan deferred the use of Lake Tiberias for storage for five years, or until 1960, when, according to the plan, "a neutral engineering board" would determine the amount of Yarmouk floodwater to be stored in Lake Tiberias based "solely on irrigation requirements of Arab lands in the lower Jordan valley."[163] The last water-storage clause allowed for a dam on the Hasbani tributary for Lebanon to use its allocated water for the Hasbani Valley. The size and type of dam would depend on a survey, which the United States would finance.[164] As we see in chapters 3, 4, and 6, discussions of a Yarmouk dam are a major component of the Jordan River political agenda from the 1960s to the present. In the late 1990s, Jordan will push for storing some of its water in Lake Tiberias and, by the mid-2000s, will be on the verge of completing a Yarmouk dam.

Division of Water

The water allocations are both the most important and most contentious part of the plan. In mcmy, the plan allows:

To Lebanon	35 from the Hasbani
To Syria	20 from the Banias
	22 from the Jordan for the Boteiha farms
	90 from the Yarmouk
Total	**132**

To Jordan	377 from the Yarmouk
	100 from the Jordan
Total	**477**
To Israel	25 from the Yarmouk

As for the residual water, the plan states that "except for the above with-drawals and deliveries, the waters of the Yarmouk River will be available for the unconditional use of the Kingdom of the [sic] Jordan, and the waters of the Jordan River will be available for the unconditional use of Israel."[165]

There are two key differences in respect to allocations between the two memoranda of understandings: the first is the quantity of Yarmouk water allocated to Israel's Yarmouk Triangle farms. The "Draft Memorandum of Understanding" between Israel and the United States allocated 40 mcmy of Yarmouk water to Israel, while the "US-Arab Memorandum of Understand-ing" provides 25 mcm. The second variation is the quality of usable Lake Tiberias water that Israel is to deliver to Jordan. Israel's memo states that Israel would provide "100 mcm of which 70 mcm would be of average Lake Tiberias salinity and the remaining 30 mcm being derived at Israel's option from the diversion of saline springs around Lake Tiberias."[166] The Arab memo states that 85 mcm of the 100 mcm must be of Lake Tiberias quality and the remaining 15 mcm may be from saline springs, as long as that water is not too salty.[167] In essence, the Arab memo gives Jordan 45 mcm more freshwater than provided by the Israel memo. Thus, a question remained over the 30 mcm of saline water, the Kingdom's Jordan River share, and Israel's Yarmouk water allocation.[168] It was the debate over Israel's summer Yarmouk allocation that pushed Jordan and Israel to secretly cooperate from the 1960s onward, as will be discussed in chapter 4.

Distribution Systems (see Map 2-2)

The plan provides for a network of irrigation canals, diversion weirs, hydroelectric dams, and electrical generation facilities for Jordan, Syria, and Lebanon.[169]

For Lebanon: Storage dam and irrigation works on Hasbani for uti-lizing 35 mcm of water.

For Syria: (1) Diversion structure and canal leading from the Jordan to the Boteiha farm area; (2) replacement of existing hydroelectric facilities on the Boteiha farm. New canals and generating facilities to supply 50 kWh of electrical power.

For Syria and Jordan: Storage dam to create a 300 mcm capacity reservoir on the Yarmouk River for irrigation, electrical power generation, and "security."[170]

For Jordan: (1) Diversion dam near Adasiya for Yarmouk water to Ghor canals; (2) irrigation canal network: East Ghor Canal running from Adasiya southward to the Dead Sea area and a West Ghor canal system that would include a siphon from the East Ghor Canal to the West Ghor canal; (3) canal from Adasiya to Lake Tiberias, if necessary, to capture and store Yarmouk flood waters in the lake; (4) distribution system to convey waters from main canals to farm lands; (5) pumping plants to raise water to lands above the primary canal; (6) drainage works for excess water and salts; and (7) works on Lake Tiberias if lake is used to store Yarmouk River flood flows.

The "US-Arab Memorandum of Understanding" fails to mention even a single water project for Israel. Yet in the US-Israeli memo it does state that "the principal Israel diversion structure will be located at or near B'not Yacov."[171] This statement is important because it gives Israel permission to divert water from the controversial location. The Arabs, especially the Syrians, did not consent in writing to this point. In addition, this contradicts a clause in both memos that states that the water plan cannot interfere with the armistice agreement and vice versa. In the end, the Johnston mission never resolved the B'not Yacov issue.[172] On another controversial issue, neither memo prohibits out-of-basin use by any of the riparians. The section regarding the division of water in both memoranda explicitly states that, except for the mentioned withdrawals, "the water of the Jordan will be available for unconditional use of Israel."[173] Thus, the plan authorized Israel to proceed with out-of-basin use and the Technical Committee agreed in writing to this point. Chapter 3 discusses the two primary Jordan River basin projects: Israel's National Water Carrier and Jordan's East Ghor Canal.

Supervision

The plan proposed the creation of an impartial engineering board together with a watermaster for supervising operation of the water system and compliance of the riparians with the plan. The engineering board would consist of three engineers who would be selected from a list prepared by the secretary general of the United Nations.[174] The participating Arab states and Israel would each choose one engineer. The two selected engineers then would pick the third member of the board and the board would choose the watermaster. The four could not be nationals or employees of the participating riparians.[175] Thus, this supervisory system would eliminate the need for direct contact or negotiations between the Arab states and Israel.[176] The engineering board would review engineering designs of diversion structures and other water-related structures and establish patterns of water withdrawals and releases to assure all participants that all water-related matters were within the framework of the plan. It would be the board's responsibility to detect violations of the agreement. Finally, the watermaster's duties would include supervising the deliveries and withdrawals of water and all monitoring facilities, and keeping records and generating reports regarding the system. As previously discussed, the watermaster was to make the computations relating to the Yarmouk water deposits and withdrawals from Lake Tiberias. If there was a violation, the watermaster was responsibile for taking the necessary steps to enforce compliance or remedy the situation. The watermaster was to have complete, unimpeded access to all areas of the watercourse. In the end, as discussed in chapter 4, Jordan and Israel found it more productive to address Yarmouk water issues face-to-face, although secretly, than through a watermaster or other third party.

At the end of the Johnston mission, three issues remained unresolved: international supervision, the allotment of Jordan water for Jordan, and the allotment of Yarmouk River water for Israel. Riparians and third party negotiators would continue to debate some of these issues long into the future. Although the differences between the parties were quite small, each issue called for limited cooperation, and, in the end, this requirement was the primary reason why the differences were difficult to resolve. On the issue of international supervision, Israel initially accepted the concept of inspection because Jordanian water was to be stored in Israeli-controlled Lake Tiberias. Even so, Israel wanted a minimal amount of international supervision, which would not involve the United Nations in any capacity. The Arabs wanted greater supervision. On the second point, the Jordan River distribution, the Johnston Plan stipulated that Jordan was entitled to 100 mcm of Jordan River water from Israeli sources. The disagreement was over the ratio of saline water to freshwater. Israel argued that Jordan was entitled to 70 mcm of freshwater and 30 mcm saline, and the United States and the Arabs argued that the allocation was 85 mcm freshwater and 15 mcm saline. There was discussion between Israel and the United States over this issue with no agreement. In the end, Jordan remained unwilling publicly to cooperate with Israel, even if it meant losing 100 mcm from Israeli sources. On the third point, the distribution of Yarmouk River water, Israeli Yarmouk Triangle farmers were allotted Yarmouk River water; however, the mediation did not resolve whether they were entitled to 25 or 40 mcmy. Unlike the other two issues, to be discussed in chapters 3 and 4,

Jordan cooperated with Israel on this issue. This cooperation was feasible because it was not public. To cooperate, Jordan merely had to allow a certain amount of the Yarmouk to flow past its canal intake to Israeli pumps downstream. In addition, Jordan depended on US assistance for its water projects, and the United States insisted that Jordan abide by the Johnston Plan, which included allowing Israel its Yarmouk allocation. In the end, it was the Yarmouk sharing that provided the focus for future Jordan-Israel water coordination.

ANALYSIS AND CONCLUSION

How did the Johnston mission succeed in convincing both sides of the Arab-Israeli conflict to negotiate for two years and arrive at an agreement on the engineering and economic aspects of a water-sharing plan? And why did Johnston fail to achieve a final agreement between the United States and all the riparians? Also, how did water scarcity stimulate acute conflict twice?

After the 1948 War, the preferences of Jordan River riparians were fairly straightforward. For Israel, because it had to fight to exist from its day of independence, its preferences were clearer than most struggling developing states. The first preference was the security of the state and its citizens; the second was the promotion of immigration of Jews from all over the world, but particularly the Middle East and war-torn Europe; and finally, the third was economic development.[177] At the time of the armistice agreements, Israel's Jewish population was three-quarters of a million, compared to the 30 million of the five Arab states it had fought. In addition, the combined Arab gross domestic product was seven times greater than Israel's.[178] As a result, Israel's preferences were interlinked and reinforced each other. Without Israeli economic development, it would be impossible to absorb immigrants and purchase needed weapons systems for the state's security. Without immigration, Israel would not be able to increase the size of its military or to grow its economic sector.

With the exception of Lebanon, no Arab state after the 1948 War instituted a government that was democratically elected and there were few, if any, liberal democratic institutions.[179] As a result, the leaders controlled most of the institutions of state power and the elites' preferences were paramount. Arab state preferences were security of the state and the regime, economic development, and addressing the Palestinian refugee problem in their state.[180] Between 1949 and 1953, there was a belief among Syrian leaders Zaim and Shishaqli and Jordan's Abdullah that resolving the Israel problem quietly while at the same time addressing the problems at home would solidify their power base.[181] In a way, this was also the case for some Israeli leaders. Prime Minister Moshe Sharett saw the Johnston mission as a way of quieting critics of his policy of halting the B'not Yacov project.[182] By 1954, a strong Arab preference developed against cooperating with Israel because, unlike the earlier leaders, such as Zaim, Shishaqli, and Abdullah, such cooperation was perceived as a detriment to an Arab leader's power. There was also, as political scientist Nadav Safran put it, the "psychological reluctance of Arab governments to admit final defeat to Israel and their fear of facing an outraged public opinion that had been encouraged in its expectations of easy victory."[183]

As for Jordan River water, it was enmeshed in each state's preference to develop economically. For all these states, agriculture was the key economic sector and, without a dependable water supply, agriculture would wither. As already mentioned, Israel and Jordan were downstream riparians and much more dependent on the Jordan/Yarmouk rivers than Syria and Lebanon. Even so, it would be an error to assume that water needs and riparian position alone would predict a state's behavior. Other preferences, such as security and immigration/refugees, are linked to the water issue and may influence preferences and therefore a state's behavior. Israel's strategy to achieve its preferences was to seek to establish final peace with its Arab neighbors and maintain good relations with all the great powers, but especially with the United States.[184] Initially, the strategy of Jordan and Syria involved secret, bilateral negotiations with Israel. When this approach did not succeed, the strategy moved toward Arab states working together, at least in international negotiations, such as the Johnston mission. These less developed Arab states also saw the value of US economic aid and were willing to make limited compromises, such as participating in the Johnston negotiations, so as to become a US aid recipient.

Johnston succeeded in using the negotiating strategies of issue linkage, facilitating regional water technocrats or an epistemic community, and two-level diplomacy for initiating cooperation during his mission.[185] He linked US economic assistance to Arab and Israeli water cooperation; he facilitated the establishment of a community of water technocrats, who did not meet directly, but had a common understanding of the problem. With US mediation, this community of technocrats was able to arrive at a technical solution.

Johnston utilized a two-level diplomacy technique in cases when riparians' domestic and international interests were pitted against each other to attain compromises from both sides to realize international cooperation.[186] This political strategy, at least in relation to Israel, also played a positive role in facilitating cooperation. There was a faction opposed to any compromise with the Arabs on the water issue, but using the linkage of improved relations with Arab states enabled the pro-cooperation faction initially to win out. In addition, the needs of Israeli agriculture helped moderate what Arabs perceived as attainable demands during negotiations and vice versa. While the *Mapai* party government coalition was strongly aligned with the agriculture sector that opposed making any water concessions, there also was a faction within the government, including Prime Minister David Ben-Gurion, that saw the political benefits of making certain water compromises with the Arabs to improve political relations and enhance the chances of a diplomatic breakthrough. The tension between the Israeli factions arguing for no compromise on water resources versus the group supporting trading water to improve political relations with neighboring Arab states was an ongoing factor. Finally, while the Arabs and Israelis were not all allied with the United States, the participants were also not yet split into two separate and opposing superpower blocs. The Arabs were all opposed to Israel, but it was not until the Soviets entered the political scene that the anti-Israel alliance became unified. All these factors contributed to Johnston's initial success.

Nonetheless, the strategies and factors that enabled Johnston to facilitate cooperation were not sufficient to maintain it. The politics of the region were becoming increasingly tense and difficult, a reality that neutralized the positive impact of the water technocrat epistemic community. By the end of the mission, the Soviets had a foothold in the region, and their growing influence reduced Arab states' dependence on US financial aid. As a result, the issue linkage became less effective. Two-level politics—in particular, the relationship between negotiators (elites) and the masses—were having an increasingly negative impact on Arab willingness for water cooperation. State elites were not politically strong enough to use this type of diplomacy for cooperation. In fact, many Arab states utilized the water issue as a means of increasing their domestic and international power base by criticizing an effort at water coordination with Israel. On the eve of the Arab foreign minister meeting in Cairo in October 1955, Johnston explained to the State Department why he was pessimistic about a positive Arab decision. First, he argued that international events, like Israel's raid on Gaza in February, the Baghdad Pact, and the Czech-Egyptian arms deal made the environment tenser. These events pushed Egypt and Syria closer to the USSR. He also argued that Syria and Lebanon did not have enough incentive to cooperate and that Jordan "lacked courage to stand up for its own best interest." Johnston noted that Syria and Lebanon advocated using the Yarmouk alone, and that Jordan's loss of 200 mcm of water was of little concern to them. Syria, for its part, would obtain its Yarmouk hydroelectric power without a Johnston plan, and Lebanon was only interested in developing the upstream Hasbani tributary to the Jordan. It could secure US aid for this project without agreeing to the Johnston Plan. By the end of the mission, the Arab governments believed they had much to lose by having any apparent contact or agreement with Israel. Johnston hoped Nasser would be his white knight, but Egypt was moving closer to the USSR.[187]

If any tactical functional water-sharing cooperation is to be effective, what changes are needed? The usual conditions for cooperation (discussed in chapter 1) are creating mutuality of interests, lengthening the shadow of the future, and decreasing the number of participants. Both Jordan and Israel had an interest in seeing the Johnston plan move forward. Both needed the water and the US financing of their water projects. Lebanon and Syria, on the other hand, were not dependent on the Jordan River water and not politically aligned with the United States. Lebanese and Syrian state elites would not jeopardize their political power for a water agreement with Israel. When analyzing their state interests, leaders believed that regional water cooperation was not worth the price of being seen as tacitly accepting Israel and abandoning the Palestinian people and the cause of Arab nationalism. Although Jordan had no wish to be seen as overtly cooperating with Israel, water was such an important consideration that Jordan was willing to take limited risks and make certain political compromises to improve its water position. Thus, Jordan and Israel had mutual interests and by eliminating, as much as possible, Syria and Lebanon's role and decreasing the number of participants, cooperation was again more likely. Thus, for limited tactical functional cooperation to occur, it needed to involve Jordan and Israel. Still, these riparians had to also lengthen the shadow of the future and, more generally, overcome the obstructive politics of the emerging protracted conflict. As will be discussed in chapters 3 and 4, a secret cooperative arrangement not only addresses the problems of the larger conflict but also enables the participating riparians to repeat indefinitely their cooperative arrangement. Lastly, both Jordan and Israel were moving closer to the West, in particular, the United States, and further away from the Soviets. While Jordan and Israel were not yet balancing threats together, they were both concerned about the growing radicalism in the region.

As for violent conflict, during this period, two separate episodes of acute conflict occurred over scarce water resources between Israel and Syria, but the precise role of water scarcity is debatable. The first and more violent conflict was over the Huleh area (spring 1951) and the second was B'not Yacov (fall 1953). Both involved disagreements about the DMZ and fears of the other obtaining the upper hand. In both cases, the precipitating cause was a struggle by Israel to develop scarce water resources and Syria's attempt to stop such projects.[188] Syria's primary issue was maintaining the DMZ status quo; it was not focused on scarce water resources.[189] However, Syria was concerned in the B'not Yacov episode about enough water reaching the Boteiha farm. Therefore, while the precipitating cause was water scarcity, the intermediate cause was Israel and Syria's different interpretation of their armistice agreement and the DMZ.[190] And, finally, the deep cause of the violent conflict was the larger Arab-Israeli conflict and the failure of Israel and Syria to reach an agreement on the question of Palestinian refugees, borders, and, in general, a comprehensive peace treaty. Therefore, it is debatable whether water was an exogenous factor in the two cases of acute conflict. Through counterfactuals, we will examine these contested causal claims.[191] After the 1967 War, the DMZs ceased to exist in any meaningful way; Israel's water scarcity continued, yet border violence did not occur between Israel and Syria. Thus, water was not an exogenous factor. However, one could also argue that during the 1967 War Syria lost most of the territory that gave it a Jordan River upstream position, thus removing the water issue as a point of friction from Syrian-Israeli relations. Therefore, it is argued here that water was a precipitating stimulus for violent conflict, in combination with the existence of the DMZs as an intermediate factor.

Finally, the failure of the Johnston mission should be attributed to Arab leaders' preference to not cooperate with Israel, and the failure of the US administration to recognize the strength of their preference. Some have argued, as discussed in chapter 1, that political issues must be addressed first before functional issues, such as water, can be resolved. During this period, there were two major attempts, Alpha and the Palestine Conciliation Commission conference, to resolve the political dispute and both failed.[192] Johnston was correct that the region was not ripe for a comprehensive peace agreement. He was also correct that friction points, such as water disputes, should be addressed so that such efforts could create peacemaking benefits down the road. Johnston's mistake was conducting his negotiations so publicly. He read well the Arab preferences for economic development through US aid. He also read well the Arab leaders' willingness to establish a Jordan Valley water plan. However, his fatal mistake was misreading the Arab public's preference for not cooperating with Israel. If he had better understood this preference and used a strategy that took into consideration this strongly felt national preference, such as secret negotiations and a secret cooperative regime, Johnston might have been successful in reaching a final agreement.

The Johnston mission ended because of a complex and overwhelming web of international and domestic politics. While the plan never became the Johnston agreement, this does not mean the US mediation was for naught. The Johnston Plan served as an important guidepost for Jordan Basin development, especially for Jordan and Israel. Had Johnston not gone forward with his negotiations, the basin would have been plagued with even greater uncertainty regarding the water issue, and no substantive guide would exist for determining an equitable division of the Jordan's waters. The plan's significance was eventually demonstrated by how it served "to damp down" tension over the Jordan waters issue.[193]

After the Arab League Council adjourned without making a decision on the Jordan Valley plan, the Israelis publicly asserted their right to resume diversion at B'not Yacov. Privately, however, Israeli leaders proposed a postponement of B'not Yacov construction for a period of two additional years if the United States granted their request for a $75 million loan from the Export-Import Bank. The credit was in part for developing Israeli water resources other than the Jordan River. The US government was receptive to this move by Israel since it wanted to delay a new round of conflict over B'not Yacov.[194] Jordan also was interested in receiving US assistance so it could move forward with its water development program.

By 1956, there was a quiet shift toward Nasser's idea of two separate plans within the Johnston Plan framework. However, the acting executive director of the advisory board for international development argued that if the United States accepted the Nasser proposal for two separate programs under the basic framework of the Johnston Plan, Jordan would lose some 200 mcm of water to Israel and to the Dead Sea due to lack of storage, leaving insufficient water for Jordan's West Bank West Ghor Canal.[195] The official warned that Jordan and refugee resettlement would suffer by accepting such a proposal.

Finally, US sources reported that, during the October 11, 1955, Arab League Council meeting, the Lebanese and Syrian delegations were not only advocating outright rejection of the Johnston Plan but also promoting diverting the upper Jordan River away from Israel. Initially rejected by most Arab states, the "Damascus Plan" involved diverting the two Jordan tributaries that rise in Syria and Lebanon. These riparians would dump the excess water that Arab states could not use into the Mediterranean or the Yarmouk so Israel could not use it.[196] As will be discussed in the next chapter, this was just the beginning of the Arab diversion plans, which would, among other events, lead to heightened tension over water resources and ultimately to acute conflict.

3

Water Development and Conflict, 1957–1967

Water politics in the period between 1957 and 1967 were shaped by three new factors: a shift in US diplomacy toward more modest goals, the growing Soviet-American rivalry that influenced the Middle East conflict, and a radicalization of Arab states' preferences toward Israel and the West. After the 1956 Suez War, the Arab-Israeli conflict became routinized and US diplomacy shifted significantly. The diplomacy of the previous period—1949–1956—had focused on moving the adversaries from conflict to cooperation with tactical functional cooperation. But during the 1957 to 1967 phase, Washington primarily focused on decreasing the chances of violent conflict or war because conflict resolution was not then viewed as possible due to the shift in Arab state preferences. Arab nationalism was on the rise and had taken the form of a Pan Arabism movement, whose primary doctrine was resistance to "colonialism, imperialism, and Zionism." Egyptian President Nasser had become the leader and symbol of this movement. Like Nasser, the Baath (Arab Renaissance) Party of Syria and later Iraq also stood for Arab unity, but as well incorporated revolutionary socialism. By the mid-1960s, the Arab world was divided between radical states, led by Nasser and supported by the Soviet Union, and status quo states, such as Jordan and Saudi Arabia, allies of the West. With Britain and France discredited after the 1956 Suez War, the United States and the USSR continued to increase their influence in the region. As the Soviet-American rivalry intensified, so did the Arab-Israeli conflict. The superpower competition resulted in an arms race between Israel and the Arab states. In addition, the Soviets attempted to exacerbate the Arab-Israeli conflict in an effort to bring more Arab states within its sphere of influence. The Palestinian cause continued to rally the Arab states against Israel.

True to earlier US concerns, regional instability increased significantly. This was in part because of both the continuing Palestinian refugees and Jordan River basin water utilization tribulations.

The first section of this chapter deals with how the United States altered its Jordan River water policy in the post-Johnston mission era to facilitate potential tactical functional cooperation, but, more important, to mitigate tension and potential conflict between the riparians. Through unilateral actions financed by the United States, Israel began building its National Water Carrier and Jordan constructed its East Ghor Canal. American financing was granted only if the riparians agreed, as Israel and Jordan did, to follow the Johnston Plan. The United States established a "low-key" cooperative arrangement between only Israel and Jordan for sharing Yarmouk water. However, at this point, Jordan and Arab preferences in general were strongly opposed to any tactical functional cooperation with Israel. As described in later sections, Israel's water program and the Arab diversion projects reaction became major sources of contention. However, as explained in the section entitled "Arab Diversions," even with US efforts, acute conflict concerning the water issue resulted. The water-related acute conflict set off a chain reaction of border clashes that are linked directly to the events that led to the 1967 Arab-Israeli War. The final section argues that within this important case, the water issue became a critical domestic preference that impacted each state's international strategy and behavior. Even so, unlike some observers, this work rejects the notion that the 1967 War was directly caused by water scarcity. In other words, the 1967 War was not a "water war."

A New Piecemeal Approach

The 1956 War sent political shockwaves through the region; in its aftermath, US diplomacy became more difficult. By March 1957, Israeli forces withdrew from the Sinai and from Gaza, but pro-western Middle East regimes were under attack. That spring, a leftist uprising threatened the rule of King Hussein of Jordan. In response, the king purged the part of Jordan's government that had drawn support from other Arab leaders and requested US financial aid to replace the now suspended Arab assistance. The White House defined "the independence and integrity of Jordan as vital" to US interests and agreed to $10 million in economic aid.[1] In contrast, during this period, Jordanian-Egyptian tensions intensified because local Jordanian authorities had arrested and deported Nasser supporters. By summer, the United States and Jordan had signed economic, technical, and military assistance agreements. In an effort to demonstrate that the United States was genuinely interested in Jordan's development, Washington clearly indicated to the king a willingness to fund Jordan's primary water project, the East Ghor Canal.[2] The challenge to US interests throughout the region was real. Anti-Western forces overthrew the Hashemite king of Iraq, who had allied his country with the United States through the Baghdad Pact. In response, US troops landed in Lebanon and British troops deployed to Jordan.

At this point, the United States tried to focus on those issues on which Arab states and Americans could agree and delay consideration of other contentious questions. For the most part, the Arab-Israeli conflict was viewed by US policymakers in the context of basic Middle East–American interests, which included access to oil, the maintenance of economic and political stability, and the protection of strategic interests against the threat of Soviet expansion. Thus, the US government sought publicly to put the water issue on hold or in the "icebox," to the extent this was feasible, so it would not become a distraction from the pivotal interests.[3] In fact, in the late 1950s, after the Suez crisis, when Eric Johnston was still an outspoken proponent of a Jordan Valley Development Plan, he offered several times to return to the region. However, with the changes in the political environment, particularly the increased Soviet influence in the region, Secretary Dulles and others at the State Department did not look on a return visit with favor. Along with the Eisenhower administration, UN Secretary General Hammarskjöld, who had been briefed a number of times on the Johnston mission, agreed that the Jordan River project was now "taboo" in the area.[4] In a memo to the secretary of state, a high-ranking State Department official concluded that the appearance of a public figure such as Eric Johnston in the region at that time would "do more harm than good in the matter of the refugees" and all other US diplomacy.[5] The consensus at the State Department was that the United States needed a new approach to the Jordan Valley development issue.[6] The United States subsequently decided to separate the water and refugee issue, which had been linked during the Johnston mission.[7]

On January 24, 1958, the National Security Council (NSC) approved a policy paper that clearly delineated a new approach to the Jordan River basin problem. The NSC paper recommended "support of the development of *segments* of the Jordan River system when not in conflict with the Unified [Johnston] Plan for development of the Jordan River basin."[8] The NSC recognized that the Johnston Plan's approach for developing the river system in a unified manner and requiring cooperation among riparians was preferable to chaotic, segmented development. However, according to the NSC, the reality of the situation was that "the tense political situation within the area makes political clearance of the Unified [Johnston] Plan, as a whole, by the interested states an impossibility in the near future."[9] In the end, American officials correctly saw a radical shift in the region's political environment. In the early 1950s, public negotiations and indirect cooperation were rightly perceived as a possibility, whereas in the late 1950s and 1960s, unilateral development, secret cooperation, and US supervision were the only serious policy options.

Consequently, the United States no longer attempted to sell the Johnston Plan or any other sweeping proposal to the Arab states. Instead, by fragmenting the Johnston Plan, the Americans hoped that they could incorporate some of its original objectives and benefits without stirring up the region further. Essentially, water became an issue for states within the region to resolve. The new US policy called for minimal involvement unless both sides requested an intermediary. Nevertheless, the United States continued its policy of tactical functional cooperation, albeit more covertly, of reducing tensions where possible.[10] The United States also focused on increasing Jordan's economic viability by creating employment opportunities and augmenting the potential for the resettlement of Palestinian refugees. Gradually, though, US policy shifted from refugee resettlement as a primary objective. Instead, encouraging the economic and political stability of states friendly to the United States, such as Jordan, became the focus of American foreign policy in the Middle East.[11]

Despite the new more piecemeal approach, the United States still used its carrot of financial assistance, including aid for water projects, to convince Jordan and Israel to abide by the original terms of the Johnston Plan. The United States, in turn, received written, sometimes secret promises from these riparians that they would abide by the plan. Israel took most of its water from the Jordan River, while Jordan utilized the Yarmouk. This arrangement was feasible because Jordan and Israel primarily obtained their water from separate rivers, making interdependence and cooperation less necessary.[12] Even so, differing interpretations of the meaning of the Johnston Plan stimulated difficulties among Jordan, Israel, and the United States, especially when it came to Israel's Yarmouk allocation and Jordan's Jordan River share.

Although the allotments of water arrived at in the Johnston negotiations were not legally binding, they nevertheless became the guiding principles by which the United States monitored Israel and Jordan on their respective plans for Jordan Valley water. American policymakers for the Jordan basin cited the international legal principle of "equitable division," requiring that the waters be utilized in a fair and equitable manner.[13] Because the two sides had accepted the Johnston Plan at least on a technical level, the United States regarded it as the most defined and operational approach available to facilitate an equitable division of the Jordan basin waters. The United States, as a superpower and a donor, went one step further in stating that it "must be the moral guarantor who assures the Arab riparian states that Israel is acting within the limits of the [Johnston Plan] and vice versa."[14] Thus, US policymakers claimed a significant degree of authority in declaring that "any departures [by Jordan or Israel] from the Johnston allocations would therefore be a most serious matter."[15]

By the 1960s, the US administration made public in *Digest of International Law* its piecemeal approach:

> In the period 1953–1955, the United States Government, through the work of Ambassador Eric Johnston, made a strenuous and generous effort to devise a plan for unified development of the Jordan Valley that would be equitable and acceptable to all riparians. Regrettably, the comprehensive [Johnston] Plan drawn up by Ambassador Johnston failed to win the immediate approval of all parties. However, in the absence of later studies of an equally comprehensive nature, we have considered that it remained useful as a model for full, orderly, and equitable utilization of an immensely important international water resource. We remain convinced of the benefits of the type of unified development embodied in the [Johnston] Plan. In the absence of agreement thereon, we have supported the right of the riparians to proceed with national water programs provided these did not conflict with the general principles and allocation patterns envisaged in the [Johnston] Plan.[16]

SECRET NOTES

Between February 1958 and January 1960, the United States negotiated and received numerous secret notes of assurance from Jordan and Israel that they would abide by the Johnston Plan in exchange for US assistance with their respective water projects. Jordan, at this point, was seeking funding for the East Ghor Canal and Israel for its National Water Carrier.

Because of its open friendship with the United States, Israel publicly and privately reaffirmed its commitment to the Johnston Plan throughout the 1950s and 1960s.[17] Israel demonstrated its commitment to the United States by postponing development of the Jordan River and particularly the B'not Yacov bridge area for a two-year period during the life of the Johnston mission. Because of this and Israel's stated commitment to abide by the Johnston Plan, the United States, in 1958, helped to guarantee a $24.2 million Export-Import Bank loan for developing Israel's water resources outside the Jordan Valley.[18] In supporting the loan, the State Department also cited the fact that the loan did not include any financing for the controversial main conduit of the National Water Carrier, which was intended to convey water out of the Jordan Valley basin. In response to the leftist coup in Iraq, during this period, Israel told the US government that it was "genuinely interested" in the survival of King Hussein's government and would most likely accept Jordan's unilateral implementation of its East Ghor Canal plan.[19]

In 1958, Jordan also assured the United States of its commitment to the Johnston Plan and, in return, Washington funded part of the East Ghor Canal. In a letter to Jordan, the United States stated that American "assistance will be extended provided there is an explicit undertaking from the Hashemite Kingdom of Jordan that it will not draw from the Yarm[o]uk River more than the share allotted it under the [Johnston] Plan."[20] The next day, through a diplomatic note, Jordan formally, yet secretly, agreed to the US terms.[21] Later that year, Jordan assured the United States that it would not oppose Israeli water development plans as long as Israel did not exceed its Johnston Plan allocations. The United States understood that Jordan's secrecy arose from the pressure it was under from the United Arab Republic (Egypt and Syria) to actively oppose Israeli water development.[22] With funding in place, by summer 1960, Jordan announced it had begun actual construction of the canal, which diverts water from the Yarmouk River slightly north of the Jordanian town of Adasiya into a 3-meter horseshoe-shaped tunnel through which water is transferred to the main canal downstream. Winding southward paralleling the Jordan, the canal uses gravity to move a maximum of 155 million cubic meters per year (mcmy) into lateral irrigation canals. The laterals run west from the main canal, and perennial side wadis also supplement the flow. The first phase of the project was completed in 1961, and the United States then provided funding for the second stage of the East Ghor Canal.[23] For this stage, Jordan planned a dam at Maqarin for water storage, irrigation, and hydroelectric power generation (see Map 3-1).

Noting US aid for the East Ghor Canal, Israel requested American support for its own Yarmouk River water projects. Israel had contended that the increased East Ghor Canal utilization would lead to greater salinity of the lower Jordan, adversely impacting Yarmouk farmers downstream.[24] Israel wanted the United States to fund the Beit Shean conduit, which would furnish an alternative supply of water from Lake Tiberias to the Yarmouk Triangle farmers.

Israel also sought US funding for the more controversial main conduit project of its National Water Carrier. The project was designed to convey upper Jordan River water out of the Jordan Valley basin by linking Lake Tiberias to the Mediterranean coastal plain and to the arid Negev in the south. In August 1958, the United States informed Israel that it would fund the project only if it proved to be economically sound, did not conflict with the armistice arrangement, was within the Johnston Plan guidelines, and did not, at this time, convey water to the Negev. Two months later, Israel compromised by deciding to move the diversion from the controversial B'not Yacov bridge area within the Demilitarized Zone (DMZ) to Eshed Kinrot at the northwestern corner of Lake Tiberias. When the National Water Carrier would be complete, Jordan River water from Eshed Kinrot was to be elevated from the lake, 212 meters below sea level, to a reservoir 40 meters above sea level in the lower

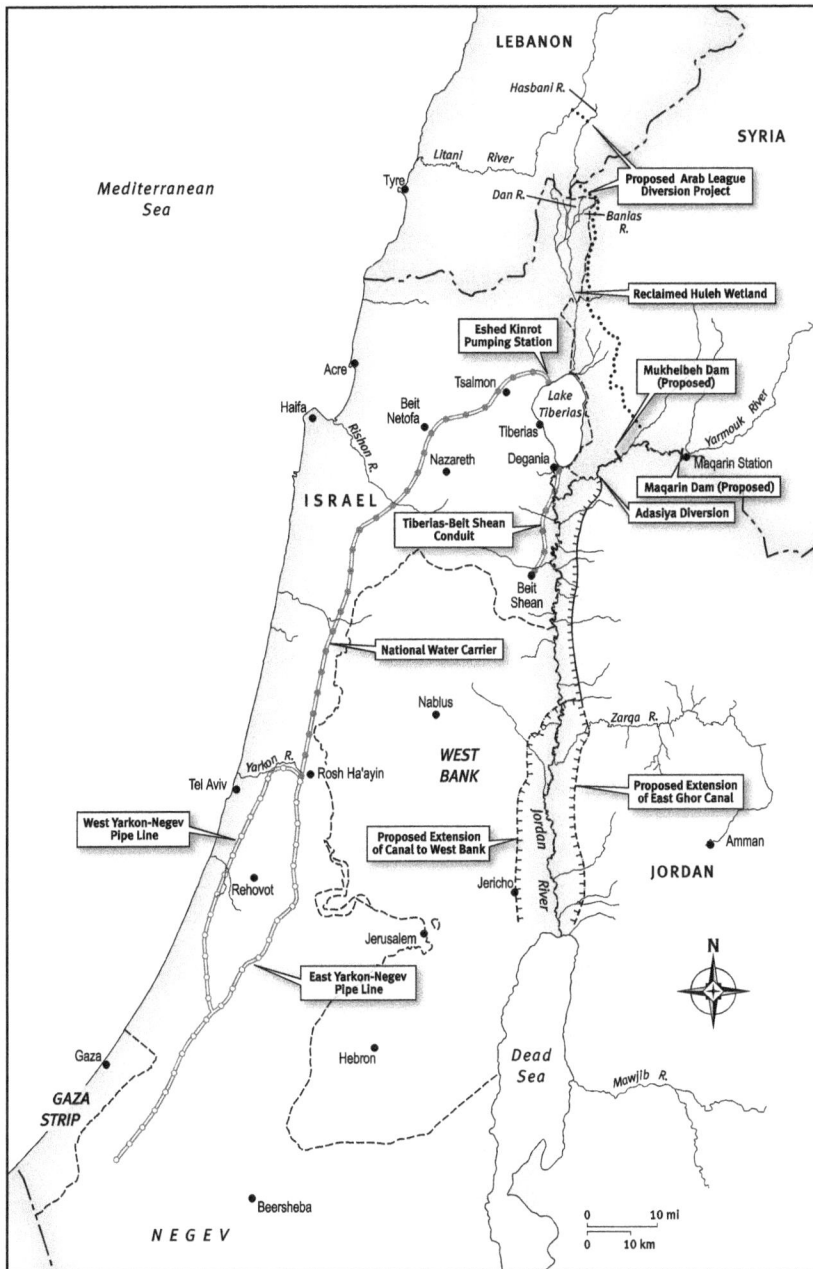

Source: US State Department.

MAP 3-1   Israel's National Water Carrier, Jordan's East Ghor Canal, and the Arab League Diversion Plan, Pre-1967

Galilee. From the reservoir, water would pass through tunnels, pipes, and open canals to the coastal plain in the Yarkon-Negev water system, and then, ideally, to the Negev itself, completing Israel's overall integrated national water scheme.[25] The guiding principle of the Israeli program was integration of most of the country's water resources to increase efficiency and allow maximum flexibility. The National Water Carrier program was designed to provide a municipal and industrial supply for three million people, water for agriculture with a continuous and regular flow, and an additional 170 million cubic meters (mcm) for increasing agriculture development.[26] Israel began construction of what would become its Lake Tiberias to Negev aqueduct or National Water Carrier on March 4, 1959.[27]

To realize the National Water Carrier, Israel was willing to make a number of major concessions. As one senior Israeli official explained, "It was obvious that the political danger of going back to the B'not Yacov [bridge] outweighed the economic costs."[28] Israeli leaders agreed, concluding that the hydrological benefits of B'not Yacov were not worth the negative political repercussions that would result from provoking Syria and antagonizing the United Nations and the United States. More important, Israel probably would not have received US economic assistance had it not moved the diversion point out of the DMZ.[29] The move was a major Israeli compromise since the original site permitted the generation of hydroelectric power. By contrast, the Eshed Kinrot project required pumping, thus consuming almost 20 percent of Israel's entire electrical power budget.[30] The new site's water also was of inferior quality because, instead of taking the water directly from the river, the water flow was mixed with that from Lake Tiberias, which was more saline.

Even with Israel's compromise, following the start of construction, the United States became increasingly reluctant to fund the main conduit of the National Water Carrier. Upon closer examination, the United States began to see "difficulties," arguing that Israel was taking 100 mcm more than was allotted in the Johnston Plan. Israeli water officials gave their US counterparts extensive documentation on their water program to clarify any remaining US concerns or misunderstandings. Israel also contended that the scheme was "in full agreement with the Johnston Plan."[31] During US–Israel technical talks in Washington in November 1959, Israel gave the United States assurances that it would continue to follow the Johnston Plan. Reassured that Israel would abide by the plan, the United States quietly approved a $15 million loan from the Development Loan Fund (DLF) for the main conduit of the National Water Carrier.[32] This was in addition to separate funding for the Beit Shean pipeline.[33] Even so, the United States requested from Israel "no publicity" for the loans and made clear that the money was for carrying surplus groundwater from the coastal plain. Behind the scenes, the United States also accepted that later the coastal waterworks would become part of the larger National

Water Carrier and carry Jordan River water to Israel's arid south.[34] At this point, Israel and Jordan had adequate funds to begin construction of their respective water projects, and both had given the United States assurances that they would adhere to the Johnston Plan.

THE CRIDDLE MISSION

By 1963, Israel was nearly ready to pump water from Lake Tiberias through the National Water Carrier, a development that was drawing increased Arab criticism. The United States responded to the growing Arab opposition, in part, by attempting to prove that adherence to the Johnston Plan was resulting in an equitable division of the Jordan basin water. The United States also committed to maintaining the sole remaining aspect of tactical functional cooperation from the Johnston Plan—that is, Jordan's allowing Israel a specified allocation of summer Yarmouk water. To satisfy its own concerns, the State Department secretly sent Wayne Criddle, the chief technical expert of Eric Johnston's mission, to Israel and Jordan during June and July 1963. Criddle had shuttled by himself through the region between Johnston's second and third trip, but the purpose of that visit was to address problematic technical issues.[35] The purpose of his 1963 mission was to provide the United States with confirmation that Israel and Jordan's water programs were still in line with the Johnston Plan and to establish remedial measures for Jordan known as the "Criddle technical formula" until Jordan's upstream Yarmouk Maqarin Dam project was completed.[36] Establishing and putting into action such practical revisions to the Johnston Plan as Criddle's "technical formula" would prove difficult given the complicated politics of the region.

Ensuring that Jordan received its proper allocation of water became a sticking point in these practical negotiations. Even before Criddle's 1963 mission, Israel approached the Americans unofficially with proposals to improve Jordan's water situation so Israel could fulfill its Johnston Plan obligations and thus increase the legitimacy of its National Water Carrier.[37] One proposal called for scheduled releases from Lake Tiberias to the Yarmouk of water allocated to Jordan under the plan via the Beit Shean pipeline.[38] This plan was not consistent with the estimates of Criddle and his associates that Jordan still needed an additional 76 mcm of water to irrigate the Jordan Valley properly. Israel's transfer of 70 to 85 mcm, Criddle believed, would fulfill most of Jordan's needs at that time as well as Israel's obligation under the Johnston Plan. As a result of a meeting in Washington in January 1964, Israel and the United States accepted a "technical formula" that addressed water allocations and salinity discharges. Together with Ahron Wiener, director of the Israel National Water Planning Authority (Tahal), Criddle developed a technical formula for delivering 100 mcm of Jordan River water to Jordan, as required by the Johnston Plan: 15 mcm from saline springs and 85 mcm from Lake Tiberias sweet water. Two-thirds was to be released at a constant flow during the summer months. Israel was to "receive an allocation of 25 mcm during the irrigation season at a maximum demand rate of 2.3 cubic meters per second [cms] from the Yarm[o]uk river." The agreement further allowed that "Jordan may use any Lake Tiberias spills and Israel may use uncaptured Yarm[o]uk waters, to the extent either exists, rather than allowing them to waste to the Dead Sea."[39] The United States specified the formula was ad referendum to a Jordanian agreement, but the idea of any cooperation between any Arab states and Israel was distasteful to most of the Arab political community. During the US-Jordanian technical formula discussion, an Egyptian water expert, Muhammad Ahmed Selim, who had led the Arab technical committee to the Johnston mission, was present and made his negative attitude toward the proposal clear to King Hussein and the American diplomats. Because of Arab pressure, Jordan refused to cooperate overtly with Israel, even if it meant not receiving the needed water that had been allocated from Lake Tiberias. So, Jordan rejected the Criddle technical formula.[40] However, a month later, King Hussein did privately tell a high-ranking US official in New York that Jordan did hope to stay within the limits of the Johnston Plan.[41]

During Criddle's missions to the region, the US engineer and mediator helped to create an effective sharing arrangement between Israel and Jordan, including a controversial secret sharing of the Yarmouk during the summer months. The necessary allotment of water for each state had been a point of conflict since the Johnston mission. At that time, Criddle wrote in a report that Israeli water officials claimed that Israel's historical use and need for the Yarmouk was 2.3 cms for the Triangle's farmers.[42] Criddle stated that, "according to the Israelis, that flow rate is needed during the peak use period, and they do not want any head gates on their diversion; thus, they want a continuous flow throughout the year. Such a demand seems unreasonable and probably should not be allowed—unless excessive use is also allowed the Jordanians. It is recommended that not more than 1,300 cm/dunum or 30 mcm be allowed for the area" and not 40 mcm, which was the Israeli total.[43] Prior to Criddle's mission, Jordan "by-passed" or allowed 30 percent of all Yarmouk water to flow past the East Ghor Canal intake to Israeli pumps, so Israel would receive its 25 or 40 mcm allotted in the two different versions of the Johnston Plan. During this period, Criddle helped to concretize for Jordan and Israel the sole cooperative regime developed because of the Johnston mission. The system called on Jordan to release approximately 2.3 cms to the Triangle during the irrigation season. At the time, this was 30 percent of the average dry season flow, which was reserved for Israel.[44] Criddle also reported that connecting the Yarmouk to the Beit Shean-Lake Tiberias pipeline was feasible and suggested to Israel that it take its

Yarmouk allocation only during the winter, using the proposed conduit. His Israeli counterpart balked, explaining that because Yarmouk water was of better quality and cheaper for Yarmouk Triangle farmers than the piped Lake Tiberias water, the Israeli government would encounter serious domestic problems with these farmers if they did not receive their historical Yarmouk allotment during the summer.[45] Even so, Criddle conveyed to Washington that both the Jordanians and the Israelis were "clearly operating within the framework of the Johnston Plan, and there was no evidence that either has any future intention of operating otherwise."[46] The United States also concluded, on the basis of Criddle's advice, that the 2.3 cms figure was part of the Johnston Plan.[47] As discussed in the next chapter, this 2.3 cms versus one-third interpretation of the Johnston Plan became a contentious issue between Israel and Jordan during the 1979 to 1994 secret talks and cooperation.

One of the unresolved issues of the Johnston mission had been the issue of the higher salinity of the lower Jordan. During a 1963 trip, Criddle examined this issue.[48] Because Jordan was diverting the Yarmouk to the East Ghor Canal and Israel was planning to shift its saline springs away from Lake Tiberias to the lower Jordan, salt levels in that part of the river were increasing significantly.[49] The new saline levels were negatively impacting Jordanian and Israeli farmers on the lower Jordan.[50] Criddle's technical recommendations called for extending the Jordanian canal system to provide needed and usable water that would replace the polluted flow of the lower Jordan. Criddle also concluded that because Jordan already was diverting large amounts of water to the East Ghor Canal, in effect driving salinity levels higher, it would be permissible for Israel to shift its saline springs to the lower Jordan and, thus, not undergo the cost of diverting the springs to the Mediterranean or elsewhere. Even so, Jordan refused to approve Israel's controversial program to shift its saline springs to the lower Jordan, thus making the water source completely unusable for Jordan's farmers. Criddle acknowledged that this was one of the unresolved issues from the Johnston mission.[51] Even without an explicit agreement, Israel began releasing saline effluents into the Jordan by the fall of 1964, but was concealing them by simultaneously releasing sweet Lake Tiberias water. The United States did not oppose the cover-up, and expressed appreciation to Israel for keeping the State Department informed and out of the public eye.[52] All this was to no avail; in a 1964 White House meeting, King Hussein complained to President Johnson about the lower Jordan salinity problem.[53]

JORDAN–ISRAEL COOPERATION AND SECRET TALKS

Pressure from their respective constituencies made it more difficult for Israel and Jordan to cooperate openly over water sharing. The Israeli Yarmouk Triangle farmers, who depended on Yarmouk water for irrigation, were concerned about Jordanian cooperation and eventually took matters in their own hands. Because Jordan was an upstream user, Israeli Yarmouk Triangle farmers needed Jordan's compliance with the Johnston Plan. Israeli leaders feared that during important crop-growing summer seasons, especially drought years, Israel's Yarmouk Triangle farmers would not receive their allocations because of upstream Jordanian utilization and a lack of storage for winter floodwater in the Triangle area. American water experts, especially after completion of the first stage of the East Ghor Canal, also agreed with Israel's assessment.[54] In fact, during the summer of 1962, Israel claimed the East Ghor Canal operation had led to a major decline in the Yarmouk water level and requested US mediation. During this period, a controversy also arose when Israeli Yarmouk Triangle farmers, without government authorization, built a weir across the Yarmouk to raise the river's level to allow Triangle irrigation pumps to draw Israel's allocated quantities. Jordan protested to the United States that they feared that the Israeli weir would serve as a tank crossing, and they doubted that Israeli pumps were "sucking air" instead of water. Jordan also protested to the Israel-Jordan Mixed Armistice Commission (MAC) and threatened to take unilateral military action against the weir.[55] Jordan's claim that Israeli tanks would cross the weir was dismissed. Israel requested that the weir be allowed to remain, but Jordan repeatedly requested its removal. Here Jordan wished to avoid any appearance of acquiescence, which Israel might use in later years as a basis for building a more permanent weir. Even so, Jordan never attempted to remove the structure.[56] Nature resolved the issue when the winter floods washed away the Israeli weir.

For its part, Jordan was feeling pressure from its Arab neighbors. By 1964, there was heightened concern among Israelis that Jordan was participating in an Arab diversion scheme. That year King Hussein publicly identified himself with those decisions of the Cairo Arab Summit Conference designed to divert Jordan headwaters from Israel. Previously, the US government had had extended talks with Jordan, as previously discussed, during which it reiterated that it would respect Israel's Yarmouk allocation.[57] In 1954, 1958, and 1959, Jordan had confirmed commitments on Yarmouk allocations and provided assurances that Israel's water supply would be protected. The United States had given Israel a verbatim record of these promises. However, in 1964 and 1965, Israel maintained that it was not receiving its Yarmouk share and asked America to use its "good offices."[58] Israel depended on the United States to pressure Jordan to guarantee its Yarmouk allocation, and the United Stats pressured Jordan to release 2.3–2.5 cubic meters per second to Israel.[59]

Initially, secret talks between Israel and Jordan to resolve Yarmouk water disputes were not an option. From Hussein's accession to 1963, Jordan and Israel did not communicate directly. In the end, King Hussein did use secret talks with Israel, in part as a way to improve his chances of achieving his political and economic objectives. Back in the late 1940s and early 1950s, extensive secret talks were held between Israel and Jordan, but, after the assassination of King Abdullah, the secret relations were discontinued for a decade. During most of the 1950s, Hussein's foreign policy was extremely cautious and relied on a skillful appeasement of the stronger Arab states as well as opponents at home. He undoubtedly allied himself with neighboring Arab states, especially in their anti-Israel stance. But, by the mid-1960s, Jordan had become increasingly dependent on the United States for support as well as more alienated from some neighboring Arab states. In the early 1960s, when a close advisor to President Kennedy asked a group of high-ranking Israeli diplomats if there were secret communications between Israel and Jordan on sharing Yarmouk water, they replied that there was so little "as to amount to 'no more than telepathy.'"[60] Syrian assassination attempts on Hussein at that time prodded him to redeploy Jordanian troops along its border with Syria; however, before he took that action he instructed his military command through a third party to receive assurances from Israel that it would not take advantage of the Jordanian troop realignment. Israel agreed.[61] With an initial level of trust established, and the understanding that Israel's clout in Washington was growing, Hussein was ready to resume Israeli-Jordanian secret talks.

Hussein directly participated in secret meetings with Israel for the first time in London in September 1963. Although little was achieved of a substantive nature, the meeting was an important breakthrough in bringing both sides together face-to-face. Hussein wanted Israel's help in securing a US military aid request. Hussein also complained about Israel's water plans, especially the scheme for diverting water from the northern Jordan River to irrigate the Negev desert by means of the National Water Carrier. The Israeli envoy tried to assure the king that Jordanian interests would not be harmed and that the existing balance of water between the two states would not be significantly altered, but the king did not agree. He believed the Israeli plan would hamper his plans for agricultural development. Despite the impasse, both countries agreed to meet again in the future, and also arranged means for exchanging messages. Still, two years would pass before the next secret meeting.[62]

In the summer of 1964, Israel complained that Jordan was excessively diverting the Yarmouk water to the East Ghor Canal and away from Israel.[63] The United States informed the Jordanians that they needed to restore the historical rate of 2.3 cms for the duration of the summer or until Israel received 25 mcm. If Jordan did not do this, it would be "breaching the letter and spirit" of previous US–Jordan agreements on water funding for adhering to the Johnston Plan.[64] Jordan's response seemed contradictory. King Hussein told the US ambassador that he was "damn" mad about the current water situation and especially "irritated by the US role as 'messenger boy' and that the proper point of appeal was through the MAC."[65] Two weeks later, however, both Americans and Israelis observed that Jordan was again allowing enough Yarmouk water to flow past the East Ghor Canal input and to the Israeli pumps. Jordan was willing to increase the Yarmouk's flow to Israel, but refused to accept the Criddle technical formula.[66] A few weeks later, the US ambassador told King Hussein that Jordan should not participate in the Arab diversion plan because it was not in Jordan's interest. He explained that Jordan might end up with less water than under the Johnston Plan. Hussein told the ambassador that he understood this, but did not feel that he alone could oppose the other Arab leaders.[67] During this period, Jordan was walking a difficult tightrope between US and Arab demands. This conflict of demands explains a Cairo radio broadcast reporting that Jordan's prime minister had made a statement charging that the United States was pressuring Jordan to abandon support of the Arab water diversion plan, when around the same time the king secretly told US diplomats that he would not oppose US policy.[68]

Several factors in the shifting political landscape led King Hussein to consider renewing secret talks. First, Israel's prime minister, Levi Eshkol, publicly warned Jordan that if it coordinated with Lebanon and Syria in diverting water away from Israel, his government would not "allow the young King to take all the sweet Yarmo[u]k" water.[69] The prime minister was taking a strong stand on Jordan's commitment to provide at least 25 mcm of Yarmouk water for Israel during the summer season because he and his party were facing a difficult election campaign. Eshkol felt that if Jordan denied this water to Israel during the summer of 1965, the Israeli government should regard the move as a hostile act marking the beginning of the Arabs' "actual" spiteful diversion of water against Israel.[70] In the past, the Israeli government had attempted to downplay the problems on the Yarmouk with Jordan or to work behind the scenes with the United States to resolve the matter quietly, but it was an election year and Israeli Yarmouk Triangle farmers were beginning to intensify their objections.[71] Again, the US ambassador to Amman protested to King Hussein to release Israel's Yarmouk allocation. The United States accused Jordan of "taking off excessive amounts of water for the East Ghor and wasting it" so downstream Israeli pumps would run dry.[72] That same year Hussein's relations with Egypt and Syria had started to deteriorate. The radical Syrian Baath party government sponsored a new round of terrorist attacks from Syrian and from Jordanian territory, which, in turn, invited Israeli reprisals against Jordan. In addition, there were clashes between Hussein's army and PLO guerrillas. Hussein also rejected an Egyptian request to station Iraqi and Saudi troops in Jordan to confront Israel. Finally, tensions had increased because of numerous Israeli border incidents, many of which related to the water issue. At this point, the king recognized the need to renew secret talks.

At the second Jordanian-Israeli secret meeting, held in Paris in 1965, the countries made substantial progress on the water issue. The king met with Foreign Minister Golda Meir, and the issues of US military assistance and water were revisited. Meir restated Israel's position that the National Water Carrier would neither injure Jordan's development nor violate the Johnston Plan. Hussein presented Jordan's economic development plan on water, including the completion of the East Ghor Canal. He also stated that these projects posed no real threat to Israel. Both sides considered the water talks useful and reached a tacit understanding that the general outline of the Johnston Plan would continue to be followed.[73] Subsequently, the United States noted that the water flow to the lower Jordan River during the summer of 1966 had permitted the Israeli pumps to draw sufficient water. The flow was enough to avoid a water crisis like that experienced during the two previous summers.[74]

At this point, the United States attempted to pressure Israel to forgo its summer Yarmouk allocation because of the continuous tension over this provision. An Israeli diplomat replied that "Jordan's dry season delivery of Yarmouk water at the rate of somewhat more than two cubic meters per second was the last real Johnston Plan link between Israel and the Arab riparians. It [was] vital to maintain [that] link, for if the Jordanians [got] away with cutting it, they [would] be emboldened to participate in diversion projects more damaging to Israel."[75] Domestic concerns also were part of the calculations of Israeli politicians. The government could not be seen as weak in its stance on the Yarmouk. As will be discussed in chapter 4, Yarmouk water cooperation would again become a US priority and an important link for Jordanian-Israeli collaboration.

ARAB DIVERSION

In the face of Arab threats to divert the upper Jordan River from Israel and Israeli plans to move water from the river basin to the Negev, the United States found itself in a delicate diplomatic position. The State Department believed that its basic objectives were to "avert a serious clash" between Jordan riparians, avoid a situation in which the United States becomes the target of Arab frustration, and continue pushing equitable division of the Jordan waters.[76] In November 1959, Israel had publicly announced a plan to pump water from Lake Tiberias for transport to the coastal plain and to the Negev. In response, the Technical Committee of the Arab League had approved a plan to divert the upper Jordan tributaries, the Hasbani and Banias, from Israeli territory (see Map 3-1). The Arab League Council reportedly decided that "it [was] necessary to utilize the waters of the River Jordan in the interest of the Arab countries and the Palestinian Arabs," and recommended "the establishment of a special organization to coordinate and implement work in this regard."[77] These statements alarmed Israel enough for it to voice its concerns to the United States. Israeli leaders considered the threats merely propaganda, but warned the United States that any action to carry out a diversion of Jordan tributaries "could lead to armed conflict."[78] Prime Minster David Ben-Gurion publicly stated that Israel would develop the Jordan water regardless of Arab reaction. The United States, however, did not take too seriously the possibility of Arab diversion of the upper Jordan from Israel. Indeed, between 1961 and 1964, the Arab diversion water program floundered because other issues took precedence, especially inter-Arab disputes and domestic instability. During this period, Syria withdrew from the United Arab Republic with Egypt, and relations between those states became strained. Egypt was preoccupied with the Yemen civil war where many of its troops participated in the conflict.

By 1964, Israel was on the verge of completing the National Water Carrier, and the project became a common concern for Arab states to unite around. Nasser at that point did not believe the time was ripe for war, but nonetheless wanted to show his leadership and reduce interstate Arab rivalry by generating solidarity on issues relating to Israel and the Palestinian cause. In January and September 1964, Arab heads of state gathered in summits to devise a plan to divert the Jordan headwaters.[79] The summits led to the establishment of a unified Arab military command, as well as a Palestinian organization and army. Even so, the Arabs did not make public the specifics of the diversion plan. During this time, Syria also continued to push for outright war with Israel, but Nasser and the Arab chiefs of staff successfully isolated the Syrians and advanced the diversion plan, which included sabotaging the Israeli pipeline system.[80] In May, Israel began test pumping through the main conduit of the National Water Carrier, and the water issue continued as the focus of inter-Arab rivalry as well as the Arab-Israeli conflict. Jordan and Egypt enjoyed improved relations, and, in 1964, besides the Arab summits, which Hussein attended, Nasser and Hussein met at least four times that year.[81] The Arab leaders, including Hussein, agreed that Israel's National Water Carrier had to be stopped.[82] Frustrated by Israel's water development, as explained earlier, Hussein took part in the Arab plan to divert water from the Jordan River's source away from Israel. The Arab states set up a $30 million fund to divert water from the Yarmouk. Syrian and Lebanese engineers began to build diversion canals; in response, Israeli artillery and jets destroyed the equipment on several different occasions. Given his new alliance with Nasser, King Hussein no longer saw a need for maintaining direct, though secret, relations with Israel.

Israel's plans to move water out of the Jordan River basin had long been a point of conflict with Arab states in the region. As early as January 1960, US diplomats in the region had requested the State Department to make an effort to reduce hostilities over the water issue. Even then, moderate Arab leaders were becoming highly sensitive to Israel's use of the Jordan River.[83] As far back as 1955, the Arab states had threatened to divert the Jordan River's headwaters, which rise in Syria and Lebanon, to block Israel's water supply for the National Water Carrier and for out-of-basin use. By the mid-1960s, the Arab states actively opposed out-of-basin use or water allocations used to irrigate the Negev desert, plans that would further Jewish immigration. According to the United States, "a fundamental principle of the Johnston Plan was that all the reasonable needs of the Jordan basin must be accommodated. It was privately understood by the negotiators and included in the 'US-Arab Memorandum of Understanding' that once allocations were made it was each riparian's own concern as to what it did with its share."[84] There was a clear understanding between Johnston negotiators in 1955, according to the US government, that Israel's Jordan River basin water share "could be used legitimately either in or out of the basin."[85] The United States also stated that if Arab states continued an "indefinite veto on a reasonable program of development by refusing to agree to equitable diversion" of water resources, the United States would support Israel's water plans.[86]

By the 1960s, Arab leaders unanimously rejected Israel's out-of-basin use of Jordan water. In diplomatic discussions, the Syrian prime minister told the US ambassador that technical means, such as the Johnston Plan, could not resolve the water conflict because "Syria and other Arabs were still at war with Israel." Syria's arguments, according to the United States, reflected a long-range strategic perspective. Israel's water scheme had to be stopped, according to the prime minister of Syria, because Negev development with Jordan River water would provide additional territory for new immigrants, who "would constitute military reinforcements."[87] In April 1964, King Hussein and Jordan's top officials met with President Johnson at the White House where they noted Arab annoyance with a speech Johnson gave at the Friends of the Weizmann Institute banquet. The president had said: "Water should not be a cause of war but of peace." The king and the foreign minister stated that the Arabs interpreted this statement as official US support of Israel's right to divert water from the Jordan, when the water was needed in other areas.[88] Other Arab leaders rejected the American and Israeli position that the Johnston Plan was equitable and acceptable. According to Arab diplomats, the plan for implementation required the consent of all riparians, and in 1956 the Arab League's political committee had decided to oppose the plan. The Arabs also rejected Israel's argument that since Jordan had constructed the East Ghor Canal, Israel was entitled to the National Water Carrier. In sum, Arab states such as Syria did not regard Israel as a party with any Jordan water riparian rights. Israeli unilateral actions, according to the Arabs, endangered Arab riparians' rights and threatened to harm the quality of the water. Since Israel had ignored Arab League warnings on this issue, the Arab states concluded that they were entitled to take counteractions, including diverting water. The Arabs accused the United States of not fully appreciating the prospect that Israel might grow to a population of five million while Palestinian refugees remained in refugee camps. They also warned that in the future Israel might eventually exceed Johnston Plan limits and disregard US requirements.[89]

With instructions from Washington to "avoid any suggestion of pressure to influence Arab leaders," the US reply to the Arab diplomats was that each riparian was entitled to an equitable share of Jordan River water.[90] And for the United States, Israel was a recognized riparian. Qualified American experts, such as Wayne Criddle, still believed the Johnston Plan was fair and realistic and that the National Water Carrier and East Ghor Canal had been developed within appropriate limits. In addition, the United States had continuously scrutinized and verified that Israel was conforming to the specifications of the Johnston Plan. The United States also argued that these limits would not support the dramatic Israeli population growth feared by the Arabs. On the contrary, the limits offered Arabs insurance against excessive Israeli withdrawal of water.[91] For their part, US diplomats met with Arab leaders and strongly advised moderation in relation to the Israeli water program.[92] The Soviet Union, on the other hand, publicly supported the Arab diversion and viewed it as a means to unify all Arab states against the West.[93] Soviet aid and engineers played a key role in developing Syrian and Egyptian water and agricultural systems.[94]

Israel's position was that the threatened Arab diversion was a hostile response meant to challenge Israel's right to the Jordan River basin. In a 1962 letter from Ben-Gurion to President Kennedy, the Israeli prime minister stressed that his country faced the threat of hostile Arab armies and consequently needed to increase its population through immigration. The best way to provide for a growing population was to develop arid Negev with Jordan water.[95] So, in addition to defending the National Water Carrier plan because it complied with the Johnston Plan, Israel also claimed it was a necessary defense against hostile neighbors. At the two Arab summits in 1964, the Arabs challenged Israel's right to the Jordan River basin. According to Israel, the Arab diversion intended to halt the headwaters from flowing through their natural channel to Israel. Lebanon was to take some 60 to 90 mcm from the upper Hasbani River, which rises in Lebanon only a few hundred yards from the Israeli border, of which 40 to 60 mcm were to be diverted to Lebanon's national river, the Litani, and 20 to 30 mcm to the Yarmouk for Jordan. The Banias, which rises in Syria, was to be diverted to the Yarmouk. Under the Johnston Plan, Syria and Lebanon were allotted a total of 55 mcm from the upper Jordan, but they now threatened, according to Israel, to withdraw 200 to 250 mcm. Israel termed the Arab actions "a spite diversion" with the aggressive intent to limit Israel's water by wasting it to the Mediterranean. If executed, the plan would reduce the supply of water to its National Water

Carrier by at least a third and would contribute to the salinity of Lake Tiberias.[96]

Israel's increasingly heated rhetoric showed the seriousness with which it viewed the conflict over the Jordan River basin. According to the Israeli government, "The diversion of the Jordan headwaters [was] not only an act of political hostility toward Israel. It was an act of physical aggression." Prime Minister Levi Eshkol made Israel's position clear in the Knesset on January 16, 1965, when he stated: "any attempt to deprive Israel of its share of the Jordan River system under the [Johnston] Water Plan [would] be considered an encroachment on our borders."[97] Eshkol told the Knesset four days later that Israel had "undertaken to remain within the framework of the quantities specified in the [Johnston] Plan and [Israel would] honor this undertaking."[98] The Israeli government viewed Arab objections as a ploy to further different ends: "What the Arab states [were] planning [had] no connection with water but only [had] meaning in the context of their denial of Israel's right to exist and their aggressive designs."[99] To the press, Eshkol stated that Jordan water is "as precious to us as the blood in our veins. We shall act accordingly."[100] Obviously, Eshkol placed great importance on water and refused to compromise on the issue. Before becoming prime minster, Eshkol had played a key role in Israel's agricultural and economic development. He was a lead negotiator at the Johnston mission talks, a finance minister, a founder of Mekorot, Israel's water development institution, an executive of the Jewish Agency's agricultural planning section, and had family roots in the agricultural sector. As a Labor Zionist, he had always placed great importance on immigration and agriculture, as well as economic development. He strongly believed that water was a critical state preference that played a dominant role in guiding Israel's economic growth and, consequently, he was willing to fight to protect it.[101] Furthermore, there was political pressure from former Israeli agriculture minister, war hero, and political competitor, Moshe Dayan, who urged Eshkol and his government to regard any attempt to divert Israeli water as an act of war.[102]

Ineffective US Diplomacy

During this period, the United States was "scrupulously avoiding a public role" to keep from becoming a target of Arab frustration in their inability to forestall Israeli water projects.[103] While trying to defuse the tension over the Jordan River water issue, the United States privately suggested to Israel that it undertake a public campaign in the international community to garner support for its position. The United States wanted Israel to publicize the scheduling of its water program, and its intentions to abide by equitable allocations (i.e., the Johnston Plan). The United States also wanted Israel to publicly state its

willingness to discuss unified development at any time, its readiness to accept
international observation (provided the other riparians also accepted monitoring), and its commitment to continue research and development to increase the
usable water resources of the Jordan River basin. Israel agreed to and publicized all of these points, except for its commitment to accept an international
observer. Israel was unwilling to give the United Nations or Arab states once
again the right or ability to block its water program. Since the United States
had complete information and had verified through the Criddle mission that
Israel was acting in accordance with the Johnston Plan, Israel did not see the
need for further international supervision.[104] The United States suggested to
Israel that its position would be enhanced if it could provide evidence that its
plan had a minimal impact on Jordan. First, the US wanted Israel to continue
providing schedules for testing and withdrawing from Lake Tiberias and upper
Jordan stream flow, as well as salinity data, to be passed on to Jordan. Second,
the United States asked Israel to agree to the US version of the Johnston
Plan—in particular, that Israel should supply Jordan with 85 mcm of Lake
Tiberias water and 15 mcm of the saline spring water instead of 70 mcm fresh
water and 30 mcm salty water for which Israel was arguing. Also, the United
States asked Israel to acknowledge that it was only entitled to 25, not 40 mcm,
of Yarmouk water.[105] In the end, however, Israel refused to accept the American version of the Johnston Plan.

The United States hoped to soften anti-Israel feeling among Arab states
by supporting Jordanian water projects. In the 1960s, when Jordan initiated
planning for the Maqarin Dam, the United States, while staying in the background, supported the dam project through International Bank for Recon-
struction and Development (IBRD, also known as the World Bank) funding.
During this period, Israel did not oppose the Maqarin Dam, but did voice concerns that such a project might injure its water rights.[106] The US argued that
without a dam on the Yarmouk to store winter water, there would not be
enough water in dry years or during some summers to satisfy both Israel and
Jordan's water requirements.[107] Between 1955 and 1963, the United States
provided some $50 million to Israel and $13 million to Jordan for water programs. The United States hoped that the Israel-Jordan aid imbalance and the
start of National Water Carrier project could be offset by US assistance in constructing the Maqarin Dam, which would cost between $65 and $85 million,
and would give Jordan critical winter storage for its Yarmouk water. Initially,
the World Bank was "sympathetic" to loaning money for the Maqarin Dam,
but the bank could not finance the entire project and was subsequently dubious of the cost/benefit ratio of a large dam, a view similar to that held by Eric
Johnston. Senior World Bank officers told the State Department that they
opposed funding the project, claiming that Jordan was ineligible for further
loans and pointing to problems in the size of the project.[108] Even so, by 1963,

Jordan concluded a feasibility and engineering contract with a Yugoslavian firm. With the design to be completed in 1965, the State Department pushed the IBRD to change its policy and become actively involved in the project.[109] The United States regarded measures to enhance Jordan's economic position, including Maqarin construction with IBRD financing, as necessary. Financial help from the United States and other Western countries would, in the long run, strengthen the Israeli and American positions against the Arab diversion plans.

In addition, the United States made other efforts to defuse the growing tensions over water even as it strongly but quietly supported Israel. It prepared papers arguing that Israel's actions were consistent with established international water practice and law, produced rebuttals against anticipated Arab arguments, and offered ongoing technical confirmation by US engineers that Israel's water program complied with the Johnston Plan.[110] The United States wanted to show that Israel was in the right, and that aggressive measures on either side were not necessary. President Lyndon B. Johnson wrote Prime Minister Levi Eshkol in January 1964 that "we stand behind you in your right to withdrawal [water] in accordance with the [Johnston] Plan."[111] Earlier, in 1962, President Kennedy had provided Prime Minister David Ben-Gurion with similar assurances.[112] The United States also promised to use its influence to keep the Arabs within their Johnston Plan allocations. In a letter from Assistant Secretary of State Frederick Dutton to Senator Kenneth Keating in June 1964, the United States clearly outlined a policy that:

> [I]n the event that other Middle Eastern states attempt to frustrate the Israeli plan by counter diversion projects, the United States would oppose such projects if it appeared that the Arab riparian states combined were offtaking water in excess of the combined allocations of the Arab states specified in the 1955 [Johnston] plan. The form of any such United States opposition would of course depend upon the circumstances prevailing at that time.[113]

Even with these strong statements of support, US officials urged restraint on Israel's part and warned that any military action against the Arab diversion would be met with US disapproval.[114] The United States believed that even if the Arabs succeeded in their diversion project, which America regarded as highly doubtful, it would not have a major impact on Israel's water supply. America's stated position was that "in spite of its aversion to the Arab Plan, we do *not* see it as constituting in itself a legitimate *casus belli* for Israel." The United States "will not condone or support the use of force in this matter; if force is used [the United States] will use [American] power and influence to bring it to a halt and to see that those who resort to it do not profit from it."[115]

In a memo from Secretary of State Dean Rusk to President Johnson, the United States recognized the difficulty of maintaining balance in the region: America has "been trying to maintain an even keel in our Near East relations in the backwash of Arab reaction to Israel's completion of its Jordan River diversion project. The Arabs have equated the diversion with the establishment of the State of Israel in Arab territory, and Nasser has used their emotional reaction to forge a solidarity."[116] The United States voiced concern that this would push Arab allies closer to the Soviet camp. The United States warned Israel on numerous occasions that continued US arms deliveries were contingent on Israel's refraining from preemptive strikes against Lebanon or Jordan. The United States hoped such threats would "keep Israel in line." [117]

The Israelis frequently expressed unhappiness over the inadequacy of US support for them on the Jordan waters issue.[118] Not satisfied that the United States was privately sympathetic with Israel's water problems, Israel was disappointed with America's lack of public support because it felt that only public US support would deter Arab aggression against Israel. Israel watched with dismay as the Kennedy administration increased US economic assistance to Egypt. In addition, Kennedy himself made several statements supporting an even-handed approach to the Arab-Israeli conflict and began a personal correspondence with Nasser.[119] Ben-Gurion, in a letter to Kennedy, warned that the Arab threat to destroy Israel was more imminent now that Egypt, Iraq, and Syria had signed an alliance pact.[120] To no avail, Prime Minister Eshkol pleaded with the US government to give public support on the Jordan water issue "as a means both of reassuring the Israeli electorate and deterring the Arabs from continuing their diversion scheme."[121] In reply, the United States maintained its objections to Israel's using force and recommended taking the water issue to the United Nations. Israel rejected the UN idea and argued that such a suggestion represented "backtracking on [US] undertakings to support the [Johnston] plan."[122] The Israeli official position, as expressed to the United States, was that it must act on the assumption that the Arabs could deprive Israel of 10 to 15 percent of the upper Jordan water and that the Arab states might cause the reduction in the near future. Full implementation of the Arab diversion plan, Israel argued, would destroy the tacit system of Jordan water division that the United States had promoted since the end of the Johnston mission. Also, the US stance put the secret agreements with Israel and Jordan in jeopardy. But most important for Israel, if the United States did not take a strong stand against aggressive Arab actions, those states would not be deterred from taking future belligerent actions against Israel.[123] By 1965, Israeli concerns were deepening because, in addition to Syria, Lebanon's participation in the diversion was increasing, while Arab coordination was improving and construction on the diversion had accelerated. Israelis believed that the water conflict was intensifying because they perceived Jordan and Lebanon as now in the radical Arab camp with Syria and Egypt.[124] Moreover, the Israeli government was under increasing domestic pressure to act forcefully because the prime minister found himself, as noted earlier, in a difficult election campaign in which he could not afford to appear weak. There was considerable support for the government to intervene militarily against the Arab diversion and to do so quickly. The Israeli government had made a "national decision" to protect its water rights as detailed in the Johnston Plan.[125]

The Lebanese president also faced extraordinary domestic pressure to act. He told the US ambassador that due to political divisions and the threat of a popular "explosion" in Lebanon, his country would begin upper Jordan water diversion construction soon. Many in the United States believed that ethnic divisions had forced the Lebanese government into this "perilous position." Beirut privately hoped that the expected Israeli raid against the Arab diversion would be on Syrian territory and not Lebanese.[126] By early February 1965, American, Israeli, and Arab diplomats believed violent conflict, if not war, was imminent over the water issue. Israeli Foreign Minister Golda Meir made clear to American diplomats that "Israel would not wait for completion of the diversion project to act."[127] She asked the United States to convey Israel's determination to the Lebanese government. In turn, the United States cautioned Israel against the use of military force to deal with the Arab diversion plans. It also, however, conveyed to Egyptian leaders that the diversion project might lead to an Israeli military response. The Egyptians replied that the United States should rein in Israel and that the United States itself had little credibility in the Arab world. An Egyptian presidential advisor said that the United States "must realize how suspicious we are of any US action regarding [the] Jordan waters."[128] A pessimistic mid-February note from the US embassy in Beirut signaled the extent of the tension: "Mideast crisis [was] in the offing. . . . Arab-Israeli tension appears to be reaching point somewhere similar to that period which preceded Suez crisis ten years ago. Key protagonists seem captive to courses which could end in collision."[129] As a result, President Johnston appointed Special Ambassador W. Averell Harriman to mediate between Israelis and Arabs so a violent conflict in the Middle East could be averted. Israel and Arab riparians rejected the US suggestion to use the UN as a means to resolve the conflict over the Jordan waters.[130] And both sides urged the United States to put more political pressure on the opposing side. Harriman, for his part, was pushing to hold Israel's "feet to the fire" to decrease chances of a military attack on the Arabs.[131] Again, Israel protested, viewing Harriman's pressure as "an apparent change in the United States position" on the Johnston Plan. Israel also argued that the US stance was contrary to the January 1964 US-Israel accord on Jordan water.[132]

Acute Conflict

In the end, the US diplomacy was ineffective. Israel no longer felt it could depend on America to protect its water interests and would have to rely on itself. Less than a month after Harriman's mission began, Israel attacked Syrian diversion equipment in the Dan and Doka areas. Israel claimed that its attacks were in response to Syrian shelling near Lake Tiberias. The United States condemned the attacks and warned Israel not to continue such actions.[133] Privately, though, Israeli actions were acceptable to the United States. American diplomats believed that Israel was going to continue small-scale attacks into Syria that would disrupt the diversion program but would appear as "normal" border incidents. Because small-scale attacks would result in less publicity, there would be less chance of Syria's successfully bringing the issue before the UN Security Council.[134] Israel confirmed to the United States that it hoped to isolate Syria on the water issue, if not in general, and committed itself, for the moment, to ignore Lebanese withdrawals. By April, the Arab states had a unified plan for retaliation against Israeli attacks. This collective security pledge suited Lebanon because it removed any rationale for deploying foreign troops on Lebanese territory to defend its diversion projects.[135] On May 13, Israel again attacked Syrian diversion works.[136]

Although Israel's attention was focused on Syria, it continued to be concerned about Lebanese diversion plans. Israel repeated its requests that the United States pressure Lebanon, which had been allied with the United States, not to link up with Syria on the diversion works. But, in July 1965, the United States became highly critical of Israel's stance on Lebanese canal construction, which the United States did not view as urgent or particularly harmful to Israel's interests. According to the United States, Israel's threat of force made American efforts to help Israel more difficult.[137] Israel, for its part, complained that the United States was accepting Arab misinformation. To prove this, the Israeli government presented the State Department with aerial photographs seemingly showing the Lebanese diversion projects still in progress. The photographs confirmed that the Lebanese were not constructing a local irrigation project, as the latter had told the United States. By that point, the diversion work was moving quickly and would shortly have had the capacity to divert a large amount of water.[138] Israeli diplomats experienced frustration because they believed the United States was still not paying adequate attention to their concerns. Indeed, in June 1966, US diplomats concluded that the Israelis were no longer focusing much attention on the water diversion projects, although an Israeli diplomat had warned the United States that the Lebanese "are playing with fire if they take water from the Hasbani."[139] Despite Israeli vehemence, in the end, there were no water-related attacks on Lebanese territory.

However, further attacks, charges, and countercharges continued to heighten tension between Israel and Syria. There were additional Israeli attacks on Syrian diversion projects on July 14, 1966, when Israeli jets struck Syrian water diversion projects near Almagor. Israel claimed that these attacks were in response to Syrian attacks into Israeli territory.[140] The Syrians stated that the raid destroyed 80 percent of the equipment, costing approximately $1.5 million in damages. Jordan, though, downplayed the Israeli attack, stating that there was only $280,000 of damages.[141] The Syrian foreign minister stated that the July 14 Israeli raid was a premeditated attack and denied Israeli allegations that Syria was aiding infiltrators into Israel. He claimed that Syria was not responsible for "stopping one million scattered Arab Palestinians from struggling to return to their country."[142] Israel's Prime Minister Eshkol responded the next day that in the last half-year Syria had shelled Israeli territory eighty-two times. In the previous two months, mines had been laid in Israeli territory and four Israelis had been killed. Israel suspected Syrian assistance. Eshkol also pointed out that Syrian equipment that was bombed by Israel was similar to the Israeli equipment that had earlier been sabotaged by Palestinians and Syrians.[143]

During this period, Jordan waterworks were hit once by Israel, but Jordan was focused on the construction of the Mukheibeh Dam and so was inclined to see the attack as accidental, which it probably was. When, on January 9, 1967, two Israeli shells hit the upper Jordan Mukheibeh Dam site in Jordan, the Jordanians reported only minor casualties and damage. They noted that an artillery confrontation had been in progress between Israel and Syria and that the shells were probably aimed at a Syrian target, which was close to the dam.[144] The Mukheibeh Dam had been approved at the September 1964 Arab summit and would store approximately 200 mcm of water. In fact, the Johnston Plan allows Jordan as much as 300 mcm of storage capacity on the Yarmouk.[145] The State Department publicly gave its support to the construction of the dam and stated that it was not inconsistent with the Johnston Plan.[146] A year earlier Israel had stated to the United States that it would not oppose the dam if it were used to store only Yarmouk water, and not divert water from the upper Jordan. Even so, Israeli diplomats said later that their acquiescence on the Mukheibeh Dam was very difficult. Israel wanted assurances from Jordan that Israeli Yarmouk Triangle farmers would obtain a fair share of Yarmouk water.[147] The construction of the dam was scheduled to begin January 1967. The United States had concerns about Soviet and Yugoslavian bids to build the dam and warned Jordan that such a development might "create serious problems for continuation of AID programs" for Jordan.[148] According to a CIA source, the only Soviet assistance for the dam was ultimately in the form of one or two technical experts. There was much talk of diverting the upper Jordan "but little activity at the Mukheibeh site besides building access roads and a construction works camp." It was predicted that the dam's construction would take four to five years.[149] Back in January 1966, Arab leaders had agreed to increase funding for the diversion of the Jordan. This money was for the construction of the Mukheibeh Dam and for the PLO.[150] By 1967, Jordan was still pursuing needed funding for a Yarmouk dam— Mukheibeh and Maqarin—but was receiving little, if any, of the Arab support that had been promised earlier.

Precipitating War

By 1966, the political landscape of the Middle East was shifting significantly, with some Arab states withdrawing from conflicts, while others—notably Syria—contributing to the escalation. By 1966, Israel was pumping water from Lake Tiberias, and Syrian and Lebanese attempts to divert the headwaters had been virtually halted, primarily because of Israeli air and artillery attacks on the diversion sites. In addition, other Arab states, especially Egypt, refused to support Syria or Lebanon and Arab funding had dried up. At this point, tensions on the Israeli-Syrian border increased. Between 1963 and 1967, Syria experienced internal economic and political instability. In an attempt to divert attention from these problems, the Syrian government exacerbated the confrontation with Israel. It also hoped to attract new resources from other Arab states.[151] Beginning with the February 1966 coup in Syria, a more radical and anti-Israel regime held power. This government, led by Salah Jadid, supported more Palestinian guerrilla attacks and DMZ skirmishes with Israel. Along the DMZ in the north, Syrian gun posts on the Golan Heights fired on Israeli farmers and settlements, with Israel retaliating on several occasions. And DMZ disputes over cultivation rights also continued. Moscow's ambassador to Syria had contended that the leadership in Damascus was well aware of the risk of forceful Israeli retaliation and had no illusions about the disparity between their two forces. Although the Syrian government became increasingly concerned about the likelihood of conflict, it also hoped to provoke the Arab world into conflict with Israel.[152]

The deteriorating situation on the borders between Syria and Israel, and between Jordan and Israel, as well as the Palestinian guerrilla activity, brought inter-Arab tensions to the surface. Despite the appearance of unity, Arab states were still divided at this point about the level of their individual commitments to fighting Israel. Nasser criticized Jordan for not supporting the Palestinian cause more actively, while Hussein countered by calling Nasser a coward for not living up to his promise to oppose Israel. In November 1966, Israel undertook a major military assault in Jordan against as-Samu and neighboring towns, killing eighteen, including three civilians. Hundreds of buildings were destroyed. The raid was condemned by the international community, including the United States, because of the scale of the attack and because it undermined King Hussein's regime. Jordan expressed disappointment that Nasser did not react more vigorously to the Israeli attack against as-Samu. Nasser was also criticized for not lending Syria or Lebanon greater support in trying to halt Israel's water program. Egypt's policy up to the spring of 1967, in fact, had been to avoid a larger conflict with Israel. Even after several months of acute conflict in the north, including air battles between Israel and Syria in which Israel shot down six MIG jets and buzzed Damascus, Nasser chose not to take part in military action. In April 1967, Palestinians responded to the Israeli attack by destroying a pumping station in northern Israel. Eshkol made clear Israel's intention to retaliate.[153]

By May 1967, Nasser began to assume a more active stance against Israel. He had three objectives: to answer Soviet and Arab criticism of his inaction, to reestablish Egypt's leadership role in the Arab world, and to divert domestic complaints from the Egyptian economy. Egypt announced that its armed forces were in a state of maximum alert with combat units to be sent to the Sinai. Egypt also requested that the United Nations remove its peacekeeping forces from the Egyptian-Israeli border, and the United Nations quickly complied. Jordan, Iraq, and Syria began to mobilize their armies. By the end of May, Nasser announced the closing of the Gulf of Aqaba to Israeli vessels and any ships carrying goods to Israel. Eshkol immediately replied that Israel would consider any interference with its freedom of shipping as an act of aggression. Egypt replied with more bellicose speeches, calling on its Arab neighbors to liberate Palestine and destroy Israel. The defense pact between Egypt and Jordan, which allowed Iraqi troops to enter Jordan in the event of hostilities, pushed Israel to launch a preemptive attack that began the 1967 Arab-Israeli War. Six days later Israel had attained a stunning victory, capturing territory that made it three times larger than its 1949 to 1967 size.[154]

ANALYSIS AND CONCLUSION

What role, if any, did water scarcity play in the advent of the 1967 Arab-Israeli War? This conflict-related case is important because it is the most often cited example of a "water war" and is a good illustration of the complex causal chain from water scarcity to acute conflict. Israeli prime minister and general Ariel Sharon stated that "people generally regard June 5, 1967 as the day the Six-Day war began. That is the official date, but in reality it started two-and-one-half years earlier on the day Israel decided to act against the diversion of the Jordan."[155] Also, in this specific case—the Arab-Israeli conflict between 1957 and 1967—there is a direct link between water scarcity and limited international violence. Most historians and political scientists, including Thomas Naff and Ruth Matson, agree that the buildup in water-related Arab-Israeli hostility was a major factor leading to the June 1967 War.[156] Some, though, such as geographer Aaron Wolf, argue that "water was neither a cause nor a goal of any Arab-Israeli warfare."[157] Both sides agree that during the 1960s there were numerous incidents of water-related acute conflict, as documented in this chapter. The fact that, as Wolf, Naff, and Matson point out, for the most part, the water-related violence ended in mid-1966, approximately a year before the June 1967 War, makes the case complicated. Wolf is correct in arguing against the thesis that the 1967 Arab-Israeli conflict was a water war, a conflict initiated because of water scarcity. Wolf, for example, correctly rejects Norman Meyers's argument that "Israel started the 1967 War in part because the Arabs were planning to divert the waters of the Jordan River system."[158] However, water scarcity did play a pivotal role in the causal chain that linked directly to the precipitating events of the 1967 War. Between 1956 and 1962, the Arab-Israel conflict was for the most part inactive. However, the inauguration of Israel's National Water Carrier provoked Arab summits. During these summits, many anti-Israel schemes surfaced, but the most important was the plan to divert upper Jordan water from Israel. Violent attacks and counterattacks by the Arabs and Israelis relating to the Arab water diversion and the DMZ heightened tension and provoked a general acceleration of the arms race between Arab states and Israel. And water resources functioned as a political tool for some states. Syria wanted to increase its Pan-Arab leadership profile and provoke other Arab states to action, especially Egypt. Syria knew quite well that if it began the Jordan diversion, Israel would respond militarily, as, in fact, it did. As political scientist Nadav Safran argues, Israel tried to halt the Syrian diversion project militarily and "the result was a prolonged chain reaction of border violence that linked directly to the events that led to war."[159] Certainly, water scarcity was not a precipitating cause of the 1967 war; Nasser's troop buildup in the Sinai, the military mobilization of Jordan, Iraq, and Syria, the closing of the Gulf of Aqaba to Israeli ships and goods, and the stationing of Iraqi troops in Jordan were the immediate causes. Nor was water scarcity a deep or long-term cause; the Arab-Israeli political and military conflict, including the Palestinian issue and the changing relative power of Israel and its neighboring states, were more long term. Water scarcity was, however, an important intermediate cause of the 1967 War. During the 1949 to 1967 period, Israel's water needs were more complex because the sources of Israel's water supplies were near or just across its border in Syria and Lebanon.

Intermediate causes of war merit attention and should not be disregarded simply because they are not immediate or precipitating. For example, to understand the advent of World War I, do we only need to understand the assassination of Franz Ferdinand at Sarajevo by a Serbian? Or do we also need to understand deep and intermediate causes, such as the changing balance of power in Europe—in particular, growing German strength, the rise of nationalism, the struggle for natural, nonrenewable resources, and the personal idiosyncrasies of British, German, and Russian leaders?[160] In the 1967 War example and in international politics in general, so many factors are at work that it becomes difficult to determine which are pivotal.

Furthermore, to better understand what happens in international politics it is useful to distinguish between three levels of causation: the individual, the state (society), and the international system. Together, these "images" help us understand international violence.[161] Specific individuals, particularly state leaders, played a critical role in turning Jordan River basin water scarcity into a divisive issue. Israeli leaders equated the water issue with national survival, and Arab leaders associated it with growing Israeli strength, Palestinian rights, and Arab solidarity. Had Syrian leaders and Eshkol been willing to attach a rational economic value to Jordan River basin water resources and, thus, decrease its perceived symbolic value, it is doubtful that the issue would have become so explosive.

The unstable nation-state system provides a good explanation for why the water issue played an important role in the hostilities preceding the 1967 War. Israelis and Arabs perceived water as an important element of Israel's state power and security, and when Arab states took action to divert Jordan River water, Israelis felt they needed to reply with force to protect their resources and deter future Arab aggressive actions. The security dilemma intensified the insecurity of the Middle East states involved. Without an understanding of the individuals and types of states involved, an accurate assessment of the role of water as a factor in the cause of war becomes difficult, if not impossible, to make. Moreover, many different types of states were involved and their character impacted their strategy to realize their preferences. Israel is a democracy, and the pressure of the election cycle prompted elected leaders such as Eshkol to act more aggressively than they might have if an election had not been in the near future. On the other hand, Syria's autocratic government lacked domestic or regional legitimacy and therefore used the water issue to improve its standing. Syria was an unstable state that was not impacted by water scarcity, yet it utilized the symbolic water issue to provoke acute conflict.

Variations in state leaders along with differing state types made a tense international system even more unstable. Israel became insecure because the Arab states were procuring arms from Soviet bloc states and Israel believed that the Arabs were becoming less deterred by its military capabilities. The United States was not willing to give Israel the assurances it felt it needed on the water issue, thus moving Israel toward a self-help policy of military action against the Lebanese and Syrian diversion project. On the other hand, Egypt, Syria, and Jordan became less secure because the United States was selling sophisticated offensive weapons systems to Israel; consequently, they were unable to stop Israeli retaliation raids, while more immigration to Israel because of an increased water supply would bolster Israel's overall power. In addition, Syria and Egypt looked to the Soviets for political and military support, and the USSR advocated diverting the upper Jordan from Israel.

In summary, the water issue was not a direct cause of the 1967 Arab-Israeli War, but it was an important intermediate factor; it increased regional instability and this instability eventually did lead to the war. When state elites and the masses perceive water as a symbol and a critical issue in determining a state's capabilities, and the international environment becomes tense and unstable, then protecting water resources emerges as a strong and sometimes irrational preference, making it more likely to be linked to international strategies of acute conflict. The US-initiated tactical functional cooperation (TFC) included a small number of players—only Israel and Jordan—and it was secret, so why did it fail? With Arab preferences so strongly opposed to water cooperation with Israel, even a strategy of limited coordination was difficult between 1963 and 1967. As detailed in the next chapter, between 1967 and 1994, secret TFC between Israel and Jordan was much more successful.

4

The Yarmouk, 1967–1994

The Yarmouk River and not the upper Jordan became the focal point of the Jordan River basin riparian dispute during the post–1967 War period. In the June 1967 Middle East War, Israel captured the Sinai Peninsula, the Gaza Strip, the West Bank, the Golan Heights, and East Jerusalem. Besides these geopolitical changes, important hydropolitical modification also occurred. Through its control of the West Bank, Israel took command of the West Bank aquifers that supply one-third of Israel's freshwater. With the control of the Golan Heights, Israel gained control of most of the upper Jordan River and expanded its rule of the Yarmouk River's northern bank; however, Syria continued to command most of the Yarmouk's headwaters (see Map 4-1).[1] Israel, rather than Syria, was now across the river from the East Ghor Canal intake, a critical source for Jordan's irrigation system.[2] Because of these geopolitical changes, Arab water disputes with Israel were no longer a high political issue and, subsequently, Jordan's preference not to participate in tactical functional cooperation with Israel mellowed in the post–1967 War period. By November 1967, Syria and Lebanon acknowledged their suspension of the diversion projects for technical and financial reasons, and Jordan began to allow a portion of the Yarmouk to flow to Israeli pumps.[3]

This chapter focuses on why cooperation and agreements occurred and endured between Israel and Jordan, and Jordan and Syria, while, at other times, coordination of water resources did not take place. This chapter will also consider why water scarcity nearly precipitated violent conflict five different times between Israel and Jordan in the midst of their secret water-sharing regime, yet peace was maintained. While the protracted Arab-Israeli conflict continued, limited water-related cooperation carried on between

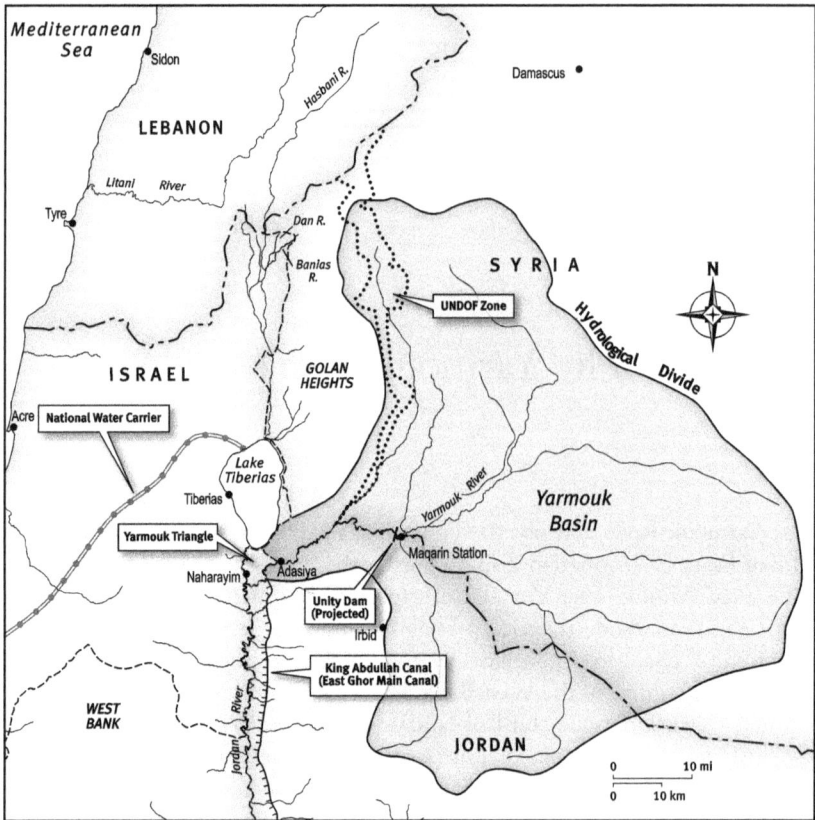

Source: US State Department.

MAP 4-1   Yarmouk Basin, Post-1967

Israel and Jordan for sharing the Yarmouk water, which assisted both of them in developing their agricultural sector. In addition, Syria and Jordan were able to cooperate at times on issues such as the Maqarin and Unity (al-Wahdah) Dam projects. Syria and Israel, however, never cooperated over water resources. These different outcomes tell us something about the conditions necessary to build tactical functional cooperation, be it numbers of players or potential for future cooperation. As discussed in chapter 1, tactical functional cooperation is an arrangement of water-related rules between states, in this instance, Jordan and Israel, that prescribe roles, constrain activities, and shape expectations. Tactical functional cooperation also provides critical information, reduces transaction costs, establishes focal points for coordination, and facilitates reciprocity. However, in a protracted conflict where trust is lacking and water-sharing rules are poorly defined, tactical functional cooperation is difficult to achieve, and misunderstandings and cheating may lead to violent conflict. Therefore, third party involvement, such as that of the United States, may be beneficial when the third party pushes the sides to better define the tactical functional cooperation rules and to comply with them. In addition, this *process* of creating rules and compliance leads to new ideas on addressing water scarcity and positive personal relationship among technocrats and elites, which is necessary for improving overall political relations.

The first section of this chapter examines the issues linked to the Yarmouk water resources of its riparians: Jordan, Syria, and Israel. The next part explains the value of Jordan Valley agricultural development and the importance of its political stability for Jordan and Israel. That section also analyzes the strengthening of Israel and Jordan's relationship due to their balancing of the Syrian and Palestinian Liberation Organization (PLO) threat. The third section reviews the difficult negotiations over building the Maqarin Dam on the upper Yarmouk in the late 1970s, and why dyad cooperation occurred but triad cooperation failed there. Around the same time, secret tactical functional cooperation between Israel and Jordan developed, and a Jordan-Israeli community of technocrats emerged, as described in the fourth section. In the mid-1980s, Yarmouk water scarcity and noncooperative actions by Israel and Jordan precipitated a mobilizing of troops and heavy arms to the Yarmouk that could have led to violent conflict but did not. The next section reviews the late 1980s negotiations on the Unity Dam, which, like the Maqarin, was an upstream Yarmouk facility that in the end was not completed during this period. The final section discusses why cooperative efforts succeeded during the Jordan-Israel tactical functional cooperation efforts, but failed during the Yarmouk Dam talks. It is argued that when all negotiating sides understand each others' preferences, this facilitates more effective international strategies for cooperation, such as rule-based international regimes. This conclusion is a departure from scholars who focus first on a riparians' river position, power, and water interests to predict state behavior and the chances for water-related cooperation.

MIXED PREFERENCES

During the 1990s, Jordan obtained about 20 percent of its water supply from the Yarmouk, making it the country's primary freshwater source. By contrast, for Israel and Syria the Yarmouk is a relatively much less significant water source. The West Bank's western mountain aquifers, the coastal aquifer, and the upper Jordan provide Israel with most of its total freshwater supply. The Yarmouk accounts for only 3 percent of Israel's freshwater and much less than a percent of Syria's supply.[4] A major share of Syria's water is from the Euphrates. Although the Yarmouk is a key water resource for Jordan, Israel and Syria also share in it, and four of the five Yarmouk sources originate in Syria. The river flows along the border of Jordan and the Israeli-held Golan, but runs briefly between Jordan and Israel before bending southwest into the Jordan River, just 6.5 kilometers (4 miles) south of Lake Tiberias. The Yarmouk is an important water source for the Jordan Valley and Israel's Yarmouk Triangle farming area—located between Lake Tiberias to the north, the Jordan River to the west and the Yarmouk to the south and east, which makes a roughly triangular area (see Map 4-1).

Jordan has struggled to maintain its Yarmouk water portion and, as the residual user, has had the difficult task of convincing Syria and Israel to refrain from taking Jordan's share of Yarmouk water. According to the Johnston Plan, Jordan's water allocation from the Yarmouk was 377 million cubic meters (mcm), Syria's was 90 mcm, and Israel's was 25 mcm per year. A dispute arose over Israel's Yarmouk allocation. As discussed in chapter 2, the Israeli government's "Memorandum of Understanding" with the US government claimed an annual allocation of 40 mcm, while Jordan and the United States contended that the Johnston Plan had allocated only the 25 million cubic meters per year (mcmy) to Israel, as stated in the "US-Arab Memorandum of Understanding." For its part, Syria never accepted the Johnston Plan allocations, but did sign three different Jordan-Syria water-related treaties in which it agreed to limit its Yarmouk use. Syria, however, only sometimes complied with these formal agreements. Although the riparians never ratified the Johnston Plan, under the circumstances, it still served as an important guidepost for Jordan-Israel water discussions on the Yarmouk.

Since the early 1960s, Jordan had aggressively pursued construction of a major dam on the Yarmouk to improve its water-supply position. All riparians agreed to the importance of the project; however, there were major political obstacles to its realization. Jordan and Syria have had a cyclical relationship, varying from friendly to openly hostile.[5] Jordan and Israel, on the other hand, have had many secret low-key functional ties including water sharing and some high-level meetings, even though a de jure state of hostilities existed. Although Syria and Israel were adversaries with few to no common bonds, Syria tacitly accepted Jordanian Yarmouk negotiations with Israel when it accorded with Damascus's preferences to do so. Arrangements on a dyad basis between Jordan and Israel were politically feasible, but triad agreements between Israel, Jordan, and Syria were not. During this period, open agreements were acceptable between Syria and Jordan, while only secret arrangements were possible between Israel and Jordan because, except for Egypt, Arab states did not recognize the Jewish state. For numerous reasons, cooperative Yarmouk arrangements between Israel and Syria were not politically feasible.[6]

JORDAN VALLEY INSTABILITY

During this period, Jordan and Israel were both more apt to cooperate on the water issue because they had achieved greater communication through secret talks and had established general principles for water sharing through the US-mediated arrangements, such as the Johnston Plan, the Criddle mission, and subsequent parallel agreements with the US.[7] Between 1970 and 1974, Israeli-Jordanian relations began to improve because of Israel's tacit support of King Hussein during Jordan's 1970 civil war and Hussein's stronger position in Jordan after the destruction of his primary domestic opposition, the Palestine Liberation Organization. The period leading up to 1970, however, would test the strength of their potential to cooperate.

Israel and Jordan held two important meetings in London in 1968. Both sessions addressed conditions for Israeli withdrawal from the territories captured during the 1967 War. Hussein explained to the Israeli negotiators that Jordan could not sign a peace treaty as long as stronger Arab states remained at war with Israel and the Palestinian question was not resolved. Israel posited that it could not pull out of the territories without a peace agreement.[8] Although they could not resolve the larger political issues, both states recognized that many functional matters needed to be addressed, with water as an important one.

Israeli-Jordanian talks in the aftermath of the 1967 War primarily focused on issues arising from Israel's occupation of the West Bank and on political stability on both sides of the Jordan River in the postwar period.[9] At the beginning of the West Bank occupation, *Fatah* and other Palestinian guerrilla organizations attempted to resist Israeli control through violent attacks and mass civil disobedience from inside the West Bank. Israel deported nearly one thousand Palestinians from the West Bank, located and eliminated *Fatah* cells, and demolished hundreds of homes associated with Palestinian guerrillas. By 1968, Israel had crushed the Palestinian resistance in the West Bank and, by 1970, resistance also had stopped in the Gaza Strip. Because Israel had neutralized the PLO within the West Bank, the Palestinians focused on the East Bank and began building what King Hussein termed a state within a state in Jordan. The PLO organized medical and educational institutions in refugee camps throughout Jordan. More important, the PLO launched numerous terror raids against Israel, which resulted in many casualties, a frustrated Israeli leadership, and a demoralized Israeli public.[10]

Between 1967 and 1971, Jordan had hoped to extend the East Ghor Canal by 8 kilometers to help strengthen its economy. The objective was undermined by mounting hostilities in the Jordan Valley between Israel, Jordan, and the Palestinian guerrillas.[11] In the summer of 1969, guerrilla fighters, known in Arabic as *fedayeen*, mounted an intense campaign against Israeli settlements in the Jordan Valley, and Israel responded militarily.[12] Israel's objective was to bring security to its borders by forcing Jordan into restraining the *fedayeen*; consequently, it refused to recognize political boundary lines, which would provide sanctuary to the *fedayeen*. Israel destroyed thousands of dunum of prime Jordanian farmland and demolished many buildings in an attempt to eliminate *fedayeen* safe havens.[13] Almost 55,000 of the Jordanian prewar population abandoned the Jordan Valley for the safety of the nearby eastern hills and urban centers.[14] Between 1968 and 1970, Israel attacked the East Ghor Canal no less than eight times: February 15, March 29, June 23, 1968; April 20, April 22, June 23, August 10, 1969; and January 1, 1970.[15] These Israeli attacks were tactical, meant to motivate the Jordanian government to be more assertive in stopping incursions into Israel. During March 1968, for example, there had been thirty-seven acts of sabotage, resulting in the death of six Israelis and the injuring of forty-four.[16] The Israeli attacks on the East Ghor Canal caused Jordanians to flee the area and threatened critical Jordanian cash crops such as citrus and bananas. Jordanian technocrats attempted to repair the canal, but Israel would breach it again, in response to another terrorist attack against Israel from Jordanian territory. After unsuccessful military efforts to stop PLO attacks, Israel again bombed the East Ghor Canal twice during the summer of 1969 and incapacitated it.[17] In September, *fedayeen* retaliated by blowing up a section of the disabled Rutenberg hydroelectric plant at Naharayim, which was in Jordanian territory. During the 1948 war, Arab troops had disabled the plant;[18] however, the turbine house served as a regulator of the Jordan's flow to Israeli water pumps downstream.[19] Because of the 1969 attack, nearby Israeli settlements were unable to pump water from the river for three weeks.

Long-standing interest in the Middle East and support for particular projects gave the United States the influence needed to help resolve the crisis. The king himself urged the United States to exert pressure on Israel to halt the attacks, and US diplomats argued that it was not in Israel's or America's interest to destroy the Jordanian economy and push the kingdom into political anarchy. Israel agreed, but countered that the *fedayeen* attacks from Jordan had to be stopped by the king first. By August 1969, King Hussein told US diplomats that "no attempt would be made to repair the East Ghor Canal without Israeli permission."[20] In discussions with Israeli officials, high-ranking US diplomats emphasized the "public relations problems" for Israel of turning the Jordan Valley into a desert and attacking the East Ghor Canal, a project the United States regarded as "the most important and visible American-sponsored and financed project in the country."[21] Furthermore, the Americans questioned whether a US-financed development project, the East Ghor Canal was an appropriate target for Israeli armed forces that were US-equipped. After a January 1970 East Ghor Canal attack, Israel and Jordan met in secret negotiations. Israel agreed not to attack Jordan or its canal system again once Jordan stopped *fedayeen* incursions.[22]

Black September

By 1970, King Hussein faced more than just *fedayeen* attacks against Israel. He was rapidly losing control of his own country—PLO guerrilla fighters set up roadblocks and harassed merchants and the middle class. The army, hard hit by Israeli retaliations and upset at the PLO's brazen activities, urged Hussein to act. The king tried to avert a civil war, but when the Popular Front for the Liberation of Palestine hijacked and blew up three airliners in Jordan, Hussein responded in September 1970. Commanding his troops to neutralize the PLO, the king destroyed the PLO's political and military power base in Jordan and forced the Palestinians to flee to Lebanon by June 1971.

During the civil war, Israel proved its commitment to the king's survival by deterring the Syrian air force from attacking Jordan. When Syrian tanks crossed the northern Jordanian border in support of the PLO, Amman sent an urgent request for support to Washington. Understanding the gravity of the situation, the Nixon White House ordered the Sixth Fleet toward the area and Washington contacted Israel to coordinate Jordan's defense. Israel not only agreed to American flights across Israeli air space into Jordan, but also to the direct involvement of Israeli aircraft in stopping the expected Syrian attack. Within Syria, the commander of the Syrian air force (and shortly president of Syria), Hafez al-Asad, opposed the invasion of Jordan and refused to commit Syrian aircraft. With control of the skies, the Jordanians were able to defeat the Syrian tanks. After the conflict, Hussein recognized that Israel had played an important role in deterring the Syrian air force and supporting the king.[23] The dramatic events of 1970 led to new levels of functional cooperation and diplomacy between Israel and Jordan. The relationship became strengthened, with both Israel and Jordan facing common threats from the PLO and Syria.

Rebuilding the Jordan Valley

For the kingdom to recover from its recent trauma, the economy had to be revived. Amman's drive to develop the agricultural sector in the East Bank's Jordan Valley was a first and important step.[24] In order for Jordan Valley development to succeed, the government understood the need for political stability and the availability of water resources for agriculture. Jordan pursued an integrated, comprehensive regional development plan that aimed to settle 100,000 new residents in the region. To prevent migration to already crowded cities while increasing the region's agricultural potential, Jordan expanded social and economic services as well as employment opportunities for the state's rural poor and especially for the valley's farmers. Being able to feed the country's population and offset large imports with exports of fresh produce were also Jordan's objectives.

The Israeli attacks and the civil war had nearly destroyed Jordan's economy, yet Jordan saw that some cooperation with Israel must be part of its
recovery effort. Even though Israel and Jordan perceived that a comprehensive
political resolution was in the distant future, both countries had similar immediate preferences, such as sharing the waters of the Yarmouk River, mining the
Dead Sea, and utilizing the Gulf of Aqaba/Eilat, which made cooperation sen-
sible. Additionally, both governments wished to manage the conflict. However,
public exposure of Jordan's secret relations with Israel would have harmed Jordan both politically and economically. For instance, according to analyst
Daniel Pipes, it may be assumed that Saudi Arabia would have cut off subsidies, Iraq would have cooled relations, and Syria would have attempted to sabotage such a relationship.[25] In addition, severe domestic dissension with the
government would have arisen, especially among Palestinians. Therefore, it is
understandable that before the 1994 Israel-Jordan peace treaty, "the most ven-
omous propaganda against Israel [did] not emanate from Damascus or even
from Riyadh; it [came] from Amman."[26] Jordan was careful publicly to
demonstrate to the Arab world that it was still a leader in opposing Israel.

With greater Jordan-Israel political stability in the post 1970 period,
socioeconomic development accelerated in the Jordan Valley. The three
Yarmouk riparians, Syria, Jordan, and Israel, were expanding their agricultural
sectors and thus their need for water. The king's younger brother, Crown
Prince Hasan, was in charge of rehabilitating and developing the valley. By
1972, the Jordanian government approved a development plan for the Jordan
Valley's rehabilitation. The plan focused on land, irrigation, and agricultural
and social development in the valley.[27] A year later, the Jordanian government
established the Jordan Valley Commission, which would become the Jordan
Valley Authority (JVA) in 1977, to oversee the social and economic develop-
ment of the area. The plan's first phase focused entirely on water resources in
Jordan's territory and included the construction of the King Talal Dam on the
Zarqa River, which was completed in 1977, and an 18 km extension of the East
Ghor Canal, which was finished in 1978.[28] The next phase, a large upstream
dam on the Yarmouk, proved much more difficult to execute.

THE MAQARIN DAM

By 1974, Jordan began Stage II of its revitalization program, which focused on
the Maqarin Dam project.[29] This phase became more urgent as Jordan began
to realize that if it did not take action to preserve its Yarmouk water share, the
country's development of the Jordan Valley would be difficult, if not impossible. Jordan's primary problem was lack of water-storage capacity; since Jordan
was unable to store much of its winter floodwater, it lost that water to Israel or

to the Dead Sea. Israel was using 60 to 70 mcm of Yarmouk water, almost twice the amount allocated to it by its own interpretation of the Johnston Plan. And over 90 mcm, on average, were lost to the Dead Sea (see Table 4-1). Jordan planned to expand its irrigated area by extending the East Ghor Canal to the northern tip of the Dead Sea and supplying Yarmouk water to Amman and Irbid. However, only by obtaining an upstream use commitment from Syria and capturing winter floodwater behind a dam would Jordan be able to realize its development objectives. Initially, cooperation between Syria and Jordan on building the Maqarin Dam was successful, but in the end failed, while Jordanian-Israeli negotiations on this project were progressing but halted because of the faltering Jordanian-Syrian track.

Meanwhile, both Syria and Israel had been increasing their use of Yarmouk water. Syria began building a series of small Yarmouk River dams in 1970 while Jordan's civil war was ending. According to Jordanian water technocrat Munther Haddadin, "it was not until 1975 that Jordan became aware of the size of the Syrian [water] project. When a Jordanian delegation . . . visited the [Syrian part of the] Yarmouk basin, [they] were shocked."[30] Moreover, during a feasibility study visit to Syria, Haddadin observed the large number of Syrian small dams and he believed the water they diverted from

TABLE 4-1
Annual Yarmouk Water Distribution between Jordan and Israel (mcm)

Year	Jordan's Canal	Israeli Pumps	Dead Sea	Total
1981	127	16	104	247
1982	144	36	34	214
1983	130	64	45	239
1984	144	57	51	252
1985	125	52	57	234
1986	125	57	47	229
1987	167	69	121	357
1988	144	39	153	336
1989	108	47	4	159
1990	99	50	9	158
1991	95	53	13	161
1992	164	35	579	778
1993	118	21	126	265
1994	99	34	33	166
Average	126	45	98	271
Percentage	47%	17%	36%	100%
Maximum	167	69	579	778
Minimum	95	16	4	158

Source: Compiled by author based on data from Israel's Jordan Valley Water Association and Jordan's Jordan Valley Authority.

Jordan was in violation of the Syrian-Jordan treaty of 1953 (see Table 4-2).[31] At the same time, Israel had completed the Beit Shean pipeline from the Yarmouk to Lake Tiberias in 1974 and was pumping winter floodwater to the Israeli national water system.[32]

In 1975, Jordan aggressively pursued the Maqarin Dam project, making it a priority for the Jordan Valley Commission's Seven-Year Plan (1975–1982). That year Jordan asked the US Agency for International Development (AID) for assistance. It recommended that the United States play an active role in feasibility studies for the proposed dam and loan one million dollars, which was two-thirds of the feasibility study's cost. Harza Overseas Engineering Company, a Chicago-based firm, conducted the feasibility study in 1978.[33] The projected cost to build the dam was $300 million, but in less than a year the price more than tripled to approximately one billion dollars.[34] The eventual plan was for a 178-meter high earth- and rock-filled dam, which would hold 486 mcm of water. A small, 5-meter high, downstream diversion weir at Adasiya was to regulate the Yarmouk's flow to the East Ghor Canal intake.[35] By 1980, AID lent Jordan $14 million to assist in financing design costs.[36]

In 1976, larger political pressures encouraged Syria to agree to work with Jordan on the Maqarin Dam project. Relations between these two riparians were improving; Syria was trying to achieve closer ties and greater influence with Jordan. Amman had been becoming increasingly isolated in the Arab world following a decision at the 1974 Rabat Arab summit that the PLO, rather than Jordan, would be the sole representative of the Palestinians. Meanwhile, Syria and Jordan overcame mutual hostilities in the mid- and late 1970s in their effort to isolate Egypt because it posed a potential threat to both states by making a separate peace with Israel. This fear surfaced when Egypt signed the Sinai II agreement in September 1975, which combined a partial Israeli withdrawal from Sinai with an agreement for demilitarized zones and a multinational force to supervise the various provisions.[37]

At that point, Syria's President Asad preferred to form a union or federation with Jordan because the benefits to both parties seemed clear. To realize

TABLE 4-2
Syrian Depletion of the Yarmouk (mcm)

	Syrian Depletions	Stream Flow at Adasiya (Remaining Flow for Jordan and Israel)
Pre-1947		454
1954	20	434
1984–1988	172	282

Source: "Syrian Depletion Versus Stream Flow" FOIA US State Department Document (circa. 1988).

this goal, Asad and Hussein established a Higher Jordanian-Syrian Joint Committee to plan the integration of the two countries in the political, military, economic, cultural, and educational realms.[38] Cooperation on the Maqarin Dam provided an obvious benefit for Jordan, and, in exchange, Asad developed closer political ties and better relations with Jordan. Additionally, the Maqarin Dam would help develop Syria's Yarmouk basin region by providing a new source of hydroelectricity and water for irrigation. In 1977, Jordan and Syria amended the 1953 Yarmouk water treaty so that Jordan received the right to utilize all the water and electricity generated from the dam, provided Jordan would supply nearby Syrian villages with water and power. This was to compensate Syrian landowners who sustained economic injury because of the dam. Jordan would also pay the construction costs.[39] In 1978, Jordan and Syria signed the Maqarin Dam Agreement, which codified the dam's design and Syrian upstream use.[40] However, specific Syrian water allocations were not part of the agreement, which proved to be a difficult obstacle for the project.

The process of raising funding for the dam exposed the project to intense scrutiny by potential donors. In 1979, Congress authorized AID to appropriate $50 million to the Maqarin Dam project, with a verbal commitment to Jordan to provide another $100 million for construction and downstream irrigation related activities.[41] An AID official stated that "our interest is in having a clear understanding that we [AID] can pass onto the Jordanians that Congress does support the project," and that other international donors should do the same.[42] According to expectations, the remaining $850 million would come from other states or from international institutions. American assistance, in other words, depended on Jordan's ability to secure firm commitments for the balance of funding required for completing the dam.[43] Funding meetings concerning the dam took place during the late 1970s and early 1980s in Amman, Washington, London, and Chicago and attempted to resolve outstanding technical issues. Sixteen prospective donors, including France, West Germany, Britain, the European Investment Bank, US AID, the World Bank, and several oil-rich Arab states, expressed serious interest in the project. The revised project cost was $1.13 billion, including $642 million just for the dam.[44] During these meetings the donors examined some of the key assumptions of the Maqarin Dam and questioned the impact of Syria's taking more Yarmouk water than previously anticipated. These discussions also made it clear that more Jordanian water would be needed for municipal and industrial use and less for agriculture.[45] By 1980, most of the technical issues had been decided, but the funds would not be released until the riparian issues were resolved.[46]

At the start of US involvement, the US Senate Foreign Affairs Committee, as well as the World Bank, made clear that funding for the dam would depend on a "firm understanding with and between Israel and Jordan" regarding water use.[47] By itself, international law was not going to resolve political problems. In fact, international law was viewed as a "side track" in riparian rights discussions.[48] The State Department-commissioned Baxter Report was correct in concluding that "the principles and factors relating to an equitable apportionment of waters are guideposts for negotiations and for third-party decision makers, such as international tribunals, but they do not of themselves provide rules about how waters are allocated."[49] The water issue, in other words, would need to be solved by negotiators, not international lawyers or judges, apart from other political issues.

Throughout most of the negotiations, Israel was the major obstacle to finalizing the project, primarily because it pursued assurances that the Maqarin Dam would not injure its interests. In the 1950s and 1960s, as discussed in chapters 2 and 3, Israel had supported the construction of a Maqarin Dam, but, by 1976, Israel's Foreign Affairs Minister Yigal Allon indicated to Secretary of State Henry Kissinger that Israel was concerned about some of the implications of the Maqarin Dam project.[50] Israel did not object, in principle, to the dam, but feared that the project "endanger[ed] Israel's entitlement to water as envisaged in the Johnston Plan."[51] In January 1977, both Israel and Jordan requested the United States to help resolve disputes on the Maqarin Dam. Initially, King Hussein opposed direct Yarmouk water talks with Israel, but the United States made clear to both sides that its role was not as one of the negotiators, but as a conduit for information between Israel and Jordan. The United States also emphasized the importance of maintaining secrecy.[52] The next month a US delegation of technical experts led by Selig A. Taubenblatt of AID began discussions with Israeli officials, including Deputy Director General of the Foreign Affairs Ministry Moshe Alon, Deputy Director General of the Water Planning Authority (Tahal) Yacov Vardi, and Israel's Commissioner for Water Menachem Kantor.[53] After reviewing the Harza Engineering Company's interim report on the dam, Israeli officials made known to US officials five concerns: "(1) Israel must [be] assure[d] that it receives its equitable share of the Yarm[o]uk, (2) The quality, quantity, and flow of the Yarm[o]uk should be sufficient for Israeli needs, (3) The hydroelectric rights of Israel should be assured,[54] (4) Ecological and environmental problems must be overcome, [including the impact on the lower Jordan and Dead Sea, and][55] (5) Provisions must be made for the West Bank's water needs."[56] Yacov Vardi questioned whether the 17 mcm allocation for Israel's Yarmouk Triangle in the Harza study would be sufficient and Menachem Kantor reasserted that Israel still held its 40 mcm interpretation of the Johnston Plan. However, according to the Jordanians, a secret "gentleman's understanding" between the mid-1960s through the mid-1970s allowed an average 17 mcmy of Yarmouk water to flow to pumps for Israel's Yarmouk Triangle during the summer.[57] Moreover, data provided by Israel indicated that only 18.2 mcmy was drawn during the summer from the Yarmouk for the Israeli Yarmouk Triangle farmers.[58]

Jordan emphasized that the dam had the potential to benefit both countries. When the Americans met with Omar Abdullah Dokghan, president of the Jordan Valley Authority, he made it clear that Jordan would not discuss political issues. They did, however, discuss Israel's five issues of concern. Dokghan replied that resolution of the questions of specific volume of water for the Triangle and the West Bank and the Palestine Electric Corporation concession's standing would have to wait for an overall Middle East political settlement.[59] Jordan argued that the dam's reservoir would mitigate summer water scarcity and regulate winter Yarmouk flows, which would also benefit Israel. As an alternative, Jordan sought a reaction from Israel on its desire to build a diversion weir near the East Ghor intake.[60] Both Jordan and Israel agreed that a diversion weir, located near Adasiya, would be the preferred means for regulating the flow to the East Ghor Canal and the Yarmouk Triangle pumps. However, operating a weir that rested on both Jordanian and Israeli controlled territory was also problematic. Jordan demanded exclusive operational responsibility, while Israel insisted on some type of joint operation, such as direct technical talks relating to the weir's operation in distributing the Yarmouk. At this point, however, overtly cooperating with Israel was too risky for Jordan.[61]

The Maqarin project received new momentum when King Hussein raised the issue of economic assistance for the project with President Jimmy Carter.[62] A month later, a US team went to Jerusalem to discuss the Israeli reaction to the feasibility study. As a result of these meetings, the Israeli government stated in writing that "the water issue allocations for both the Yarmouk Triangle and the West Bank were of such pressing importance that they could not be deferred to undefined future construction stages or for resolution in the context of the some future political settlement."[63] Moreover, during the negotiations Israel indicated that it was willing to compromise on most of the five issues, including the 40/25 Yarmouk Triangle summer allocation dispute, but not on the 2.3 cubic meters per second (cms) flow rated during the summer months for the Yarmouk Triangle.[64] Jordan, on the other hand, argued that in times of drought Yarmouk water would have to be shared on the basis of demand.

Sustaining talks on the Maqarin Dam was complicated in 1977 by a change of governing parties in Israel. That year Likud defeated the Labor-led government for the first time. The new government did not have the same close type of relations with King Hussein. Nonetheless, Maqarin Dam negotiation continued. In July 1977, the United States circulated a draft working paper in an effort to jumpstart the negotiations. Jordan agreed to a summer flow rate of "up to" 2.3 cms to Israel's Yarmouk Triangle, but only if a dam was operating and there was no drought.[65] There was considerable disagreement about how much direct contact should exist between the two countries. In an effort to manage the Yarmouk waters, Israel insisted on direct talks and written agreements with Jordan. King Hussein emphatically stated to US Ambassador Thomas Pickering that Jordan would only discuss technical matters with the Israelis and would avoid all direct political contacts.[66] At this point, the Jordanians were resisting Israel's request for direct technical talks because their disclosure might threaten Syrian Yarmouk cooperation and Arab financial support. Since neither Jordan nor Syria recognized Israel as a sovereign state, AID did not believe a formal agreement was appropriate for proceeding with the Maqarin Dam. Arab leaders were particularly sensitive to such political matters due to Egyptian President Anwar Sadat's visit to Jerusalem. The US negotiating team concluded that Israel's insistence on direct technical talks "was not a negotiation position, but rather a *sine qua non* for further movement."[67] The US negotiators told the Jordanians that they needed to resolve outstanding issues with Israel in order to assure congressional support for financing the Maqarin Dam.

Despite these potential setbacks, the Maqarin Dam negotiations seemed to be making progress by 1979. Jordan, the World Bank, and other donors asked the United States to use its "good offices" to help reach an agreement with Israel on the project. In December 1979, the negotiations were advancing with an AID official leading the US delegation in "separate, unpublicized" talks with Israel and Jordan on the Maqarin Dam.[68] By late 1979, America had come to view the Maqarin talks with greater importance, as a means of advancing the Jordan-Israel peace track. The Egypt-Israel Camp David Peace Accords were recently signed, and the United States was hopeful that Jordan would be next. The United States also wanted to keep Jordan as a pro-Western friend and therefore feared the latter's moves toward closer relations with Soviet-aligned Syria. All this energy and willingness to negotiate led to higher level talks that came close to an agreement, but in the end failed.

The Habib Mission

The efforts began in mid-May 1980, when Ambassador Philip Habib, Senior State Department diplomat and Special Representative of the US Secretary of State for the Maqarin Dam, along with AID representative Selig Taubenblatt, launched their mission. They met with Israel's Prime Minister Menachem Begin and Agriculture Minister Ariel Sharon in Jerusalem before going to Amman for talks with King Hussein, as well as Jordan's prime minster and minister of state for foreign affairs.[69] Some participants described the Habib talks as "Middle Eastern horse trading."[70] The primary issues discussed were Yarmouk Triangle water allocations, a downstream diversion weir, Yarmouk water for the West Bank, and the form the agreement would take. According to Habib, "both the Israelis and Jordanians expressed positive and constructive attitudes in trying to find ways to resolve their differences."[71] Habib's major accomplishment was that Israel and Jordan agreed to 25 mcm as Israel's Yarmouk summer water allocation.[72] However, Habib failed to resolve Israeli-Jordanian differences over how much Yarmouk water should be allocated to the West Bank. This issue of Yarmouk water for the West Bank was the most difficult issue of the negotiations, according to US diplomats, because of the political spillover.[73] Prime Minister Begin expressed a positive attitude toward the Maqarin Dam and claimed that a formal agreement was not necessary, but insisted that there be a precise and binding understanding on allocations.[74] In particular, a West Bank allocation was necessary because of the mixed population on that land. According to Begin, Israeli settlements would be supplied with water from Lake Tiberias.[75] The Israeli concern was that in the future Israel alone would be responsible for the water needs of West Bank Arabs. Without an agreement on the quantity of Yarmouk water for West Bank Palestinians, Israel was unwilling to accept the Maqarin Dam.[76] For these negotiations, Israel made it clear that political considerations involving the territories' final status were secondary to the water issue.[77]

Although both Israeli and American officials said they were happy with the progress of the negotiations, the actual report of the Habib mission struck a more cautionary note.[78] The report concluded that Jordan was avoiding addressing the issue of a Yarmouk-West Bank allocation because such a public agreement might negatively impact Amman's relations with Syria, the Palestinians, and the major Arab donors to the dam. Jordan was reluctant to reopen discussions on the allocations specified in the Johnston Plan. This refusal was fed by the fact that, according to the Johnston Plan, Jordan was allocated 100 mcm from the upper Jordan, which it had yet to receive. Jordan made it clear that it would not recognize Israel or its West Bank occupation and refused to become a negotiator for West Bank interests. Jordan feared that any agreement with Israel on a Yarmouk allocation for the West Bank would not remain secret.[79] In the end, Israel would not agree to a dam or to a downstream weir without a clear West Bank allocation.[80] Habib's view, according to his report, was that "the ball is now in the Jordanian court, and Jordan will have to decide what is in its best interest."[81] He concluded that Jordan could either find a creative and diplomatic means to address the West Bank allocation issue so as to realize the dam project or continue not to move on the issue and deadlock negotiations. At this point, it was Jordan's higher preference not to compromise on the Palestinian question than to realize the Maqarin Dam. Both issues were politically significant, but Jordan viewed strengthening its fraying ties to Arab states as paramount.

To make matters worse, Jordanian-Syrian relations were deteriorating, and Damascus was seriously reassessing its Maqarin policy. Syria understood that it would benefit from the Maqarin's hydroelectric power and the additional irrigation water, but its primary reason for agreeing to the project had been to improve relations with Jordan. As early as 1977, Jordanian-Syrian relations were showing signs of strain. King Hussein—and Saudi Arabia—refused to join the Asad-initiated Tripoli Bloc, which included Libya, Algeria, South Yemen, and the PLO. Syria had engineered the bloc in order to reject the Camp David Peace Accords and form a newly configured alliance to oppose Israel. Hussein sided with Asad in opposing the peace accords, but was unwilling to join the anti-Western bloc. In an attempt to exert pressure on Jordan to follow Syria's lead, Asad, in mid-1978, dispatched PLO guerrillas into Jordanian territory to carry out operations against Israel. To counter Asad's continued pressure on Jordan, Hussein allowed a major opposition group to the Syrian regime, the Muslim Brotherhood, to operate within Jordan in 1979. A year later, Jordan became the first Arab state explicitly to side with Syria's archenemy Iraq in the Iran-Iraq war, and Jordan subsequently permitted Iraq to send weapons across Jordanian territory to Lebanon's anti-Syrian Christian leader, Michel Aoun. By late 1980, a serious rift had developed between Jordan and Syria. With Syria's growing domestic problems with the Muslim Brotherhood, Asad deployed his troops along the Jordanian border in December 1980. Hussein retaliated with his own mobilization. Relations worsened, and in early 1981 the Jordanian attaché in Beirut was kidnapped and a plot to assassinate Jordan's prime minister surfaced. Jordan accused Syria of instigating all these attacks and schemes.[82]

Because of the tense political and military environment, Syria was unwilling to discuss the Maqarin project with Jordan. By 1981, AID told Congress the "continuing inability to resolve riparian rights issues makes it impossible to begin construction of the project."[83] The agency, therefore, made no request to Congress for more funds for the Maqarin Dam. Technical and financial issues had, for the most part, been resolved, but the political riparian questions remained unanswered. An AID official explained to Congress that "with the current state of relations there's no way to reach agreement with the Syrians on the construction of the dam."[84] "There remain issues to be resolved with Israel," but discussions were continuing. Then AID concluded that in the final analysis, "in light of the Syrian problem, it is not fruitful to pursue that [project]." Building a Yarmouk dam was put on hold by the Jordanian and US governments.[85] Despite the stalled talks about the dam, Jordan was still interested in a deal with Israel so it could build a downstream weir and manage the summer flow.[86]

THE YARMOUK FORUM

As the Maqarin Dam negotiations began to falter on the Jordanian-Syrian track in 1979, Jordan and Israel commenced secret talks on the division of Yarmouk water. Until the Yarmouk dam was built, the functional objective of the Yarmouk forum or secret talks was to mitigate conflict by dividing and maintaining the flow in a manner that both sides could accept—on average, a

30 percent water distribution for Israel and 70 percent for Jordan during the summer irrigation months (see Table 4-3). These secret meetings continued until the signing of the 1994 Israel-Jordan peace agreement. Most often, Jordanian and Israeli water experts met at a Jordanian picnic table on the Yarmouk's bank near the Canal's intake or at an Israeli Allenby Bridge immigration shed. Between three and eight meetings took place each year, and the issue most often discussed was summer water allocations. At times, this was a slow and difficult process of developing rules for cooperating, but after fifteen years of secret on-site meetings, Israel and Jordan not only mitigated the chance for acute conflict over water but over time also developed confidence and trust between water technocrats and state elites. In other words, an epistemic community was emerging, a professional group of experts who share a common understanding of a problem (there is not enough summer water for both the Yarmouk Triangle and Jordan Valley) and its solution, and who meet on a routine basis to divide the scarce water in an equitable fashion. This Israeli-Jordanian international strategy of water cooperation was possible because Jordanian elites had a strong preference for mitigating Jordanian water scarcity by increasing its quantity of water from the Yarmouk. On the other hand, Israel's predominant preference, in this instance, was improved diplo-

TABLE 4-3

The 70/30 Water-Sharing Regime

Israel's and Jordan's Yarmouk water perrcentages during the summer season (May 15 to Oct. 15)

Year	Israel	Jordan
1981	33	67
1982	25	75
1983	36	64
1984	31	69
1985	36	64
1986	27	73
1987	28	72
1988	29	71
1989	32	68
1990	38	62
1991	37	63
1992	28	72
1993	32	68
1994	26	74
1995	25	75
Average	31	69
Maximum	38	75
Minimum	25	62

Source: Compiled by author based on data from Jordan's Jordan Valley Authority

matic relations with Jordan. It is also important to note that Israel had a strong preference for providing Yarmouk Triangle farmers and Lake Tiberias with Yarmouk water, and Jordan had a strong preference not to be seen, in any way, as cooperating with Israel. The US government's tactical functional cooperation preference was mitigating the chances of water-related conflict, while at the same time building confidence so a peace treaty would be more probable in the near future.

The area of focus for the negotiations was what Israelis called Point 121, near Adasiya (see Map 4-2) across from Jordan's East Ghor Canal intake.[87] This Israeli-controlled land was "disputed territory" in that the land had been within the Palestine mandate but was a demilitarized zone under Syrian control in 1949. Israel took control of it in 1967.[88] Just a few meters upstream from the intake is an island of debris formed by winter floods, and downstream from the intake is a weir of sandbags. Jordan and Israel together manipulate the canal gates and the sandbag weir, which straddles both the Israeli and Jordanian riverbanks. This arrangement is necessary during the summer to influence the flow to Jordan's canal and downstream Israeli pumps. Managing the flow by these means was the focal point of their secret water talks. Even with this cooperation, water relations between the two countries occasionally became extremely tense. In 1979, 1986, and 1987, Israel and Jordan mobilized their troops on the Yarmouk's banks because of disputes over water allocations and scarcity. As the Yarmouk forum rules became more established and confidence and transparency increased, the sides gauged the flow on a biweekly basis, jointly cleaned the riverbed annually, and exchanged technical data on river flows, as well as an information on the upstream dam.[89]

Between 1970 and 1979, little or no secret on-site cooperation had occurred between Jordan and Israel, but there was tacit water-related coordination. Secret diplomatic water-related meetings regarding Yarmouk allocations took place in Europe and the United States from 1967 onward, although they did not involve joint Israeli-Jordanian measuring or weir adjusting in the field.[90] During June and July 1974, Prince Hasan asked the US government to provide Jordan with Israeli hydrological data. For the United States, this was the first known instance when a Jordanian official sought water development information from Israel via the United States. In the end, the State Department warned Hasan that his request might leak to the Israeli press. The crown prince subsequently decided against pursuing the matter. Even so, the State Department believed the exchange of hydrological "data could be the beginning of a useful exchange" between Israel and Jordan if Israel would guarantee that such matters remained secret.[91] A minimal Jordanian-Israeli cooperative arrangement worked between 1967 and 1978 because Yarmouk water demand, while increasing, was still manageable. During this period, Israel allowed Jordanian farmers to unilaterally build temporary weirs out of

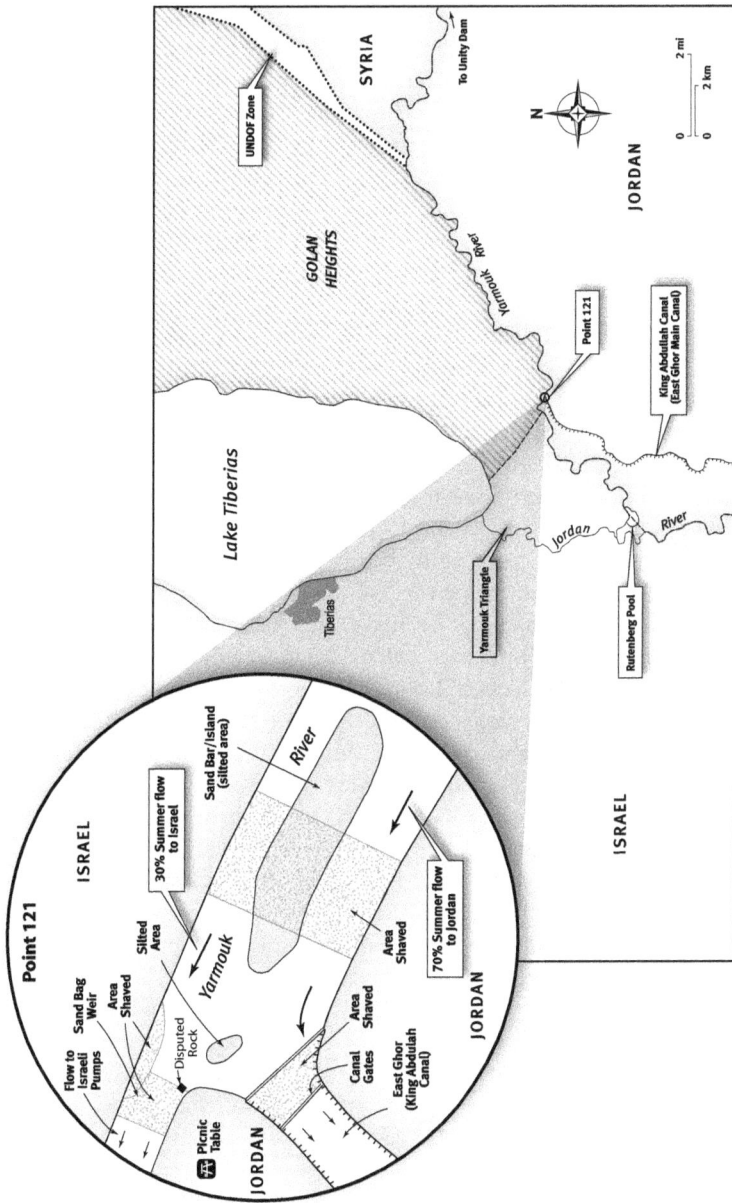

Source: Tahal and US State Department.

MAP 4-2   Lower Yarmouk Valley and Point 121/East Ghor Canal Intake

stones near or at Point 121. And the Jordanians permitted Yarmouk water to flow to downstream Israeli pumps. However, occasionally, as in July 1976, Jordanians dammed up the entire river with rocks, and thus prevented Israeli Yarmouk Triangle farmers from obtaining water needed to irrigate their fields. Consequently, the Israelis periodically dismantled the Jordanian weir to secure their share of the water flow.[92] During this period, Israel publicly maintained that it was entitled to 40 mcm of the Yarmouk water during the summer, but rarely, if ever, took that much. This water-sharing arrangement worked for a time, but when greater water scarcity occurred, the riparians required enhanced cooperation.

CONFLICT BEFORE THE YARMOUK FORUM COOPERATION

During the summer of 1979, the Yarmouk basin was in a severe drought, and relations at Point 121 were extremely tense. In fact, this was the severest drought since the East Ghor Canal began operations in 1962. As the Yarmouk flow declined, both riparians tried to obtain as much water as possible. The summer season, between May 15 and October 15, was the most contentious time.[93] The Yarmouk in winter usually floods, and more water rushes downstream than can be absorbed by the canal's intake, but during the summer literally every liter of water is used. To make matters worse, upstream Syrian extraction was increasing, Jordan completed an East Ghor Canal extension and was expanding its irrigation area, Israeli and Jordanian farmers were demanding water for their crops, and the Maqarin Dam negotiations were beginning to falter.[94] Furthermore, at times Jordan's intake failed to receive its share of flow because of uncleared debris that had accumulated from winter floods. Prior to 1967, thanks to the Syrians, Jordan had easy access to the Yarmouk riverbed and cleaned debris when needed.[95] However, since 1967, when Israel became Jordan's new Point 121 neighbor, there had been no agreement on dredging the area. Year after year, rocks and sand accumulated into a sandbar, partially obstructing the East Ghor Canal intake. On June 21, 1979, the Jordanian minister of state for foreign affairs asked the US ambassador to Jordan, Nicholas Veliotes, to question Israel when Jordan could remove the detritus. Within a week, the US ambassador to Israel, Samuel Lewis, passed along the Jordanian request to the Israeli government. Jordanian and Israeli technical experts met midstream to discuss flow measurements and devise a plan for removing part of the sandbar.[96] On July 10, Israel told the US that Jordan could shave part of the sand bar "provided that Israel's water interests relating to the Yarmouk will be fully safe guarded" and that the oral agreement between technocrats at midstream was followed.[97] Israel was very specific in what the Jordanians were permitted to do. The day after the cleaning, the

Israeli government protested that Jordanian bulldozers had violated the agreement. They argued that the Jordanians had widened the riverbank, deepened the channel, blocked the flow of water to Israel for a limited time period, and reduced Israel's flow by two-thirds.[98] According to one State Department lawyer, at this point "the US lent its good offices to resolve a potentially dangerous confrontation between Israel and Jordan when unilateral Jordanian actions sharply depleted Israel's share of the Yarmouk flow."[99] After investigating the issue, Munther Haddadin, JVA vice president (and acting president because Dokghan was out of the country), determined that Israel was entitled to an additional 200 liters per second.[100] Israel rejected this offer and argued that since the US good offices had obtained Israel's agreement for the cleaning, it was the United States' responsibility to encourage Jordan to fix the problem and gave Jordan until July 17, four days, to resolve the matter by restoring the status quo ante water flow. In turn, the United States urged Israel not to take unilateral action.[101]

With Syria increasing its upstream utilization, thereby decreasing the downstream flow left to Jordan, Jordanian officials understood that dividing the flow proportionately was preferable to guaranteeing Israel a specific flow, such as 2.3 cms, drought or not. Haddadin argued to the Americans that, prior to the removal of the debris, Jordan was receiving less flow than its fair share. In fact, it had a right to two-thirds of the flow immediately above the East Ghor Canal diversion plus one cubic meter, with the remainder—one-third minus one cubic meter—going downstream to Israeli Yarmouk Triangle pumps.[102] Israel had never accepted such a system and made clear that it was unacceptable now. American diplomats pointed out that the only reference to the two-third/one-third formula was in the 1950s Tennessee Valley Authority Main proposal that Israel had rejected long ago.[103] Moreover, Wayne Criddle said that the two-third/one-third formula was never discussed during the Johnston mission talks.[104] Haddadin insisted that the cleaning agreement with Israel was for 25 percent of the flow or .75 cms of 3 cms to the Yarmouk Triangle.[105] The change in the flow since the Criddle mission of 1955 was also a factor in Israel's rejection of the two-third/one third formula. When the East Ghor Canal first began operation in 1962, the Yarmouk's summer flow had been 7.7 cms of which 2.3 cms or 30 percent went to Israel.[106] During the summer of 1979, the flow was approximately 5 cms of which 30 percent is 1.5 cms, much less than 2.3 cms. After researching the issue, US diplomats concluded that its records did not support the Jordanian contentions of proportional division of the flow.[107]

This disagreement directly led to a heightening of political tensions. Munther Haddadin asserted that Jordan would not clean the river, but would meet for the first time with the Israelis to negotiate the matter. The Israelis argued to the United States that the JVA authorities were intentionally "dragging their feet" to obtain more water. The Jordanians believed that, with the sandbar, "the Israelis had previously taken more than their share," so stalling for more water was justified.[108] According to the US embassy in Tel Aviv, however, Israel was receiving a flow of 1.1 cms out of 5.2 cms. The State Department knew Israel would not tolerate the present situation, and Washington pointed out to the Jordanians that the current flow did not "satisfy the spirit of the 1958 [Jordan-US] understanding."[109] The Americans appraised the situation correctly. During the night of July 19, 1979, Israeli soldiers crossed the Yarmouk into Jordan, captured the Jordanian soldiers on guard, and allowed Israeli farmers to readjust some rocks in the riverbed, "correcting the distribution" from what the Jordanians had done originally. The Israeli government explained that it had sent troops to protect the Israeli workers.[110] After being notified of the crisis, Haddadin drove from Amman to the East Ghor Canal intake and saw across the river Israeli "infantry, personnel carriers, tanks, artillery, and machine guns."[111] The Jordanians had matched the mobilization, and only 200 meters separated the forces. The Israelis were videotaping the entire crisis.

Jordan's actions at this point would determine whether the crisis would escalate or resolve itself peacefully. After being briefed by Haddadin about the Israeli actions, the Jordanian prime minister ordered Haddadin to return to the river to determine whether the Israeli cleaning was fair and Jordan was receiving its share of the flow. Initially, Haddadin rejected the Israelis' contention that Jordan had widened the channel and reiterated that it only removed debris that had accumulated over the last four years. In the end, however, Haddadin eased his stance and recognized that this crisis was the result of Jordan's noncompliance with its agreement with Israel. Noah Kinarti, the lead Israeli farmer who conducted the unilateral readjustments, argued that the reason the Jordanians did not fight was that the JVA head knew that the Israeli "recleaning" had merely followed the understanding established previously between Israel and Jordan.[112] Direct Jordanian-Israeli talks were important to Israel, especially in the context of Israel and Egypt signing a peace treaty in Washington just three months earlier. But Israel would not stand for redistributing the flow. Haddadin had miscalculated Israel's response to the diversion and stalling, but had the experience and savvy not to jeopardize the East Ghor Canal and Jordan Valley development with a shortsighted response.[113] Less than a decade earlier, the canal had been incapacitated by numerous Israeli attacks, and Haddadin did not want a return to those days of instability. Both sides understood that Israel was far superior militarily and that both would lose a great deal from a military battle over Yarmouk water.

Haddadin concluded that Jordan's only remaining nonmilitary option available was to continue contact with Israel through the UN Armistice Commission. Almost two years earlier, the United States had suggested the UN

Joint Mixed Armistice Commission (MAC) as a possible venue to hold talks relating to the Yarmouk.[114] In response to the Jordanian army's standing down, Israel agreed to pull back its forces and continue meeting with the Jordanians. This episode marked the dramatic beginning of fifteen years of on-site secret meetings between Israeli and Jordanian technocrats concerning the Yarmouk water issue.[115]

During the crisis, a great deal of discussion took place about the rules for dividing the flow. The first part of the dispute centered on the question of how to interpret the Johnston Plan of several years earlier and the various parties' agreement to its terms. The United States argued that the "historical record, precedent, and the February 1958 exchange of notes obliged Jordan to respect the Triangle's senior use right to a 2.3 cms summer flow rate irrespective of controlled conditions or drought."[116] Jordan promised to satisfy this obligation if the United States showed it the documents of the Jordanian commitment.[117] In fact, in 1958 Jordan had committed to adhere to the Johnston Plan, and in exchange the United States pledged to fund the East Ghor Canal. Wayne Criddle, who was a technical advisor for the Johnston mission and who later returned to the region to resolve some water-related differences between Jordan and Israel, stated that, according to the negotiations, Israel was guaranteed a summer rate of 2.3 cms with a gross entitlement of 25 mcm. Criddle maintained that lack of an upstream dam or existence of a drought did not free Jordan of this obligation.[118] As it turned out, the United States did possess documents that evidenced that Jordan accepted the Johnston Plan, but Washington did not have papers that Jordan had agreed to a 2.3 cms flow to the Yarmouk Triangle during the summer. Criddle's statements about a Jordanian commitment to a 2.3 cms flow were recollection and not a written agreement.[119] With this room to maneuver, Omar Abdullah Dokghan, president of the JVA, had returned to Jordan and argued that the Johnston Plan allocation of 25 mcm to the Yarmouk Triangle would only apply if an upstream dam and downstream weir controlled the Yarmouk's flow but not before. According to Dokghan, Jordan would follow the 2.3 cms obligation after the dam and weir began operations.[120]

Five days after the crisis started, Israeli and Jordanian officials met under MAC auspices to consider the water dispute. In the past, Jordan and Israel had accepted that ad hoc arrangements had to be made when droughts occurred, but the tension surrounding these meetings made agreement difficult.[121] Dokghan offered an 0.2 cms increase flow to Israel.[122] Two days later, Israel countered that it was willing to accept a little more than 2 cms, the amount it was receiving prior to the Jordanian cleaning. According to Israelis, once this was resolved, it was ready to consider practical means to address the drought conditions.[123] The next day, Israeli representative Vardi stood firm that Israel should receive 2 cms, but the Jordanian representative Fuad Natour—director of irrigation for the JVA—responded that, under the present drought conditions, 2 cms for Israel were not feasible. At this point, JVA heads Dokghan and Haddadin would not meet face-to-face with the Israelis. Three days later, though, Natour and Vardi did meet, but did not conclude an agreement.[124] Even so, the atmosphere was civil and a follow-up meeting was scheduled, according to the UN official present at the meeting.[125] Since the on-site negotiations were stalled, US Ambassador to Jordan Nicholas Veliotes met with the chief of the royal court and Dokghan. The ambassador had also recently met with King Hussein to discuss the Yarmouk water crisis. At the same time, the Israelis lowered their water demand to 1.9 cms and again stated that, once the flow was established, Israel was prepared to negotiate long-term arrangements.[126] On July 27, 1979, after a meeting between Jordanian and Israeli representatives, Dokghan ordered an increase in the flow to the Yarmouk Triangle.[127] Three days later Israel informed the United States that the flow had increased to almost 2 cms and that the "harsher part of the dispute was over."[128] A week later, Dokghan complained to US officials that "Israel is now happy and satisfied. We are suffering."[129] Calm had been maintained, but it was a fragile one.

A little more than a month after the conclusion of the July–August predicament, a new crisis erupted from an unexpected quarter. It began September 14 when a group of Yarmouk Triangle farmers led by Noah Kinarti, who were upset by a return to a lower Yarmouk flow to their pumps, decided to block the channel to Jordan's East Ghor Canal intake with rocks. This was meant to be a statement to both the Jordanian and Israeli governments that the Israeli Yarmouk Triangle farmers were not willing to "lose the Yarmouk waters" to the enlarged East Ghor Canal or to the proposed Maqarin Dam. Reaching the river was relatively easy for Israeli farmers because the Israeli army had recently cleared Point 121's river banks of mines and had paved a road to the river so farmers could better observe Jordanian actions on the river.[130] The Jordanians were irate that the Israeli farmers were damming the river and immediately contacted the Americans and again mobilized troops on the Yarmouk's banks. Jordan complained that the Triangle was receiving 2.6 cms and Jordan was receiving only 2.1 cms. For their parts, Israeli government representatives and water technocrats were also infuriated by the Yarmouk Triangle farmers' unilateral actions.[131] The Israeli government had not authorized such a move; nonetheless, Israel matched the Jordanian mobilization. At a September 16 Jordanian-Israeli meeting, Israel promised to rectify the situation.[132] As a result, Israel and Jordan agreed to build a sandbag weir of some 60 to 70 centimeters, which covered the entire width of the Yarmouk, approximately 15 feet west of the East Ghor Canal intake. The sandbags would be manipulated to adjust the flow to the East Ghor Canal and Yarmouk Triangle pumps.[133]

Initially there was little trust between Israelis and Jordanians. Both sides tried cheating and neither side would allow the other to act unilaterally. For example, the sandbags were moved only after an agreement was reached and while both sides were present. With the failure of the Maqarin Dam negotiations and the advent of the picnic table talks, Jordanian officials asked for US assistance in building a permanent weir near Adasiya and a second East Ghor Canal inlet to channel more water to their water system. Israel resisted the immediate construction of the weir without a package agreement on Yarmouk water matters, in particular, on the Maqarin Dam. Jordan rejected the idea of a quid pro quo of Israeli acceptance of building the weir for a comprehensive agreement.[134] In the absence of a comprehensive agreement, the secret talks would continue as the venue for addressing the distribution of the Yarmouk flow between Israel and Jordan.

DIVIDING THE FLOW

After the dramatic events of 1979, the secret talks largely settled into a routine. The primary issue discussed and investigated was "what the flow per second would be" and how it impacted the farmers on each side of the river.[135] The parties took measurements and made distribution arrangements, such as moving sandbags and adjusting the gates of the East Ghor Canal intake. Meetings concerned only summer water allocations and usually occurred during that season. At the beginning of summer, participants discussed a schedule of monthly flow rates for the entire irrigation season. Then they jointly reviewed each other's current water requirements in order to reach an equitable sharing arrangement. Conflict management was a shared goal of both parties, so meetings occurred whenever either party had a problem, such as when orchards needed additional water immediately. Winter water was not as scarce, and without an upstream dam Jordan could not store much of it, so there was less need for cooperation during that season. Additionally, Jordan considered the entire winter water supply as its own; thus "there was nothing to discuss."[136] Haddadin, now acting director of the JVA, did, however, complain to US officials about Israeli pumping of residual Yarmouk winter flows and thus taking more than was allotted to Israel in the Johnston Plan.[137]

The bureaucratic details of the meetings were quite similar to those of peaceful neighbors working out resource management together, except for the elaborate means of communication. The number of meetings held each year ranged from three to eight. One meeting was held at the beginning of each summer season and one at the end for planning. Additional meetings were dispersed throughout the summer to address specific problems as they arose.[138] The water authority of either side could call a meeting, and intermediaries, usually the United Nations, would normally arrange the rendezvous. For example, if the Jordan Valley Authority wanted to hold a meeting, its representatives contacted the Jordanian army liaison, who in turn called the UN Armistice Commission office in Jordan, who then notified members of their office in Israel who contacted the Israeli army liaison, who then called the Yarmouk Triangle Water Association. Even with such a convoluted communication system, they could arrange meetings, if necessary, in only two hours time.[139]

When Israel or Jordan needed to check facts in the field, such as measuring the river's flow, representatives would meet at Point 121. A temporary bridge was placed across the Yarmouk so the Israelis could cross to Jordan where both sides would meet at a picnic table near the riverbank. If the meeting did not involve fieldwork, participants would meet at the Allenby Bridge to discuss issues such as the water flow schedule.[140] The meetings were small, usually comprising one representative each from Jordan's JVA, Israel's Tahal (the Water Planning Authority), Israel's Water Commissioner's Office, as well as the head of the Yarmouk Triangle Water Association. Experts on specific issues were present when necessary.[141] Army liaisons from both Jordan and Israel were present along with a representative from the United Nations who observed the proceedings.[142] The river's flow was measured at two points, upstream and downstream from the East Ghor Canal intake.[143] The intake gates managed the water along with the movement of twenty or so sandbags that were just below the canal.[144] At the end of the summer, the technocrats removed the bags from the river so the winter floods would not wash them away.

The cooperation between Jordan and Israel extended beyond simply maintaining the equitable flow arrangement and providing an exchange of information. Through such cooperative actions as "water loans," which began in 1979, the riparians tried to help one another.[145] When Jordan occasionally needed extra water during the summer for a specific crop, usually orchards, it made a request at a secret meeting and, more often than not, Israel would approve the loan.[146] Later in the summer, Jordan allowed Israel's flow to be increased to repay the debt. By the end of the season, the distribution was back to normal, on average 30 percent for Israel and 70 percent for Jordan (see Table 4-4).[147]

Just as the cooperation was kept secret, the paper trail was informal. No formal agreements were made, and all arrangements became "non-agreements," "non-papers," or gentlemen's agreements. Neither side signed documents, and meeting minutes were handwritten merely for personal records. There were no official meeting minutes or protocols.[148] Even so, the unofficial records were very detailed, specifying agreement dates, flow measurements, and loan requests. They also recorded discussions of larger issues such as debates over the Johnston Plan and the Yarmouk dams.[149] The participants made most of the day-to-day decisions on-site. Larger issues such as water

TABLE 4-4
Yarmouk Winter (Oct. 15 to May 15) Water Loans from Israel to Jordan (mcm), 1980–1989

Jordan (mcm)	
1985/1986	9.13 ([first loan] 2 + [second loan] 7.13)
1987/1988	7.75
1988/1989	7.75

Source: "Yarmuk Water Data for Winter Seasons (15.10–15.5)" FOIA (photocopy).

loans were referred back to the respective capitals. In Israel, the prime minister's office, as well as that of the water commissioner, always received a briefing on the Yarmouk secret meetings. The same was true in Jordan, where the prime minister's office and the palace were kept informed.[150] However, the meetings were "always local initiatives."[151] When the respective water authorities wanted to discuss matters, ranging from future dam construction and drought conditions to the position of sandbags and difficulties with measurements, a meeting was held. The arrangement worked because both sides developed confidence that when problems arose they would be addressed without difficulty and that the meetings and cooperation would continue into the future.[152]

This level of cooperation built only gradually. Confidence developed little by little and only as time progressed could it be said "there was lots of trust."[153] For the first two years, for example, army escorts accompanied the Israeli and Jordanian participants. By 1983, the Israelis deemed this unnecessary, but acquiesced to the Jordanians having escorts.[154] At the beginning of the talks, between 1979 and 1984, the JVA sent the second in charge, Fuad Natour, to the picnic table to meet with the Israelis, while the JVA president Haddadin remained 200 meters away in a tent. If the deputy had questions, he would walk back to the tent, confer with the president, and then return to the picnic table.[155] By 1985, though, the JVA head was participating directly in face-to-face negotiations with the Israelis. This trust, sustained over time, produced other potentially valuable dividends from the secret water talks. For example, during Point 121 meetings, the Israeli and Jordanian army liaison would occasionally walk away from the picnic table and privately discuss other issues.[156]

Secrecy was critical to the Yarmouk forum's success. Jordan was willing to participate to benefit its water interests but, for political reasons, could not be seen as cooperating with Israel. Therefore, so long as the arrangement remained secret, Jordan would participate. Israel also had important water interests, although less critical than those of Jordan. For Israel, the priority was managing the conflict that might arise from water scarcity, maintaining a steady water flow for its Yarmouk farmers and Lake Tiberias, securing the Jordan Valley so that terrorist incursions such as those in the 1967–1971 period did not recur, and improving diplomatic relations with Jordan when feasible. The secret nature of these meetings permitted greater cooperation between Israel and Jordan. However, at least twice over the fifteen years of the secret picnic table talks, Israeli politicians leaked aspects of the talks to the Israeli press. These leaks had a greater impact on the Maqarin and Unity Dam negotiations. The suspected leakers were from the Israeli political right, such as Minister Ariel Sharon and Water Commissioner Yishay Tzemach. American diplomats assumed that the leaks aimed to push the Jordanians toward normalization of relations with Israel or were meant to negatively impact the Jordanian-Syrian dam negotiations.[157] The Jordanians rejected this pressure and rightly complained to the Americans about the leaks, but Amman did not end the talks, in part because of the limited nature of the disclosures.

The United Nations, which gave Jordan's participation in the meetings legitimacy or at least political cover, played a critical role in the secret talks. If the secret Yarmouk meetings had become overtly public, Jordan was in a position to argue that it was acting under the 1949 Israel-Jordan Armistice Agreement, which stated that the UN Armistice Commission would facilitate meetings between the two countries. Jordan did maintain that the Yarmouk forum fell under the Armistice Agreement and that the whole arrangement "was not a big deal"[158] and was "the graceful and peaceful solution of [technical level] problems, which threatened the truce."[159] Nonetheless, Jordan still believed UN legitimacy did not provide sufficient political cover and, therefore, it required a high level of secrecy even with the United Nations' participation. Jordan's leadership believed that its own public and its Arab neighbors would never accept that the meetings only concerned Jordan's water interests and were not an effort to normalize relations with Israel.[160] For Israel, UN participation was a "tolerated formality." Since Jordan had participated in the 1967 War, Israel argued that Jordan had voided the Armistice Agreement.[161] However, Israel understood Jordan's political constraints and was willing to cooperate.[162] During the Point 121 meetings, the UN representative sat at the table, but rarely contributed to the discussion.[163]

The United States played an important role in assisting the talks, even though it had no representatives present at the meetings. Both sides recognized that the United States had a legitimate function as an ally of both Israel and Jordan and a provider of financial assistance to important Jordanian and Israeli water projects.[164] The Amman and Tel Aviv US embassies and the State Department "were always in the picture."[165] The United States usually played a passive role by speaking with both sides to get "readouts" or summaries of the past picnic table meetings. Periodically, the United States also played a more active role by generating ideas for resolving specific problems or contacting high-ranking leaders when Yarmouk politics became tense. As already seen, the United States had a major part in the Maqarin Dam shuttle-diplomacy negotiations. For Israel and Jordan, the United States' most important role was as a guarantor. Relations with the United States were important to both states, and thus the superpower had a critical position in guaranteeing the integrity of the arrangement. This was especially important to Jordan, the weaker state. Amman made a much greater effort than it might normally have done to inform the United States on water-sharing developments and conflict. Even so, Jordan was careful not to let the United States force the process forward more quickly than Amman believed was in its best interest.[166]

CLEANING THE SANDBAR/ISLAND

Between 1979 and 1984, the parties were unable to agree on how to deal with the issue that caused the first crisis in 1979—removal of the island/sandbar that was impeding the East Ghor Canal intake. Israel considered the obstacle in front of the East Ghor Canal an island because they saw it as something permanent, whereas the Jordanians viewed it as a temporary result of their inability to clean the riverbed. During a picnic table meeting, Vardi showed the Jordanians a 1946 aerial photograph of the Yarmouk with an island next to the location where the East Ghor Canal inlet is located today. For Israel, this was evidence that the obstacle was permanent. For Haddadin, the construction of the canal inlet had altered the Yarmouk's flow patterns, thus producing a non-permanent sandbar. By the mid-1970s, the sandbar had become an island because Jordan was kept from cleaning the riverbed and inlet channel, as it had done in the past.[167] Because of the obstacle, Jordan was unable to obtain its share of the summer flow. Without a dam in place, Jordan still refused to provide the Yarmouk Triangle with 2.3 cms and certainly would not consider it in times of drought. Haddadin argued that since Israel pumped more than 25 mcm annually from the Yarmouk for storage in Lake Tiberias, Israel could release water to the Triangle during the summer. American officials still countered that there was a strong historical record that Jordan had accepted a 2.3 cms summer flow until Israel received 25 mcm as the amount for the Triangle during the summer.[168] The United States did, however, agree with Jordan that Israel had no permanent right to Yarmouk winter floods.[169]

During a May 1983 picnic table meeting, Jordan's JVA vice president for irrigation, Dr. Fuad Natour, met with Vardi and again proposed to the Israelis the removal of the 30 to 40 meter-long sandbar that was obstructing the Yarmouk water flow to the East Ghor Canal's inlet. Israel insisted that any work on the island required "careful technical and engineering study." At the meeting, Jordan reluctantly agreed to an alternative—to establish a new sandbag weir so Jordan would receive a more satisfactory flow.[170] Israel also rejected a second East Ghor Canal inlet until Jordan came to an agreement on riparian rights.[171]

By the winter of 1984, Washington feared that the impasse over the sandbar would lead to more serious conflict, given the other pressures on water resources at this time. Extreme Jordan Valley water scarcity might lead to heightened tensions between Israel and Jordan over sharing Yarmouk water. Rainfall in Jordan was well below average and consequently all small reservoirs were empty, and Jordan's only large reservoir, the King Talal Dam, held only 20 mcm, only 40 percent of its capacity. The wet season was quickly coming to an end, and Jordanian farmers were already being advised not to plant a spring vegetable crop.[172] On the political side, Jordan was insisting that the Israelis were deliberately dragging their feet. During the Habib mission, both sides accepted that Israel had a right to 25 mcm annually of Yarmouk water and that the residual belonged to Jordan. According to Haddadin, the summer flow was not the problem. Israel and Jordan measured and adjusted the allocation and shared the shortfall. The issue was the winter flow, which belonged to Jordan, but, with the sandbar in front of the East Ghor Canal inlet, this island provided an obstruction.[173] The sandbar, among other considerations, restricted the Yarmouk flow and decreased the amount of winter water available to Jordan's reservoirs. Jordanian officials argued that Israel dragged out the sandbar negotiations to exploit Jordanian vulnerability over water and force higher-level direct bilateral talks. The high-ranking Jordanians told US diplomats that such strong-arm Israeli tactics would fail and could result in a confrontation over the water issue that would have serious political implications.[174] By the summer of 1984, JVA president Munther Haddadin had made it clear to US ambassador Viets that no progress was taking place on the sandbar issue with Israel and therefore Jordan was reassessing its options—one of which was the immediate unilateral removal of the sandbar. Haddadin hoped the United States would help Jordan in this matter so that a potential violent conflict could be averted.[175]

The US government increasingly feared that if the sandbar issue did not reach resolution, the important direct talks between Jordan and Israel were not the only element in peril. Even more alarming for the United States was the possibility of unilateral action—"i.e., Jordan's clearing the island without Israel's agreement," which could lead to a break in talks or an open confrontation.[176] To mitigate the crisis, Washington asked its ambassadors to bring the sandbar issue to the attention of the Jordanian and Israeli leadership at the highest level. A week later US Ambassador to Israel Samuel Lewis met with Prime Minister Yitzhak Shamir. Shamir agreed that the contacts with the Jordanians were important and that they could be useful for resolving other current problems, such as Jordanian pollution in the Gulf of Aqaba/Eilat. Shamir indicated that he would look into the matter and would seek to improve the climate between Jordan and Israel.[177]

The Israelis were, in fact, interested in discussing larger water-resource questions and feared that resolving the sandbar issue would end Jordan's willingness to meet. A few weeks after Ambassador Lewis's visit, the Israeli ministry of foreign affair's legal advisor, Eli Rubinstein, contacted the US embassy and indicated that the prime minister was very interested in continuing its talks with Jordan over water. However, Israel insisted on a broader water action plan, including building a permanent weir and means for dividing the water, not just the removal of the island as Jordan requested. Rubinstein's fear was that, once Jordan had removed the island, it would take all the winter flows and Israel would be left with less water. Also, Israel had a political problem with Yarmouk Triangle area farmers who were fiercely opposed to the removal of the island and worried that they would lose access to the winter flows. Rubinstein insisted that if any negotiation were to be successful, a Jordanian who had the authority to negotiate in a comprehensive manner had to be in place. Israeli interlocutors respected Jordanian negotiator Natour, but he lacked the necessary authority to complete a deal.[178]

Meanwhile, water scarcity in 1984 drove the Jordanians to cheat on water use, taking a stealthy course of action that might have led to greater conflict but did not. With the grass on the riverbanks high enough to make Israeli oversight difficult, the JVA had twelve men secretly dig a small channel to the canal's intake to increase Jordan's water supply. Soon after the ditch's completion, the US attaché at the embassy in Amman arranged a meeting with the JVA president. The US diplomat showed him satellite photos of Point 121 and questioned him about the ditch canal.[179] The Israelis did not react to the Jordanian canal.

The Jordanians eventually gave in to pressure that a higher-level Jordanian official meet with Israelis to discuss broader cooperation on water issues. Secretary of State George Schultz visited Jordan soon after the channel incident and included on his list of discussion items the dredging of the Yarmouk. Until 1984, Jordan had sought the dredging, but wanted it done unilaterally. Amman was hesitant to undertake such a major project with the Israelis. For its part, Israel wanted Jordanians of higher rank involved in the secret meetings. In fact, Israelis wanted a face-to-face meeting with the JVA head, Haddadin. But now another factor influencing the Jordanians to dredge with the Israelis was the proposed installation of a new Israeli pumping station at Tabya in 1984. This was to be the fourth such station, and the Israeli Water Commissioner explicitly stated his intention to draw Israel's full allocation of 25 mcm during the summer and any "desirable amount during the winter."[180] Under US and Israeli pressure, the JVA president informed an AID representative in Amman that he would meet with the Israelis to discuss the dredging.[181] That same year, Shimon Peres became prime minister of Israel in a national unity government with Likud, a development that would positively influence these talks. Peres sought a breakthrough on peace negotiations with Jordan. Both King Hussein and Peres privately agreed to expand Israeli-Jordanian secret functional ties, hoping

eventually to move toward a peace settlement.[182] While not prompting an overall breakthrough, Peres's actions further helped the dredging talks.

Differences over the sandbar continued for another year, but on September 10, 1985, at the Allenby Bridge, Israeli and Jordanian representatives
agreed on the work to be done on the Yarmouk riverbed near the inlet to the
East Ghor Canal. The technocrats signed no documents but adopted a course
of action, which is described later, for the cleaning operation. A computer
model from Delft University in the Netherlands provided the basis for the initial discussions on how best to clean the river and facilitate the "normal" flow.
By the end of the negotiations, though, a split had erupted in the Israeli delegation. The Jordanians could hear the Israeli delegates "arguing loudly" in a
separate, closed room at the immigration shed near the Allenby Bridge.[183] The
Israeli members representing farmers opposed the arrangement because they
would receive less water while the members representing political interests
argued in favor because of the benefits to Israel of closer cooperation with Jordan.[184] Jordan and Israel finally agreed to work together to reduce the buildup
of soil and debris in the river, solve the riverbank's erosion problem, remove the
island, and restore an equitable flow.[185] Israel agreed to the removal of the
sandbar/island if the removal was part of a larger package that would safeguard
Israel's low flow during the summer months. To do this, after the island was
removed, a hydrological pool near the canal intake was to be established, and
the Yarmouk River bed would be dredged. The result was that Israel would
receive a "normal" flow without a sandbag weir and with East Ghor Canal
gates open.

The following is a summary of the agreed on points between representatives of Israel and Jordan regarding the cleaning of the Yarmouk, according to
a document from the Israel ministry of foreign affairs legal advisor. The document was sent to the US embassy in Tel Aviv.

> On September 10, 1985, a meeting was held between representatives
> of Israel and Jordan at the Allenby Bridge, concerning work to be
> done in the Yarmouk riverbed at the entrance to the EGMC [East
> Ghor Canal]
>
> The following points were agreed upon:
> a) The whole island will be removed [sea level].
> b) A stilling pool at the entrance of the EGMC will be created
>   between cross-section DD, YY and ZZ (see attached agreed upon
>   map [Map 4-2])[186] with an elevation of – 206.85.
> c) Between the bottom of the newly created stilling pool and the
>   existing riverbed upstream of it, a gradual slope will be created.

d) In the downstream reach of the river, the riverbed will be excavated and adjusted so as to restore the present flow. According to our estimates this will be achieved by creating a straight uniform bottom slope between cross sections ZZ and III.

e) This assumption will, however, be rechecked at the conclusion of the works so as to assure a flow of 1.7 cms (without any artificial obstacles in the riverbed and with EGMC gates fully open) downstream out of a total of 4.4 cms. According to our estimate, this flow would correspond to about 2.3 cms out of a total of 5.5 cms that is considered to be "normal" low flow of the river.

f) Periodic inspections will be performed in order to establish the flow distribution in the river.

g) The works at the island and at the downstream channel will be carried out in one stage and simultaneously except for the eastern half of the island, which may be removed separately prior to the rest of the above described works.

h) Jordanian equipment will perform the works on the island, and Israeli equipment will work on the downstream channel.[187]

Israel feared that, with only the island removed, all the summer water would flow to Jordan. Israel did not want to depend on Jordan to close the canal gates so water would flow to the Yarmouk Triangle. Yacov Vardi clarified to the Americans that Israel did not feel it could rely on the "current goodwill" between Jordan and Israel to guarantee the summer Yarmouk Triangle share; however, this "pool package" satisfied the needs of both sides. In the end, Jordan agreed.[188] Even so, the *modus operandi* of the previous five years would continue: altering the sandbag weir along with the Canal intakes gates during the summer months to control the flow to Israel and Jordan, according to picnic table decisions.[189] In the agreement with Jordan, Israel asserted its right (according to the Johnston Plan) to a flow of 2.3 cms during "normal" low flow but compromised on drought periods.[190] Jordan, on the other hand, maintained that Israel had a right to only 1.7 cms. This difference would subsequently lead to discord.

For a five-day period, from October 16 to 20, 1985, Israel and Jordan worked together to dredge the river. At least five large bulldozers and other heavy earthmoving equipment cleared away rocks, sand, and accumulated debris. A UN soldier was present to provide Jordan with political cover. A number of Israeli and Jordanian soldiers also observed the dredging on their respective sides of the river. At times, Israeli and Jordanian technocrats even rode the bulldozers together. Relations were friendly; at times, JVA President Haddadin and his Israeli counterpart, Vardi, talked and smoked Marlboro cigarettes side-by-side.[191]

"THE ROCK"

The dredging would have been a success, had it not been for a disagreement over the displacement of a large boulder.[192] At the end of the cleaning, Haddadin was not on site, and Vardi and Mohammad Bani Hani, JVA vice-president and second in command, were assessing the finished work. Vardi and Bani Hani agreed that the primary work, the removal of the island and the creation of stilling pool, was completed. Vardi suggested that the Israeli bulldozer clean some rocks and debris downstream that were hindering the flow to Israel, in exchange for the same bulldozer clearing rocks and debris from the entrance to the East Ghor Canal. Later on, Bani Hani complained to the United States that Israel had done a comprehensive job for itself downstream, including the removal of one large boulder that was more than a meter across. According to Bani Hani, Vardi's reciprocal cleaning was superficial and partial and Vardi refused to do more. This led to considerable shouting and some shoving. Once informed, Haddadin was furious because he felt betrayed by the Israelis. He told Bani Hani that because of his mistake, the careful negotiations with Israel since 1979 had now been compromised. Haddadin argued that the removal of the "large rock" and debris would allow an additional flow rate of 600 to 800 liters per second to pass downstream. Haddadin also maintained that Vardi took advantage of Bani Hani's lack of experience with the Yarmouk discussions and that Israel had breached the "pool package" agreement. For Haddadin it was also a breach of confidence. Haddadin made it clear that there would be no more meetings until the "symbolic rock" was returned to the riverbed.[193] On the other hand, Israel argued that removal of the rock and debris was not a violation of the agreement because the supervising Jordanian, Bani Hani, had given approval for its removal and that the reciprocal cleaning was fair.[194]

Because of the rock episode, picnic table relations were at their most tense since 1979. The actions taken during this period tended to be unilateral or secret in nature, rather than the result of mutual negotiations. All parties understood that the 1986 summer was going to be dry and politically difficult. Kinarti and his negotiator reported that Haddadin was still angry about the removal of the large rock, and, as a result, Jordan dragged its feet on manipulating sandbags and cleaning again the riverbed after the 1985–1986 winter floods. This delay was in opposition to the 1985 agreement. In response and under Israeli army military protection, the Yarmouk farmers, along with other Israelis, removed the sandbags. Again, the Jordanian army moved troops to the river, Haddadin assessed the situation and requested that the Jordanian military stand down so the matter could be resolved at a picnic table meeting. Haddadin sent the following message to his Israeli counterparts via UNTSO:

On Thursday 22nd of May 1986 your side approached the Yarmouk River accompanied with a force, and under its protection removed all the sacks from the riverbed unilaterally. This unilateral action on your part is against the long-standing procedure that the two sides followed to resolve disagreements. As we protest this unilateral action we expect a meeting to be convened on June 2 and request that the sacks be placed back by your side before that meeting.[195]

Israel did return the bags, but considerable disagreement was expressed on the flow rate to Israel during this season. There was also disagreement on how to dredge the riverbed prior to winter. While upset about the unilateral sand-bag move by Israel, throughout the summer the Jordanians still focused on the return of the rock.[196] Even so, as the summer progressed, the atmosphere improved somewhat between Jordanian and Israeli negotiators.[197] However, relations became tense when, once again, Jordan dragged its feet on dredging the Yarmouk prior to the winter, and Israeli farmers responded by using a bulldozer to dredge the riverbed for the winter flows. This unilateral act was again under Israeli army military protection. In response, Haddadin asserted that he would not meet with the Israelis and was not sure if his superiors would continue to support talks with Israel. Because it was November and winter rains were beginning, Jordan was under no real pressure to respond. However, as an American diplomat pointed out, the winter flow would alter the riverbed and the only way to properly address it is a cleaning in the spring. That would only occur in a peaceful manner if, as one US diplomat quipped, "an outbreak of infectious sanity" among Israelis and Jordanians occurred between now and then.[198]

Relations between Israel and Jordan did not improve much during the spring and summer of 1987, even though some individuals on both sides recognized the importance of keeping negotiations open. In fact, on the morning of August 13, Israel executed another unilateral dredging of part of the Yarmouk riverbed. Both Jordanian Prime Minister Zaid Rifa'i and senior military officers pointed out to the United States that Israel's actions came extremely close to provoking an armed confrontation near the entrance to the canal.[199] That afternoon, US diplomats met with Israeli representatives, including Director General of the Foreign Affairs Ministry Yossi Beilin, to determine what had occurred and to assert that the United States was "surprised and disappointed" by the Israeli action. Beilin explained Israel's action by reiterating why unilateral action was also taken the previous year: Jordan was intentionally stalling negotiations at the picnic table over cleaning the Yarmouk so the canal could receive the maximum flow possible during the summer season. Beilin stated that Israel was not even receiving a flow equivalent to Jordan's interpretation of the 1985

TABLE 4-5
Israeli and/or Jordanian Military Mobilization at Point 121 Related to Water Scarcity

| July 19, 1979 |
| September 14, 1979 |
| May 22, 1986 |
| November 23, 1986 |
| August 13, 1987 |

agreement. In fact, according to Beilin, Israel, prior to that morning's dredging, was receiving only 20 percent of the flow, not the expected 30 to 38 percent. The flow would result in only 12 mcm, not the expected 18 to 25 mcm by the end of the summer season.[200] Even though, just three weeks prior, Bani Hani had proposed a four-step package to deal with clearing the pool, the proposal included restoring the controversial rock, which was a non-starter for the Israelis. The Israelis, in fact, considered the proposal a stalling tactic.[201] Despite Israeli hostility, however, Beilin asked US representatives to emphasize to Jordan that the unilateral action was reluctantly taken and only because the Israeli government was under severe pressure from the Yarmouk Triangle farmers to resolve the immediate problems of the low summer flow. Beilin had already pointed out to US representative that those in the government who understood the importance of continuing to develop relations with Jordan were not happy with the action and its possible ramifications (see Table 4-5).[202] These forces of cooperation would gain the ascendancy by the end of the decade.

"AN OUTBREAK OF INFECTIOUS SANITY"

By 1988, the water-sharing system and rules were fully in place, and new individuals who were more cooperative with their counterparts were in charge: Bani Hani represented the JVA and Eli Rosenthal, a senior hydrologist for the Israel Hydrological Service, represented the Israeli water-negotiating team. By this time, real trust and confidence had built up, and no crises developed even during one of the worst droughts in the area's history. By the spring of 1988, Bani Hani was JVA acting president, replacing Haddadin, and Vardi was semi-retired.[203] By early June, both sides agreed to a plan of excavating the stilling pool and successfully executed it. Bani Hani expressed to the Americans his hope that with the establishment of terms agreeable to both sides, including an authoritative reference map, future clearing operations would take place without the debate and conflict on the terms and arrangements that had occurred in the past.[204]

Bani Hani was correct. Together, Rosenthal (with Vardi) and Bani Hani created a much more transparent system that led to greater confidence on both sides of the Yarmouk. In addition to the dredging and creating an authoritative river cleaning plan, both sides established an effective gauging system as well. In 1990, Vardi told Harza and the United States that since the 1988 cleaning, Israeli and Jordanian teams measured the flow with only minor discrepancies. Vardi went on to say that the Jordanians were reliable and on time. During the irrigation season, both sides took measurements every two weeks and compared the results, right then and there. If results differed, the teams took measurements again, but this time together.[205] Even though neither side could agree to a fixed formula for the flow, both sides understood the changing needs of the other and the conditions of the river, which meant that, after the June 1988 dredging, both were willing to show "good will" and adjust the flow when needed.[206]

Although an engineer by training, Bani Hani turned out to be an effective negotiator. He tried to create a positive atmosphere at the picnic table. Many important documents relating to Yarmouk dam project passed across the picnic table.[207] Consequently, not only did he move the Unity Dam negotiations forward, he also maintained, if not increased, the summer flow and percentage of water Jordan received in 1987 and 1988.[208] He also understood the great value and advantage of keeping the United States in the loop on the picnic table talks. In meetings with the Americans, he provided an insight into the evolving role of the technocrats at the picnic table meetings, and generally made clear his feelings toward his different interlocutors: Vardi, Noah Kinarti, and the Syrians. Kinarti, who represented the Yarmouk Triangle farmers and led most of the unilateral actions concerning the Yarmouk, turned out to be Bani Hani's most difficult negotiating partner. Bani Hani complained that Kinarti "conveniently and consistently forgets past discussions/gentleman's agreements reached regarding water sharing, especially during periods of adversity."[209] On the other hand, Bani Hani, and, for that matter, Haddadin, both indicated that they held Yacov Vardi in the greatest respect as an individual, professional, and engineer.[210] According to Bani Hani, Vardi created a much better, more congenial negotiating atmosphere and was someone to be trusted.[211] As for the Syrians, Bani Hani had many successful meetings concerning a Yarmouk dam but, by 1989, Syrian upstream pumping had become so problematic and negotiations were so difficult, he told US diplomats that "much of the time, I would rather deal with the Israelis than the Syrians."[212] Bani Hani saw himself as a Jordanian engineer who wanted to put politics aside as much as possible.[213]

Establishing a fixed percentage of the flow for each side, though, continued to elude the negotiators. During a July 1989 picnic table meeting, Bani Hani passed to Vardi tables of month-by-month Yarmouk flow rates to Israel and Jordan for the years 1980–1988. The tables showed proportions of one-third to Israel and two-thirds to Jordan. As in the past, Vardi rejected the one-third/two-third as the official sharing regime and argued that the sharing ratios should be left to further discussion and to the good will and understanding between negotiators.[214] Jordan continued to be a strong advocate of a proportional system because of increasing upstream Syrian use and the decreasing downstream summer flow. Israel, on the other hand, did not wish to acquiesce to less than what it argued was its 25 mcm Johnston allocation.[215] In the end, while Israel continued to argue for 25 mcm, from 1981 to 1994 the division was closer to 30 percent for Israel and 70 percent for Jordan.

PICNIC TABLE IN CHICAGO

The Bani Hani period of Yarmouk negotiations culminated in an unusual meeting of all parties in the United States, convened to discuss engineering issues for an upstream dam on the Yarmouk. By the late 1980s, Jordan had restarted negotiations for such a dam on the Yarmouk. To finance the project, Jordan needed World Bank funding and support. At the outset, the bank stressed that Israel must be informed of the technical details of the project. That way, the Israeli government could determine if the project would cause appreciable harm. As a result, the secret meetings at the picnic table on the Yarmouk briefly moved to Chicago for a US-sponsored meeting of Israeli and Jordanian technical experts at the offices of Harza Engineering, held December 6–8, 1989. The two-man US team—L. P. Bloomfield and Fred Hof—met for three days with lead picnic table negotiators: Jordanian JVA Secretary General Bani Hani and Israeli water experts Vardi, Eli Rosenthal and Foreign Affairs Ministry counsel Alan Baker. The US objective was for Israel to receive all information about the dam it needed. These meetings were significant because they involved face-to-face contact about the Yarmouk dam, but they were not at the picnic table or near the Allenby Bridge, and US rather than UN representatives were present. Jordanian Prime Minister Bin Shaker had accepted the US proposal to host the meeting at which Jordan would allow Harza to pass to Israeli representatives the operating plans for the dam and intensive discussion about the project would go forward among all the representatives—Jordanian, Israeli, Harza, and US government. To say the least, there was political risk for the Jordanians. During the meetings, the Israelis pledged that the Chicago meeting would remain secret and it did.[216] The atmosphere among the participants was very positive. For example, on the evening of December 7, all participants had dinner together at the Metropolitan Club of Chicago in the Sears Tower, with no discussion of mediation issues.[217] At the conclusion of the meeting, Bani Hani stated that he and his

Jordanian colleagues had friends on the other side of the Yarmouk. Both Israel and Jordan face difficult water problems, he asserted, and "we must work it out."[218] Vardi responded that he agreed with Bani Hani's statement and appreciated that his Jordanian counterpart was so straightforward. Vardi went on to say that he would continue to seek ways to meet demands without injuring Jordan's interest.[219]

This successful meeting of minds, however, did not last long past the Chicago meeting because of personnel changes. Less than half a year later, Bani Hani was no longer JVA head or a picnic table negotiator, but relations remained cooperative. He was moved to municipal affairs and rural development. During the summer of 1990, the JVA was in the midst of a corruption scandal, but, according to US diplomats, there was no evidence that could be linked directly to Bani Hani.[220] Initially, there were concerns among Americans and Israelis that Bani Hani's replacement, Dr. Abdul Aziz al-Wishah, lacked the necessary knowledge of the issues and the negotiating record or the experience in dealing directly with Israeli counterparts.[221] When al-Wishah took control, the Americans became concerned that there had not been a picnic table meeting in some time.[222] After the United States made some high-level contacts, the first meeting took place a month later, in August 1990. Vardi told the Americans that al-Wishah was well briefed, and Vardi was impressed with his knowledge of the issues. The biweekly gauging meetings continued at the diversion at Adasiya.[223] As time progressed, though, Israeli negotiators such as Rosenthal and Kinarti developed reservations about al-Wishah and his intentions to cooperate with Israel.[224] Even though the region was in the midst of political and hydrological crisis, biweekly gauging and frequent picnic table meetings took place. Relations between the Jordanian and Israeli technical teams remained very good. For example, during a February 28, 1991, picnic table meeting the Jordanians brought gifts for Noah Kinarti's fiftieth birthday. At that meeting, the "Vardi Bridge" was dedicated. This was a small, retractable structure that was constructed to allow easier access to the picnic table from the Israeli side of the Yarmouk. Vardi was present and appreciated the tribute.[225]

Despite the ongoing success of Jordan-Israeli negotiations, a major problem for Jordan and its development plans throughout this period was Syria's increased annual utilization of upstream Yarmouk water. In 1983, the CIA estimated that Syria was using nearly 50 percent of the Yarmouk's average flow.[226] Jordan was caught between Syria's increasing utilization of the Yarmouk and Israel's demand for water that it believed had been guaranteed to the Yarmouk Triangle through the Johnston Plan and subsequent Jordanian agreements with the United States. During picnic table negotiations, Israel's Vardi told Jordan's Natour to "talk to the boys upstream about the problem" of not having enough Yarmouk water for Jordan during the summer.[227] And when Jordan did ask Syria for a greater summer portion of the Yarmouk, Damascus's reply was less than what Jordan hoped for.[228] As a result, Jordan attempted to restart negotiations with Syria for an upstream dam.

THE UNITY (AL-WAHDAH) DAM

By the mid-1980s, Syrian upstream usage became a critical issue for the Jordanian government because it was growing dramatically (see Table 4-2). Using Yarmouk water, the Syrian government developed artificial lakes and canals to establish agriculture settlements in the southern Syrian Yarmouk basin. Syria hoped these new towns would help reduce Damascus's overpopulation, employ army veterans, and decrease Syria's dependence on Jordanian produce.[229] During April 1987, Israeli military intelligence briefed US diplomats on Syria's rapid development of Yarmouk water. According to the Israelis, Syria was using 150 mcmy and by 1990 would be using 250 mcmy out of 346 mcmy available from the Syrian part of the basin. This prediction was based on a Syrian "master plan" that was initiated in 1981 and scheduled for completion in 2000.[230] Even so, Jordanian-Syrian diplomatic relations began to improve. Syria hoped to reduce its political isolation and improve relations with the West. Jordan understood that the Yarmouk was one of its last underdeveloped water resources. By controlling Syrian usage and building a Unity Dam, Jordan calculated that the Yarmouk contribution to the Jordanian water budget would increase from 20 to 32 percent. Again, both parties believed a dam project would serve their respective interests.

In subsequent discussions with US diplomats, Prime Minister Rifa'i indicated that in 1987 the Unity Dam negotiations were logjammed because the Syrian bureaucracy and local farmers opposed cooperation with Jordan, but Asad was receptive to the project. Rifa'i personally negotiated with Syria and had staked his political future on the success of this project. As a result, Rifa'i approached President Asad directly to attain Syrian acceptance of the project. Rifa'i told Asad frankly that Jordan would have to allocate water to Israel. According to Rifa'i, Asad acknowledged the point by saying, "I did not hear you; you did not say it; but do what you must."[231]

In September 1987, Jordan and Syria signed a Unity Dam treaty and codified its design and operation.[232] The dam site was near the old Maqarin Dam location, but, at 100 meters tall, it was about half the size of the earlier Maqarin project.[233] Since these negotiations were so important to Jordan, it made a series of notable concessions to Syria. Jordan agreed to allow Syria to build a series of twenty-four small dams upstream,[234] and take 75 percent of the generated hydroelectricity.[235] Jordan also allocated 140 mcm of water to Syria, a dramatic increase and break from the Johnston Plan's allocation of 90 mcm.[236] Amman, though, was solely responsible for finding the funding for the project's construction and maintenance.[237] In protest over all these concessions, JVA president Munther Haddadin resigned from his post.[238] Nonetheless, the Jordanian government felt it had to do something to slow Syrian upstream utilization before it was too late. The government could only hope that Syria would abide by this agreement. The Jordanian agriculture minister explained that "at present we can't give Jordan Valley farmers water all year round, so they will have two harvests a year. When we have a dam, more water will reach each unit, and farmers will be able to grow summer crops."[239]

Again, Jordan was faced with the daunting task of raising the funds to build the project. As it did ten years earlier, AID provided one million dollars to help fund the feasibility study by Harza Engineering Company. Harza also prepared the final design. Jordan hoped international agencies would finance more than half the dam's cost and hosted a lenders' conference in Amman in an effort to raise $260 million, with the remaining $180 million to be paid by the Jordanian treasury.[240] When this issue was resolved, the World Bank anticipated that it would provide leadership in a donor consortium and fund the project with no more than $25 million.[241] In addition to limited World Bank and US funding, Jordan was pursuing loans and grants from Japan, West Germany, Kuwait, and Saudi Arabia.[242] In 1988, Jordan sought World Bank support for the project. The United States was in the midst of a budget crisis, and, unlike the 1970s Maqarin Dam project, was not to be a lead financer. Following its guidelines, the bank advised Jordan to provide all relevant details of the project to Israel in order for Israel to determine whether the project would cause it "appreciable harm."[243] Before proceeding with the project, the bank wanted Israel to assert that it posed no objection. The intent of the Israel-Jordan-US-Harza meeting in Chicago, December 1989, discussed earlier, was to satisfy the Bank's information requirement. The United States sought an Israeli letter to the World Bank stating that satisfactory technical information on Jordan's project had been received.[244] In fact, shortly after the Chicago meeting, Israel did inform the bank that it had received additional information but that Israel "shall be requesting further clarification and further detail."[245]

Unlike the Israel-Jordan track, the State Department concluded that it would be best "to let the Jordanians deal with the Syrians directly."[246] The Jordanian-Syrian Joint Commission for the Unity Dam met for technical talks four times—May, August, and October 1989, and February 1990.[247] Mohammad Bani Hani, JVA secretary general, led these negotiations and gave the United States briefings known as readouts of each meeting. The United States gave Jordan advice and, more important, satellite and technical information on Syrian noncompliance, which the Jordanian brought to the Syrians' attention during this meeting.[248]

The Armitage Mission

Securing Israel's agreement to the project proved more difficult. Since, at this late point, Israel had not yet given its approval, the World Bank decided to suspend its activities with respect to the Unity Dam.[249] In 1988 and early 1989, the State Department conducted "low level and low key" separate talks with Israel and Jordan. Disappointed with the lack of progress, King Hussein asked President George Bush, during their April 1989 meeting in Washington, to help move the project forward.[250] Jordan's Prime Minister Rifa'i told US diplomats that the Soviet Union had offered to build the dam on a "turnkey" basis, but that Jordan did not want to accept the offer.[251] In September, Secretary of State James Baker named senior American diplomat Richard Armitage to mediate the dam issue between Jordan and Israel so the project could go forward. The State Department saw Armitage as a "highly skilled deal-maker" who had close working relations and "high credibility" with both Israel and Jordan.[252] Armitage shuttled between the two riparians four times between September 1989 and August 1990.[253] The United States, Israel, and Jordan completed considerable analytical work, and Israel received reams of project details from Jordan. Significant progress took place: Jordan's obligation to Israel during the summer irrigation period took shape—25 mcm at a rate "up to" 2.3 cms. The downstream diversion weir was cancelled because of political problems.[254] Instead of an international treaty, the parties also decided that the agreement would take the form of two parallel US diplomatic notes to Israel and Jordan.[255] By July 1990, the Israeli team indicated to the United States and the World Bank that it needed one additional "project detail" before it could determine that it would experience no harm, and that detail was Israel's winter water allocation. Jordan was unwilling to provide such an allocation. Jordan argued that, according to the Johnston Plan, it was entitled to all of the Yarmouk's winter water it could capture. However, Jordan conceded that it did not concern itself with flows it could not divert. Israel claimed that it pumped, on average, about 60–70 mcm annually from the Yarmouk River to Lake Tiberias and the Yarmouk Triangle. The Israeli position was that it needed to be "no worse off" as a result of the Unity Dam. According to the United States, on average, Israel pumped about 17 mcm from the Yarmouk during the summer and about 45 mcm during the winter. Jordan maintained that, on average, 40 mcm of winter water would pass the King Abdullah intake annually. This water would flow to Israeli pumps. However, Jordan would neither officially recognize nor guarantee this winter water allocation for Israel, especially since much of the Israeli water would arrive in the form of floods only partially capturable by Israel. During the last round, Israel and the United States discussed ideas such as rehabilitating the Rutenberg Pool for capturing and storing floodwaters that in the past had escaped and improving the conveyance system from the Yarmouk to Lake Tiberias.[256]

The Americans concluded that the Israeli government was negotiating in good faith. The United States was pleased that the West Bank Yarmouk allocation issue, which stymied the Maqarin negotiations, was sidestepped by Israel.[257] Nonetheless, US diplomats made clear to Jordan and Israel that the Unity Dam mediation "does not prejudge [West Bank] water issues that will need to be addressed in any overall peace settlement."[258] Furthermore, Israel had acknowledged "as a point of fact, [that] Israel controls 100 mcm of Jordan water beyond that originally allocated to it" under the Johnston Plan.[259] In fact, it had benefited from the status quo of a river without a dam and had little reason to make major concessions on this issue. As stated earlier, Israel's starting position during these negotiations was that it was willing to sign off on the dam, but only if it was guaranteed winter Yarmouk allocation between 50 and 70 mcm, with 25 mcm in the summer months. The day before the Iraqi invasion of Kuwait, Israel reduced its winter water demand to 42.5 mcm, but Jordan never responded.[260]

Armitage wrote Secretary Schultz that he believed there were two primary reasons why Jordan was unable to be more flexible in the negotiations with Israel. First, the politics of the region were again becoming unsettled. During the negotiations, much domestic tension arose because in 1989 the Jordanian people elected a parliament with a strong group of Islamic parties, thirty-one of eighty seats.[261] This parliament took an activist posture, opposed to any agreements with Israel and critical of the government's handling of water resources, including the scandals involving officials of the JVA, the extension of the King Abdullah Canal (KAC) to new farmland, but without the water to irrigate it, and general water shortages in all sectors.[262] To make matters worse, Jordan-Israeli relations were poor. Prime Minister Yitzhak Shamir was making comments regarding the need for a Greater Israel to accommodate the influx of Soviet Jewish immigration. Israel and Jordan were in the midst of a serious drought and less willing to make compromises.[263]

Second, Jordanians were showing a greater tendency to dig their heels in concerning the Johnston Plan. In the just mentioned letter to the secretary of state, Armitage indicated his frustration with Jordanian inflexibility during negotiations:

The "Johnston Plan" has become, within Arab political circles, a mindless incantation to be recited whenever the subject of riparian relations with Israel comes up. It is a shorthand way of saying, "we cannot deal directly with Israel on this subject; our legal rights are enshrined in a document we were never willing to ratify; we waived those rights with respect to Syria when it suited us; but the US is still obliged to force Israel to recognize what remains of our rights."[264]

Armitage's frustration was understandable, especially considering the time and effort he and his associates had put into the mission. However, the United States did have parallel agreements with Israel and Jordan but not Syria regarding the Johnston Plan. On many occasions, the United States pressured Jordan to adhere to the plan's provision that assured Israel summer water from the Yarmouk. It is understandable that Jordan should expect Israel to adhere to Washington's interpretation of the Johnston Plan's provisions—especially that Yarmouk winter water belongs to Jordan. Although Jordan was historically not able to capture much of this water, it never acquiesced its rights to it. In fact, during the negotiations, US Ambassador Brown told the Israeli team that the "winter flow of the Yarmouk to which Israel has access and has made use in the past is not an allocation to which Israel has a legal right." This US position is long-standing and unchanged (see Table 4-6).[265] Nonetheless, Armitage was correct that Jordan, as well as Israel, needed to show more pragmatic flexibility when it came to dealing with winter water, such as ways in which Israel could catch floods and ways Jordan could tacitly lose water to Israel. This would finally happen when the two sides sat down to negotiate the 1994 Jordan-Israel Peace Treaty water provisions.

ANALYSIS AND CONCLUSION

In 1979 and beyond, a harmony of water and political preferences between Jordan and Israel proved elusive. In fact, there was much discord. But once both

TABLE 4-6
Yarmouk Water Data for Winter Season (Oct. 15 to May 15) (mcm), 1982–1989

Year Captured	Flow Past KAC Inlet	Israeli Pumping	Large Scale Releases or Loans	Potential Pumping	Israel's Percent
1982/1983	30.5	21.7		26.04	71
1983/1984	77.3	53.66		64.39	69
1984/1985	90.81	73.1		87.72	80
1985/1986	53.6	48.2	9.13	66.46	90
1986/1987	206.4	41.54	33	82.84	20
1987/1988	178.3	47.57	104.88+7.75	64.83	27
1988/1989	36.7	31.81	7.75	47.47	87

Source: "Yarmuk Water Data for Winter Seasons (15.10–15.5)" FOIA (photocopy).

sides understood each other's preferences better and actively attempted to adjust policies to meet the demands of the other, cooperation emerged. When cooperative preferences were understood, Israel and Jordan formulated international strategies to realize their preferences. The Yarmouk forum became less conflictual and more cooperative as soon as the rules for summer Yarmouk flow sharing became clarified in 1988. This was thanks to the work of Yacov Vardi and, in particular, Mohammad Bani Hani, that included joint flow gauging, agreed topography of the diversion pool and joint operations for cleaning it, and the exchange of technical data on river flow and plans for the dam.[266] When both sides had a system of rules that provided a perception that cooperation would last long into the future, and not just for a short time, they began to share common expectations and gain transparency in negotiations.[267] The result was that coordination emerged in place of noncompliance. This new environment resulted in no more cheating, unilateral actions, or military mobilizations on the banks of the Yarmouk.

During the same period, the Maqarin and Unity Dam projects failed to materialize because, unlike the Yarmouk forum, Israel and Jordan were unable to reach an understanding of each other's preferences and thus devise an effective international strategy for resolving their differences. A complicating aspect was the number of players relevant to the dam negotiations. The Yarmouk forum principally involved Jordan and Israel; the dam negotiations also included Syria. Prospects for cooperation erode as the number of players increase. The presence of more players makes it harder for the riparians to identify the other's preferences or to negotiate an international agreement.[268] Had Israel or Syria not been part of the dam negotiating process, it is fair to assume that a Yarmouk dam would have been in place long ago.

During the 1967 to 1994 period, the Yarmouk negotiations provide an interesting example of how a relatively weaker, downstream riparian can still make great gains for itself. Jordan's dependency on this water source forced Amman to pursue means that would protect its water interests. Syria's and Israel's relative power placed Jordan at a disadvantage. Jordan used its greater preference intensity on the water issue to overcome its relative vulnerability in this asymmetrical interdependence. The more powerful and/or better positioned riparians—Israel and Syria—did not always win in the manipulation of water and political interdependence. Jordan, a weaker and downstream state, had a greater concern about its Yarmouk water allocation than Syria or Israel, and even with its inherent geographical and capabilities disadvantages, it did well. Jordan often prevailed in a number of disputes because it was willing to threaten retaliatory actions, such as ending political relations, unilateral action, or involving the United States, that sometimes deterred Israel and Syria from taking all of Jordan's Yarmouk water. The Jordanians would have suffered much more if their actions had led to a full dispute, but Jordan felt it was better to risk occasional retaliation from the stronger states than to agree to water-related rules that would permanently put them at a disadvantage.[269]

The Yarmouk forum was successful because the talks addressed Israel's and Jordan's limited but important common preference of maintaining a stable flow of water, avoiding any inadvertent conflicts over that scarce resource, and allowing the Yarmouk basin and the greater Jordan Valley to develop socioeconomically (see Table 4-7). Both states wanted as much water as they could obtain, but were willing to make policy compromises.[270] Israel's understanding of Jordan's predicament also helped make the arrangement successful. Like Jordan, Israel's primary objective was to maintain direct talks between Jordanian officials and its own people. This group would manage water-related conflicts and encourage Jordan Valley development, even if this limited development on Israel's side of the river, which it did.

There were confounding factors. When Yarmouk Triangle farmers successfully asserted their power, Israel's overall preference to cooperate decreased, and Jordan, for its part, did not want to cooperate with Israel. However, for many reasons, it was in Jordan's interest to develop the Jordan Valley, and that would only happen with a stable water-sharing arrangement with Israel. In the end, it was Jordan's preference to cooperate so long as that arrangement was secret and America served as a guarantor. When a more anti-Israel Jordanian parliament came to power in the late 1980s, however, Jordan's overall preference to cooperate with Israel diminished. Israel did not try to use the Yarmouk forum as a means to dramatically change the overall situation between itself and Jordan by demanding Jordan's recognition of Israel.[271] However, Israel did utilize the Yarmouk forum to improve diplomatic relations with Amman as much as was politically feasible. Jordan understood that Israel wanted to normalize relations and used that as a key bargaining chip.[272] Also, Jordan was aware of the split between Israel's farm and political interests and attempted to

TABLE 4-7
Jordan's Jordan Valley Development Indicators

	1973	1991
Population	64,000	200,000
Population's potable water service	10%	98%
Paved roads	60 km	2,500 km
Irrigated area	137,000 dunum	295,000 dunum
Usable irrigation water	152 mcm	300 mcm
Crop production	342,000 tons	706,000 tons

Source: "Department of Statistics and Jordan Valley Authority" as cited in "International Symposium on Water Resources in the Middle East: Policy and Institutional Aspects" (Urbana-Champaign: University of Illinois, 1993), 25.

use that division to its advantage. Both parties recognized that Israel had superior military, political, and economic capabilities and that the relative power of the two states played an important role in shaping each side's international strategies or means to realizing their preferences. Through preference intensity, issue linkage and relations with the United States, Jordan's power shortcomings were somewhat offset, and it was able to realize some of its policy objectives. In fact, Jordan received many water-related concessions from Israel. For example, although the Johnston Plan allocated 25 mcm of water to Israel during the summer, Israel rarely, if ever, took the full amount because it tacitly honored the 30/70 sharing arrangement established between the two countries. Furthermore, Israel held a veto over removing the sandbar and, as the more powerful state, had water-related reasons not to remove it; yet it did. The explanation for this can only be Jordan's issue intensity relating to water and the issue linkage to nonwater-related issues that were important to Israel, such as improving Israel-Jordan political relations. Israel could have easily used its military superiority to obtain whatever allocations it wanted, but its relations with the United States and its policy goals with Jordan often checked its military advantage. On the other hand, Israel understood the importance of Yarmouk water to Jordan and the benefit river dredging would provide to Jordan's water supply. Israeli negotiators used these bargaining chips to improve Israeli-Jordanian relations, a process Jordan otherwise would not have initiated.

There are examples of Israel's use of military force during this period that may seem to challenge this view that common water preferences and tactical functional cooperation kept two potential combatants at peace. Between 1967 and 1970, for example, Israel used its military might against Jordan's East Ghor Canal, but it is important to recognize that those attacks were tactical in a military sense. They were efforts to push Jordan into stopping guerrilla attacks from Jordanian territory and not water-scarcity-related actions. Between 1979 and 1987, Israel again used its military might, and these unilateral moves *were* water scarcity related. However, Israel only took these actions when it believed Jordan was being noncompliant with agreed rules. In that case, the fundamental desire of both parties to keep open water negotiations led them to choose cooperation over greater heightening of the conflict.

On the other hand, because of the Israel-Egypt Sinai II agreement, Jordan and Syria improved relations and therefore became more willing to explore other issues on which to cooperate. At this point, they preferred not to make peace with Israel. Maintaining Jordanian-Syrian water cooperation depended on stable and good political relations. When Syria was interested in improving diplomatic relations, it was willing to cooperate with Jordan on Yarmouk water sharing, but when political relations deteriorated the political water linkage disintegrated. Syria generally did not follow formal water agreements with Jordan. One explanation is that Syria is a stronger upstream state in relation to

Jordan; therefore, it would demand the agreement it wanted at a time it deemed desirable. But Syrian farmers and bureaucrats did not believe water cooperation with Jordan was in their interest. However, power and riparian position were only part of the reason for subsequent Syrian noncompliance. By 1980, Damascus and Asad in particular were not receiving from Jordan what it really wanted: greater Syrian influence over Jordan. In the end, Syria was not willing to give up its water bargaining chip to Amman without nonwater-related political benefits. By 1987, these benefits seemed again attainable to Asad, and he overcame domestic obstacles to realize his preference for closer relations with Jordan.

In 1989, a senior State Department official wrote "our goal is to resolve the forty-year-old issue of Jordan water sharing in a manner that will facilitate an eventual Arab-Israeli peace settlement, by turning a long unresolved problem into a vehicle for a bilateral Jordanian-Israeli cooperation and enhanced contact."[273] The time and effort put into the secret water talks not only increased lines of communication, clarified rules, built confidence, mitigated conflict, and spurred development of an epistemic community on water issues, it also helped lay the foundation for a future water section in the Israel-Jordan peace treaty, which will be discussed in chapter 6. As discussed in chapter 1, this was tactical functional cooperation. The Yarmouk forum, by itself, did not lead to peace, as a functionalist might predict. However, the *process* did lead to conflict mitigation and confidence-building on a pivotal and difficult issue, which is a key tactical achievement on the long road to peace.

5

The West Bank and Gaza, 1948–1992

From the Johnston mission's focus on resettling Palestinian refugees to delays in the construction of the Maqarin Dam in part because of a West Bank water allocation dispute, the Palestinian question has continued to play an important part in the politics of the Jordan River basin. With that said the material available to this researcher and incorporated within this book positions the West Bank and Gaza—the prospective future Palestinian state—along with Syria and Lebanon as secondary case studies with respect to the main Jordan-Israel issue. There is much more reliable and available data on this primary case with these lessons than what is applicable to the politically unresolved secondary cases.[1] This chapter focuses on the West Bank and Gaza during the period just after 1949 and before the 1993 Oslo breakthrough. An important question discussed in this chapter is whether Israel can relinquish control of all or part of the West Bank without jeopardizing one of its primary sources of freshwater and the security that comes with it. Some argue that water interests make it almost impossible for Israel to give up control of the West Bank. I argue that Israeli water security issues will not necessitate its control of the vast majority of the West Bank. This analysis is based on data in Israeli government documents.

The West Bank of the Jordan River commands the strategic high ground that rises 1,200 meters above potential invasion routes into the narrow coastal plain that is home to two-thirds of Israel's population and most of its commerce.[2] About the size of Delaware, the West Bank is 560,000 hectares (2,000 square miles) of mostly rocky slopes and deserts. The area's only natural resources are 200,000 hectares (500,000 acres) of cultivatable land—an Iowa county's worth— and 500 to 750 millimeters (mm) (20 to 30 inches) of annual rainfall on the mountain highlands that feeds three underground aquifer systems.

141

The aquifer located in the east is almost entirely within the West Bank and supplies the largely unoccupied, arid eastern half, known as the Jordan Valley that Arabs and Jewish settlers farm. The other two aquifers flow into Israel and supply it with a third of its growing water needs.[3] The mountain highlands, where much of the rain falls to feed the aquifers, are also home to nearly all of the West Bank's one million Arab residents. Palestinian farmers cultivate almost all the valleys and terraced steep hillsides in the rainy mountain regions. For them, the West Bank aquifers provide about 90 percent of their annual water consumption.[4] Thus, the competing demands of Israelis and Palestinians mean that the delicate balance of resources could easily be upset.

If new wells were drilled by the Palestinians between the West Bank mountain recharge area and the coastal plain Israeli wells, Israel's critical and already overexploited groundwater supply would be reduced or even cut off. Additional pumping would lower the water table levels and allow some salty water from greater depths to seep in, polluting what was left. Though important in themselves, West Bank groundwater politics are intertwined with the larger territorial issues of the Arab-Israeli conflict and, in particular, the Palestinian-Israeli struggle. During the 1967 Arab-Israeli War, Israel captured the West Bank from Jordan and the Gaza Strip from Egypt. Israel's original intent was to trade occupied land for peace with neighboring Arab states pursuant to UN Security Council Resolution 242.[5] Since June 1967, however, Israeli government rationales for building West Bank Jewish settlements have changed. Some Israelis argue that religious, heritage, and historical reasons give them the right to the land; that they need the land for strategic defense from the west or for local-tactical defense, for economic reasons, or because of water needs.[6] Although water is considered a critical issue for the West Bank, it certainly is not the only consideration.

Most analysts believe that, unlike its interests in the West Bank, Israel has no vital requirements in the Gaza Strip. "In all key sectors—security, water, demography, heritage and economy—the Gaza Strip is for Israel a burden rather than an asset."[7] Israel does not share important water resources with Gaza as it does with the West Bank, but Gaza Arab residents do experience severe water shortages. During Israel's 1967–2005 control of Gaza, unfair taxes, discriminatory water regulations, and general repression including unequal distribution of water resources between settlers and the Arabs were important sources of Palestinian-Israeli tension. According to a Palestinian perspective, West Bank water, like its land, is in the process of being permanently annexed by Israel.[8]

This chapter examines the development of Israeli-Palestinian tension over the West Bank and, to a much lesser extent, over Gaza water resources. The first section focuses on the 1949 to 1967 period of Jordanian rule of the West Bank. During this period, the Jordanian government never challenged Israel's growing use of the shared West Bank aquifers. Tensions did not arise because Jordan invested little into developing the West Bank, and Palestinian water demand remained relatively low through 1967. After the 1967 War, the Israeli Labor-led coalition preference at this time concerning the West Bank was to trade captured territory for peace with its Arab neighbors. On the other hand, subsequent Likud governments preferred to maintain control of the captured territory. The second section explains how Israel, under a Labor-led government, had severely limited Palestinian access to additional water resources after it took control of the West Bank in 1967. The next section analyzes how a growing Palestinian population and economy have led to a need for increased water use; however, because of Israeli consumption and regulation of West Bank water, an inequitable distribution of water resources has resulted under Likud governments. The West Bank and water preference of Likud, unlike Labor, make compromise and cooperation much more difficult. The final section also examines how Israel has now become so dependent on West Bank water resources that some of its policymakers fear an effort to redistribute water would severely injure Israel's economic and security interests. Thus, if Israeli-Palestinian tensions over water are to be reduced, the parties must find a balance between Palestinian needs for equitable utilization and Israeli demands for protection from injury to its economic and security interests. In fact, numerous Israeli studies have proposed policy options for dividing the West Bank and thus its groundwater between Israel and Palestinians.

Steps in this direction are under way, spurred by gains in Palestinians' bargaining power. Prior to the 1980s *intifada*, Israel's control of Palestinian affairs was so great as to keep Palestinians from reciprocating effectively for Israeli actions. Palestinians lacked the capabilities to push Israel into serious negotiations regarding the West Bank water issue. The *intifada* altered the political equation. Israel became more open to changing the post-1967 West Bank and Gaza Strip hydropolitical status quo. Consequently, international strategies emerged, developed for compromise on the water issue between Israel and the Palestinians. An interim water agreement resulted and is discussed in chapter 6.

HYDROLOGY

The West Bank's geography, climate, hydrology, and demography vary significantly among its different regions, and these differences determine the ease with which water can be collected. Topographically, the western slope rises 200 meters above sea level from the coastal plain and includes the towns of Tulkarm and Kalkilya; the mountain ridge rises 1000 meters above sea level and includes the urban centers of Hebron and Bethlehem; and the Jordan Valley descends 400 meters below sea level to the Jordan River and the Dead Sea.[9]

Most of the precipitation, approximately 700 millimeters of rain and some snow annually, falls on the central mountain ridge section. The western slope has annual rainfall of 500 mm, and the Jordan Valley receives only 100 mm or less of annual precipitation.[10] Most of this precipitation evaporates and approximately 5 percent runs off the land surface and floods into area rivers and seas. The rainy winter season extends over a six-month period with some 70 percent of annual precipitation falling between November and February. The amount of rainfall fluctuates sharply both within the year and between years, making profitable non-irrigated agriculture even more difficult.[11] Precipitation that is not lost to runoff or evaporation percolates down through soil and rock into the groundwater system.

A large portion of the West Bank's precipitation falls on the mountain ridge, making this area the primary zone for recharging—or feeding—the aquifers with water. The groundwater flows from the recharge area down to the storage—or pumping—area of the aquifer, or to springs, at the foot of the hilly region. The vast majority of wells are located above the storage area, which is situated at a lower elevation because pumping is more accessible and less costly there.[12] The groundwater flows down from the mountain heights in either a westward direction toward the coastal plain, northward toward the Yizrael and Bet Shean valleys, or eastward toward the Jordan Valley. Based on this water flow, West Bank groundwater is divided into three major basins: the western basin (*Yarqon-Tanninim* in Hebrew), the northeastern basin (Nablus-Gilboa), and the eastern basin. Together, these basins are also known as the mountain aquifer. The western basin has the largest renewable yield, 350 mcm per year, and supplies the highest quality water of the three-aquifer system. The V-shaped northeastern basin provides an annual renewable yield of 140 mcm. Of the three basins, the eastern basin has the lowest quality water and the lowest yield at approximately 100 mcm (see Map 5-1).[13] The mountain aquifer's groundwater flow does not follow political boundaries. Water from the western and northeastern basins flows from the mountain recharge area inside the West Bank across the Green Line into Israel.[14] However, the eastern basin is almost entirely within the West Bank.

THE WEST BANK UNDER JORDAN, 1948–1967

During Jordanian rule of the West Bank from 1948 to 1967, Jordanian investment in West Bank agriculture and Palestinian groundwater use remained low. By contrast, Israel was dependent on the western and northeastern basin aquifers for approximately one-third of its total freshwater consumption by June 1967. Meanwhile, it was also using most of the groundwater that flowed naturally into its pre-1967 territory. At the end of the 1800s, most of the

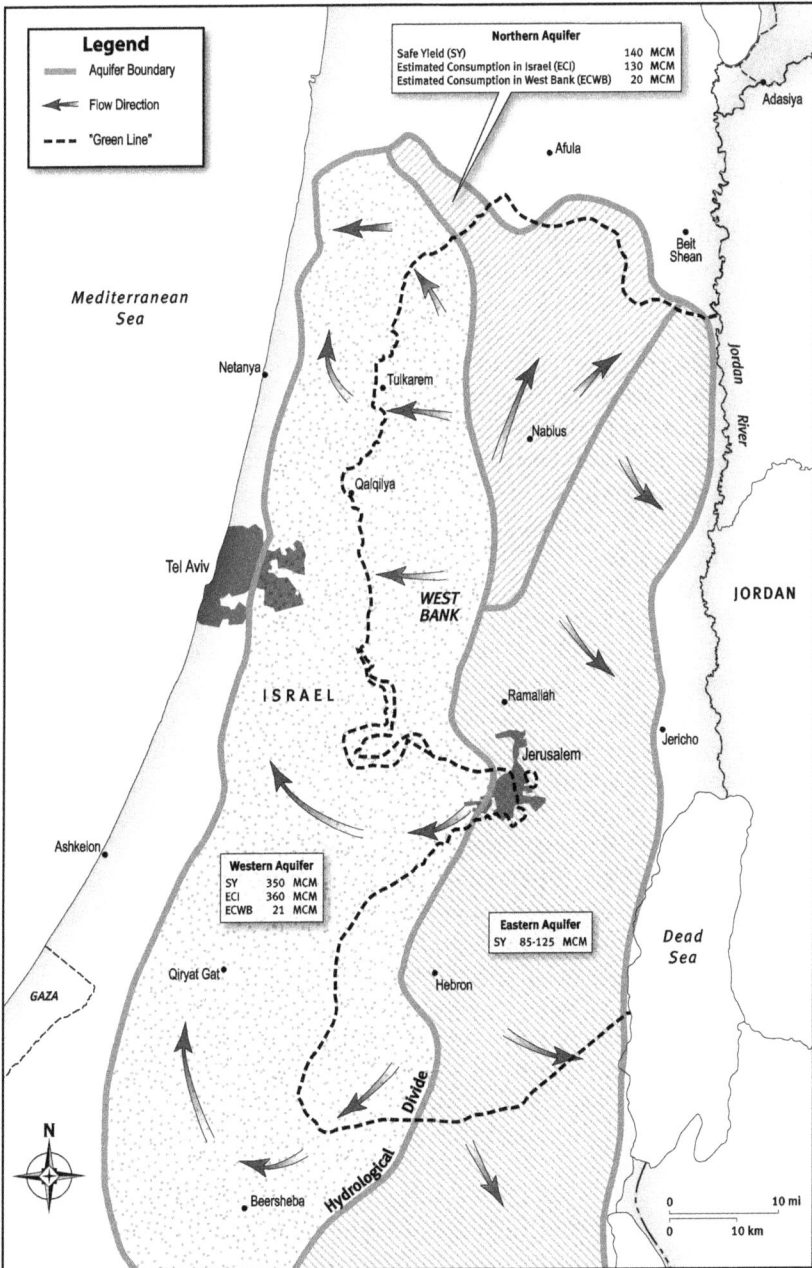

Legend

- Aquifer Boundary
- Flow Direction
- "Green Line"

Northern Aquifer

Safe Yield (SY)	140 MCM
Estimated Consumption in Israel (ECI)	130 MCM
Estimated Consumption in West Bank (ECWB)	20 MCM

Adasiya

Afula

Mediterranean Sea

Beit Shean

Netanya

Tulkarem

Nablus

Qalqiya

Tel Aviv

WEST BANK

JORDAN

ISRAEL

Ramallah

Jericho

Jerusalem

Ashkelon

Western Aquifer

SY	350 MCM
ECI	360 MCM
ECWB	21 MCM

Eastern Aquifer

SY	85-125 MCM

Dead Sea

GAZA

Qiryat Gat

Hebron

N

Beersheba

Hydrological Divide

Jordan River

0	10 mi
0	10 km

Source: Government of Israel

MAP 5-1   Mountain Aquifers: 1984 Quantities

western basin's groundwater flowed either into the Mediterranean or into swamps. During the early 1900s, Zionist farmers drained the swamps, regulated the springs' flows, and developed agriculture and urban projects to use the water. Since the 1950s, Israel has used all of the available renewable groundwater, and, by the early 1960s, was overusing the western aquifer groundwater sources. However, around the same time Israel also began to recharge the western basin aquifer with Lake Tiberias winter water through the National Water Carrier.[15] Before June 1967, Israel used 340 of the 360 mcm of water annually pumped from this basin. West Bank Arabs used only the remaining 20 mcm, primarily for irrigation in the Tulkarm and Kalkilya areas.[16] Zionist farmers in the 1930s also developed the northeastern basin aquifer. Before 1967, Israelis used about 115 mcm annually and the West Bank Arabs used 25 mcm.[17] Thus, prior to 1967, Israel established a historical pattern of use of the western and northern aquifers. Under Jordanian control, the eastern yield was approximately 58 mcm annually and primarily used by West Bank Arab farmers. During Jordanian rule of the West Bank, neither the Jordanian government nor the Palestinian West Bank inhabitants challenged Israeli utilization of the western or northern aquifers.

Even though the West Bank supplied most of Jordan's produce, the kingdom chose to spend most of its scarce development resources on the East Bank. West Bank Arab agriculture remained primitive and primarily rain-fed. The limited irrigated agriculture was dependent on a few springs and wells, due in great part to the topology of the populated mountain ridge area.[18] This elevated area did not have access to most springs and pumping was not a viable option. Consequently, the West Bank inhabitants consumed a relatively small amount of groundwater. In fact, before June 1967, the overall West Bank groundwater consumption was 80 to 100 mcm annually with 75 to 95 percent allocated to agriculture and 6.5 percent for domestic and municipal sectors.[19] According to estimates, about 40 percent of the groundwater was lost to inefficient irrigation practices of flooding fields, using permeable soil canals, and a lack of effective water storage. The Jordanian government provided minimal assistance to make West Bank agriculture more productive. Mechanization, pesticides, and fertilizer usage were not promoted. The Jordanians did not initiate modern water drilling on the western slopes until the mid-1960s. Their work to prepare sites that would pump additional water from the western slopes to Jerusalem and Ramallah ended in 1967 when Israel captured the territory.[20]

LABOR GOVERNMENT, 1967–1977

West Bank water did not become a major source of tension between 1967 and 1977, as might have been expected. The impact of Labor's restrictions on

Palestinian water development was offset by a strong Middle East economy, which absorbed Palestinian labor; Israeli assistance in West Bank agricultural development, which increased agricultural output and profitability, and optimism that "land for peace" was still a viable option. Once the Israeli government altered the equilibrium established among these factors, however, West Bank water became a greater source of tension between Israel and Palestinians.

After Israel took control of the West Bank in 1967, it limited the Palestinian water use by administration of the territory and the water system. This policy helped to maintain Israel's historical usage of West Bank groundwater and matched the broader Labor government's security-oriented policy for the territory. Labor's approach, which was delineated in the various versions of the Allon Plan, sought to create settlements that doubled as security buffers between Israel, Jordan, and the large Palestinian population on the mountain ridge.[21] On the west side of the mountain ridge, settlements were placed so as to widen Israel's narrow mid-section, gain control over east–west transportation routes, protect approaches to Ben-Gurion International Airport, and secure groundwater resources. Israel developed Jordan Valley settlements on the mountain ridge's east side to separate the Palestinian population from Jordan. A band of settlements in the Jordan Valley was established to defend against a potential invasion from the east.[22] Israel also included the Gush Etzion bloc of settlements within the Allon Plan's boundaries. The bloc lies between Bethlehem and Hebron and was in Jewish hands before being overrun by the Jordanian Legion in 1948. The preference and guiding principle of Labor's West Bank policy was that Israel must retain sections of the West Bank to have defensible borders. However, they did not settle in the densely populated Arab hill regions, anticipating that this area would be traded in a territorial compromise agreement with Jordan.

Security was not the only motivation driving Israel's settlement effort. This initiative was also based on agriculture, in accordance with the Labor-Zionist movement's traditional emphasis on farming the land as a prerequisite for security. The Jordan Valley was the focal point of West Bank Israeli farming. Some in the Labor government hoped to settle as many as two million Israelis in the Jordan Valley, viewing these settlements as a security asset and a source of Israel's future economic prosperity.[23]

The Israeli government adopted numerous restrictive policies that prevented Palestinian development of West Bank resources. These policies served to maintain Israel's control of the eastern aquifer for Jordan Valley settlements and to ensure that the western and northeastern aquifers would be protected for continued use within Israel. First, the regulations limited water usage. They permitted a minimal increase from 1967–1968 water allocations for Arab agriculture and only a small addition for domestic needs. According to a Ministry of Defense report, "The ban on further drilling and pumping in fully used basins was applied to water for irrigation purposes; water for domestic use received a definite priority and drilling and pumping permits [were] granted whenever necessary to establish municipal water systems that meet modern sanitation requirements."[24] The water bureaucracy was more flexible with Arab water allocations from the eastern basin because it was neither overexploited nor a shared aquifer with Israel.[25] After 1967, Israel tapped certain springs before they became salty, thus increasing the basin's yield from 58 to approximately 100 mcm. Israel allocated most of the additional supply to Jordan Valley Jewish settlements for irrigation with some water reserved for Arab and settler domestic use. Second, the regulations required Palestinians to obtain government permission to drill wells in the West Bank, as was the policy for Israelis in Israel. Drilling authorization had to be obtained from the civil administration, Tahal, Israel's national water planning company, which oversees engineering, planning, and design of water projects, and Mekorot, Israel's national water authority, which is responsible for construction of irrigation and water supply projects. Third and finally, the regulations called for water agencies to meter and monitor all water pumped in the West Bank, as in Israel.[26] However, unlike in Israel, strict water allocation limits were enforced for Palestinians. Overall, Israeli policy restricted the number of permits granted for digging new agricultural wells in a double effort to preserve water resources for Israel and increase Palestinian water efficiency.[27]

Israel's policy was to fully utilize West Bank groundwater that flowed naturally across the Green Line into Israel and protect the flow by restricting Palestinian water use, but not to artificially transfer West Bank water to Israel. Jewish settlers could use indigenous West Bank wells, but Mekorot was not permitted to drill within the West Bank and pump the water to Israel.[28] However, water was permitted to be pumped from Israel to the West Bank. By the early 1980s, approximately 3 mcm per year of water were transferred from Israel to West Bank Arabs.[29]

For Labor to maintain its policy option of "land for peace," it needed to ensure political and economic stability among West Bank Arabs. Under the leadership of Defense Minister Moshe Dayan, after the 1967 War, Israel assumed a low profile in the West Bank and Gaza. The Labor-led government kept Israeli military forces out of Arab-populated areas, allowed continuity of Jordanian administrative personnel, law, and law enforcement agencies, quickly removed curfews and other security restrictions, restored essential services disrupted by the war, and encouraged local authorities to assert themselves when it came to public welfare projects. All these practices became part of Dayan's "Open Bridges" policy that included the free movement of Palestinians and Palestinian goods across the Jordan River to facilitate trade and family contacts with the rest of the Arab world and with Israel proper.[30] Israel's civil administration of the territories argued that it should diligently develop services for the welfare of the population and encourage local and external initiatives in the economy and the development of the new projects—this, of course, provided that there was no conflict with the economic and security interests of Israel.[31]

In essence, the policy of the Department of the Civil Administration of the West Bank was to improve agricultural productivity by more efficient use of existing resources and to increase control over water use at the individual farm level.[32] And, in fact, during the two decades of West Bank rule, the civil administration introduced modern irrigation and cultivation techniques that, according to Israel, resulted in the doubling of irrigated areas using the same water quantities.[33] Agricultural production growth from 1967 to the mid-1980s averaged about 10 percent in the West Bank compared with 5 percent in Israel. Until June 1967, approximately 45 percent of the Palestinians worked in the agricultural sector, but this number dwindled with increased mechanization. Before 1967, farming methods had been relatively primitive, with crops harvested primarily by field workers using donkeys instead of tractors. Much of the water used for irrigation flowed through open canals and evaporated or percolated into the ground. Palestinian farm workers used a minimal amount of fertilizer and guidance by the Jordanian government was negligible.[34] After the 1967 War, Israel introduced modern irrigation, fertilization, mechanization, and pest control methods. As a result, "production per unit of land and water doubled in field crops, orchard fruits and vegetables between 1967 and 1985," according to a Defense Ministry report.[35] Increased mechanization reduced the demand for agriculture-sector labor. By 1978, only 27.7 percent—down from almost 45 percent in 1967—of the workforce was engaged in agriculture, and the surplus workers were absorbed in Israeli, Jordanian, and Gulf states' higher income labor markets.[36]

Over time, agriculture's importance to the West Bank's economy decreased, creating changes in work patterns that might have led to tension. Both agriculture as a percentage of West Bank Gross Domestic Product (GDP) and agricultural-sector employment as a percentage of total West Bank employment consistently declined during the late 1970s and early 1980s.[37] Initially, Israeli government restrictions on Palestinian water use were not overly problematic for West Bank inhabitants. This was because Palestinian workers found higher paying jobs outside the West Bank, and Israeli programs were able to increase Palestinian agriculture productivity.

During the Labor government period, Israel's West Bank water policies reduced the possibility of water-related Israeli-Palestinian tension. For the most part, the Labor government refrained from constructing settlements on the Arab populated mountain ridge. Under domestic pressure, Labor permitted the establishment of a few "heritage" settlements, notably Kiryat Arbah, just outside Hebron, and Elon Moreh. Both settlements are located in the heavily Arab-populated mountain ridge area. In general, Labor governments emphasized strategic security. Their goals were to secure greater Jerusalem, where they settled some 150,000 Jews,[38] and to preserve the option of territorial compromise with Jordan. By the end of 1977, Labor had established twenty-one settlements, mostly agricultural cooperative *kibbutzim* and *moshavim*, in the Jordan Valley and along the Eastern slopes. The Jewish population of the West Bank and Gaza numbered approximately 5,000.[39]

LIKUD, 1977–1992

In contrast to Labor's "land for peace" policy, Likud's leadership argued against territorial compromise and in support of "peace for peace."[40] The Likud coalition was not concerned with maintaining the West Bank status quo. Between 1977 and 1992, Likud-led governments—at times in a national unity government partnership with Labor—increased Israel's resources devoted to enlarging the West Bank's Jewish population. Government preference and policy moved from Labor's security-based settlement plan to Likud's religious-historical-heritage settlement approach.[41] The objective was to increase settlements as a means of maintaining Israel's control over the West Bank.

The *Gush Emunim* (bloc of the faithful) settler group, evoking religious and historical sentiments, called for the absorption of the West Bank as part of what had been *Eretz Israel* (Land of Israel), the biblical term denoting the Promised Land. It called for settling the Arab-populated heartland of the mountain ridge area to prevent any future possibility of dividing the territories and to encourage the area's eventual annexation by Israel.[42] This approach was ideologically motivated and based on religious and historical claims to the land. While Labor had strenuously opposed such policies, Likud built more mountain ridge settlements. Led by cabinet minister and former general Ariel Sharon, Likud's settlement faction sought to establish roots on the mountain ridge. Ultimately, though, Jews were settled outside of heavily populated Arab urban areas—with the exception of Hebron. Under Sharon, Likud attempted to "sever and fragment" the continuity of Arab towns on the mountain ridge by placing Jewish settlements on hilltops near major Arab urban areas such as Nablus and Ramallah. In the "Sharon Plan," approximately 50 percent of occupied land would be left for Palestinian rule in the form of enclaves around the cities and towns of Jenin, Nablus, Tulkarm, Kalkilya, Ramallah, Bethlehem, Hebron, and Gaza—all separated from one another by Israeli-controlled roads and settlement zones.[43]

The essence of the Sharon Plan was to shift settlement priority from sparsely populated areas along the Jordan River to the densely populated mountain range.[44] Sharon's idea was to lure middle class, non-ideological Israelis to the West Bank by building bedroom communities near Jerusalem and Tel Aviv. With the assistance of government subsidies, city dwellers moved to spacious accommodations across the Green Line to upgrade their standard of living.[45] For many, the move was motivated financially rather than ideologically. With 100,000 West Bank settlers by 1992, Palestinians clearly viewed Likud's settlement policy as creeping Israeli annexation of the West Bank.[46] Because of this change in policy, West Bank Arabs became increasingly suspicious and anxious about all of Israel's West Bank policies, including water.[47]

Likud continued Labor's policy of strict control over Palestinian water use. Likud's motivation, though, was to restrict Palestinian water use so that more water would be available for the increasing number of settlements. Thus, Likud's new policies resulted in heightening Palestinian tension over water. Unlike Labor's "Open Bridges" policy, under Likud, Arabs had to depend more and more on Israeli utilities, and a general Israeli presence was felt much more.[48] Mekorot, which in 1982 was given the responsibility of managing the West Bank water system, developed water sources primarily for settlements and made water use increasingly difficult for Palestinians.[49] For example, the state comptroller's office—Israel's official watchdog agency—reported one case where Mekorot expropriated land from an Arab owner to drill a well for a nearby Jewish settlement. The company failed to obtain permission from the civil administration and initially did not compensate the owner for his land. Only later, after some news reports of the case surfaced, did the company offer to compensate the owner.[50] Israeli drilling of new, deep wells in the West Bank to supply water for irrigation of Jewish agricultural settlements in the arid Jordan Valley lowered water tables and dried up some springs and shallow wells used by Palestinians. One example of the impact of this drilling was that two-thirds of the farmers in the Jordan Valley village of al-Ouja had to abandon their land when their 150-year-old spring went dry.[51]

In some instances, the Likud government did not follow a consistent policy of increasing domestic Arab allocations where needed. Drilling permits for drinking water became increasingly more difficult to obtain. In 1986, for example, the comptroller reported that when Tulkarm began suffering from a shortage of water for domestic use, the civil administration turned down the mayor's request to sink an additional well.[52] Conversely, Israel drilled approximately five wells for Jewish settlements on the already overexploited western and northeastern basin aquifers.[53] The civil administration issued forty-six drilling permits to West Bank Palestinians between 1967 and 1990; eight wells were drilled for agricultural purposes, twenty-eight for domestic purposes, and the remaining ten involved unsuccessful drillings. All but one of the agricultural wells were drilled on the eastern aquifer—Jordan Valley or Jiftlik districts. During the same period, Israel granted seventeen permits for West Bank settlers, most of which were in the Jordan Valley.[54] The state comptroller reported that Jewish farmers were overusing their water quotas by as much as 44 percent, while Arab allocations continued to be strictly monitored. Additionally, because of subsidies in 1987, Jewish settlers obtained their water at a lower price than the Palestinians.[55] The Likud government made developing land in the West Bank increasingly difficult for Palestinian farmers and increasingly easy for Jewish settlers.[56]

During this period, subsidizing West Bank settlements became the government's priority, and development initiatives for Arab agriculture dried up.[57] The rate of farm production grew, but per capita income decreased in the West Bank Arab agriculture sector. Furthermore, Israel reduced government assistance for West Bank agriculture—and Israeli agriculture, for that matter. By the mid-1980s, West Bank Palestinian farming could no longer function properly, given the existing water and economic constraints imposed by the Israeli government. At this point, Arab agricultural productivity began to decline. With a general economic downturn in the Middle East, Israel, Jordan, and the Gulf States' job markets were no longer able to supply employment opportunities to West Bank and Gaza Palestinians. The shrinking Palestinian agriculture sector did not have the capacity to hire the returning laborers.[58]

Rising Palestinian unemployment combined with the Likud settlement policy intensified Palestinian awareness of the inequitable water distribution between Israel and the West Bank and between Palestinians and settlers. According to Brigadier-General F. Zach, Israeli deputy coordinator for the Occupied Territories, West Bank Palestinians consumed 119 cm of water per capita, while Israeli settlers used almost three times that amount in 1990.[59] In Gaza, unequal water distribution and general scarcity of resources were even worse than in the West Bank.

THE GAZA STRIP

Although the Gaza Strip does not share a major groundwater source with Israel and Israel ended its occupation in 2005, severe water scarcity has heightened tensions and instability between Gaza Palestinians and Israel. The Gaza Strip is on the coastal plain bordering the Mediterranean Sea, Sinai desert, and Israel. The climate is arid, with less than 200 mm of precipitation annually. Surface water is only available following rainfall and groundwater is contained in two shallow aquifers. Unlike the West Bank's aquifers, Gaza's are shallow and easy to tap. Palestinians in Gaza pump water from more than 2,000 wells, primarily for irrigation purposes. They withdraw approximately 110 mcm per year, while the natural recharge provides only 55 to 70 mcm annually.[60] With hundreds of illegal wells, farmers use approximately 90 percent of the Gaza groundwater. Intense water consumption is needed for citrus fruit, which accounts for two-thirds of Gaza's agriculture and remains

Gaza's economic mainstay. The ongoing problem of overpumping has resulted in saltwater intrusion, both from the Mediterranean and from lower saline aquifers. Additionally, heavy fertilizer and pesticide use and poor sewage control have polluted the aquifer. As a result, many Gaza residents have been consuming contaminated water and are unable to use water from their taps at home.[61]

Before 1977, Israel attempted to regulate Gaza water usage to prevent any further deterioration of the supply that occurred with the overpumping permitted by the Egyptian administrators prior to 1967. However, under the Likud government in the late 1970s, Israel also became more lax in regulating Palestinian pumping. As a result, the hydrological situation in Gaza deteriorated even further. This policy may be attributed to the fact that Gaza's drinking source was not connected to Israel's.[62] Along with severe poverty, Gaza Strip Palestinians experienced a scarcity of clean drinking water on a daily basis. Just before the *intifada*, in 1986, estimated per capita annual consumption by Gazans was 142 cm, while that of the settlers was 2,240 cm.[63]

From 1967 to 1987, Israelis often disregarded the economic and political needs of Arabs living under their control and even came to look upon Palestinians as passive subjects.[64] The inclination of the political leadership to ignore growing problems such as Gaza and West Bank water scarcity was part of this picture. The Palestinian uprising or *intifada* forced Israelis to pay greater attention to the plight of the Palestinians and eroded Israeli public support and preference for maintaining the status quo.

THE 1990 STATE COMPTROLLER'S SPECIAL REPORT

During the *intifada* and the 1989–1991 drought, Israel's state comptroller disclosed that the country has significantly mismanaged the West Bank aquifers. A special report by the comptroller contended that "the [1990] water crisis is not the result of natural factors, but of actions of man."[65] The comptroller and water experts principally attribute Israel's water deficit not to years of drought but rather to uncontrolled exploitation and mismanagement of resources. Influenced by the Israeli agricultural lobby, the Agriculture Ministry and the Water Commissioners Office, the guardians of Israel's water, failed to comply with the water management guidelines and laws.

For the previous twenty-five years, the water planners at Tahal and other national and international institutions had recommended that the water bureaucracy reduce Israeli agricultural water quotas by a substantial amount. Until 1990, such advice was all but ignored. According to the comptroller's report, overexploitation had caused the average level in the mountain aquifer to drop "during the period beginning in the early 1970s to 1990s, by about four meters—each meter of the aquifer's water level is equal to approximately 100 mcm" of water.[66] With these declines in the water level, most of the aquifer's water reserves were depleted. For example, between 1985 and 1990, the average amount of water that was safe to use was 25 mcm. But, in November 1990, there was a deficit or negative storage of 30 mcm, meaning that if water were pumped below the red line, saline water would pollute the freshwater. According to the comptroller, decades of excessive use coupled with a three-year drought left water resources depleted and in danger of irreversible damage. The comptroller estimated that Israel's water overdraft was equal to more than one year's use (1.6 billion cubic meters). With no real effective storage because of overuse, "every one or two consecutive dry years are liable to bring about a serious crisis in the water situation."[67] In 1979, 1986, and 1990, Israel experienced serious water shortages. The 1990 crisis was the most critical, in part because of the exhaustion of the mountain aquifer's effective storage capacity. During these crisis years, the danger of damaging the reservoir increased. Due to the dropping water levels, close to and even below the danger lines, the threat of penetration by polluting salty water increased. "A drop below the danger line can destroy the aquifer's groundwater."[68]

The comptroller found that many settlements were exceeding their water quotas. The Jordan Valley, for example, exceeded its 1986 water allocations by 35.6 percent, and settlements in the West Bank's southern district surpassed their quota by 44.8 percent. Together, settlements in these two regions used almost 10 mcm more water from the eastern aquifer than was allotted to them.[69] Israel had also failed to adequately protect the mountain aquifer from man-made pollution, such as sewage and pesticides. In many West Bank towns, Israel was not treating sewage, thereby threatening groundwater quality. The government continued to build many settlements and towns above the western aquifer on both sides of the Green Line. One noted Israeli water official said that "it's only a matter of time before we are drinking our sewage."[70] There are continuing signs that sewage effluents from the Israeli settlements are polluting the western aquifer in the area of Kalkilya and Kfar Saba and of Tsofin and Alfei Menashe along the Western ridge.[71]

To address the water scarcity problem, the Ministry of Agriculture, led by Minister Rafael Eitan, slashed water allocations for 1991–1992 by 1.3 mcm per year. Moreover, more than half of the water cutback applied to agriculture. At first, farmers ignored the reductions, but, by June, the water bureaucracy, backed by public opinion, cut 1991 allocations by as much as 60 percent and threatened to turn off violators' taps altogether. Production of high-water-consuming crops, such as cotton, was reduced and greater use was made of treated water. During this period, the water crisis became so severe that the government forced farmers to reduce consumption during the farming season. This, however, caused more economic harm than if the water bureaucracy had cut water quotas before the planting season so the agriculture sector could plan appropriately.[72]

Gradually, administrative edicts and more judicious crop selections ameliorated the immediate water crisis. The abundant rainfall in late 1991 and early 1992 filled surface reservoirs and did much to replenish groundwater sources. The political changes triggered by the water emergency, however, were more long lasting for agriculture. The government targeted the farm lobby for dictating water prices, subsidies, and allocations. In reaction to the water crisis and the state comptroller's report, Water Commissioner Yishay Tzemach was pressured to resign. Professor Dan Zaslavsky, who was not considered overly sympathetic to the farm lobby, replaced him. According to the *Israel Yearbook and Almanac*, "Agriculture lost its primacy as a trademark of Zionism and Israel. It had become merely one interest group among many, and its prerogatives came under attack."[73] Additionally, segments of the agriculture lobby were experiencing a serious fiscal crisis, which weakened them politically. Many privileges for the agriculture sector were reduced, including subsidies for water, price supports, and regulations that supported agriculture product-market monopolies. While the 1990 drought might have decreased agriculture's political power, it also increased Israeli awareness of their country's water vulnerability and, therefore, heightened fears of future water scarcity.

As these fears increased in the early 1990s, the problem of Israel's West Bank territory came to the fore. As talk of West Bank territorial compromise increased, Agriculture Minister Eitan, a secular right-wing former general, publicly argued that relinquishing control over West Bank water supplies would "threaten the Jewish State." During the 1990 drought, the Agriculture Ministry, led by Eitan, took out full-page advertisements in the international press describing the connection between West Bank water and Israel's security. The ad concluded that "it is important to realize that the claim to continued Israeli control over Judea and Samaria is not based on extremist fanaticism or religious mysticism but on a rational, healthy and reasonable survival instinct."[74] In the hope of influencing the mostly secular Israeli public, security hawks who were opposed to territorial compromise used the water issue as a key arguing point rather than emphasizing the religious-historical rationales. In the end, the advertisement raised an important question: could Israel relinquish control of all or part of the West Bank without jeopardizing one of its primary sources of freshwater and the security that comes with it?

As far back as 1977, Prime Minister Menachem Begin, who was preparing for Camp David Peace Accord negotiations on West Bank autonomy, instructed Israel's water commissioner to draft a study considering whether Israel might relinquish control if water resources were the only consideration. The study, which had not been made public, concluded that only about one-third of the West Bank needed to remain under Israel's control to ensure water security. Israel could cede control over most of the eastern basin, which includes the Jordan Valley, without jeopardizing its supply that flowed across the Green Line into Israel.[75] As for the western and northeastern basins, the water commissioner concluded that a "red line" could be drawn along the West Bank's western side where Israel should maintain control. The analysis was based on the assumption if Palestinians chose to pump many wells that were more than 100 meters deep for the sake of harming Israel, it would be too expensive and technically difficult.[76] It is also fair to assume that international funding agencies would not support such projects.

Jaffee Center Report

In 1991, less than a year after the publication of the Agriculture Ministry advertisements, Tahal, in cooperation with the Tel Aviv University Jaffee Center for Strategic Studies, completed a study entitled "The Water Problem in the Context of Israel-Arab Agreements." Like the earlier study ordered by Menachem Begin, this project also concluded that Israel did not need to retain the entire West Bank to ensure its water security. The study contained maps outlining possible withdrawal lines from the West Bank that would still safeguard water sources used by Israel.[77] When Eitan learned that an agency, Tahal, which was indirectly associated with his ministry, had coauthored the study, he quickly classified the study as secret. Two years later, the new Labor government leaked excerpts of the report and the maps to the press.[78]

The Jaffee Center report was important because it reflected the new reality that both Israel and the Palestinians might be forced to cooperate because of their interlocking needs. Because of the mutual Israeli-Palestinian dependence on West Bank groundwater, the Jaffee Center report argued against full Israeli withdrawal without a comprehensive commitment from the Palestinians for cooperation with Israel on the water issue. Such an arrangement was not necessary for Gaza. The concern was that Palestinian overexploitation and pollution would severely damage one of Israel's primary water supplies, the West Bank aquifers. However, with full cooperation, border adjustments and verification and monitoring of drills and groundwater exploitation, joint management of the shared aquifers was possible and could benefit both sides. The report recommended border modifications, similar to the study for Begin, so Israel could ensure control over West Bank water resources even if Israeli-Palestinian cooperation should fail at some point. In other words, the border modifications reflected the maximum amount of land Israel could cede while still minimizing the possible damage to its water supplies. The border modifications included retaining most of the area near Tulkarm-Kalkilya to protect the western aquifer, some of the area to the north of Jenin to safeguard the northeastern aquifer and a belt around Jerusalem to protect part of the eastern basin.[79]

ANALYSIS AND CONCLUSION

Palestinians could rightly argue that they were not receiving a reasonable and equitable portion of the shared water. Although "equitable does not mean equal,"[80] it does suggest that factors such as population, geography, and similar factors should be considered in determining water allocations. On the other hand, Israel also has a legitimate claim on the water. The western and northeastern aquifers are integral parts of the Israeli water network. These aquifers supply drinking water to most of Israel's population and have become the most important multiyear reservoir of the water system. This is due to the grave situation, in both qualitative and quantitative terms, of the coastal aquifer, Israel's other major groundwater source. Additionally, the shared aquifers play a critical role in storing surplus winter water for dry summers.[81] The shared aquifers are critical to Israel; any sudden or significant decrease in their availability would cause harm to Israel's economy and its security. "Harm" to a state's water supply can also come from within the state, as was detailed in the 1990 state comptroller report discussed earlier.

To understand Israel's West Bank water policy, one first must understand, not the international system as realists argue, but the domestic preferences of its two major parties, Likud and Labor. As discussed in this chapter, both parties had different preferences concerning the West Bank and therefore its water resources. Likud has been determined to maintain Israel's control of the territory, and Labor has shown more willingness to negotiate this land for peace.

When a player has control over the other and reciprocity is not a viable option, then cooperative strategies will not be long lasting. As described in this chapter, Israel initially worked with Palestinians to aid or at least not cripple the Palestinian agriculture sector. However, after ten years, a new Israeli government led by Likud began a policy that not only did not assist the Palestinians but at times injured their water interests. The Palestinians had no effective means of challenging the Likud water policies and those policies continued. The relationship had become noncooperative and nonreciprocal. Robert Axelrod demonstrated that prisoners' dilemma strategies that emphasize cooperation despite the other side's behavior will tend to bring out the worst in the other player as he realizes that he can exploit the opponent's action to his own benefit.[82] With the initiation of the *intifada*, this began to change.

In contrast, as described in earlier chapters, reciprocity does not need to be between actors with equal capabilities. Israel is a much stronger state than Jordan, yet the operation of reciprocity played an important part in maintaining cooperation. Without reciprocity, the conditions for cooperation such as mutuality of interests and lengthening the shadow of the future are usually not effective. Thus, tactical functional cooperation is difficult to maintain. The operation of reciprocity also helps develop a feeling of trust and fairness between participants. Without it, the controlled party experiences a sense of frustration, which occurred between Israelis and Palestinians.

The Jaffee Center report put water negotiation at the center of any security plan. The report concluded that no security arrangements were possible without solving the water problem. It went on to argue that Israel must do all it can to safeguard its existing water assets in the territories.[83] The report advised the Israeli government not to make any concessions on the water issue unless Israel was compensated by clear and unambiguous political benefits. The report also suggested that Israel link any concessions on water to an explicit commitment from donor countries for desalination projects. The Jaffee Center report refuted many past arguments against Israeli territorial compromise based on a water security rationale.[84] With the advent of the *intifada*, both Israel and the Palestinians now had the mixed interests needed to negotiate the West Bank water issue. Still, not until the Madrid Peace Process and the Oslo breakthrough, which is discussed in the next chapter, would the water Palestinian-Israeli issue start to be addressed.

6

The 1990s Madrid Peace Process
and After, 1991–2006

Not since the 1950s and the Johnston mission did Jordan River riparians negotiate and resolve so many water-related issues as they did through the 1990s Madrid Peace Process. Even so, water remains a difficult political and economic issue for the Jordan riparians. Some of the water agreements ratified in the 1990s have a tactical functional cooperation foundation, which facilitated a cooperative process of confidence building in a tense political environment. Elements of this process were the providing information, reducing transaction costs, making commitments more credible, establishing focal points for coordination, and facilitating the operation of reciprocity. Nonetheless, the protracted conflict among all the riparians has yet to be resolved, and the same is true of the many water disputes. Certain water matters have not been properly addressed, and water scarcity remains a part of the political landscape. Water has been a central issue during the peace process. It alone temporarily deadlocked the negotiations for two major agreements: the Israel-Jordan Peace Treaty and the Israel-Palestinian Interim Agreement on the West Bank and Gaza Strip (Oslo II), and continues to be a primary obstacle to Syrian-Israeli negotiations. This chapter first examines the Middle East peace process and the organization of the 1990s Madrid process. The next five sections analyze the four tracks of the peace process—the Palestinian-Israeli, Jordanian-Israeli, the Syrian-Israeli, the Lebanese-Israeli, and, finally, the multilateral track. In each section, we will review the important role third party involvement has played and explain the continuing importance of the process of tactical functional cooperation on the water issue, even before the overall political issues are resolved.

OVERVIEW OF THE 1990S PEACE PROCESS

For almost half a century after the 1948 War, the Arab-Israeli arena was mired in a smoldering, protracted conflict. In a stunning breakthrough, Israel-Egypt negotiations led to the 1978 Camp David Accords and the 1979 Peace Treaty. However, after President Anwar Sadat's assassination, Israel's invasion of Lebanon, and Likud's aggressive West Bank settlement policy, the evolving peace process halted and relations between Israel and Egypt cooled. A decade later, the Gulf War and the breakup of the Soviet bloc dramatically altered the politics of the Middle East. Israel's vulnerability to Iraqi scud missiles had shaken that state. Jordan and the PLO became weakened and isolated by wealthy Arab allies and by the United States because they did not back the 1990 US-led Gulf coalition against Iraq. Syria, on the other hand, had supported the coalition, but, with the Soviet Union's disintegration, Damascus had lost its strongest supporter and initially looked to the West for new allies.

Taking advantage of the political opportunity after the Gulf War, the United States went on a diplomatic offensive for resolving the Arab-Israeli conflict. In a diplomatic tour de force, US Secretary of State James Baker made eight trips to the Middle East during the eight months following the Gulf War. He and his team formulated the Madrid framework, which they conveyed in a "Letter of Invitation," jointly issued by the United States and the Soviet Union, now Russia.[1] They invited Israel, Syria, Lebanon, Jordan, and the Palestinians, the core parties, to an opening conference, from October 30 to November 1, 1991, in Madrid, Spain. The letter's text detailed the structure of the Madrid process, which would become the framework for the Middle East peace negotiations in the 1990s. The letter stressed the ambitious goal of their meetings: "The United States and the Soviet Union are prepared to assist the parties to achieve a just, lasting and comprehensive peace settlement, through direct negotiations along two tracks, bilateral and multilateral, between Israel and the Arab states, and between Israel and the Palestinians, based on United Nations Security Council Resolutions 242 and 338—the land for peace formula. The objective of this process is real peace."[2] The opening conference in Madrid served as a forum for all participants to make speeches and meet face-to-face publicly for the first time. It also served as the location for the first round for the bilateral talks. The Madrid conference, as stated in the invitation, had no power to impose solutions or veto agreements reached by the participants, nor would the conference convene without the consent of all parties. The core parties accepted the invitation. At Israel's request, the Palestinians attended as part of a joint Jordanian-Palestinian delegation. Egypt and the European Community, now the European Union, also took part, and the Gulf Cooperation Council and the United Nations served as observers.

The multilateral track sought to raise the Middle East of the future by addressing regional issues and building confidence through addressing less political matters. Delegates from the Middle East and from the international community attended these talks, which opened in Moscow in January 1992. This track focused on the key regional issues of water, the environment, arms control, refugees, and economic development (see Figure 6-1). The United States designed this forum to build confidence among the various regional parties and maintain momentum when the bilateral negotiations slowed.

The bilateral track sought to resolve the conflicts of the past, but it initially stagnated. Immediately following the Madrid conference, on November 3, 1991, the first public and direct diplomatic talks began between Israel and Syria, Israel and Lebanon, and Israel and Jordan, present with a Palestinian delegation. The "Letter of Invitation" offered a clear framework for negotiations between Israel and the Palestinians. Talks would be "conducted in phases, beginning with talks on the interim self-government arrangements." The interim self-government phase would last for five years, and during that time a "permanent status agreement would be negotiated based on the land for peace formula or UN Resolutions 242 and 338."[3] After the Madrid bilateral

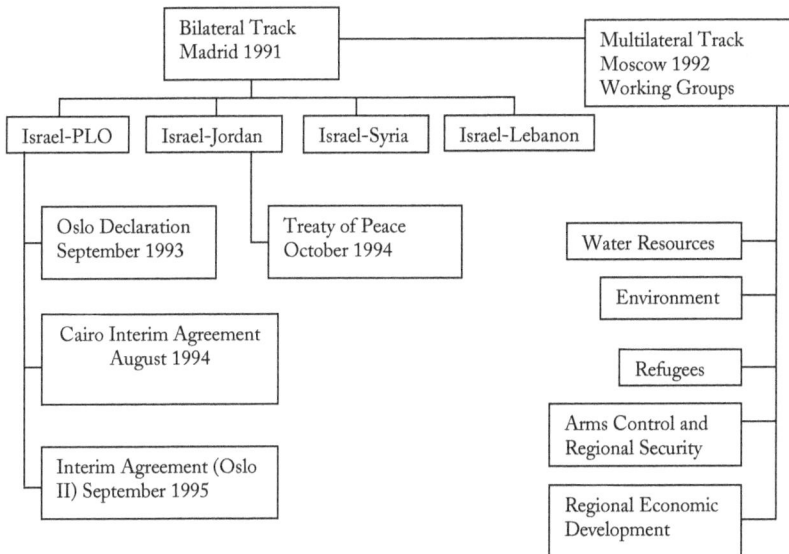

Source: "From Contention to Cooperation: A Case Study of the Middle East Multilateral Working Group on Water Resources," paper provided by the US Geological Service (Feb. 2000), 2.

FIGURE 6-1   The Structure of the 1990s Middle East Peace Process

round, the talks then moved to Washington where numerous sessions took place at the US State Department. But after the first two years of negotiations there, little in the way of substantive negotiations took place, and the talks thus became deadlocked. Then, with the Labor Party's electoral victory in the 1992, the bilateral peace process track began to make progress.

THE PALESTINIAN-ISRAELI TRACK

The crux of the water negotiations incorporated Israel's efforts to protect its historical water supply and the Palestinians' to increase their existing water source and have Israel recognize their water rights to West Bank groundwater. As discussed in chapter 5, Israel and the West Bank share an important groundwater source, which includes almost all of the West Bank Palestinians' water supply and one-third of Israel's water budget. Up to this point, Israel had complete control of West Bank water resources, and thus there was no Palestinian-Israeli water cooperation. However, by the end of the 1990s, a process of negotiations and water-related cooperation was leading to greater trust and confidence between Palestinian and Israeli water technocrats. That process continues, although slowed by the Israeli-Palestinian violence and political instability of the early and mid-2000s.

After secret negotiations in Oslo, Norway, Israel and the Palestine Liberation Organization (PLO) reached a political understanding of mutual recognition, which was the political breakthrough that propelled the Madrid process forward. The basis for negotiations was security for Israel and self-government and statehood for the Palestinians. On September 9, 1993, PLO Chairman Yasser Arafat sent a letter to Prime Minister Rabin, stating that the PLO recognizes the right of Israel to exist in peace and security. In effect, Arafat accepted a peaceful resolution of the conflict, and renounced the use of terrorism and other acts of violence. In response, Israel recognized the PLO as the representative of the Palestinian people. Four days later, in Washington, a joint Israeli-Palestinian Declaration of Principles (DOP) was signed, outlining the proposed interim self-agreements. The DOP provided for immediate Palestinian self-rule in Gaza and Jericho, new rights and obligations for West Bank Palestinians, and an agreement on self-government. The interim arrangement was scheduled to last five years, at which time a permanent status treaty would be negotiated and finalized by 1999.[4] The Israelis and Palestinians negotiated the interim agreement in three stages: first, the Gaza-Jericho Agreement, also called Oslo I, signed May 4, 1994; second, the preparatory transfer of power and responsibilities completed August 29, 1994; third, and most important, the Israel-Palestinian Interim Agreement on the West Bank and Gaza Strip, or Oslo II. This last agreement, signed September 28, 1995, has been to date the most extensive agreement involving the water issue.[5]

During the Oslo II negotiations, water became one of the most contentious issues, paralyzing the entire talks for almost two months. Rabin even testified before the Knesset Foreign Affairs and Defense Committee that "if the [water] issue is not resolved satisfactorily, we will not sign [Oslo II]."[6] Before the intense Oslo II water negotiations, both sides developed inflexible positions on which they said they would not compromise. The Palestinian position from the outset of the Madrid process was that Israel must recognize Palestinian water rights—meaning that Palestinians should gain control of the West Bank's water when it gains control of the West Bank. Israel initially refused to discuss Palestinian water rights in the bilateral talks, seeking to discuss only water allocations. The Israeli position was that the Palestinians would not receive additional water for agriculture from the western or northern aquifers that flow into Israel.[7] Instead, the Palestinian Authority (PA) would receive additional water from parts of the eastern aquifer, thereby maintaining the current supply level to Israel since this aquifer is not shared.[8] At the negotiations, Noah Kinarti, the leader of the Israeli water team made it clear to Palestinian counterparts that Israel would discuss joint management and control of shared aquifers and a larger quota for Palestinians. But he warned that there would be no discussion of a division of the water or water rights.[9] Essentially the same position surfaced at a negotiating round hosted by Egypt's President Hosni Mubarak. This meeting attempted to break the Oslo II negotiation's stalemate, with Chair Yasser Arafat and Foreign Minister Shimon Peres attending. Repeating Israel's position, Peres told reporters that any new water arrangements would not come at Israel's expense, stating that "what is clear is that there will be no division of what already exists, but rather we are talking about an effort to create new water sources."[10] Peres continued by saying that the Israelis and Palestinians are "negotiating over levels of water each side needs, not about water rights."[11] As a gesture aimed at creating new water sources, Peres said that Palestinian drilling for the eastern aquifer water was negotiable. The foreign minister also spoke of loans from Germany to fund a Gaza desalination plant, which would provide some 50 mcm (million cubic meters) of water annually at a cost of approximately one dollar per cubic meter. This idea alone did not resolve the difference, and the Oslo II deadlock persisted.

The importance of verification and compliance were also issues stressed during the Oslo II negotiations. Israel emphasized to the Palestinians that it could not permit unsupervised water drilling in the West Bank. After Israel withdrew from the Gaza Strip, some Palestinians drilled hundreds of unlicensed wells, and it seemed clear to Israel that the Palestinian Authority had lost control over its own people in the water sphere. Israeli policymakers feared that such uncontrolled drilling would seriously damage the shared West Bank groundwater if Palestinian wildcat wells were not halted.[12] Agriculture Minister Yacov Tsur stated that "there is no doubt that we will not be able to leave the [West Bank] area without supervisory measures to prevent [illegal] drilling."[13] He also said "Israel can't leave the area without the question of water being fully defined." These arrangements must include monitoring water pumping and quality. "We have to check what they are pumping. We also have to check the sewage. If they don't treat the sewage, it will affect the groundwater." Tsur pledged to keep supplying West Bank settlements with water. Major settlements would continue to be linked to separate Mekorot lines, and smaller settlements would be connected to the Palestinian Water Authority but provided with emergency reserves in case the Palestinians were to interrupt their supply.[14]

On August 11, Israel and the PLO reached a partial settlement on an interim agreement, but it did not include water. However, in the days that followed, Palestinian shortages on the ground would spur the Oslo II negotiations. At the initialing of the document, Israeli Foreign Minister Director General Uri Savir maintained Israel's negotiating line on water, stating that Israel still opposed altering the present distribution of West Bank water.[15] In the midst of completing the Oslo II negotiations, Israel Television reported that the West Bank city of Hebron had been largely without running water for four months, a revelation that embarrassed the Israeli government and shocked the Israeli public. Two days after the report, the Israeli cabinet met. Afterward, Prime Minister Rabin ordered the civil administration for the West Bank to resolve the Hebron water shortage problem. Army and private tankers brought in water to solve the immediate crisis. Israeli water technocrats complained that Hebron was receiving enough water to serve its 100,000-person population, but that the water delivery network was so old and dilapidated that much was lost to leaky pipes and theft.[16] The television report was important because it challenged the notion that West Bank Palestinians had an adequate water supply for their daily lives. As a result, Israeli negotiators were told by the government leadership and by the United States to be more generous with the Palestinians.

The Palestinian position was very different from the Israeli one. From the outset of the Madrid Peace Process, Palestinians demanded equitable utilization of water resources. The Palestinians pointed out that Israel consumed 1.5 billion cubic meters of water, or six times the water consumed by Gaza and West Bank Palestinians. A major part of the Oslo II agreement provided for the PA to take full control of the urban West Bank centers. The Palestinians negotiated for control not only of the land evacuated by Israel but also of the water underneath the autonomous Palestinian territory. In particular, Tulkarm, Kalkilya, and the towns and villages in close proximity sit on top of the western aquifer. Palestinians asserted that only with access to the western and northern aquifers could their economy improve and the peace process succeed.[17] The Palestinians also argued that Israel must increase the Palestinian water allocation dramatically and that the PA's water rights had to be recognized. A Palestinian negotiator and hydrologist pointed out the multiple issues surrounding water resources: "The problem is that we are suffering too much from water shortages in the West Bank and Gaza. It is an acute problem for us. We don't get enough water for our daily needs. In Gaza almost all the water is polluted. At present desalination is too expensive for both Israelis and Palestinians. It is not going to solve our immediate problems."[18] During the negotiations, Jamil al-Tarif, a senior Palestinian negotiator on water, insisted that the first point on the agenda should be Israel's recognition of Palestinian's water rights. He further pointed out that, while Palestinians were pushing for this recognition, Israel during most of the negotiations had failed to negotiate this issue.[19]

During the Oslo II talks, Noah Kinarti was a lead Israeli negotiator on the water issue, a man who was eventually able to gain the respect of the Palestinians. Because of his background as a picnic table negotiator with Jordan and an Israel regional water authority manager, Prime Minister Rabin brought his old and trusted friend in not only to negotiate with the Jordanians but also with the Palestinians. He was Rabin's advisor on settlement affairs and for water and infrastructure. Uri Savir, Israel's chief negotiator with the Palestinians from 1993 to 1996, recalled how Kinarti was initially "rough, rigid, and suspicious" of fellow Israeli negotiators who were not part of Rabin's inner circle, as well of the Palestinian negotiators. Savir recalled how Kinarti "insulted the entire Palestinian delegation by saying that a Palestinian uses a quarter as much water as an Israeli does (implying that [Israelis] were cleaner)."[20] When Savir recommended to Kinarti that he be less difficult with the Palestinians, he replied, "Let me do it my way. We'll reach an understanding in the end. Because without an understanding on water, there won't be an Interim Agreement."[21] During the final push for an agreement, Agriculture Minister Yacov Tsur and military officer Oren Shachor joined Kinarti's water team. Chief Palestinian negotiator Abu Ala, also known as Ahmad Quray, established a good rapport with the Israeli team, and Savir recalled that in the end Kinarti built a good working relationship with Nabil al-Sherif, the lead Palestinian negotiator on water. Savir concluded that "when I got to know Kinarti better, I found that under his rough exterior was a warm, caring, and astute man who had lost a son in uniform and was genuinely striving for peace."[22]

In a breakthrough that moved the Oslo II Agreement forward, Israel conceded and recognized Palestinian rights to West Bank water in writing. With this recognition, the two sides agreed to put off the issue until final status talks. Chief water negotiators Abu Ala and Yacov Tsur signed a joint statement that reads, "Israel recognizes the water rights of the Palestinians in the West Bank. The issue will be determined in the final status negotiations and will be included in the final status issues as it relates to the different water sources."[23] Not only was this agreement a breakthrough for the water talks, it was also the breakthrough needed to finalize the entire Oslo II agreement. Recognizing Arab water rights was an Israeli policy change. For example, throughout the Jordanian-Israeli negotiations, Jordan also demanded that Israel recognize its water rights, but, in the treaty, Israel was able to bypass the issue by recognizing only Jordan's "rightful allocations." Despite Israel's apparent change in attitude during Oslo II, Palestinian water rights have yet to be defined by either side. One of Israel's water negotiators, Tsur, praised the talks for producing "an honorable solution, as is required, which will provide water for the growing population's needs, so that we don't return to the scenes we witnessed in Hebron."[24] He went on to discuss ways of creating new water sources, such as recycling water and desalination. The Palestinian negotiator, Abu Ala, also indicated that the agreement was important because Palestinian water rights were recognized by Israel in writing. He stated, "The main obstacle that hindered negotiations over practical issues has been removed."[25]

During the Oslo II talks, Israeli negotiators made clear that they spoke of West Bank water rights, not rights in the Jordan River basin, as the Palestinians demanded. The reason for this distinction is clear. Political analysts have argued if Palestinians take control of the West Bank's Jordan Rift Valley, they, as Jordan River riparians, would be entitled to 150 million cubic meters of water per year (mcmy) from the Jordan River in accordance with the Johnston Plan.[26] With sovereignty over the entire Gaza Strip and West Bank, they also would claim rights to the Yarmouk River, storage and fishing in Lake Tiberias, and access to the Mediterranean and Dead Sea, in addition to "sovereign control of Gaza and West Bank groundwater."[27] Currently, Israel and Jordan negatively impact the flow of the lower Jordan by siphoning off water to their canal system or releasing saline water to the river. If the Palestinians took control of the Jordan Rift Valley, they would have the right under international law to demand improved quality and quantity of the water flow. This would be no different from Israel and Jordan demanding that Syria maintain quality and quantity of flow for the Yarmouk. Claiming the rights of Jordan River riparians, the Palestinian negotiators have proposed several criteria for dividing the West Bank groundwater. These criteria included divisions based upon area and the size of the groundwater basin, a division according to the future pace of population growth, or allocations based on agricultural development needs.[28] Though not incorporated into the interim agreement, these demands might be discussed in the final status negotiations.

In sum, the primary goal of the water section of the Oslo II Accords was to establish a framework in which Palestinians could increase their water supply by developing untapped West Bank groundwater using international funding. Of equal importance was the establishment of a joint management regime, which would safeguard West Bank groundwater from pollution and overutilization, an Israeli preference. The Oslo II agreement includes an eleven-page section that codifies the water and sewage accord between Israel and the Palestinian Authority.[29] The pact provides the Palestinians with additional water and establishes a verification system to allay Israeli fears of Palestinian noncompliance. The arrangement assures an additional 28 mcm of water for Palestinians while guaranteeing that all necessary measures will be taken "to prevent any harm to water resources including those utilized by the other side."[30] Schedule 10 in Oslo II describes the "existing extractions and estimated potential of West Bank aquifers"—see Map 6-1.

In the Oslo II agreement, both parties estimate the future needs of the Palestinians in the West Bank to be between 70 and 80 mcmy.[31] Palestinians receive 28 mcm for domestic use only, of which the pact allocates 5 mcm from Israel to Gaza, to lessen urban water scarcity there. The Palestinians will develop the remaining 42 to 52 mcm from the eastern aquifer and other designated sources in the West Bank. The Palestinians have the "right" to use the remaining water for domestic and agriculture purposes.[32] Thus, Israel was largely successful in limiting an increase in Palestinian irrigation allocations.

To implement the agreement and manage the jointly shared groundwater, the Israelis and Palestinians established a Joint Water Committee (JWC), a pivotal idea in overcoming the deadlock that was blocking an Oslo II agreement, according to Uri Savir.[33] The JWC comprises an equal number of Palestinian and Israeli representatives, and all JWC decisions are reached by consensus.[34] Only technical issues are to be brought before the JWC—not political ones. The committee also determines allocations during droughts when less water is available and approves all plans for new water and sewage systems. Under the control of the JWC are five Joint Supervision and Enforcement Teams (JSETs) for the West Bank. The JSETs' mission is "to monitor, supervise and enforce the implementation" of the water section.[35] Both sides have "free, unrestricted and secure access to all water and sewage facilities and systems."[36] To verify compliance, JSET visits must take place within twenty-four hours of a request or complaint. All problems that JSETs are unable to rectify are to be referred to the two JWC chairs for a ruling.[37] During the interim or transitional period, Israel and the PA tested this institutional structure, which gave both sides a better idea of how to improve the compliance system for the final status arrangement. Serious problems still needed to be worked out, but, by the spring of 1998, the Palestinian and Israeli JSET members developed good personal working relations, and inspections were going smoothly.[38] In general, according to political scientist Alwyn Rouyer, "Palestinians and Israelis working to implement the water accords are in

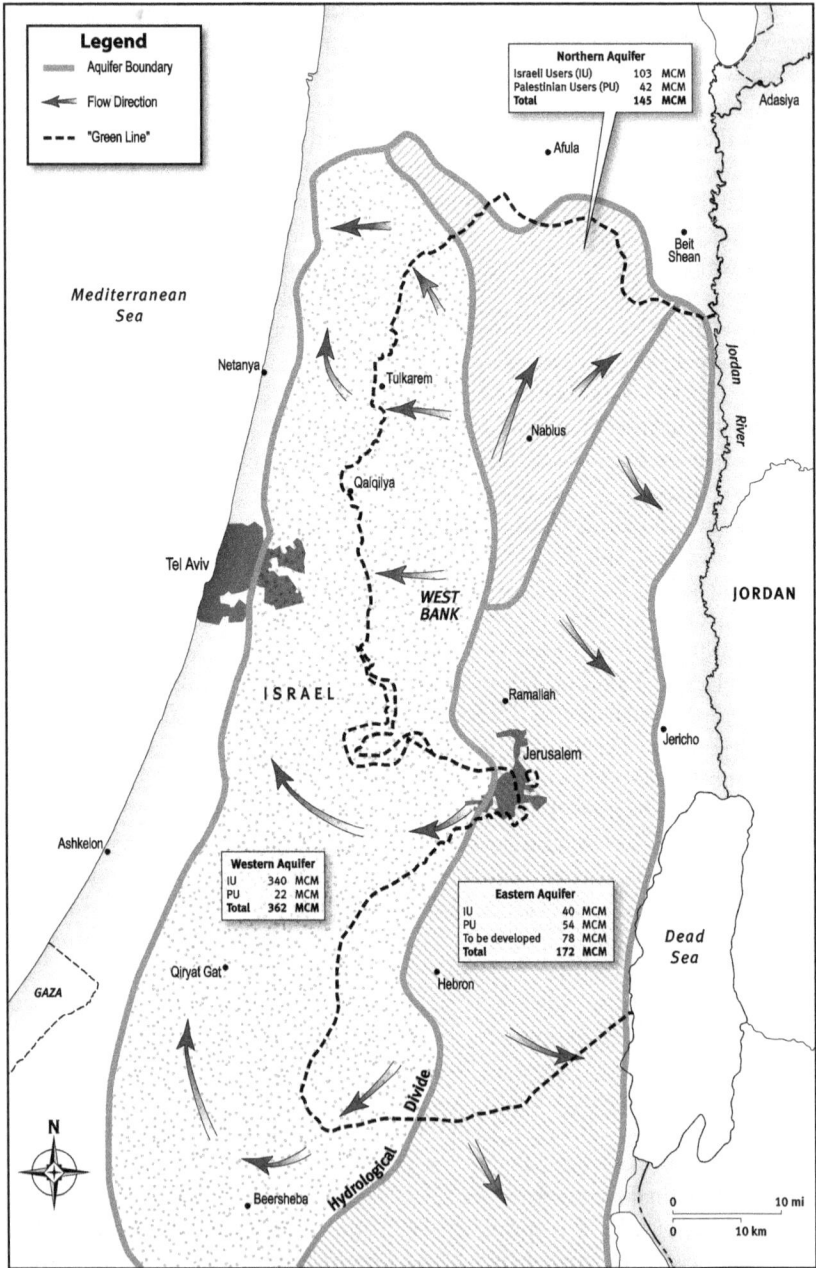

MAP 6-1   Oslo II: The Shared Palestinian-Israeli Mountain Aquifers

daily contact with each other, if not in person then over the telephone . . . middle-level officials on both sides stress the fact that they have a good working relationship on a personal basis with their counterparts."[39] Beyond the obvious functional benefits, this system also creates the means for establishing trust and good working relations between Israeli and Palestinian water technocrats, an environment that was virtually nonexistent prior to the Madrid Peace Process. For example, in December 1995, Israel complained about illegal Palestinian water drilling in the West Bank town of Jenin. After a Joint Palestinian-Israeli inquiry, Agriculture Minister Tsur concluded that they resolved the matter amicably and that he was satisfied with the Palestinian cooperation.[40]

After Oslo II was ratified and prior to the outbreak of the *al-Aqsa intifada*, Israeli and Palestinians water technocrats met regularly in a rule-based environment, but disputes surfaced. Although a Palestinian water bureaucracy, the Palestine Water Authority, was taking root during this period, a great deal of frustration existed on the Palestinian side over the slow pace of developing and providing West Bank Palestinians with additional water. These delays were caused by Israel's JWC veto power in issuing drilling permits and by location disputes with the Israeli civil administration for the West Bank. Israel, on the other hand, complained about Palestinian activities that have reduced the quality of West Bank groundwater, such as poor sewage management, and charged that Palestinians were stealing water by tapping into Israeli pipelines for irrigation without permission or paying.[41]

Along with other international development aid, the United States played an important role in moving the Oslo II water negotiations forward and promoting cooperation. During the water talks, the US provided the Palestinian Authority with $11 million for the first stage in developing a $40 million wastewater processing plant.[42] Beginning with Egyptian-Israeli talks on Palestinian autonomy in the late 1970s, the United States had argued that the Palestinians must receive water rights in the West Bank, to which Israel did not initially agree. The United States also put pressure on Israel to allocate much more water to the Palestinians.[43] Most of the proposed Palestinian water projects are in Gaza, where water scarcity is most serious. As discussed in chapter 5, Israel and Gaza do not share major water resources, except when Jewish settlements were within Gaza. The Oslo-Jericho redeployment gave the PA control of all water resources within Gaza except for the Jewish settlements. Between fiscal year 1994 and 1998, the United States promised almost $200 million of financial assistance for water projects, more than half of the total US aid obligation to the Palestinians.[44] The US AID assistance to Palestinian water projects has continued through the mid-2000s.[45]

In the summer of 1996, Israeli elections resulted in Labor's defeat by the Likud Party, and Benjamin Netanyahu becoming prime minister. As a result, the peace process slowed, and water issue differences became more prevalent. Netanyahu appointed former Defense Minister Ariel Sharon as national infrastructure minister and Israel's lead water negotiator. Netanyahu was consistently more hawkish on the water issue with the Palestinians than his Labor Party predecessors. The Likud prime minister argued that the Palestinians should have self-government, but not all the powers that come with state sovereignty, "such as control of airspace or control of underground water resources," which might someday threaten Israel.[46] In May 1997, Netanyahu provided a detailed plan of a final status arrangement for the West Bank and Gaza. The Netanyahu Plan proposed to transfer control of less than 40 percent of the West Bank to the PA. Some of the central water-related principles of the plan were that most of the Jordan Valley and major water sources in the West Bank remain under Israeli control.[47] Sharon, a key Netanyahu cabinet member, had influenced the water-related provisions of the Netanyahu Plan by arguing that Israel should annex large tracts of the West Bank that are above important groundwater sources. Sharon had advocated Israel's maintaining control over all groundwater, and not giving Palestinian water rights. However, Sharon said that Israel should offer the Palestinians a substantial increase in water allocations to their urban areas, so that water consumption levels would be equal to those in Israel.[48] Despite this seemingly generous gesture, he failed to specify a source for this additional allocation of water. His plan also recommended that Israel require the Palestinians to build water recycling and sewage systems to protect the West Bank groundwater and to increase available water for Palestinian agriculture. Again, Sharon failed to explain how the Palestinians would fund such expensive projects. Since the beginning of 1997, Sharon had obstructed the US plan to dig three wells in the area of Herodian for Palestinian use. This project was a provision of the Oslo peace accords to be funded by the US government. Israel blocked the $46 million project when Sharon's national infrastructure ministry and the West Bank's civil administration added new conditions for issuing a permit, insisting that Palestinians first submit a sewage treatment plan.[49] Sharon said that "the Palestinians in Hebron . . . I would even say on purpose are polluting our water sources by directing sewage through the Hebron stream." He added, "Our most important aquifer is being polluted by sewage."[50] Although Sharon's sewage accusations seemed somewhat politically motivated, there were some genuine concerns about Palestinian theft of water resources. Israeli news reports have alleged that Palestinians were illegally connecting to Israel's Mekorot West Bank pipelines of the National Water Carrier. It is believed that West Bank Palestinians were stealing 10 mcm of water a year. This water was used by Palestinian growers to irrigate orchards and came at the expense of both Palestinian and Israeli consumers.[51]

During this period, Palestinian frustration with the JWC system and the water scarcity in the West Bank and Gaza increased as did the political rhetoric. Important Palestinian water projects were frustrated by Israeli JWC vetoes.[52] According to the deputy chairman of the Palestinian Water Authority, the Israelis refused to give clearance on more than 130 projects, including 42 wells, 62 lines, and 14 sewage networks worth some $200 million. Some of these projects cleared the JWC, but were held up within the Israeli bureaucracy.[53] Isa Atallah, head of the Palestinian Water Authority in Hebron, said: "It is really frustrating when your children are going thirsty and you see the settlers next door watering their gardens and swimming in their pools."[54] The deputy mayor of Bethlehem noted that "the next war will be over water. I say so to everyone, what kind of peace can there be while we have no water."[55] During the drought summer of 1999, hundreds of Bethlehem Palestinians protested in the streets and burned tires outside of a Palestinian refugee camp, shouting, "We need water" and blaming Israel for the shortages.[56] In fact, by 1999, the per capita use of water in Israel continued to be more than three times that in the West Bank and Gaza Strip.[57] According to Palestinian news reports, the water shortage was a result of Israel's dragging its feet in approving draft plans for many of the proposed West Bank Palestinian water projects. During Netanyahu's term, overall trust and cooperation between Israel and the PA decreased. The Palestinians had been unreceptive to the Netanyahu Plan and had intended to hold Israel to its written commitment to recognize Palestinian water rights. However, until substantive final status negotiations begin on water, this commitment would be almost irrelevant.

In 1999, a Labor-led coalition that was more receptive to negotiating returned to power and Ehud Barak became Israel's prime minister. During this period, there was an intensive push to finalize an Israeli-Palestinian treaty. Back in October 31, 1995, Yossi Beilin, a top aide to Foreign Minister Shimon Peres, and Mohammed Abbas, also know as Abu Mazen, one of Yasser Arafat's closest advisors, completed a secret document subsequently known as the Beilin-Abu Mazen draft accord. The draft was an extensive outline for a final status agreement and the basis for a final peace deal between the Israelis and Palestinians, and it included a short water section. The document was to be delivered to Rabin for review, but on November 4, 1995, an Israeli assassin killed the prime minister, and no action on Beilin-Abu Mazen was taken until the Camp David negotiations of 2000. President Clinton led the final push at Camp David for a treaty and considered the Beilin Abu-Mazen draft a "core idea."[58] However, these negotiations failed and by February 2001, President Clinton's term in office had ended, Ariel Sharon had defeated Ehud Barak in Israel's prime minister election, violence between Israel and Palestinians had resumed, and final status negotiations had ceased.[59] Sharon made clear that the Israeli position during Camp David and subsequent talks was now null and void. George W. Bush's administration pursued a much less active role in promoting progress toward peace. In March 2001, the Bush administration made clear it would not appoint a special Middle East envoy to replace the outgoing Dennis Ross. Secretary of State Colin Powell said, "The United States stands ready to assist, not insist. Only the parties themselves can determine the pace and scope and content of any negotiations."[60]

During the initial phase of the Palestinian *al-Aqsa intifada*, there were nine incidents of West Bank waterworks being intentionally damaged, but there was also an effort to maintain a level of cooperation on water matters between Israel and the PA.[61] The emergence of a community of technocrats during less violent times built confidence that lasted during the *intifada*. During this tumultuous period when many Israelis and Palestinians were killed, when most agreements were being broken, and little confidence existed on either side, the two heads of the JWC—Noah Kinarti for Israel and Nabil al-Sherif for the PA—signed a joint declaration in the presence of American diplomats indicating that water and sewage infrastructure should be spared from the Palestinian-Israeli violence. The declaration called for the two sides to continue to treat sewage and supply water, and for the public not to harm infrastructure or personnel who maintain or repair waterworks.[62] During this time, the declaration translated into many concrete examples of cooperation between Israeli and Palestinian water workers. Chlorine for purifying drinking water was produced in the Haifa area and Mekorot workers continued to meet with their Gaza and West Bank Palestinian counterparts so the chlorine could be delivered to purify Palestinian drinking water. Israeli columnist Zeev Schiff observed that among water technocrats "a unique relationship is being maintained even during this difficult period of military conflict."[63] The presence of this important community of water technocrats has maintained confidence during periods of violent conflict and explains what Schiff called the "unlikely cooperation" of protecting water infrastructure during the cycle of Israel-Palestinian violence.[64] In December 2002, Palestinian Authority's Water Minister Nabil al-Sherif stated that "the only area in which Israelis and Palestinians are continuing cooperation, in spite of 25 difficult months of *intifada*, is water."[65]

As stated earlier, the basis for negotiations is linking security for Israel and self-government for the Palestinians. Therefore, it is not surprising that Israel would bargain for assurances to protect its water resources and the Palestinians would negotiate for greater autonomy in the water sphere, including water rights. Despite these sometimes conflicting demands, the interim agreement has established a formal mechanism for an epistemic community, facilitated increased international aid for Palestinian water projects, and, in general, established focal points for coordination. Even though the political process has disintegrated, Israeli-Palestinian water cooperation continues.[66] It has also been maintained on the multilateral track, as will be discussed. Both sides are highly interdependent on many issues, including water. As in the past with Jordan, the United States or another third party might play a role in linking the water issue to economic or political assistance so that the water issue does not increase political tensions. Rather, it can serve during this transitional period to build confidence so a future political settlement on the water issue will be less difficult. With that said, as in the Jordan-Israel case, the Palestinian-Israeli track is an uneven and imperfect process: Palestinians continue to be frustrated by Israeli vetoes of Palestinian projects in the JWC and in the Israeli bureaucracy, lack of adequate drinking water and agriculture water supply, lack of waterlines to many West Bank villages, absence of access to wells due to Israel's security regulations and the separation fence/wall, and Israeli settler sewage and general pollution of West Bank groundwater. Israelis are frustrated by weak Palestinian water institutions, water stealing, West Bank pirate wells, dangerous and unregulated Palestinian sewage that pollutes shared groundwater, and unpaid water bills owed to Israeli institutions.[67]

THE JORDANIAN-ISRAELI TRACK

After three years of on-and-off negotiations, Israel and Jordan signed a peace treaty in 1994. Israel-Jordan bilateral talks began at the Madrid Conference and continued in Washington for almost two years.[68] By September 1993, immediately after the Oslo breakthrough and following serious movement on the Palestinian track, Israel and Jordan signed a "common agenda," which was a blueprint for a peace treaty. Just after the signing, King Hussein and Prime Minister Rabin met publicly for the first time and signed the Washington Declaration, which, among other things, terminated the state of belligerency between Jordan and Israel, with both states agreeing to seek "a just, lasting and comprehensive peace based on UN Resolutions 242 and 338."[69] Starting in July 1994, bilateral delegations met regularly in the region to negotiate issues of security, water, refugee, border, and territorial issues. On October 26, 1994, less than four months after intense negotiations began, the prime ministers of Israel and Jordan signed a peace treaty, which included thirty articles, six maps, and five annexes.[70] Middle East analysts, such as Robert Satloff, have called the peace accord "a remarkable document" in that "it is filled with mature, creative and principled solutions to common problems."[71] Cooperation is the cornerstone of the agreement, with many references to mutuality and joint efforts. This tone is especially evident in the water-related sections.

From the outset of the negotiations, Jordan stressed the importance of increasing its water supply and improving its economic situation, and Israel emphasized its preference for having a formal peace treaty and "normalization" with a second Arab neighbor. As always, water was an important issue to the Israelis, but, as in the past, it was secondary to the political considerations inherent in a peace treaty with Jordan. For Jordan, several factors, including economic ones, made it necessary to pursue negotiations. The politics of a formal peace treaty were less risky now that the DOP agreement had been signed between Israel and the PLO. Even though there was little movement on the Syrian track, King Hussein felt the time was ripe for an Israel-Jordan peace treaty.[72] After the 1991 Gulf War, US-Jordan relations were strained, and Jordan's economy deteriorated severely. King Hussein understood that a treaty with Israel would greatly improve its relations with the United States, which, in turn, would lead to much needed debt relief and economic assistance.[73]

During the four months of hard negotiations, water and territorial issues were the most difficult matters to resolve. In the end, Jordan held out on the water issue until offered an additional 50 mcm of water a year by Israel. This helped convince King Hussein to sign the treaty. Two months earlier, Israel gave Jordan 4 mcm of water at the request of Prime Minister Rabin. This gesture was aimed at easing Jordan's severe water shortage and creating a better atmosphere for moving the treaty negotiations forward.[74] In a speech before the Knesset, prior to the signing of the treaty, Prime Minister Rabin stated that "Israel agreed to transfer to Jordan 50 mcm of water annually from the northern part of the country."[75] In the end, linking water resources use to normalization played a pivotal role during the talks.

A cornerstone of the Jordanian negotiating strategy was to pursue Johnston Plan allocations and projects in negotiating the treaty with Israel.[76] Jordanian officials endorsed the Johnston Plan during the spring of 1993.[77] In fact, Jordan claimed that the treaty's water sections closely followed some basic principles of its interpretation of the Johnston Plan. First, Jordan received the Yarmouk's water and Israel the Jordan River's. Second, Israel was allocated 25 mcm of Yarmouk water. Third, Jordan stored some of its Yarmouk water in Lake Tiberias. And fourth, Jordan and Israel were to build waterworks to store and divert Yarmouk and Jordan winter water.

Claiming that the water annex precisely follows the Johnston Plan, however, would be inaccurate. The treaty allocates 25 mcm of Yarmouk water plus another 20 mcm to Israel, giving it 45 mcm of Yarmouk water. In addition, under the treaty, Israel is allocated 10 mcm from Jordanian aquifers in the south. During the Johnston negotiations, the riparians did not discuss this water or any other groundwater matters. The additional 50 mcm offered by Israel, according to Haddadin, "was new and not part of the established rights defined under the [Johnston] Plan."[78] In explaining the treaty to the Jordanian Council of Ministers, Haddadin responded to the statement by the minister of water and irrigation that the Johnston allocations were better for Jordan:

> No, sir, they are not better than what we got when we respect the [king's] decision of disengagement [from representing Palestinian interests]. The share of 100 mcm from Tiberias earmarked for the

Kingdom in the Johnston Plan belong[s] to the West Bank, and the reduction in our flow from the Yarmouk is due to Syrian abstraction. Israel's share in it is now confined to 25 mcm per year, split into 12 in the summer and 13 in the winter, better for Jordan than the Johnston Plan by which the Israelis claim their share to be 40 mcm. Besides, we are not entitled to 50 mcm per year of water of drinkable standards. This is above what the Johnston Plan earmarked for Jordan.[79]

Implicit in the Haddadin statement is that the Israelis, not the Jordanians, are responsible for making future water concessions to the Palestinians.

In the end, the Jordanian-Israeli negotiations involved some creative compromises, and water allocation tradeoffs were a major part of the negotiations. First, as with Palestinians, Jordan wanted water rights to be recognized, and Israel wished only to address water allocations.[80] As a compromise, the treaty speaks of "rightful allocations."[81] Second, Israel negotiated for its historical Yarmouk utilization of 40 mcm a year. However, for the past forty years, a central point of Jordanian water negotiations had been that Israel was entitled to only 25 mcm annually from the Yarmouk. Both sides received what they wanted. Israel was allotted 12 mcm during the summer and 13 mcm during the winter.[82] Thus, Jordan was able to argue that Israel's combined summer and winter allocation from the Yarmouk was 25 mcm, the same amount cited in Eric Johnston's 1955 "US-Arab Memorandum of Understanding" on the Jordan Valley Plan, which is considered an integral part of the Johnston Plan.[83] However, Jordan "concedes to Israel" 20 mcm from the Yarmouk during a wet winter in exchange for Israel's transferring 20 mcm of good quality Jordan River water during a dry summer. Thus, Israel ends up with its historical Yarmouk usage of 45 mcm. Finally, Jordan negotiated for more water for its northern city, Irbid. Here Jordan bargained for the transfer of 10 mcm of desalinated water from an Israeli source for Irbid's municipal and industrial sector.[84] In exchange, Jordan allowed Israel to drill wells in the south and pump 10 mcm of water beyond the 7 mcm currently being extracted by Israeli farmers on land under Jordanian sovereignty.[85] For Israel, transferring water from the north to the south is expensive; thus, the increased pumping from the desert aquifer had an economic benefit, making the 10 mcm trade worthwhile, even if the groundwater is of lesser quality (see Table 6-1).[86]

Selling the treaty to the public was of critical importance to the Jordanian government. Since increasing Jordan's water supply was a key peace dividend, Jordanian water experts quickly publicized the water increase after the treaty was signed. Water experts anticipated that, by 2003, 215 mcm more water annually will be available for Jordan. This is equivalent to 26 percent of Jordan's 1994 total water consumption. However, in 1995, Jordan was receiving only 110 to 120 of the expected 215 mcmy. For Jordan to realize its water gains

TABLE 6-1
Allocations in Israel-Jordan Peace Treaty (mcm)

Jordan	Israel
Yarmouk River residual for Jordan	Jordan River residual for Israel
20 from Jordan River Deganya Gates (summer)*	20 from Yarmouk (winter)
10 from desalinated water in north (10 from Deganya Gates (summer) until plant constructed)	10 from Arava groundwater in south
	3 from Jordan River flood storage
50 "additional water"	
	25 from Yarmouk (12 summer; 13 winter)

* The treaty is silent on water distribution during drought years. However, Water Commissioner Gidon Tsur stated that if Israel was unable to pump its 20 mcm from the Yarmouk because of a drought, then Jordan would not receive its 20 mcm from Lake Tiberias ("Officials View Water Section of Treaty with Jordan," *Davar*, 27 Dec. 1994, 7 [FBIS-NES 94-249, 28 Dec. 1994, 32]).

in the treaty, it would need to build two small dams, a desalination plant, and a water transmission system that were specified in the treaty for Jordan, but could only be realized with international funding.[87]

Israel also put the best face on the outcome of the treaty negotiations. Israel's water commissioner Gidon Tsur argued that the treaty would not hurt Israel's water balance: "as far as Israel is concerned, this does not really constitute giving up any water we formerly had, although in long-term hydrological terms this agreement may necessitate a more intensive utilization of the Lake Tiberias basin, on the basis of long-range reservoirs left for the water economy."[88] In fact, Israel was giving up 50 to 90 mcmy of Yarmouk winter water, which Jordan had been unable to capture and store. This water was piped to Lake Tiberias for storage and used in the National Water Carrier. Also, the storage of 20 mcm in Lake Tiberias was a concession because that meant that Israel had that much less space to store its own water.[89]

Until a desalination plant can be built to fill Jordan's rightful water allotment according to the treaty, it must rely on Israel to make up what water cannot be gotten from the Jordan Basin. In June 1995, Israel began supplying water to Jordan following the opening of a pipeline between Lake Tiberias and the King Abdullah Canal. The 3.5 km (2 miles) pipeline, a $5 million project that was jointly financed by the Jordanian and Canadian governments, initially supplied Jordan with 20 mcm over a five-month period. The water is stored in Lake Tiberias during the winter and pumped to Jordan over the summer.[90] According to the treaty, Jordan is also entitled to 10 mcmy of desalinated water. Until the desalination plant is in operation, Israel is transferring an additional 10 mcm during the winter using the same pipeline. Although Lake Tiberias is an important water source in the region, the salinity of its water is a problem and makes the construction of a desalination plant an urgent priority. A total of 20 to 30 mcm of saline spring water from Lake Tiberias is currently diverted to the lower Jordan River in an effort to control the salinity of Lake Tiberias. To desalinate all 20 to 30 mcmy of saline water in the Lake Tiberias region would cost an estimated $100 million with a water cost of $0.50/cm.[91] The 10 mcm for Jordan will be supplied through the Deir-Alla pipeline to improve Amman's urban water supply. In addition to the desalinated water, the Deir-Alla pipeline will also make possible the reclamation of the lower Jordan. Prior to the treaty, it was a dumping ground not only for the 20 to 30 mcm of saline water but also for polluted water from agricultural and industrial sources. Cleaning up this section of the river will facilitate construction of a better system of water storage.

A Jordan River reservoir would benefit Jordan by capturing some of the estimated 90 mcm that is annually lost to the Dead Sea. By building a dam or series of dams on the lower Jordan to capture Yarmouk and Jordan winter floodwater, Jordan plans to secure 20 mcm. According to the treaty, the boundaries of this storage system would be delineated by the confluence of the Yarmouk River and the Jordan in the north and by Wadi Yabis in the south.[92] The primary water sources, which in the past flowed to the Dead Sea, are Yarmouk winter floodwater not absorbed by the King Abdullah Canal (KAC), return flow from agriculture, and overflows from Lake Tiberias and from wadis flowing into the Jordan. After the riparians rehabilitate the river, Jordan is planning to capture an additional 40 mcmy of water suitable for irrigation. Although the reservoir will primarily benefit Jordan, the pact guarantees Israel 3 mcm from this source, and the Israeli government will pump the water southward to irrigate land near the Dead Sea.[93] A total of 60 mcmy would become available to Israeli and Jordanian consumers from this reservoir under current plans. At present, Jordan has completed the Karama Dam at Wadi Malaha and three storage dams southeast of the Dead Sea. All these projects were started after the 1994 Treaty signing and are a Jordanian effort to store more winter flood water.[94]

In other ways, Jordan has already gained more control over its water supply. A weir completed in 1999 directly downstream of the Point 121/Adasiya diversion area for the KAC replaces the sandbags that prior to the treaty controlled the Yarmouk's flow into the KAC.[95] The Adasiya diversion dam, which straddles both the Israel and Jordan side of the Yarmouk River, improves the efficiency of the water flow to Jordan and Israel's water systems.[96] As discussed in earlier chapters, the weir had been a Jordanian priority delayed because of political disputes with Israel prior to 1994. Even with the peace treaty, this important project became enmeshed in political concerns. In fact, the ceremony to inaugurate construction of the weir did not take place until the fourth anniversary of the signing of the peace treaty.[97] Originally scheduled for a year earlier, the project encountered delays when Israel claimed the weir location would destroy an important Israeli archaeological site. The Israeli government preferred a different site, which was on disputed territory claimed by both Syria and Israel.[98] In the end, the weir construction, funded by Jordan, took place on Israeli, nondisputed territory.

A critical provision of the treaty was the stipulation that an additional 50 mcm of water go to Jordan. In the treaty, Jordan and Israel were to cooperate "in finding sources for the supply to Jordan of an additional quantity of 50 million cubic meters per year of water of drinkable standards."[99] By 1996, only 30 mcm of Lake Tiberias water (10 winter, 20 summer) were stored and subsequently transferred to Jordan, far less than the total of 50 mcm of "additional water" to be negotiated after the signing of the treaty.[100] At the time of the treaty signing, Israel was already in a position to pump its allotted 45 mcm from the Yarmouk. And a year after the treaty signing, Israel did begin pumping the Arava groundwater. But for Jordan to use its allocated Jordan River water and augment its share of the Yarmouk River, new water facilities would have to be built as stated in the treaty.

After ratification, some analysts became concerned that Israel in the future might not feel bound to provide this 50 mcm allocation of water. This is because the treaty text does not identify the country or source of the water.[101] As stated previously, this provision was of pivotal importance because it was this commitment by Israel that moved the treaty process forward.[102] According to the treaty, the issue of additional water was to have been resolved by 1995, but, for many reasons, including the Rabin assassination, negotiations were not completed. By the 1996 second anniversary of the signing of the peace treaty, rumblings of discontent began to emerge from Amman. A Jordanian ambassador to Israel was quoted saying that "there has been no translation of the hopes into hard economic facts on the ground—or certainly not at the pace we wanted."[103] The ambassador was referring to the delays in implementing the treaty on matters relating to water and trade. According to a poll conducted by al Sabeel, the Islamic movement's paper, which opposes relations with Israel, 64 percent of Jordanians support terminating the peace treaty with Israel and 74 percent believe that Jordan's water scarcity problems have not improved because Israel is not implementing its obligations under the treaty.[104] But, by 2005, the eleventh anniversary of the signing of the peace treaty, Israel was emphasizing the growing interdependence with Jordan. In fact, two-way trade had reached $185 million dollars. Jordan's government maintained that peace with Israel was an "irreversible strategic choice." Even so, there is still a vocal coalition of Jordanian groups that are strongly opposed to any coordination with Israel.[105]

Jordan used the same international strategy it had employed in the past to realize its preference for increasing its water supply: threatening to cut its political relations with Israel. Prior to the dry 1997 summer, the additional 50 mcm issue reached crisis proportion when, in response to Israeli foot dragging, Crown Prince Hasan canceled his participation in the dedication of a "peace center" he had been scheduled to attend together with Prime Minister Benjamin Netanyahu. This center was at the site where a Jordanian soldier had gunned down seven Israeli schoolgirls. Soon after the cancellation, Netanyahu and King Hussein conducted a secret meeting in Aqaba to resolve the crisis and begin serious negotiations for the 50 mcmy of water.[106] Subsequently, Likud's national infrastructure minister and lead water negotiator, Ariel Sharon, concluded a deal with his Jordanian counterpart Munther Haddadin. The deal was for Israel to send 25–30 mcmy to Jordan from Lake Tiberias and the entire 50 mcmy was to follow from a desalination plant in three years.[107] By May 1997, a total of 55 to 60 mcmy of water began to flow from Israel to Jordan. King Hussein held a public ceremony in which he thanked the Israelis for their cooperation and spoke of the fruits of peace.[108] Sharon indicated that Israel would transfer 50 mcmy of saline water from Israel to Jordan, where the two countries would jointly desalinate it.[109] Until the desalination project was completed, Israel had agreed to supply 25 mcm from Lake Tiberias. This would be in addition to the 30 mcmy that Israel already supplies to Jordan under the first phase of the water agreement.[110]

During the spring and summer of 1997, the controversy over water sharing came to a head. That spring, the Israeli daily *Haaretz* reported that Munther Haddadin and Ariel Sharon had hammered out an agreement to replace specific reservoirs in the Jordan Valley with storage in Lake Tiberias. As discussed in chapter 2, storing Jordanian water in the Israeli lake was a basic but controversial concept from the Johnston Plan, and many of the concerns voiced five decades earlier again stimulated debate after the public learned about the negotiations. The broad idea was again scuttled.[111] As a stopgap measure, Jordan agreed to store 30 to 55 mcm of its water in the lake or from its basin, to be transferred by Israel each year to Jordan, while Lake Tiberias continues to be under exclusive Israeli sovereignty.[112] That summer Jordan experienced an intense heat wave and continued severe water shortages. To make matters worse, water pumped to parts of Amman was contaminated and caused people to be become ill. Several water ministry officials were faulted and charged with negligence. Water Minister Munther Haddadin was relieved of his duties. The water scandal soon led to the fall of the government, which was replaced with a new prime minister and cabinet.[113]

During the spring of 1999, Israel and Jordan were still in the midst of severe drought when Israeli officials proposed that they should not transfer that year the full 55 mcm agreed on up to this point because Israel did not have enough water for its own needs and could not meet its commitment to Jordan. In fact, Israel was slashing its water quota to its farmers and Lake Tiberias was at its lowest level since 1908. The Israeli water commissioner Meir Ben-Meir proposed that the Jordanian cut ought to be proportional to the shortfall in the Israeli supply.[114] The Jordanian prime minister quickly rejected Israel's decision to reduce the water it supplies Jordan, arguing that "the water deal is an official agreement signed by two sides, and we will insist on its implementation as it is."[115] A month earlier King Hussein had died of cancer and his eldest son Abdullah II took the throne. This was the new King's first dispute with Israel. As Ben-Meir noted, a shortcoming of the peace treaty is that it "did not take into account such a crisis."[116] There was considerable domestic political pressure on the Jordanian government and on its new king to reject Israel's attempt to reduce the supply it committed to deliver to Jordan. In a public declaration, Jordan's parliament admonished Israel, stating that "Jordan's water belongs to it by right—it is not a donation or gift of kindness for Israel to grant or withhold as it pleases." Members of the lower house stated that if Israel did not supply the obliged water, such action would represent a "violation—indeed an evasion—of all its peace accords" and "casts doubts on the sincerity of Israel's intensions." The Jordanian prime minister responded to parliament that his government would "accept no concessions" on this water issue.[117] After five weeks of negotiations, Israel decided to convey all the water it committed to supply Jordan. For its part, Jordan agreed to change the water distribution schedule. Israel could give the water to Jordan in the winter instead of the summer and, to Jordan's benefit, supply the water from the Yarmouk instead of storing it in Lake Tiberias where its quality deteriorates.[118] This interim solution was worked out by the Joint Water Committee, some of the same people who worked through difficult problems at the picnic table.

No matter how successful the negotiations were, it was clear that water would remain a contested resource until new facilities for storing water could be constructed. Back in 1996, Jordanian information minister Marwan Muasher had noted that even after Jordan gets everything stipulated in the treaty, it will still have water problems and is looking for other sources. Muasher went on to say that "Jordan's only alternative is to seek additional water sources."[119] He added that while Israel and Jordan would continue to discuss options for increasing their water supply, Jordan was also waiting for financing from countries like Germany because new funds would be needed for water conservation. Lack of funds had prevented Jordan from upgrading its internal pipeline network, which was so old that "about 55 percent of the water goes to waste due to the inefficient distribution network."[120] Germany, through the EU, supported plans to develop some $600 million in water projects in northern Jordan. Germany funded a master plan, which included dams, storage and conveyance plans, and wastewater treatment plants. In 1995, German Chancellor Helmut Kohl promised to support water projects during a visit to Jordan and Israel. In the past three decades, Germany has helped build many of Jordan's water and irrigation programs.[121] In addition, Israeli Prime Minister Rabin, immediately after the treaty signing, asked Japan to provide Jordan with financial assistance in building water projects on the Yarmouk River.[122] Prime Minister Netanyahu also pledged a "financial package" from Israeli and international sources to fund the projects.[123] In 1997, Israel's and Japan's prime ministers met in Tokyo, and Netanyahu appealed for Japanese funding for Jordanian water projects.[124] However, much of these funds have yet to materialize.

Jordan's major water resource project, the building of the Unity (al-Wahdah) Dam on the Yarmouk, has been complicated by the need for Jordan to work with two feuding riparians, Israel and Syria. Jordan's problems with Syria in part stem from Jordan's signing of the peace treaty with Israel. According to some Jordanian officials, Syria is "withholding" from Jordan about 130 mcm of water annually from the Yarmouk River.[125] When King Hussein made a reconciliation visit to Syria in 1996 to try to solve this problem of depletion, it was his first trip to Damascus since relations were strained by Jordan's signing the 1994 peace treaty with Israel. Damascus had accused Jordan of weakening Syria's position by signing a separate agreement with Israel and even went so far as to call Jordan's pact an "apostasy (*kufr*) [and] . . . shamefully wrong."[126] On the 1996 visit, Hussein brought his water minister and other high-ranking officials to conduct serious talks on water and security issues with President Hafez al-Asad.[127] After the success of the reconciliation meeting between Asad and Hussein, a joint Jordan-Syrian panel was reactivated to continue planning for the Unity Dam project. The committee affirmed the commitment of both sides to build the dam. The tunnel on which the body of the dam will be built was already in place, but construction stopped because of funding difficulties and the advent of the 1991 Gulf War.

Since international donors required the approval of all Yarmouk riparians, Jordan had to obtain Israeli consent to the project as well. Even with the Israel-Jordan treaty, members of the Israeli government still indicated reluctance to accept a large Yarmouk dam. After the Asad-Hussein meetings, Israel's agriculture minister Rafael Eitan of the Likud-led government criticized the proposal, publicly maintaining that the decision to renew dam construction on the Yarmouk contradicted the Israel-Jordan peace treaty.[128] By 1998, however, Israel's public statements on the Unity Dam were much more accepting. For example, Israel's water commissioner Meir Ben-Meir told the *Jerusalem Post* that he did not think that Israel's water resources were likely to be affected by the project.[129]

Prospects for the Jordanian dream of a large upstream Yarmouk Dam have improved. Prior to the 1994 treaty, Israel had a de facto veto because, in part, international donors, including the World Bank and the United States, were not willing to finance such projects unless all the riparians approved. At present, Jordan has Arab donors who do not require Israeli acquiescence. The Kuwait-based Arab Fund for Economic and Social Development is providing 80 percent of the funding for the dam. The Abu Dhabi Fund in the United Arab Emirates is funding 10 percent and Jordan is paying the remaining 10 percent. Even so, the treaty with Israel states that "artificial changes in or of the course of the Jordan and Yarmouk Rivers can only be made by mutual agreement."[130] In so doing, the treaty creates a framework for discussing new water projects, including an upstream dam, that would affect other riparians. Israel no longer voices public objections to the Unity Dam, and Syrian-Jordanian relations have continued to warm.

In mid-2003, construction began on the Unity Dam and the project was scheduled to be completed in 2006. However, Syrian-Jordanian disputes over Jordan's Yarmouk water rights and other various reasons have delayed the project's completion.[131] During Israel's 1999 dispute with Jordan over water, Jordan took the initiative to further mend relations with Syria. In April 1999, King Abdullah met with President Hafez al-Asad in Damascus. With political relations improving, bilateral talks focused on issues such as the Unity Dam.[132] In June 2000, Bashar al-Asad became Syria's new president following the death of his father Hafez al-Asad. Both Abdullah and Bashar showed an interest in building stronger bilateral ties. As a means of improving relations, Bashar al-Asad released between 3 and 8 mcm from a Yarmouk dam each year from 1999 to 2001 during the summer to help Jordan with its water shortages and committed to continue to cooperate on building the Unity Dam.[133] Between 2002 and 2004, the two young leaders did not meet, but in early 2004 King Abdullah and President Bashar al-Asad formally launched the Unity Dam project with a ceremony in which the cornerstone and commemorative plaque were unveiled at the dam site.[134] In 2005, Syria and Jordan signed a water memorandum of understanding to increase their water-sharing cooperation. The cost of the dam is $125 million, and it will be 116 meters high and store 110 mcm of water, of which Amman would receive 50 mcmy and Jordanian agriculture 30 mcmy. Syria would receive most of the electricity generated by the dam. In the future, the second stage of the dam construction will raise it to an elevation of 140 meters with a storage capacity of approximately 225 mcm and the dam will generate 18,000 megawatts per hour of electricity.[135]

Another recent water resource project that Jordan plans to embark on with Israel regards an idea that predates the Johnston Plan: to supply Mediterranean or Red Sea water to the Dead Sea. Water planners have long understood that if the upper Jordan flow is diverted for human use, then less water would flow to the Dead Sea. In fact, the Dead Sea has shrunk by almost a third in the past twenty years. The shoreline in some places has receded over one mile. Jordanian water expert Elias Salameh said that "if we don't move fast, there will be no Dead Sea."[136] A project Jordan has been pursuing is to increase the water supply to the Dead Sea through a "Red–Dead" project. A pipeline or canal from the Red Sea—or Mediterranean (Northern or Katif alignment)—would raise the water level of the Dead Sea, and take advantage of the 1,320 foot difference in height between the Red Sea's Gulf of Aqaba and the Dead Sea to generate electricity to desalinate seawater for Jordan (see Map 6-2). A canal would be more expensive, costing three times as much as a pipeline, but would increase tourism to southern Jordan.[137] During a September 2002 Johannesburg Summit Meeting on the Environment and Development, Israel and Jordan announced an accord to build a Red Sea to Dead Sea 200-mile pipeline. The estimated cost for the pipeline is $1 billion and would take two to five years to build.[138] The World Bank will underwrite the pipeline, but an additional $3 billion to $4 billion will be needed to build desalination plants. These plants will produce 850 mcmy of drinkable water, of which two-thirds would be allocated to Jordan and the rest to Israel and the Palestinians.[139] In 2005, the World Bank agreed to partly fund a $20 million feasibility study.[140]

The cooperative, professional relationship established over the previous quarter-century between Jordanian and Israeli water technocrats and policymakers facilitated creative thinking and the rapid negotiations as well as implementation of the treaty.[141] In place of secret meetings, the Joint Water Committee established by the treaty enables Israel and Jordan to better cooperate, communicate, and verify compliance of the agreement.[142] Having worked together for the last quarter century, Israeli and Jordanian water experts not only have confidence in each other but also are well aware of the problems and policies faced by the other side. This awareness, in turn, facilitates quicker and more effective action when conflict or crisis arises over the implementation of the treaty.

The treaty has been successful because both sides have continued to prefer cooperation to conflict. Since the signing of the treaty, there have been a number of water-related differences, but the Joint Water Committee and the political leadership have been able to resolve the issues. Jordan was upset over Israel's slow implementation of the overall water section of the treaty. When Israel did not deliver the 50 mcm of "additional water," Jordan responded by freezing political relations with Israel. As a result, Israel finally began to negotiate seriously on the 50 mcm. By May 1997, the Netanyahu government amicably resolved these issues, and Jordan and Israel began to implement the second stage of the water agreement.[143] Difficulties in implementing the treaty and water shortages will continue, but as long as both sides maintain the preference for water cooperation, international cooperation strategies will continue.

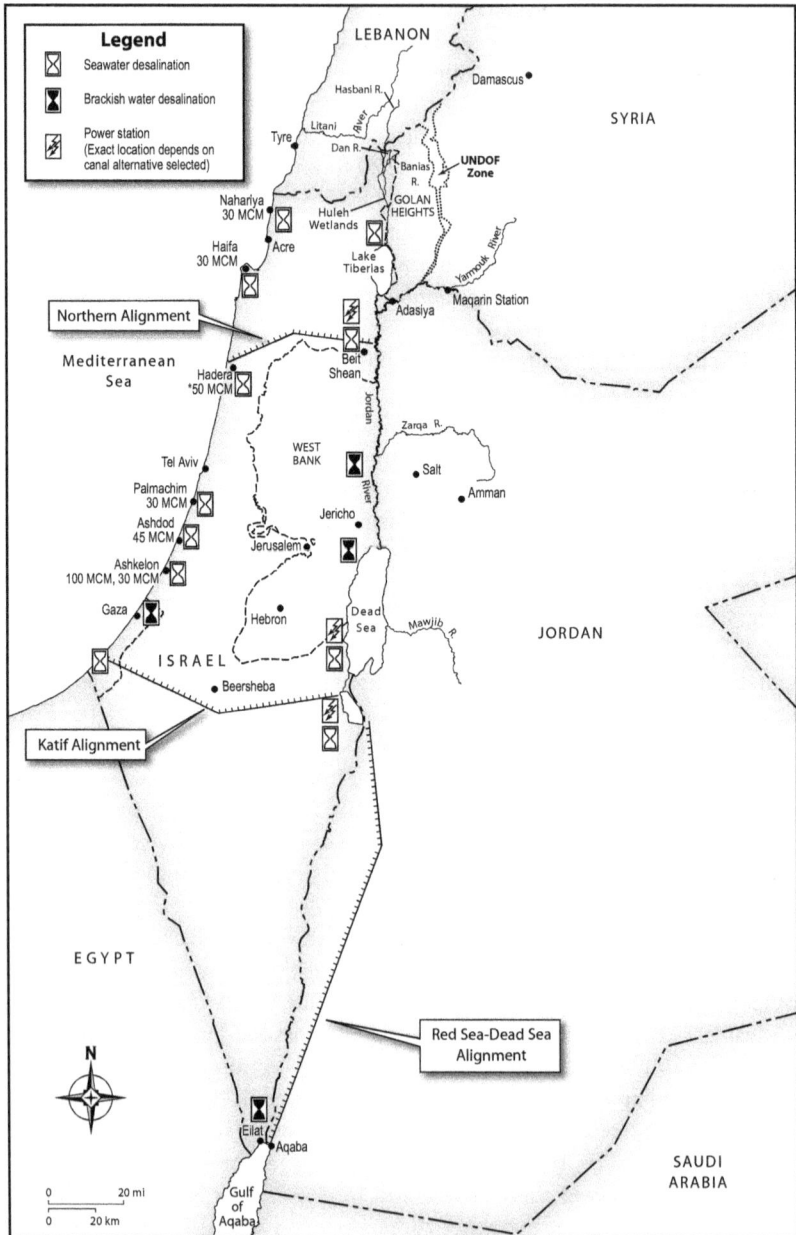

Legend

Seawater desalination

Brackish water desalination

Power station
(Exact location depends on
canal alternative selected)

LEBANON

Damascus

SYRIA

Hasbani R.

Litani
Tyre
Dan R.

Banias
R.
UNDOF
Zone

GOLAN
HEIGHTS

Nahariya
30 MCM

Huleh
Wetlands

Haifa
30 MCM   Acre

Lake
Tiberias

Northern Alignment

Adasiya   Maqarin Station

Mediterranean
Sea

Hadera
*50 MCM

Beit
Shean

WEST
BANK

Zarqa R.

Salt

Tel Aviv

Palmachim
30 MCM

Jericho

Amman

Ashdod
45 MCM

Jerusalem

Ashkelon
100 MCM, 30 MCM

Gaza

Hebron

Dead
Sea

Mawjib R.

JORDAN

ISRAEL

Beersheba

Katif Alignment

Red Sea-Dead Sea
Alignment

EGYPT

N

Eilat
Aqaba

SAUDI
ARABIA

0   20 mi

0   20 km

Gulf
of
Aqaba

*Option available to double production capacity to 100 MCM.
Source: Governments of Israel and Jordan and *Jerusalem Post*.

MAP 6-2   Possible Water Projects

THE SYRIAN-ISRAELI TRACK

Given the different position of the riparians, both ideologically and geograph-ically, than that of Israel and Jordan, the Israel-Syrian negotiations have been more contentious and overtly political. The water resources of the Golan Heights are more critical to Israel than to Syria: a third of Israel's water flows from the Golan Heights area. In addition, Israeli-Syrian relations, unlike Israeli-Jordanian, have always been tense and confrontational.[144] Syria made it clear from the outset of the Madrid process that its primary focus in the negotiations was Israel's withdrawal from the Golan Heights to the border that existed to June 4, 1967. Although security became a primary focus of Israeli-Syrian negotiations, the water issue has also received considerable attention.

Like the Palestinian and Jordanian talks, Syrian-Israeli negotiations began slowly but by the mid-1990s became serious and comprehensive. Following the Madrid Conference, Israeli and Syrian representatives negotiated in Washing-ton within the Madrid framework. In February 1994, talks continued in Wash-ington and moved up to the ambassadorial level. Meetings on security arrange-ments took place between the Israeli and Syrian chiefs-of-staff in December 1994 and June 1995. In December 1995 and January 1996, Israeli-Syrian talks resumed at the ambassadorial level outside Washington at Wye Plantation in Maryland. These discussions became detailed and dealt with not only security matters but also the quality of peace, normalization, and water issues. While no direct talks took place during the Benjamin Netanyahu administration (1996–1999), the election of Ehud Barak restarted the negotiations. Prime Minister Barak stated that Israel would resume negotiations with Syria so as to establish a full peace that would bolster the security of Israel, and would be grounded in UN Security Council Resolutions 242 and 338 that established the land for peace formula. Barak also made it clear that the peace treaty would be submitted to the Israeli people for approval in a referendum.[145] This com-mitment underscored Israel's position that return of the Golan was certainly not ruled out at this point, even though that area had been formally annexed by Israel. The Israeli-Syrian negotiations resumed in December 1999 from the point where they had halted in January 1996.[146] Discussions included Presi-dent Clinton in Washington followed by a round of talks between Prime Min-ister Barak and Syrian Foreign Minister Farouk al-Shara in Shepherdstown, West Virginia, January 3 to 11, 2000. The negotiations were to have resumed on January 19, but were called off. In March, President Clinton attempted to restart the talks at a meeting with Hafez al-Asad, but the summit did not result in a resumption.

Prior to the Wye Plantation round, Syria had made it clear that its focus in the negotiations was political: Israel's withdrawal from the Golan Heights to the border that existed prior to June 5, 1967. But these political negotiations over the border relate directly to the water issue. Syrian representatives consequently showed no interest in Israeli demands for normalization of relations between the two states or a withdrawal to the 1923 international boundary of Palestine, which would leave the Syrian border 10 meters from Lake Tiberias. The lead Syrian negotiator, Ambassador Walid al-Moualem, claimed that the issue is not strategic but an issue of sovereignty: "Every inch of our land is sacred to our people."[147] The 1967 border demanded by Syria would extend its territory virtually to the northeastern waters of Lake Tiberias. The French and British colonial powers in 1923 had set international boundaries for northern Palestine that did not include Syria almost bordering on Lake Tiberias' water line. These borders were subsequently altered when the Syrian army took control of some of the territory during the 1948 Arab-Israeli War. Syria did withdraw its forces from some disputed areas that subsequently became demilitarized zones. If Israel agreed to return to the 1967 line extending to the lake, it feared that Syria would then demand Lake Tiberias water and fishing rights. Israel would also lose the water-rich Hamat Geder enclave, part of the Yarmouk River bank, the cliff overlooking the southern Lake Tiberias basin, and the area around the Banias falls.[148] So the 1967 border that carried so much political weight also delineated who would get precious water resources.

Although Israeli negotiators recognized the division of water resources as a fundamental element of a successful peace treaty, they did not insist on tackling this issue at the Wye Plantation talks. Prime Minister Rabin said that the greatest danger Israel has to face in the talks with Syria was the possibility of Israel's losing control of the Golan Heights' water resources.[149] When Peres became prime minister, he said that "without a solution to the water problem, we will not have any agreements."[150] Israeli analyst Zeev Schiff agreed, arguing that water is "of the highest strategic importance." However, during the Wye Plantation talks, Peres government negotiators did not define water as an important agenda item.[151] The Rabin government was prepared to withdraw to the 1923 international border in exchange for suitable security arrangements and full normalization of relations, which Israel termed a qualitative peace. Rabin negotiated for the demilitarization of large areas and a reduction in the Syrian military.[152] He also made clear that approval of a treaty would depend on national referendum. Israeli negotiators for both the Rabin and Peres governments had accepted the principle of withdrawal from the Golan Heights in the context of a peace settlement. This peace settlement with Syria should address key issues for Israel, including: (1) the depth of the withdrawal; (2) the schedule and duration for withdrawal; (3) a link between political and economic normalization and withdrawal; and (4) agreement over security arrangements.[153] At these meetings, the Syrians agreed for the first time to negotiate on what full peace for Syria would entail. The quality of peace, normalization of relations, and water were discussed.[154] While they conducted a detailed negotiation, Syria and Israeli negotiators made few of these details public.[155] According to lead Israeli negotiator Itamar Rabinovich, Israel planned to negotiate possible water-sharing plans with the Syrians during the 1996 Wye talks, but, according to Rabinovich, Syrian envoy Walid al-Moualem's message was that "if Israel and the United States undertake to help Syria with its water problems with Turkey, there will be no water problem between Syria and Israel."[156]

The 2000 Shepherdstown negotiations were halted indefinitely because, in general, Syria said it would not return to the negotiations until Israel agreed to withdraw to the June 4, 1967, border. Barak indicated that disagreement came down to Israel's control of Lake Tiberias and security arrangements following a withdrawal from the Golan, including the status of the early warning station on Mount Hermon.[157] The primary obstacle to an Israeli-Syria peace treaty was disagreements over Syria's water rights to Lake Tiberias. By demanding the June 4 border instead of the 1923 border, Syria would gain a small slice of land on the northeast coast of the lake, which Barak feared would give Syria access to Israel's primary reservoir of freshwater. Such a concession might, among other things, negatively impact the outcome of an Israeli referendum on the treaty.[158] In numerous speeches, Barak pledged that no Syrian soldiers would "wash their feet in the Kinneret (Lake Tiberias)."[159] At a press conference with President Clinton, after the end of Shepherdstown talks, Foreign Minister David Levy said that "the entire Sea of Galilee, including the northern shore, must remain under full Israeli sovereignty."[160] In response, Hafez al-Asad is reported to have told President Clinton that "I have held barbecues at the Sea of Galilee, swam in its waters, sat on its shores, and eaten fish from it. I have no intention of giving it up."[161] The ruling Baath party's newspaper *al-Baath* stated in a front-page editorial that "Syria will defend those meters and all its rights in water with everything in its hand, and she is ready to wait for many years for these meters."[162]

After the Shepherdstown talks ended, the Israeli newspaper *Haaretz* published a leaked draft of an Israel-Syria Peace Treaty, which the US government put together for review by the parties and which shows how close the parties had come to a lasting agreement. Although the detailed annexes were not part of the document, there was a section on borders and water.[163] According to Israeli negotiator Yossi Beilin, the proposals "were essentially opening positions that still required extensive negotiations."[164] Unfortunately, those negotiations never took place. At present, important bridging ideas are needed to resolve differences on the water issue.

The water resources of the Golan region are critical to Israel but less so to Syria, which is much more concerned about its Euphrates supply. Six hundred mcm, or one-third of Israel's water, comes from the Golan region and almost 500 mcm flows from the upper Jordan tributaries.[165] Approximately 110 mcm of the remaining water either flows as springs to Lake Kinneret (60 mcm) or is used for Golan settlements from wells or artificial reservoirs on the heights (35 mcm) or from Hamat Gader (15 mcm). Since 1967, Israel has utilized all of the 110 mcm of water that previously flowed into Lake Tiberias through its bottling industry and a system of water reservoirs.[166] If Israel withdraws from the Golan, and Syria builds reservoirs for rainwater and drains the Banias River flow for Damascus, Israeli analysts believe the potential water loss to Israel could be as much as 200 mcmy. However, this scenario would require the Syrians to build large and expensive waterwork projects. On the other hand, Syria could use some 110 mcmy from the existing Israeli infrastructure without much effort or investment. During the Peres government, Foreign Minister Ehud Barak stated that Israel would leave the Golan water industry, which previously flowed to Lake Tiberias, to the Syrians if they guaranteed Israel's remaining water rights.[167] Furthermore, Israel is concerned about future pollution. Water Commissioner Meir Ben-Meir stated before a Knesset committee in January 2000 that "if the Syrians settle the Golan with hundreds of thousands of inhabitants, who do not handle sewage and pollution in a proper fashion, this will spell doom for the Kinneret—without any doubt."[168]

Although Syria was a water-rich country, it now faces serious problems in this area. In 1970, Syria's population was 6 million; by 2006, it had tripled to almost nineteen million. Official forecasts put the 2010 total at 24 million. According to a professor of hydraulic engineering at the University of Damascus, in 2001 "full supply matches full demand." In fact, according to the head of the Syrian water agency, summer demand in Damascus is now fifteen times the amount available.[169] The supply is roughly 20 billion cubic meters, a figure that dwarfs the Israeli, Jordanian, and Palestinian supply, which together adds up to a little more than 3 billion cubic meters. The Yarmouk and even all of Lake Tiberias are insignificant compared to Syria's primary source of water, the Euphrates. Still, the Syrian capital Damascus alone needs some 273 mcmy, but receives only half that. Damascus, like Amman, is now known for its draconian water rationing.[170] In large part, poor Syrian water management has created summer water shortages in Damascus and Aleppo. In 1977, the World Bank could not account for an estimated 30 percent of the domestic water supply in Syria's nine largest cities. According to Syrian sources, the discharge of sewage systems and industrial effluents contaminates most small- and medium-sized rivers in the country. Groundwater in Aleppo and Damascus is also highly polluted.[171] To make matters worse, Turkish water development upstream has continuously decreased the Euphrates flow to Syria.[172] In 1996, Syria started implementing relatively small projects sponsored by the UN Development Program to conserve and protect water resources. The five-year

$9 million program rehabilitated a number of water networks and controlled some of the pollution.[173] By the mid-2000s, Syria was receiving from Japan and Germany development aid to improve its domestic water infrastructure.[174] Because of water shortages, Syria has in turn aggressively developed the Yarmouk basin using water that would have flowed to Jordan and Israel.

Prime Minister Shimon Peres said that the issue of water between Israel and Syria required a two-tier solution: first, Turkey must supply water to Syria, and, second, Syria must increase the river flow to Jordan and Israel. In the late 1980s, as part of its Southeast Anatolia Development Project (GAP), Turkey reduced the Euphrates flow into Syria from 850 cm/second to 500 cm/second. This reduction created tension between the two states. Some argued that Syria's past support of the Kurdish rebels in Turkey was an effort to pressure Turkey to increase Syria's Euphrates' flow.[175] This history between Turkey and Syria complicated negotiations with Israel. During the Syrian-Israeli negotiations in early 1996, an aide to Prime Minister Peres told reporters that the Americans were talking to Israel about a water arrangement between some of the Euphrates and Jordan riparians. The scheme "would not necessarily mean a pipeline from Turkey, but rather an agreement on how much water should be transferred among the states."[176]

The Jaffee Center report, discussed in chapter 5, offered a model for settling this conflict that balances Israel's need for verification with the problem of territorial control. The Jaffee Center report insists that any security arrangement with Syria would be impossible without a solution to the water problem.[177] The report recommended that Israel do its utmost to retain the water sources currently under its control and make concessions in this domain only if diplomatic benefits are guaranteed. The report added that Israel's water compromises would be conditional on a clear promise from international donors that they would fund Israeli importation of water from an outside source and finance water desalination projects. The report also recommended that Israel preserve its right to supervise water sources and basins so as to ensure water supply and quality. The threat of water pollution of Lake Tiberias and overexploitation of the area water supply make it necessary for Israel to verify Syrian compliance in an agreement. It emphasized that if Israel returned to the 1967 borders, "Golan water—40 [to 100 mcmy]—will switch from Israeli to Syrian hands. Without appropriate cooperation arrangements, the threat that the Jordan River sources might be diverted will rise again."[178] The study stated that Syria was likely to develop the Golan region—in a manner similar to how it has developed the Yarmouk basin—and retain increasing quantities of Lake Tiberias basin water in its territory.

In sum, the report implies, but does not explicitly state, that, with supervision and verification, territorial control may not be necessary. Thus, the report suggests an "ultimate withdrawal line," which would leave Israel only a small portion of the Golan, not far from the 1967 border. This line would nonetheless enable Israel, in a noncooperative environment with Syria, to preserve minimum control over its Golan water resources. With full cooperation, the report states, it would be possible to supervise the exploitation of water resources in the Golan. The study recommends that a Syrian agreement should provide that Damascus streamline existing facilities and not enlarge Golan water reservoirs. Israel should demand "maximum supervision of the Jordan's resources, including the Hermon tributary of the Banias, and the Wazani fountains, which feeds the Hasbani. Israel should ensure supervision of water exploitation in the Golan throughout the territory west of the basin line along the waterfall's axis."[179] During the Israel-Syria peace talks in Shepherdstown, the cost (which Israel would ask the United States to pay) to cover the withdrawal and evacuation of Israeli settlements, and to aid in the expansion of the Israeli water network, including the construction of desalination plants to replace water lost because of the withdrawal, would amount to $17.4 billion.[180]

The proposed solution to the Israel-Syria water disagreement, which is holding up the treaty, is that Syria would agree not to take water from tributaries of the Jordan River, but would obtain a greater supply from the Euphrates. This would depend on Turkey's cooperation. To compensate Turkey for increasing the flow into Syria, Washington would increase its financial aid to Ankara.[181] Turkey's response to these proposals, however, was far from enthusiastic. Turkish diplomatic sources stated that "Israeli-Syrian peace cannot be reached through Turkey."[182] In other words, the idea of Ankara making concessions on the water issue was out of the question at this point. Since there is no community of Syrian-Israeli water technocrats, it is up the academics or the US government to come up with ideas to bridge the gap between Israel and Syria on the water issue.

THE LEBANESE-ISRAELI TRACK

Because of Syrian influence over Lebanon's policies, it is doubtful that there will be movement on this track until there is approval from Damascus. Within the Madrid framework, Israel and Lebanon engaged in more than a dozen rounds during bilateral talks between 1991 and 1994 in Washington. Since 1994, there have been no Israeli-Lebanese negotiations. According to the Israel Ministry of Foreign Affairs, "Israel has clarified to the Lebanese that it makes no claims to Lebanese land or resources, and that its primary concern is for security on its northern border."[183] In the past, water has been a secondary issue in Israeli-Lebanese relations. However, protection of the upper Jordan's Hasbani tributary, which rises in Lebanon, is now an Israeli concern, while Lebanon will probably seek assurances from Israel that it has no future claims on Litani water.[184] Shortly after the Israeli army withdrew from southern Lebanon in May 2000, it was reported that the Lebanese had constructed a pipeline from the Hasbani. By March 2001, the Israeli government had protested to Lebanon and Syria via the United Nations over the building of a pumping station and pipeline.[185] The United Nations and the United States initially rejected Israel's complaints; the US ambassador to Lebanon said that "Lebanon [is] perfectly entitled to use the water." A UN spokesman said that the Lebanese are "building a four-inch pipe to carry water from the [Hasbani] river to a poor village lacking water. You don't divert a river with a pipe so small."[186] Even though Lebanon says it will be pumping no more than 10 mcmy, much less than the 35 mcmy allocated to it under the Johnston Plan, the Israelis are skeptical. According to Mekorot chairman Uri Saguy, the long-term plan of the Lebanese is to pump 50 mcmy, which is unacceptable to Israel. By fall 2002, Prime Minister Ariel Sharon warned the Lebanese government that their water project could become a "*casus belli*." Lebanese President Emile Lahoud responded that the Hasbani use was "final and irreversible." A Hezbollah official warned that "the hand of Israel would be cut off" if it interferes.[187] The United States, France, and United Nations facilitated an end to the crisis, but the division of the Hasbani will need to be addressed.[188]

THE MULTILATERAL TRACK

The multilateral track was designed to bring states outside the region into contact with the core states, as a way to pool resources and ideas. The multilateral track has played an important role in organizing a broader community of water experts who have created new ideas for solving old water problems and providing a forum for international donors and core states to work together, while developing the foundation for water-sharing institutions. The multilaterals will not resolve the region's political issues, but the process does have important long-term peacemaking value in that material issues are addressed and greater confidence is established among core party technocrats and elites. On the other hand, like bilateral negotiations, multilaterals often are held hostage to events on the ground or larger political considerations.

In January 1992, at the Moscow opening meeting for the multilaterals, the architect of the Madrid Peace Process, US Secretary of State James Baker, explained the aim of the multilateral negotiations. In his opening remarks to the first organizational meeting and the starting point for this track of the peace process, he stated that, first, the multilaterals are "intended as a complement to the bilateral negotiations: each can and will buttress the other."[189] The multilaterals will build confidence that will facilitate further cooperation among the parties. Second, the multilaterals are to "address those issues that are common to the region and that do not necessarily respect national boundaries."[190] The five multilateral working groups were water resources, the environment, refugees, arms control, and security and regional economic development. These issues require technical multilateral cooperation and have the potential of providing mutual benefits. Third, the multilateral track was meant to widen the reach of the negotiations: "these issues can be best addressed by the concerted efforts of the regional parties together with the support of the international community and the resources and expertise that it can provide."[191] Unlike the bilateral negotiations, the multilaterals invite participation by states other than the core actors—Israel, Jordan, Syria, Lebanon, and the Palestinians. As Baker pointed out, the organizers had intended the multilateral talks to create an avenue in which the international community could provide help in the process. Beyond the expertise and experience available for resolving these regional issues, the financial resources of the international community would continue to be an important incentive to encourage the core states to continue the Madrid Peace Process.[192] In sum, the objective of the multilaterals was to find solutions for key regional problems and normalize relations among Middle Eastern states by negotiating in a multilateral forum, which included states from outside the region.

Prior to the Oslo breakthrough, the multilaterals held additional workshops and other activities between rounds of the multilaterals, even during those periods when the bilateral negotiations were disrupted or deadlocked due to events or politics in the region. The multilaterals maintained the idea that the peace process was still alive during this time. Finally, when political breakthroughs occurred, such as the Palestinian-Israeli DOP and the Jordanian-Israeli Peace Treaty, the multilaterals helped accelerate the entire process. The multilateral negotiations provided an important forum for expressing concerns, developing solutions, and assessing reactions. By continuously interacting and exchanging information and opinions, the participants better understood the central negotiating issues. Through this learning process, the participants discovered which ideas and projects would work and what would not, and how to cooperate in solving problems.

The system of working groups promoted consideration of functional, nonpartisan issues, leaving political issues for the bilateral talks. Each working group functioned on a consensus basis, with every participant having a veto. This policy limited discussions to only noncontroversial issues. In addition, official minutes of the proceedings were not recorded and media access was minimal. The goal was to allow participants to raise issues and concerns without the handicap of political bargaining and posturing for the press. In fact, the water group did most of its work between the meetings, including training

seminars, organizational meetings, and preparation for the larger studies. At
the end of each meeting, the gavel holder, which was the name given to the
party responsible for chairing meetings, defining the agenda, and preparing
documents, also produced a one or two-page statement outlining the achievements of the meeting.[193] Even though these were publicly distributed documents, they provided little insight or understanding of the proceedings or the
working group.

The United States was the gavel holder for the working group on water
resources and treated it as a chance to build expertise among the participants.
The group met formally nine times between 1992 and 1996.[194] Between these
plenary meetings, the water group held frequent intersessional programs.
These intersessional gatherings continue today, even though there has not been
a plenary session since 1996.[195] Workshops that trained professional water personnel were an important part of the water working group's intersessional programs. The working group organized fourteen priority courses, including a UN
track on regional water cooperation and management. The seminars also
included a US workshop on weather forecasting, an Australian seminar on
rainfall enhancement, and a Dutch training course on groundwater modeling.
While these workshops served an important function by educating Middle
East water personnel, they also created lasting personal relations and broke
down decades' old psychological barriers to cooperation. Initially, however,
some participants, criticized the seminars because of the disparity in the technical capabilities of the trainees and the problems inherent in having key personnel away for extended periods.[196]

Larger political considerations often constrained the effectiveness of the
multilaterals. For example, there was consensus that to manage the water
resources of the Jordan River properly, basin-wide cooperation and agreements
were necessary. However, Syria and Lebanon had refused to participate in all
multilateral talks, including those on water, until there was progress in their
bilateral negotiations with Israel. Syria also attempted to pressure other Arab
states to do the same. Damascus's position was an ongoing obstacle to properly
addressing water scarcity problems, in particular because Lebanon and Syria
were upstream riparians.[197] To further complicate matters, from the Madrid
Conference until October 1992, Israel's Likud government insisted that the
Palestinians participate as part of the Jordanian delegation. The new 1993
Labor-led coalition did not object to Palestinian delegates from the Diaspora
to attend meetings as long as they were not members of the PLO. With the
September 1993 Oslo breakthrough, Israel did not object to PLO members
being active and leading participants.

Prior to the Oslo I agreement and the Israeli-Jordanian Peace Treaty signing, political issues often bogged down the multilateral talks, especially concerning the question of water rights. In the early rounds, the Jordanians and

Palestinians were determined to address water rights within the multilateral framework. The Palestinians, however, linked the multilateral to the bilateral negotiations: "The question of water within regional cooperation, which this working group will be dealing with, cannot be separated as far as we are concerned, from the question of water in a bilateral Palestinian-Israeli issue."[198] During the May 1992 Vienna round, the Palestinians even hinted that they might boycott important intersessional multilateral activities "if Israel [did] not return to the Palestinians' water rights." After the Vienna meeting, Dan Zaslavsky, the head of the Likud's appointed delegation and the Israeli water commissioner, attacked the Palestinian position, stating that "the Palestinians did not speak about water even once throughout the conference. They only spoke about politics."[199] The Israelis had hoped that these talks would focus on technical issues and joint water projects, with the bilateral talks addressing the political issue of water rights. The politics of Palestinian water rights, however, dominated the first four rounds of the multilaterals.[200] As late as April 1993, the Palestinians were still threatening a boycott, but, by May 1993, they and the new Labor-appointed delegates quietly worked out their differences. The Israeli and Palestinian delegations signed an agreement to create a water working group as part of the bilateral talks. In return, Palestinians agreed to continue their participation in the multilaterals. In the fifth round, water rights continued to be discussed, but did not dominate the talks as the issue had in the past.[201] Jordan, too, occasionally used the multilateral talks to air a political grievance. A year after the Palestinian challenge, in April 1994, Jordan boycotted the water talks, sending only one observer in protest over the US inspections of shipping bound for Jordan's Aqaba port. The inspectors were mandated by UN sanctions on Iraq. Jordan threatened to block any progress at the Muscat round by using the consensus rule to stymie the negotiations.[202] The water rights debate and the Jordan protest against US inspections are both examples of how participants can hold the multilateral talks hostage to political issues.

As the water working group progressed, so did Israeli water policy. In the initial multilateral rounds, the Likud government maintained the traditional, anti-interdependence, "go-it-alone" Israeli water policy. Zaslavsky stated that "Israel doesn't want to become dependent for water on any neighboring country, even in peacetime."[203] With the election of Labor and its new negotiators, however, a dramatic shift occurred in water policy, even before the Oslo breakthrough. During the November 1993 Beijing Working Group meeting, the new Labor government brought in former Agriculture Minister Avraham Katz-Oz to be the lead Israeli delegate. He surprised the Palestinians and Jordanians by indicating Israel's willingness for close cooperation with other core states. Katz-Oz tied the policy change to Israeli's recognition that the growing regional populations will need an additional billion cubic meters of water a year in the near future.[204] Most surprisingly, he changed Israel's negotiating policy without consulting the team responsible for bilateral negotiations with Palestinians. Because of Katz-Oz's efforts, the multilateral talks resulted in the recognition of Palestinian water rights and helped to establish the Palestinian Water Authority. While all these developments had a significant impact on the peace process and would not have occurred without the multilateral track, these changes were mostly a result of competitive, noncoordinated Israeli bureaucratic politics.[205]

The water working group covered many important issues and, unlike the bilateral negotiations, addressed many future water problems. In a paper presented to the water working group, the US delegates outlined the objectives for the group in the "gavel holder's thoughts on water in the future." The United States stated that water scarcity is a difficult, long-term problem that has "no easy fixes." Solutions will be expensive, require careful planning and analysis, and "painstaking negotiations." According to the gavel holder, the role of the working group is to identify the extent of the problem and then to begin substantive discussion and action on addressing those problems. The essential question for the water working group is "how to supply adequate water to a growing population at an affordable cost."[206] By 1998, the participating parties reached a consensus that "although each core party has some limited potential of unexploited local water resources and can improve efficiency of water use, the future gap can only be covered through provisions on new and additional water to the region."[207] The working group's agenda items include: (1) enhancement of data availability, (2) water management and conservation, (3) enhancement of water supply, and (4) concepts of regional cooperation and management.[208] The group's work focuses on these themes and the multilateral projects are organized within these four categories (see Figure 6-2).

The first agenda item for each meeting was the enhancement of data availability. For a region to better plan for the future, it critically needs reliable and verifiable water data. Water planners and managers require dependable data to prioritize water projects. By sharing such information, participants also establish greater trust between users of shared water resources. The project is also designed to improve technical capabilities of core party technocrats, especially capacity building in the PA.[209] In an effort to improve regional water information, the United States, Norway, EC, France, Canada, the Netherlands and the core parties established an Executive Action Team (EXACT). The project charged Israeli, Jordanian, and Palestinian water officials with establishing a reliable, standardized system for regional water data collection. This data bank gives water planners access to reliable data, a weak area prior to the peace process and one that still needs much work.[210] In the early and mid 1990s, most ideas for this project and related activities came from the donors. More recently, Palestinians, Jordanians, and Israelis have become the driving force. Now, according to David Satterfield, a high-ranking US State Department official,

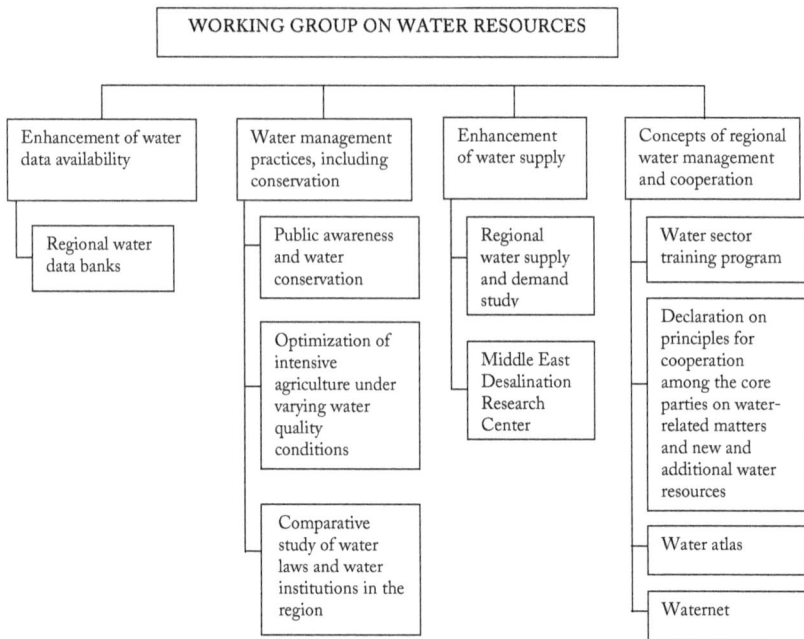

Source: "From Contention to Cooperation," 9.

FIGURE 6-2   The Project Portfolio of the Multilateral Working Group on Water Resources

the core parties "meet among themselves regularly to discuss and agree on a direction for the [regional water data banks] project and new activities they want to propose to donors."[211]

The second item was "efficient use of supplies," or better water management, efficiency, and conservation. The water working group approved several projects aimed at improving the efficient use of water for agriculture, the major water consumer in the region. Luxembourg headed a study that examined how to increase Gaza farmers' income under varying water conditions.[212] Austria supported a program to study how better to use marginal water for irrigation. Both the United States and Britain examined projects for wastewater treatment methods in small communities and their potential value for agriculture. The working group also approved an Israeli-led project for the increased efficiency of municipal water supply systems in the region. This was the first time that an Israeli proposal had been accepted within any of the five multilateral working groups. The objective of the project was to examine a number of medium-sized communities in the region for water loss because of old, low-quality pipes and pumps. With some towns losing more than 60 percent of their water to poor delivery systems, the plan recognized that improved systems could significantly increase the supply of water.[213] The World Bank also undertook a related survey of water conservation in the West Bank, Gaza, and Jordan. The working group tried to involve the public. Civic awareness increased through television, radio, and print messages on the need to conserve water. Since 2002, the United States has led a public awareness and water conservation project that incorporates into the Israeli, Jordanian, and Palestinian school curriculums a regional perspective to understanding water scarcity.[214] The working group even considered a more controversial suggestion by the US gavel holder "that domestic pricing policies, to the extent possible, [should] more accurately reflect the true costs of water for all."[215] The working group has largely failed to examine water pricing, for the most part because it is so politically controversial in Israel, Jordan, and the PA areas.

Academic, or second track talks, took up some of these questions that were too controversial for the negotiating groups. Since 1992, there have been numerous conferences and meetings among scholars on the water issue.[216] More recently, programs such as the Harvard Middle East Water Project have actively brought together Israeli, Palestinian, and Jordanian experts to discuss water-related issues and new ideas. This project, in particular, has focused on the pricing issue, arguing that domestic water pricing systems, which more accurately reflect the true cost of water, would make for more rational international negotiations.[217] Also, the Palestine Consultancy Group and the Harry S. Truman Research Institute for the Advancement of Peace at Hebrew University have come together for workshops on the "Joint Management of Shared Aquifers" and have already made substantive contributions to the Palestinian-Israeli negotiations.

The third agenda area for the working groups was to "develop additional water resources," including water importation, marketing, and desalination.[218] The US gavel holder emphasized the importance of carefully studying the long-term political, technological, and economic implications of each of these projects. One of the first projects of the Working Group was a German and World Bank sponsored study of supply and demand in Israel, Jordan, Gaza, and the West Bank. The objective was to establish specific proposals for increasing the water supply to the region through a comprehensive long-term demand forecast, a plan for future regional water management, and an action program for increasing the water supply.[219] As discussed later, this project recommended, among other ideas, the joint development of prototype desalination plants on the Mediterranean and Gulf of Aqaba.[220]

The ambitiousness of the water importation plans this working group considered varied according to the political outlook and economic circumstances of the time. Water importation plans, including moving water overland through pipelines (such as the Turkish "peace pipeline") or by sea in tankers or large bags, received considerable attention prior to the initiation of the Madrid Peace Process.[221] The first five rounds of the multilaterals generated much discussion about these and other mega projects. The "peace pipeline" was to convey water from Turkey to Jordan River riparians and to the Gulf states. The price of the pipeline just for Israel was an estimated $500 million.[222] As noted earlier, the United States, Jordan, and Israel discussed different canal proposals in their trilateral negotiations, including proposals for canals and pipelines between the Dead Sea and the Red Sea and the Dead Sea and the Mediterranean (see Map 6-2). These ambitious projects received attention at the first two economic conferences, but were barely mentioned in the literature circulated by the core states during the third economic conference in Cairo. By the April 1994 Water Working Group meeting in Muscat, substantive discussion shifted from mega projects, or so called pipe-dream endeavors, to smaller projects that would be less expensive. The belief in a massive peace dividend had waned and Middle East water technocrats began to have serious doubts about the design of the mega projects, as well as their economic and political feasibility. The multilateral talks during this period steered water delegates toward pursuing more "practical and realistic" projects.[223] Emphases shifted again at the end of the 1990s. With a multiyear drought and renewed attention given to the shrinking Dead Sea, there was new interest in pursuing larger projects. In 2002, Jordan and Israel agreed to build a $3 billion to $5 billion Red–Dead pipeline and 780–850 mcmy desalination system, as mentioned above. That same year Israel and Turkey signed a $1 billion agreement over a 20-year period for Israel to buy Turkish water (50 mcmy) and for that water to be delivered in cleaned fuel tankers. By 2005, both Israel and Turkey agreed to cancel the deal because it proved prohibitively expensive.[224] That same year, ministers from Jordan, Israel, and the Palestinian Authority signed a feasibility study agreement for the implementation of the Red–Dead Canal. The World Bank is a key donor for the study and for the project.[225]

Other creative solutions to water shortages or surpluses have included innovative marketing ideas and new technologies for utilizing existing water resources. The working group has proposed setting up water markets, where Jordan River basin riparians might sell or trade surplus water to water poor riparians. Although the United States emphasized that surplus states would not lose their water rights, the scheme is problematic at this point because Syria and Lebanon, the only two riparians that might have a water surplus to sell or trade, are not presently participating in the multilateral peace process.[226]

The working group has also considered large-scale seawater desalination as a way to make use of previously unusable water resources. Oman has led the effort and established a Middle East Desalination Research Center in Muscat whose goal is to develop technology to make desalinated water a more cost-effective option for the Middle East. The center has also provided training and education for desalination-related activities. The Water Working Group has continually and enthusiastically backed the center: The United States, Oman, South Korea, Japan, and the EC have developed an action plan and funded the multimillion-dollar project.[227] Such a project shows how the multilateral track provides a venue for regional actors, in the case the Gulf States, to play an active role in the peace process. For both Israel and Oman, mitigating water scarcity and expanding political relations are common interests. Thanks to advances in seawater desalination, Israel has decided to aggressively increase its Mediterranean coast desalination capabilities (see Map 6-2). This is possible, in part, because of the reduction in cost. At an Ashkelon plant, for example, high-quality drinking water will cost approximately $0.52 a cubic meter. This is half the price for desalinated water in 2000. Advances in reverse osmosis technology and innovations such as building a power plant as part of the unit have reduced the energy costs of desalination.[228] Aiman Jarrar, head of the Palestinian Water Authority's regulatory directorate, stated that "the Palestinians realize that one of the solutions of water shortages in [the]Gaza Strip is desalination." According to news reports, Israeli and Palestinian officials have quietly been discussing the possibility of increasing the output of the Ashkelon desalination plant to 120 mcmy, with 20 mcmy being piped five miles to Gaza.[229]

In some cases, the working group's effort to develop existing resources has focused on a particular region's serious water shortages. There have been numerous projects to enhance Gaza's water supply, for example. The Netherlands headed a project to construct a dam on a seasonal river, Wadi Aza/Nahal Besor, to recharge the Gaza aquifer system. The EC is the leader on developing a brackish water desalination plant in Gaza; Canada is heading the Gaza rainwater catchments system project; and US AID has actively supported Palestinian wastewater treatment projects.[230]

The fourth item for each meeting of the working group was regional cooperation and management. According to the gavel holder, "For the region to make the optimal and most efficient use of its water, it will be necessary to establish some form of regional cooperation or management structure."[231] On the conceptual side, the United States hopes the working group will establish "principles or guidelines" defining states' responsibility in relation to water. Jordan proposed establishing a "water charter" for the region, but this has received little support from Israel. The Swiss government headed a committee for all multilateral groups to discuss civil, political, social, economic, and cultural rights, and to develop an intercultural understanding for the multilateral process. Norway facilitated negotiations between Palestinians, Israelis, and Jordanians in an effort to codify principles for cooperation on water-related matters discussed in the working group. In February 1996, the core parties signed a Declaration on Principles. The agreement is a joint declaration on regional cooperation in developing new water sources and coordinating water infrastructure in the region. However, the accord does not deal with water rights or division of water resources, weakening its importance in some eyes. Jordan's head delegate, Munther Haddadin, while agreeing to initial the document, dismissed it as meaningless. "What they produced was a lukewarm, loose text that means nothing. There is nothing in the text about water sharing so I wouldn't give it [much] importance."[232] Even so, the Norwegians have established a "Waternet" project to help the core parties implement part of the declaration on principles.[233]

At present, as it has throughout its existence, the water working group is attempting to determine its future role. According to the US gavel holder, "It seems unlikely and impractical that the working group would actually undertake to implement any of these [proposed] large scale projects. However, the working group might become the body that considers various options, help[ing] regional parties set priorities and mak[ing] recommendations to outside funding agencies."[234] In addition, it will be critical for the private sector to be involved in order to "ensure, in some degree, that the projects undertaken are economically viable."[235] In other words, the water group's role would be to analyze and prioritize projects, while regional and international economic development institutions might be a better avenue for finding funding. Even though the 1990s Madrid Peace Process has halted, quiet cooperation on water scarcity continues and this functional coordination will not only decrease the impact of water shortages but could make the path to Arab-Israeli peace less turbulent. In 2004, before Congress, Satterfield, a high-ranking State Department official, summed up the continuing value of the water multilaterals and the worth of tactical functional cooperation:

> By focusing on problems related to regional water scarcity, the participants in the process have been able to transcend the realm of competing interests and create a situation in which all parties share benefits. Because the multilateral water working group has kept its work focused on technical issues (while leaving the "political" water issues to the bilateral track), the regional projects developed by the working group on water resources have been able to withstand the vagaries of the political process. The robustness and success of this approach is most clearly demonstrated by the fact that during the last three and a half years of violence and instability in the region due to the *intifada*, during which time political negotiations have largely been in abeyance, Israeli, Palestinian, and Jordanian water officials and experts continue to work together on a range of regional water projects.[236]

The analysis for this chapter will follow in chapter 7.

7

Conclusion

This chapter summarizes the results of this study's investigation into what leads states in a protracted conflict to cooperate or to compete over scarce water resources. By examining contemporary international security, environmental studies, and US foreign policy literature, this book identifies several prominent debates and arguments that help explain how states in a protracted conflict behave in relation to scarce water resources.

This chapter offers answers to the questions posed in chapter 1, includes a summary of the analysis contained in chapters 2 through 6 relating to TFC (tactical functional cooperation), third party involvement, domestic institutions, hegemonic stability theory, and acute conflict, and also marshals the book's defining arguments. It concludes by outlining the lessons that third parties, as well as Jordan riparians, may draw from these results.

TACTICAL FUNCTIONAL COOPERATION

This section discusses the effectiveness of tactical functional cooperation, addressing: *(1) what are the components of TFC that make it effective in maintaining cooperative efforts? (2) does TFC have peacemaking value?* Once cooperation has been initiated, riparians are able to maintain it through TFC. As with formal and informal institutions, TFC plays a critical role in managing cooperative efforts between states. Without the establishment of rules and the means to reciprocate, the evidence suggests that coordination would have been short-lived. As reviewed next, TFC also facilitates the exchange of information, lengthens the shadow of the future, and provides an avenue to continue issue linkage.

Altering the payoff structure assumes an important role in TFC when third parties such as the United States provide incentives to maintain cooperative efforts and penalize cheating. Without TFC, a focal point for third party action is absent with no means to judge whether participating parties play by the rules. While the Johnston mission failed to secure a signed agreement, for example, the Johnston Plan and subsequent secret notes between the United States and Jordan, as well as the United States and Israel, did provide the parties an important framework within which to cooperate (see chapter 3). American officials believed that the Johnston Plan was fair and realistic and that subsequent Israeli and Jordanian waterworks were within the rules of the plan. At first, the Johnston Plan led to disagreements over certain provisions for sharing water. Because the protracted conflict was ongoing and certain rules not clearly defined, TFC was initially difficult to achieve, and on a few occasions misunderstandings and cheating nearly led to violent conflict between Israel and Jordan. In 1979, 1986, and 1987, Israel and Jordan mobilized troops on the Yarmouk's banks because of disputes over water allocations and scarcity. As the Yarmouk forum rules became well established, though, and confidence and transparency increased, the parties gauged the flow on a biweekly basis, jointly cleaned the riverbed annually, and exchanged technical data on river flows. Both sides built a reputation of reliability and good will through solving the problems and addressing the needs of the other riparian. As a result, the participating states (Jordan and Israel in this case study) came to understand that cheating was not to their advantage. This example shows that, beyond the benefit of better water management, TFC also offers an opportunity for improved conflict management. In this instance, neither state wanted a conflict over water, and TFC became the best means available for realizing their mutual preferences. The fifteen-year process of TFC provided additional nonmaterial benefits of building confidence, trust, and a better understanding of the other side's water problems. Because Jordan and Israel worked together during the 1970s, 1980s, and 1990s to manage their water scarcity problem, each state achieved an important common understanding not only of its own problems, but also of the difficulties experienced by its rival. This process helped move Jordanians and Israelis from seeing each other as faceless enemies to regarding each other as good partners who had similar water problems. With TFC comes new ideas to solve common problems. If the sides had not met and discussed their common difficulties, it is doubtful that they would have had the stimulus and information needed to look for new ideas for solving old water-sharing problems.

Lengthening the shadow of the future has two important results relative to TFC. First, as discussed in chapter 1, it decreases the temptation to cheat because participants understand that cheating today would draw sanctions tomorrow and cooperation at present would bring benefits in the near and distant future. Second, lengthening the shadow of the future creates greater trust and confidence between participants with multiple common interests. Linkage plays a significant role in shaping a state's calculations on cheating, since the state knows that its partner would reciprocate on another issue linked to water cooperation. In all these elements, reciprocity is the key for maintaining cooperation. For example, even though Israel and Jordan now have a peace treaty, both states still link water for Jordan with good political relations for Israel, as discussed in chapter 6.

The small number of participants in this case study certainly made TFC more attainable. Fewer participants facilitate identifying and realizing common interests. This requirement is especially true in a protracted conflict setting. Even Israel and Syria might have achieved greater multilateral cooperation had they been more interdependent. In most instances, decreasing the number of participants facilitates cooperation.

In the short term, TFC ought to provide conflict management and better water management for cases of this kind. In the long term, TFC enables states not only to reduce tension on the critical water issue but also to establish means for solving the difficult technical aspects of the problem. When Israel and Jordan negotiated a peace treaty, their past TFC made an important difference in the successful completion of the negotiations. This was true not only for the water issue, but for the whole treaty as well because water, a pivotal issue, could have scuttled the overall negotiations. By contrast, no TFC took place between Israel and the Palestinians prior to 1993. This turned water into a more complex issue for these parties to negotiate. Nevertheless, as discussed in chapter 6, Palestinian and Israeli water technocrats had worked together since 1995, continuing even in 2000 when there had been a complete political breakdown in relations between Israel and the Palestinian Authority.

During a protracted conflict, what is the value of rivals first cooperating on functional issues, such as water scarcity? As discussed in chapter 1, some scholars argue that it is better first to resolve the security and political or high politics issues, which would have been the Palestinian conflict and territorial disputes, and then address functional or low politics issues such as sharing water. This case study shows, however, that there is value to efforts by parties in a protracted conflict to creating rules, building confidence, and reducing tensions through improving water management. The TFC here did not resolve the Arab-Israeli conflict, but it did move the parties in that direction. It certainly helped to keep an issue such as water from festering into something that could make the conflict more protracted and violent. Often states that are not yet ready for a peace treaty will still prefer not to let an issue such as water drag them into an unintentional war. For forty-five years, this was true for Jordan. King Hussein and his water technocrats saw water cooperation with Israel as a political gamble, but also showed reluctance to ignore Israel in this potentially explosive issue. Another Jordanian leader might have taken a different path, one in which Jordan absolutely refused to cooperate with Israel. This case supports the notion that such a policy would have been less successful and very costly to Jordan and its people. Over time, many Americans, Israelis, and Jordanians appreciated the value of TFC as an intermediate measure. For example, both Johnston and Dulles, at least at the outset, understood that an Arab-Israeli peace settlement was unrealistic (see chapter 2). Dulles spoke of a step-by-step approach that built confidence and reduced tensions. Johnston agreed, hoping his efforts would eliminate certain points of friction. In fact, Johnston's efforts were initially successful precisely because he convinced many of the Arab negotiating partners that the United States was seeking a water solution, not a resolution of the larger conflict. Of course, a political settlement to a protracted conflict is preferable, but that is not always a possibility at a certain point in time, and TFC is the intelligent second-best policy choice.

Thanks in part to the secret TFC process, Israeli and Jordanian technocrats today have a cooperative and professional relationship. The TFC experience facilitated creative thinking and rapid negotiations, as well as implementation of the Israel-Jordan treaty. Instead of secret meetings at a picnic table, the Joint Water Committee established by the treaty meets, sometimes publicly, and is the forum that enables Israel and Jordan to better cooperate, communicate, and verify compliance of the water section of the treaty. Having worked together for the past three decades, Israel and Jordan have confidence in one another's water experts. This confidence, in turn, should facilitate quicker and more effective action when conflict or crisis arises over politics or the implementation of the treaty provisions, as occurred in the late 1990s.

Part of the success of the multilateral talks of the 1990s came from following many of the tactics used by the Yarmouk forum. Many of the meetings took place out of the public's eye, and participants were careful to limit their goals. A major objective was to create a process where water experts could meet, learn about the water challenges of the other riparians, generate new ideas, and provide a forum for international donors to become more involved. Like the Yarmouk forum, the multilaterals did not come into being to resolve the overall political issues, but to address the water issue and in the process create greater confidence and trust among core party technocrats and elites, which is of a long-term peacemaking value.

THIRD PARTY INVOLVEMENT

Should third parties such as the United States concentrate on resolving the protracted conflict while leaving the functional issues for later resolution? In other words, why waste time and political capital on low politics such as water cooperation, prior to resolving the high politics or political disputes of a protracted conflict? In this case study and over the past half-century, the US government consistently executed policies that promoted Jordan-Israel water sharing and rejected the all-or-nothing approach.

An appropriate counterfactual experiment is to imagine the result if the United States did attempt to resolve the political dispute before encouraging negotiations over functional issues. In fact, in the past the United States did so twice and both attempts failed. Prior to the 1990s, the 1949 to 1956 period was the most advantageous time for a resolution of the larger conflict, yet both the Alpha Peace Plan and the Palestine Conciliation Commission conference failed to realize their objectives. Not only did Alpha not succeed, as discussed in chapter 2, it also played an important role in scuttling the Johnston mission. Johnston and many succeeding US diplomats understood that friction points, including the water disputes, should be addressed first in order to facilitate the peacemaking process down the road. The United States took the stance that to ignore the water issue until after resolution of the political questions would probably lead to more violent conflict. The historical record supports this position.

Gavel holder, conduit for information, moral guarantor, good offices, facilitator, negotiator, and source of information were some of the hats the United States wore during its efforts to promote water cooperation between Arabs and Israelis, in particular Israel and Jordan. At different times, changing its role was appropriate. Both sides recognized that the United States had a legitimate function because it was an ally of both Jordan and Israel, had provided financial assistance to important Jordanian and Israeli water projects, and offered important technical and political support. Officials from the US embassy often met with water technocrats and, when a political crisis arose over water, the United States placed high-ranking officials on both sides of the river before violence erupted. For Israel and Jordan, the United States' most important role was as a guarantor of the water-sharing regime. Jordan, especially, felt the importance of this since it was the weaker state. The United States continued this role, although more publicly, as gavel holder for the multilaterals. Interestingly, because of this past TFC, the Jordan-Israel water peace treaty negotiations did not require active US participation.

The most common preference for the United States was to promote cooperation and mitigate the chances for violent conflict, even when this meant allowing minor infractions to pass without comment or, on the other hand, punishing its allies. In an effort to decrease the chances of conflict at one point in the 1950s, the United States cut off aid to Israel and at another in the 1960s the United States participated in Israeli water-related cover-ups. The United States believed such a policy would decrease the chances of violence in the region. For example, the United States knew its aid funds were to be used for the controversial National Water Carrier, even though Israel publicly said that its US loans were only for the coastal plain pipelines. The United States had learned that Israel was releasing saline effluents into the lower Jordan in 1964 but concealed them by simultaneously releasing sweet Lake Tiberias water. Also during this period, US diplomats believed Israel would continue small-scale attacks into Syria disguised as minor border incidents in order to disrupt the Arab diversion program. The United States understood that these attacks would result in less publicity, minimizing the likelihood of Syria's successfully bringing the matter before the UN Security Council. These seemingly contradictory policies make sense when viewed through the lens of the overwhelming US preference for Middle East stability and nonconflict.

DOMESTIC INSTITUTIONS

What place do domestic institutions and political parties have in determining whether a state will move toward cooperation or opt to fight over scarce resources? The results of this case study challenge the neorealist assumption that states are unitary actors that speak with one voice. The results also question the liberal-democratic notion that liberal democratic institutions always promote peace. Through the past half-century, a small number of Israeli farmers in the Yarmouk Triangle have had a disproportionately important influence on the water politics of the Yarmouk, showing that a powerful interest group can operate within a democratic system and help undermine the peace. At times, the Israeli government wanted to improve its relations with Jordan and, for that matter, the United States, by being more flexible with its utilization of the Yarmouk. At many critical points, however, Yarmouk farmers challenged the government's position. At other times, when the government did not take actions that the farmers preferred, the Yarmouk farmers took matters into their own hands. On three different occasions, the farmers undertook a unilateral action, such as altering the Yarmouk's flow without the permission of the governments of Israel or Jordan. As described in chapter 4, such actions led to military mobilization on both sides of the Yarmouk. These crises occurred because an interest group had considerable political power and operated within a democratic system. By the 1990s, the Israeli agriculture sector lost much of its disproportionate political influence in Israeli politics, allowing the Israeli government to make important water concessions to Jordan during the peacemaking process. It is doubtful that the Israeli government would have been able to make the concessions it had in the 1994 Peace Treaty had the negotiations occurred twenty or thirty years earlier when the Yarmouk and other Israeli farmers were at the apex of their political power.

THE WEAKNESS OF HEGEMONIC STABILITY THEORY

What are the weaknesses of the variant of hegemonic stability theory discussed in chapter 1? Some analysts argue that water cooperation begins and is maintained "if the dominant power in the basin will benefit from regional cooperation in water utilization."[1] This variant of hegemonic stability theory is primarily a power-based approach. Cooperation occurs when it is in the interest of the most powerful riparian. Riparian position on the river and its water needs are also part of the power calculation. This approach is parsimonious and although important insights are drawn from it, it falls short of adequately explaining state behavior. This viewpoint ignores the impact of politics beyond the river basin and preferences beyond the water issue. In particular, it pays no heed to the balancing of threats regionally and internationally and dismisses the impact of weaker states and third parties to alter dominant states' behavior through linking issues.

Unlike the variant of hegemonic stability theory, the liberal approach described in this book is not primarily based on power politics but on a state's preferences because this approach takes into account a number of factors that are disregarded in power politics analysis. An analyst using the hegemonic stability approach would ignore the preferences of nondominant states, for example, because they are extraneous. It would be unnecessary, for instance, to examine Jordan's water and political preferences because it is weak and downstream. As the case study illustrates repeatedly, weaker states' interests may greatly impact more powerful riparians' behavior. In contrast, the variant of hegemonic stability ignores the significance of regional and international power distribution. Both factors, however, influence the way states, both weak and strong, calculate their future actions.

Furthermore, *why would a riparian that is politically, militarily, and economically more powerful still choose to cooperate and even to compromise on a critical issue, such as scarce water resources, with a state with which it has, at best, strained political relations?* The answer, based on the case study material, is that powerful states have many preferences, with water being only one of them. If a state can achieve important policy aims without jeopardizing vital water interests, then it should be willing to make necessary compromises, even with a state with which it has poor relations. Cooperation becomes worthwhile if it achieves additional objectives, such as improving political relations, even if that means strengthening a former foe. In the final analysis, the variant of hegemonic stability theory explains the fifteen-year cooperative water arrangement between Jordan and Israel only with difficulty. The liberal approach provides a better elucidation for why the Jordan River riparians either cooperated or did not work with each other.

This section of this chapter examines why states are more likely to initiate water cooperation when they are balancing with a partner against a common threat and, in addition, when they have mixed interests to link. *How does the balancing threat/issue linkage proposition make up for the shortcomings of the hegemonic theory approach?*

As the case study demonstrates, states most often join together to balance against external threats. Political leaders seeking to counter threats form alliances by adding the power of another state to their own.[2] Once states have established a relationship through defending against a threat together, they are more likely to cooperate on some additional issues, even when they are still in a formal protracted conflict. Balancing together creates an environment of greater interdependence. After such balancing, even rival states in a protracted conflict understand that both have an interest in the survival, if not the well-being, of the partner state. This new relationship facilitates the initiation of cooperation in other issue areas. Several examples illustrate this premise. When Jordan and Israel were in a protracted conflict, they still were able to cooperate once both perceived a common regional threat—the PLO/Syria. This also was true for Jordan and Syria in the 1970s. Both viewed Egypt's signing of the Sinai II agreement with Israel as a potential threat and, thus, initiated a new round of cooperation with one another. Clearly, even when states are balancing, it does not necessarily mean they are willing to cooperate on all issues. However, it does mean that cooperation is more likely to occur because they have better relations. The issues on which they cooperate reflect whether one state considers the matter to be important while another state has mixed interests that it is willing to link. In one of the previous examples, Jordan and Syria were balancing the Sinai II threat of a separate peace between Israel and Egypt. However, Jordan needed to store Yarmouk water and Syria was willing to cooperate in order to build the Maqarin Dam, but only if it received political concessions from Jordan. Jordan-Israel cooperation also followed the same pattern, as discussed in chapter 4.

How Acute Conflict Begins

How and why conflict occurs over water is considered in this section: *(1) Why have there been so few cases of acute conflict over the water issue to date? (2) What factors contribute to water related acute conflict? (3) What is the relationship between water-related political tension and international relations in general?* The lack of sufficient water in the Jordan basin has led to the perception that water is a potential source of conflict in the region. Still a popular assumption that Jordan River riparians will fight the next regional war over water instead of oil is *not* supported by this book's research. In addition to benefiting from improvements in water management techniques, the riparians are increasingly indicating their awareness that while there is a potential for acute conflict over water, war will not solve the long-term problems inherent in regional water allocation. Nonetheless, water has been a serious source of political tension. Water scarcity has provoked "saber-rattling" statements in the past from politicians and even limited military mobilizations, as we saw on the banks of the Yarmouk in the 1980s, as discussed in chapter 4. Still, rather than seeking to increase their water supply through warfare, Jordan River basin governments instead have tried to better manage water scarcity, despite the political challenges inherent in this stance. Indeed, some leaders have gone from threatening conflict over water to cooperating by facilitating cross-border flows. While a future outbreak of war over Jordan River water is unlikely, riparians still face some formidable challenges on this issue.

In this case study, two major incidents led to acute conflict over water between Israel and Arab states, but it is important to recognize the complex web of factors that made water so important. In the first case, violent conflict concerning the demilitarized zones in the 1950s related in part to the water issue. In the second case, acute conflict was triggered in the 1960s by Israel's initiating its National Water Carrier and by the ensuing Arab diversion of the upper Jordan. As discussed in chapters 2 and 3, the water issue was a contributing factor to acute conflict, but to understand water's relationship to conflict one must also examine regional and even global strategies. A key factor in these Jordan River basin examples of acute conflict was strong evidence that domestic preferences created the foundation for water-related tension. In turn, competitive water-scarcity strategies made regional and international relations unstable.

While the 1960s acute conflict relating to water ended almost a year prior to the outbreak of the 1967 Arab-Israeli War, significant vestiges of the water issue played a pivotal role as an intermediate contributing factor to the advent of that war. In the history of the Arab-Israeli conflict, this connection between water and war is the exception. While the water issue rarely resulted in acute conflict, it did create frequent political tension. Such tension will be especially significant to regions that are already politically unstable and prone to conflict. Unfortunately, in the past, much of the environmental security literature, as discussed in chapter 1, has focused on water's relation to war or acute conflict, overshadowing the important impact on international relations of political tension between states. Similar to arms races and trade wars, environmental related scarcity does not have to be the primary cause of war to be significant for world politics. Political tension on many issues decreases the likelihood of cooperation and increases the chances of escalating conflict. Although not the immediate cause of military conflicts, shrinking natural resources shared between states should continue to be a source of diplomatic stress and limited violence.

As the case study demonstrates, water's relation to state preferences within the context of a particular nationalist ideology is significant in understanding state behavior. Comprehending the value political leaders and the masses place on an issue such as water gives important insights into how or why a state acts the way it does. In both cases of acute conflict, states overrated water's economic value. In this case study, nationalistic ideology became a primary reason why political leaders exaggerated the value of water and agriculture. As a result, this preference led to political tension and sometimes to acute conflict.

POLICY IMPLICATIONS

What are the future policy implications for this area of study? The propositions developed in this book indicate a great deal about state behavior in relation to scarce water resources and protracted conflicts. This work posits two central policy hypotheses: (1) even for states in a protracted conflict, third party efforts to reduce water-related tensions may be productive; (2) the possibility of acute conflict over a water issue depends not only on scarcity of water as well as the power or position of riparians, but also, and most important, on domestic preferences. Therefore, policies that promote water cooperation preferences deserve considerable attention. Since the end of the cold war, the United States and the rest of the developed world have attempted to reduce tensions and end numerous protracted conflicts. Also, policymakers have striven to better understand the relationship between the environment and national security. With that in mind, five policy implications follow from this research.

First, the United States, the World Bank, and other third parties should aggressively lay a foundation for issue linking, such as developing financial aid for future water management programs in exchange for international cooperation. Once a situation with potential for cooperation arises, third parties should be proactive in assisting the negotiation process. For example, prior to the 1991 Gulf War, third parties had not actively sought a solution for the Euphrates dispute involving Syria and Turkey. The period immediately following the Gulf War would have been a ripe opportunity for third party involvement and a resolution of this difficult water-sharing dispute, but it was missed. The same could be said about the present stalemate between Israel and Syria and the absence of a badly needed third party push toward negotiations, as well as new efforts to generate and think through new ideas for resolving the complex water dispute between the two states.

Second, the multilateral track should be promoted. A multilateral, nonpolitical approach is appropriate in bringing states together in dry regions to generate new technologies, elicit international financial aid, and develop an institutional structure that would help reduce water scarcity. A less political, multilateral approach can stimulate a needed TFC process. In this case study, the multilateral track of the Madrid Peace Process helped to develop noncontroversial but nonetheless important projects for each party to reduce its own water demand; this, in turn, led to decreased regional scarcity. The multilateral track has currently gone underground, but the United States and the rest of the international community should continue to support various multilateral projects to reduce scarcity and increase tactical functional cooperation. However, when attempting to negotiate a difficult and political water agreement, a bilateral approach is preferable. As shown in this study, a smaller number of players improves the chances for cooperation.

Third, while ideology can be an obstacle to TFC, it is not always an impenetrable barrier. States that experience water scarcity are willing to make compromises on ideology for the sake of a national well-being preference. However, donors should not pressure weak regimes to make ideological compromises if it means their legitimacy among their own population will be threatened. As already pointed out, if a riparian calculates that other preferences supersede water-related cooperation, it is doubtful that coordination will occur. For example, an important element in water cooperation has been foreign aid.[3] Assistance has been a popular policy instrument in the Middle East. During the cold war, both superpowers provided extensive economic and military aid to a variety of states in the region. Aid for water projects proved most effective in initiating and maintaining cooperation when donors and patrons had similar political preferences. When patrons attempted to use aid as leverage on issues the recipient regarded as important, especially if vital to the survival of the political leadership, the riparian did not cooperate. For example, before 1994, Jordan was willing to cooperate on the water issue secretly, but was not prepared to upgrade coordination to a formal peace with Israel, even under US pressure. Israel and Jordan were highly dependent on the United States for water project financial assistance. Water projects were considered important, if not vital, to recipients. Such assistance gains influence for donors and causes the riparians to become more flexible and more willing to compromise, but it does not outweigh an aid recipient's deep preferences, even when that party is weak and dependent. By better understanding aid recipient's preferences, third parties can gain a better idea of how hard to pursue a given negotiation. As Dennis Ross, US envoy to the Middle East, 1988–2000, has pointed out, "understanding the core needs on each side is a precondition for shaping an outcome to this [Arab-Israeli] conflict."[4]

Fourth, in the past, secrecy has played a key role in water TFC. While third parties ought not to underestimate the significance of this specific technique, they should examine the importance of other creative statecraft to avoid obstacles to cooperation within a protracted conflict environment. They should also understand that the secret TFC will only create a bond between technocrats and possibly national leaders. It will not achieve the important people-to-people confidence and trust that is needed to end a protracted conflict and for a peace to prove enduring.

A final implication is that TFC is clearly preferable to acute conflict. In conveying the lessons learned during the 1990s, Dennis Ross stated that the United States' most important role may be in encouraging the sides to "talk and not to shoot"—and this will only come about with "active American diplomacy," he added.[5] Not withstanding the extraordinary frustrations on both sides of the Israeli-Palestinian negotiations since the ratification of Oslo II, there still has been TFC cooperation. Palestinians and Israelis have been working on water in the interim by remaining in daily contact with water technocrats on the other side. If this interaction continues, like the Jordanian-Israeli TFC, it could have long-term payoffs when final status talks are ultimately concluded. Until then, TFC should decrease the chance that water disputes alone will lead to violent conflict. The United States ought to fund and take part as much as possible and comprehend, as in the Jordan-Israel case, that TFC is not a short-term fix, but a long-term investment in time and resources.

This work has sought to resolve important debates about state behavior and water scarcity. Neither water cooperation nor conflict is certain in any situation, but, by using insights provided in this book, policymakers may increase the likelihood for achieving their policy objectives. These goals are only attainable if diplomats are proactive and do not wait for the water-related political tensions to intensify into a political crisis.

Notes

CHAPTER 1: INTRODUCTION

1. John F. Turner, Assistant Secretary, Bureau of Oceans and International Environmental and Scientific Affairs, US State Department, "Water Scarcity in the Middle East: Regional Cooperation as a Mechanism Toward Peace." House International Relations Committee (serial no. 108–118) [108th Congress, second session, 5 May 2004], (Washington, DC: US Government Printing Office, 2004), 19.

2. "'Water Factory' Aims to Filter Tensions," *BBC News* 7 Sept. 2004.

3. See Arun Elhance, *Hydro-Politics in the 3rd World* (Washington, DC: US Institute of Peace Press, 1999).

4. Charles Lipson, "Why Are Some International Agreements Informal?" *International Organization* 45:4 (Autumn 1991), 526–527.

5. Andrew Moravcsik, "Taking Preferences Seriously: A Liberal Theory of International Politics," in Charles Lipson and Benjamin Cohen, eds., *Theory and Structure in International Political Economy* (Cambridge: MIT Press, 1999), 41, and Hans Morgenthau, *Politics Among Nations*, 6th ed. (New York: McGraw-Hill, 1985), 5.

6. Moravcsik, "Taking Preferences Seriously," 33.

7. See, for example, John Bulloch and Adel Darwish, *Water Wars: Coming Conflict in the Middle East* (London: Victor Gollancz, 1993). Also see John Cooley, "The War over Water," *Foreign Policy* 54 (Spring 1984) and Joyce Starr, "Water Wars," *Foreign Policy* 82 (Spring 1991), 17–36. For more recent policymaker statements, see Nimrod Raphaeli, "The Looming Crisis of Water in the Middle East," *Middle East Media Research Institute Inquiry and Analysis Series* No. 124 (21 Feb. 2003).

8. Aaron Wolf, "Conflict and Cooperation Along International Waterways," *Water Policy* 1:8 (1998), 255 and Aaron Wolf et al., "Water Can be a Pathway to Peace, not War" *The Woodrow Wilson Center Environmental Change and Security Program Navigating Peace* 1 (July 2006).

9. For a more detailed discussion, see Jeffrey Sosland, "Understanding Environmental Security: Water Scarcity, the 1980s' Palestinian Uprising, and Implications for

Peace" in Tami Amanda Jacoby and Brent Sasley, eds., *Redefining Security in the Middle East* (New York: University of Manchester Press, 2002), 116–123.

10. See the "Water and Conflict Chronology" worldwater.org/chronology.html

11. David Singer, "The 'Correlates of War' Project," *World Politics* 24:2 (Jan. 1972), 243–270.

12. Wolf, "Conflict and Cooperation Along International Waterways, 255." Also see Mark Giordano et al., "International Resource Conflict Mitigation," *Journal of Peace Research* 42: 1 (2005), 47–65.

13. *Understanding International Conflicts*, 3rd ed. (New York: Longman, 2000), 70–71.

14. Homer-Dixon defines acute conflict as "involving a substantial probability of violence." ("On the Threshold: Environmental Changes as Causes of Acute Conflict," *International Security* 16:2 (Fall 1991), 77).

15. Gunther Baechler, "Why Environmental Transformation Causes Violence: A Synthesis" *The Woodrow Wilson Center Environmental Change and Security Project Report* Issue, 4 (Spring 1998), 30–31.

16. Nadav Safran, *Israel: The Embattled Ally* (Cambridge: Belknap, 1978), 381–413.

17. Charles Lipson and Benjamin Cohen, eds., *Theory and Structure in International Political Economy* (Cambridge: MIT Press, 1999), ix.

18. Andrew Moravcsik, *The Choice for Europe: Social Purpose and State Power from Messina to Maastricht* (Ithaca: Cornell University Press, 1998), 20.

19. Moravcsik, "Taking Preferences Seriously," 37.

20. Moravcsik, "Taking Preferences Seriously," 39–40.

21. Moravcsik, "Taking Preferences Seriously," 40.

22. Ivan Arreguin-Toft, "How the Weak Win Wars: A Theory of Asymmetric Conflict," *International Security* 26:1 (Summer 2001), 97.

23. Moravcsik, "Taking Preferences Seriously," 44.

24. *Bridging the Gap: Theory and Practice in Foreign Policy* (Washington, DC: US Institute of Peace, 1993), 111–113.

25. Aaron Wolf, *Hydropolitics Along the Jordan River* (New York: United Nations University Press, 1995).

26. Wolf, *Hydropolitics Along the Jordan River*, 3.

27. See Robert Lieber, *Theory and World Politics* (Cambridge: Wintrop, 1972), 41–50. This is somewhat of an odd theoretical debate considering that the theory of functionalism and neofunctionalism has been regarded as obsolete, even by its supporters, for the past twenty years (see, for example, Ernst Haas, "The Obsolescence of Regional Integration Theory," Research Series No. 25 (Berkeley: Institute of International Studies, University of California, 1975)). Even so, the related policy

debate is relevant: should the focus of Arab-Israeli peacemaking be on functional issues like water cooperation or should it be on resolving the larger political issues first?

28. Miriam Lowi, *Water and Power: The Politics of a Scarce Resource in the Jordan River Basin* (New York: Cambridge University Press, 1993), 9; "Water Disputes in the Middle East," *The Woodrow Wilson Center Environmental Change and Security Project Report*, Issue 2 (Spring 1996). Lowi makes the same argument in other articles: "Bridging the Divide: Transboundary Resource Disputes and the Case of West Bank Water," *International Security* 18: 1 (Summer 1993); and "Rivers of Conflict, Rivers of Peace," *Journal of International Affairs* 49:1 (Summer 1995).

29. Lowi, *Water and Power*, 164–166.

30. Lowi, *Water and Power*, 200.

31. Garfinkle makes a similar argument in "Hung Out to Dry or All Wet? Water in the Jordan Valley," *Orbis* 39:1 (Winter 1995), 134–138.

32. Term first used by Yehuda Lukacs, *Israel, Jordan, and the Peace Process* (Syracuse: Syracuse University Press, 1997), 5–6.

33. Dalia Dassa Kaye, *Beyond the Handshake* (New York: Columbia University Press, 2001), 7.

34. Robert Keohane, "International Institutions: Two Approaches," *International Studies Quarterly* 32:4 (December 1988), 383.

35. Robert Keohane and Lisa Martin, "The Promise of Institutionalist Theory," *International Security* 20:1 (Summer 1995), 42.

36. For regime theory see, for example, Stephen Krasner, "Structural Causes and Regime Consequences: Regimes as Intervening Variables," in Stephen Krasner, ed., *International Regimes* (Ithaca: Cornell University Press, 1983); Keohane, "The Analysis of International Regimes" in Volker Rittberger, ed., *Regime Theory and International Relations* (New York: Clarendon Press-Oxford, 1995), Friedrich Kratochwil, "Contract and Regimes: Do Issue Specificity and Variations of Formality Matter?" in Rittberger, *Regime Theory and International Relations*; and Lipson, "Why Are Some International Agreements Informal?" For a more recent critique of regime theory, see Ken Conca, *Governing Water: Contentious Transnational Politics and Global Institution Building*, (Cambridge: MIT Press, 2006).

37. See, for example, Judith Goldstein and Robert Keohane, eds., *Ideas and Foreign Policy* (Ithaca: Cornell University Press, 1993).

38. Robert Keohane, "Reciprocity in International Relations," *International Organization* 40:1 (Winter 1986), 8. Helen Milner argues that reciprocity also minimizes the fear that cooperation might overly strengthen other states. In other words, proportional absolute gains due to reciprocity imply no major relative gains ("International Theories of Cooperation Among Nations: Strengths and Weaknesses," *World Politics* 44:3 (April 1992), 470–473).

39. Rittberger, ed., *Regime Theory and International Relations*, 68 and 206.

40. As for defining central terms, this book characterizes "cooperation" as a situation that contains a mixture of conflicting and complementary interests. Cooperation is not meant to indicate cases in which two or more states have identical interests. Rather, it is when countries adjust their behavior to the preferences of other states (Robert Axelrod and Robert Keohane, "Achieving Cooperation Under Anarchy: Strategies and Institutions," in Kenneth Oye, ed., *Cooperation Under Anarchy* (Princeton: Princeton University Press, 1986), 226).

41. This is the "malign" view of hegemonic stability theory associated with Robert Gilpin's work, *War and Change in World Politics* (Cambridge: Cambridge University Press, 1981), 9–11. This variant does not necessarily provide a public good.

42. Lowi, *Water and Power,* 5 and 10; and similarly Thomas Naff and Ruth Matson propose a model that examines the factors of interest and issues, riparian position, and external and internal power. *Water in the Middle East: Conflict or Cooperation?* (Boulder: Westview Press, 1984), 192–196). In a qualitative study done by Wollenbaek et al. they argue that water scarcity is also associated with the upstream/downstream relationship "which appears to be the form of shared river resources most frequently associated with conflict. But these results are not very strong." ("Shared Rivers and Interstate Conflict," *Political Geography*, 972).

43. Some important realist and neoliberal institutionalist studies do not support the argument that a single overwhelming power actor is necessary for cooperation: Joseph Grieco, *Cooperation Among Nations* (Ithaca: Cornell University Press, 1990) and Peter Haas, *Saving the Mediterranean* (New York: Columbia University Press, 1990). For a critique of hegemonic stability theory, see Robert Keohane, *After Hegemony* (Princeton: Princeton University Press, 1984), 5–17, 31–64, 135–216; Duncan Snidal, "The Limits of Hegemonic Stability Theory," *International Organization* 39:4 (Autumn 1985), 579–614; Arthur A. Stein, "The Hegemon's Dilemma: Great Britain, the United States and the International Economic Order," *International Organization* 38:2 (Spring 1984), 355–386; Bruce Russet, "The Mysterious Case of Vanishing Hegemony; or, Is Mark Twain Really Dead?" *International Organization* 39:2 (Spring 1985), 207–232; Timothy J. McKeown, "Hegemonic Stability Theory and Nineteenth Century Tariff Levels in Europe," *International Organization* 37:1 (Winter 1983), 73–91.

44. Walt, *The Origins of Alliances* (Ithaca: Cornell University Press, 1987), 5.

45. See, for example, chapter 4; Aharon Klieman, *Statecraft in the Dark: Israel's Practice of Quiet Diplomacy* (Boulder: Westview Press, 1988) and Lukacs, *Israel, Jordan, and the Peace Process.* Laurie Brand argues that the origins of alliances may often be better explained by examining economic variables, such as a state's financial imperatives, rather than solely focusing on security-related threats, such as those Walt focuses on (*Jordan's Inter-Arab Relations: The Political Economy of Alliance Making* (New York: Columbia University Press, 1994), 3).

46. Arthur Stein, "The Politics of Linkage" *World Politics,* 33: 1 (Oct. 1980), 62–81. Also see Keohane, *After Hegemony,* 91; Kenneth Oye, Donald Rothchild, and Robert Lieber, *Eagle Entangled: US Foreign Policy in a Complex World* (New York: Longman, 1979), 13–17; Ernst Haas, "Why Collaborate? Issue Linkage and International

Regimes," *World Politics* 32:3 (April 1980); Robert Tollision and Thomas Willett, "An Economic Theory of Mutually Advantageous Issue-Linkage in International Negotiations," *International Organization* 33:4 (Fall 1979).

47. John Holmes et al., "Boundary Roles and Intergroup Conflict," in Stephen and William Austen, eds., *Psychology of Intergroup Relations,* 2nd ed. (Chicago: Nelson-Hall, 1986), 356, as cited in Milner, "International Theories of Cooperation Among Nations," 485. Also see Robert Keohane and Joseph Nye, *Power and Interdependence,* 2nd ed. (New York: HarperCollins, 1989), 30–32.

48. David LeMarquand, *International Rivers: The Politics of Cooperation* (Vancouver, BC: Westwater Research Centre, University of British Columbia, 1977), 14–15.

49. Moravcsik, *The Choice for Europe,* 65–66.

50. See, for example, Kenneth Oye, "Explaining Cooperation Under Anarchy," in *Cooperation Under Anarchy*; Kenneth Oye, ed. Robert Axelrod, *The Evolution of Cooperation* (New York: Basic Books, 1984); Robert Axelrod and Robert Keohane, "Achieving Cooperation Under Anarchy: Strategies and Institutions," in Oye, ed., *Cooperation Under Anarchy.*

51. Oye, "Explaining Cooperation Under Anarchy," 11.

52. Helen Milner argues that the iteration condition depends "on the rate at which players discount anticipated gains: the more heavily the future is discounted, the less likely is cooperation" ("International Theories of Cooperation Among Nations," 474).

53. Oye, "Explaining Cooperation Under Anarchy," 12–18, and Dale Copeland, "Economic Interdependence and War: A Theory of Trade Expectations," *International Security.* 20:4 (Spring 1996), 5–41.

54. This depends on the distribution of interests. There are cases when additional partners can facilitate cooperation through issue linking. See Lisa Martin, *Coercive Cooperation: Explaining Multilateral Economic Sanctions* (Princeton: Princeton University Press, 1992). Others suggest that large numbers of participants increase likeliness and robustness of cooperation. See, for example, Krasner, ed., *International Regimes.*

55. Oye, "Explaining Cooperation Under Anarchy," 18–22.

56. Michael Brown, et. al, *Theories of War and Peace* (Cambridge: MIT Press, 1998).

57. See, for example, the diverse Jordan River literature: Lowi, *Water and Power*; Wolf, *Hydropolitics Along the Jordan River*; Natasha Beschorner, *Water and Instability in the Middle East* (London: The International Institute for Strategic Studies, 1992) *Adelphi Paper* no. 273; Nurit Kliot, *Water Resources and Conflict in the Middle East* (London: Routledge, 1994); Arnon Soffer, *Rivers of Fire: The Conflict over Water in the Middle East* (Lanham, MD: Rowman & Littlefield 1998); Daniel Hillel, *Rivers of Eden: The Struggle for Water and the Quest for Peace in the Middle East* (New York: Oxford University Press, 1994); and Naff and Matson, eds., *Water in the Middle East: Conflict or Coopera-*

tion?; Franklin Fisher et al., *Liquid Assets* (Washington, DC: RFF Press, 2005). Also, multibook reviews: Ofira Seliktar, "Water in the Arab-Israeli Struggle: Conflict or Cooperation?" in Kevin Avruch and Walter P. Zenner, eds., *Critical Essays on Israeli Society, Religion, and Government: Books on Israel,* vol. 4 (Albany: State University of New York Press, 1997) Garfinkle, "Hung Out to Dry or All Wet?" and Jeffrey Sosland, "The Domestic-International Confluence: The Challenge of Israel's Water Problems" in Laura Zittrain Eisenberg and Neil Caplan, eds., *Review Essays in Israel Studies* (Albany: State University of New York Press, 2000), 221–240. For books that focus on the West Bank and Gaza, see Alwyn Rouyer, *Turning Water into Politics* (New York: St. Martin's, 2000), Julie Trottier, *Hydropolitics in the West Bank and Gaza Strip* (Jerusalem: PASSIA, 1999), Fadia Daibes, ed., *Water in Palestine: Problems-Politics-Prospects* (Jerusalem: PASSIA, 2003), Sharif Elmusa, *Water Conflict: Economics, Politics, Law and Palestinian-Israeli Water Resources* (Washington, DC: Institute for Palestine Studies, 1997), and Jan Selby, *Water Power and Politics in the Middle East: The Other Israeli-Palestinian Conflict* (London: I. B. Tauris, 2003).

58. Walt, *The Origins of Alliances*, 51.

59. Walt, *The Origins of Alliances*, 79.

CHAPTER 2: STATE-BUILDING AND WATER DEVELOPMENT, 1920–1956

1. Michael Brecher, *Decisions in Israel's Foreign Policy* (New Haven: Yale University Press, 1975), 193.

2. For an extensive discussion on the negotiations over borders and water during this period, see Aaron Wolf, *Hydropolitics Along the Jordan River* (New York: United Nations University Press, 1995).

3. The modern effort to settle Palestine with Jews began in 1882. However, a small Jewish community lived in cities throughout the area before modern Zionism. In 1919, at the Paris Peace Conference, Zionist leaders negotiated for improved borders for Palestine. One demand was to include more water sources to improve the economic capabilities of Palestine.

4. The *yishuv* also elected an assembly and had a defense organization, the *Haganah.* The community had its own tax collection agency and judicial system.

5. "The Jordan Valley Water Question 1919–1984," Historical Research Project No. 1403, US State Department, Bureau of Public Affairs, Office of the Historian (August 1984) [hereafter HRP], 3 (5 March 1926). This document was attained through a Freedom of Information Act petition. It gives the chronology of related events based on State Department documents and some secondary material.

6. Thomas Naff and Ruth Matson, eds., *Water in the Middle East: Conflict or Cooperation?* (Boulder: Westview Press, 1984), 30.

7. Miriam Lowi, *Water and Power* (New York: Cambridge University Press, 1995), 42; HRP, 2 (21 Sept. 1921); Also see Sara Reguer "Rutenberg and the Jordan River: A Revolution in Hydro-electricity," *Middle East Studies* 31:4 (Oct. 1995), 691–729, and Munther Haddadin, *Diplomacy on the Jordan* (Boston: Kluwer, 2002), 15–17.

8. HRP, 2 (21 Oct. 1921).

9. *Foreign Relations of the United States 1945: The Near East and Africa*, vol. 8 (Washington, DC: US Government Printing Office, 1969), 678, and HRP, 6 (2 Dec. 1943).

10. HRP, 9 (3 April 1946).

11. HRP, 13 (14 Feb. 1949).

12. *Foreign Relations of the United States 1946: The Near East and Africa*, vol. 7 (Washington, DC: US Government Printing Office, 1969), [hereafter FRUS 1946], 663.

13. FRUS 1946, 663.

14. HRP, 8–11.

15. See, for example, Benny Morris, *The Birth of the Palestinian Refugee Problem, 1947–1949* (Cambridge: Cambridge University Press, 1987).

16. A. Konikoff, *Transjordan: An Economic Survey* (Jerusalem: Economic Research Institute of the Jewish Agency for Palestine, 1946), 18; Peter Gubser, *Jordan: Crossroads of the Middle Eastern Events* (Boulder: Westview Press, 1983), 11–12.

17. Gubser, *Jordan*, 88–99.

18. Howard Sachar, *A History of Israel* (New York: Knopf, 1976), 409–411.

19. Meron Medzini, ed., *Israel's Foreign Relations: Selected Documents 1947–1974* (Jerusalem: Ministry for Foreign Affairs, 1976), 472–473.

20. Hans Morgenthau, *Politics Among Nations*, 6th ed. (New York: McGraw-Hill, 1985), 130.

21. Aron Soffer discusses no less than seventeen "significant" Jordan-Yarmouk water development plans from the 1910s to the 1960s (*Rivers of Fire* (Lanham, MD: Rowman & Littlefield, 1999), 154–175).

22. M. G. Ionides, *Report on Water Resources of the Transjordan and their Development* as cited in American Friends of the Middle East, *Jordan Water Problem: An Analysis and Summary of Available Documents* (Washington, DC: American Friends of the Middle East, Inc., 1964), 12; M. G. Ionides, "The Disputed Waters of Jordan," *Middle East Journal* 7:2 (Spring 1953), 155. Also see "Jordan Valley Irrigation in Transjordan," *Engineering*, 13 Sept. 1946.

23. M. MacDonald, "Report on the Proposed Extension of Irrigation in the Jordan Valley" (London: M. MacDonald and Partners, 1951) as cited in American Friends of the Middle East, *Jordan Water Problem*, 27–31.

24. This program, proposed by President Truman in January 1949, was an attempt to help underdeveloped states help themselves through US technical assistance.

25. Omar Z. Ghobshy, *The Development of the Jordan River* (New York: Arab Information Center, 1961), 13–15.

26. A cubic meter of water is equal to 264 gallons.

27. Ghobshy, *The Development of the Jordan River*, 13–14. Also see American Friends of the Middle East, *Jordan Water Problem*, 32–34.

28. HRP, 32 (30 March 1953).

29. "Treaty Between the Hashemite Kingdom of Jordan and the Syrian Republic for the Utilization of the Waters of the Yarmouk River: Damascus, 4 June 1953" [hereafter Yarmouk Treaty], US National Archives [hereafter USNA], Johnston files, box 4, file 40, Article 2. Also the Treaty assumed that the Maqarin Reservoir would hold 300 mcm [HRP, 34 (4 June 1953)].

30. Yarmouk Treaty, Article 8.

31. Yarmouk Treaty, Article 9.

32. HRP, 32 (24 April 1953).

33. HRP, 33 (8 May 1953).

34. HRP, 31 (4 March 1953).

35. Israeli historical Yarmouk rights are primarily based on the Rutenberg concession. As discussed earlier, the Palestinian Electric Corporation (PEC) built a power station just below the confluence of the Jordan and Yarmouk. Between 1932 and 1948 it supplied electricity to the region. However, in 1948, during the Arab-Israeli War, Jordanians destroyed the internal machinery of the power station (Soffer, *Rivers of Fire*, 155–156). As Jordan and the UNRWA were completing their 1953 agreement to build an upstream Yarmouk dam, legal representatives of the PEC wrote to Henry Cabot Lodge, US Permanent Representative to the UN that the PEC was "entitled to full recognition in the implementation" of the agreement [HRP, 35 (3 July 1953)]. The British Embassy in Washington responded to a US State Department request for clarification of the PEC matter. The British noted that "although the corporation was registered in Israel, much of its capital was British, its concession in Jordan was still valid" [HRP, 38 (11 Sept. 1953)]. The British and subsequently the United States concluded that the corporation's rights were a matter for the corporation to resolve with Israel and Jordan [HRP, 38 (11 Sept. 1953)]. Therefore, because of the Rutenberg concession and because it was a riparian, Israel had water rights to the Yarmouk; however, those rights could only be defined within negotiations with Jordan, and for that matter, Syria. According to Haddadin, the Jordanian government canceled the Rutenberg concession in 1953 (*Diplomacy on the Jordan*, 55). Israel, Britain, and the United States did not recognize this unilateral act as legal because no compensation was made. For more discussion of the Rutenberg concession, see HRP, 31 (4 March 1953) and 48 (27 Nov. 1953).

36. HRP, 30 (31 Dec. 1952, 9 and 23 Jan. 1953).

37. HRP, 33-4 (15 May 1953).

38. Walter C. Lowdermilk, *Palestine: Land of Promise* (New York: Harper and Bros., 1944), 170–179.

39. HRP, 7 (4 Jan. 1945) and 8 (10 March 1945). Also see Ze'ev Schiff, "Israel Looks for Water," *New Outlook* 5:4 (May 1962), 27.

40. Hays also worked with J. L. Savage; James B. Hays, *TVA on the Jordan: Proposals for Irrigation and Hydro-Electric Development in Palestine* (Washington, DC: Public Affairs Press, 1948) as cited in American Friends of the Middle East, *Jordan Water Problem*, 16–26. Savage was favorable to Hays's plan; however, the State Department initially shelved Savage's report because the issue of Palestine had become so controversial [HRP, 8 (10 April 1945)]. In March 1946, the Anglo-American Committee of Inquiry concluded that the proposal made by Hays and Savage had technical, financial, and political shortcomings (HRP, 9 (March 1946)).

41. National engineering and planning were subsequently taken over by Tahal (Water Planning for Israel), a corporation owned by the government of Israel in partnership with the Jewish Agency and the Jewish National Fund.

42. Medzini ed., *Israel's Foreign Relations*, 468, also see 472–475.

43. *Jisr Banat Ya'qub* in Arabic and the Bridge of Jacob's Daughters in English.

44. "Introductory note by Leslie Carver," in *The Unified Development of the Water Resources of the Jordan Valley Region* (Boston: Charles T. Main, Inc., 1953).

45. "Introductory note by Leslie Carver," *The Unified Development of the Water Resources of the Jordan Valley Region*.

46. See, for example, Itamar Rabinovich, *The Road Not Taken: Early Arab-Israeli Negotiations* (New York: Oxford University Press, 1991), 111–167.

47. Shaul Ramati, "Negotiating with Syria—A Historical Perspective," *Jerusalem Post*, 2 Feb. 1996, 9 and Rabinovich, *The Road Not Taken*, 65–110.

48. Rabinovich, *The Road Not Taken*, 168–208.

49. HRP, 12.

50. See Aryeh Shalev, *Israel-Syria Armistice Regime 1949–1955* (Boulder: Westview Press, 1993).

51. *Foreign Relations of the United States 1950: Near East, South Asia, and Africa*, vol. 5 (Washington, DC: US Government Printing Office, 1978), 993–1010, 1020–1021, and 1027, and Shalev, *Israel-Syria Armistice Regime 1949–1955*, 201.

52. HRP 21 (11 Aug. 1951).

53. Rabinovich, *The Road Not Taken*, 65–110, and HRP, 28–29 (3 Nov. 1952).

54. Aryeh Shalev, *Israel and Syria: Peace and Security on the Golan* (Boulder: Westview Press, 1994), 45.

55. Shalev, *Israel and Syria: Peace and Security on the Golan*, 44.

56. Shalev, *Israel and Syria: Peace and Security on the Golan*, 49.

57. Shalev, *Israel and Syria: Peace and Security on the Golan*, 49.

58. *Foreign Relations of the United States 1951: The Near East and Africa*, vol. 5 (Washington, DC: US Government Printing Office, 1982) [hereafter FRUS 1951], 589–590.

59. FRUS 1951, 693–696.

60. FRUS 1951, 700–703 and 727. Also see Shalev, *Israel and Syria: Peace and Security on the Golan*, 159.

61. HRP, 23 (27 Feb. 1952).

62. HRP, 28–29 (3 Nov. 1952) and Shalev, *Israel and Syria: Peace and Security on the Golan*, 159.

63. HRP, 22 (Jan. 1952), 23 (12 April 1952), and 24–25 (11 May 1952).

64. Isaac Alteras, *Eisenhower and Israel: US-Israel Relations, 1953–1960* (Gainesville: University Press of Florida, 1993), 52–81.

65. Eisenhower Library, Whitman File, Dulles-Herter Series, box 1, 17 May 1953; Dulles Papers, box 73, 29 May 1953.

66. For entire speech, see Department of State Press Release #517 or Eisenhower Library, White House Office NSC Series, Policy subseries NSC 5428 Near East [deterrence of the Arab-Israeli War (1)].

67. HRP, 33 (4 May 1953). Dulles had a similar conclusion at the end of his mission [HRP, 34 (1 June 1953)].

68. Arthur Gardiner, the political and economic advisor for the Office of Near Eastern, South Asian and African Affairs, testifying on 4 June 1953. US Congress, House Committee on Foreign Affairs, *Hearings: Mutual Security Act* Extension, 83rd Cong., 1st session (Washington, DC: US Government Printing Office, 1953), 1035.

69. "Palestine Refugee Program," Hearings before the Subcommittee on the Near East and Africa of the Committee on Foreign Relations, United States Senate, 83rd Cong, 1st session, 20, 21, and 25 May 1953 [hereafter Palestine Refugee Program] (Washington, DC: Government Printing Office, 1953), 24–25.

70. Palestine Refugee Program, 27.

71. Estimates of dead from raid range from forty-five to sixty-six (*Foreign Relations of the United States 1952–1954: The Near and Middle East*, vol. 9, part 1 (Washington, DC: US Government Printing Office, 1986) [Hereafter FRUS 1952–1954], 1358–1359).

72. Benny Morris, *Israel's Border War 1949–1956* (Oxford: Clarendon Press, 1993), 244.

73. Brecher, *Decisions in Israel's Foreign Policy*, 189–191. As part of the Rutenberg concession, a dam was built at the southern end of Lake Tiberias to manipulate the flow for the downstream power station. The dam gates also stop water from flowing out of the lake's southern outlet to the lower Jordan. Jordan depended on the flow of the Jor-

dan River to irrigate much of the east and west banks of the Jordan River (Haddadin, *Diplomacy on the Jordan*, 31).

74. HRP, 20 (7 June 1951) and HRP, 20–21 (25 June 1951).

75. E. L. M. Burns, *Between Arab and Israeli* (New York: I Obolensky, 1962), 111. However, Aryeh Shalev, who was an Israeli negotiator during the B'not Yacov dispute, states that "not a single shot was fired" (Shalev, *Israel-Syria Armistice Regime 1949–1955*, 179).

76. Also see, for example, Donald Neff, "Israel-Syria: Conflict at the Jordan River, 1949–1967" *Journal of Palestine Studies* 23:4 (Summer 1994), 26–40.

77. For a bibliographical history of B'not Yacov crisis, see FRUS 1952–1954, 1321, nt. 1. Also see *Yearbook of United Nations, 1953* (New York: UN, 1954), 224.

78. FRUS 1952–1954, 1317 and 1320–1325.

79. USNA, State Department Central Files [hereafter SDCF] 611.84a/9–2553, p. 3.

80. HRP, 42 (20 Oct. 1953).

81. *Yearbook of United Nations, 1953*, 225–226.

82. FRUS 1952–1954, 1390–1391.

83. HRP, 40 (7 Oct. 1953).

84. For a short biography, see "Eric Johnston," *The National Cyclopaedia of American Bibliography*, vol. H (1947–1952) (New York: James T. White, 1952), 98–99.

85. George Barnes, "$200 million for what?" *The Reporter*, 7 Feb. 1957, 25–26.

86. FRUS 1952–1954, 1348 nt. 1.

87. FRUS 1952–1954, 1348–1349 also see FRUS 1952–1954, 1238. The second objective was resolving the problem of Jerusalem, but the State Department later decided to focus only on water for this mission.

88. "The Jordan Valley Plan," 30 Sept. 1955 (photocopy), 1 [provided to author by former State Department officer]; also see FRUS 1952–1954, 1238 and 1270–1275.

89. "The Jordan Valley Plan," 3.

90. "The Jordan Valley Plan," 3–5.

91. "Subject: The Johnston Mission," USNA, Johnston files, box 1, files 1, 1–2 (13 Oct. 1953).

92. "Subject: The Johnston Mission," 1–2; FRUS 1952–1954, 1352–1353.

93. FRUS 1952–1954, 1271.

94. FRUS 1952–1954, 1351; for framework of negotiations see FRUS 1952–1954, 1348–1353.

95. "Subject: The Johnston Mission," 1.

96. Eric Johnston, "My Mission to the Near East: Peacemaking on the Jordan," *New York Herald*, 14 Feb. 1954, 8.

97. Johnston, "My Mission to the Near East," 8.

98. Johnston, "My Mission to the Near East," 8–9.

99. FRUS 1952–1954, 1419.

100. FRUS 1952–1954, 1313–1315, 1319, also see 415. Miriam Lowi makes similar arguments in *Water and Power*.

101. FRUS 1952–1954, 1316.

102. FRUS 1952–1954, 1314.

103. "The Jordan Valley Plan," 4.

104. *Foreign Relations of the United States 1955–1957: Arab-Israeli Dispute 1955*, vol. 14 (Washington, DC: US Government Printing Office, 1989) [Hereafter FRUS 1955], 442.

105. "The Jordan Valley Plan," 5.

106. FRUS 1952–1954, 1677–1678; FRUS 1955, 110.

107. "The Jordan Valley Plan," 3.

108. FRUS 1952–1954, 1422.

109. HRP, 43–44 (26 Oct. 1953).

110. Also, for a detailed summary of the first round of negotiations, see FRUS 1952–1954, 1418–1423.

111. See Ghobshy, *The Development of the Jordan River*, 15–19 and see American Friends of the Middle East, *Jordan Water Problem*, 64–69.

112. Brecher, *Decisions in Israel's Foreign Policy*, 196–197 and HRP, 49–50 (8–9 Feb. 1954).

113. Georgina Stevens, *Jordan River Partition* (Stanford: Hoover Institute, 1965), 23–28.

114. "Guidelines for the second Johnston mission included: (1) not pressing for precision in the allocation of water until ground surveys, land classification studies, and similar technical investigations had been concluded; (2) considering the Adasiya Diversion dam a priority project; and (3) withholding allocations of economic assistance for Israeli and Arab water projects in conflict with the comprehensive plan and making the allocation of other types of aid contingent to some degree on Israeli and Arab cooperation on the Unified Plan" (HRP, 52–53 (4 June 1954)).

115. FRUS 1955, 22.

116. HRP, 72 (10 March 1955).

117. FRUS 1955, 43.

118. FRUS 1955, 44.

119. FRUS 1955, 22.

120. FRUS 1952–1954, 1727.

121. FRUS 1952–1954, 1728.

122. HRP, 55 (6 July 1954).

123. HRP, 57 (28 Sept. 1954).

124. HRP, 59–60 (ca. 15 Dec. 1954). Also see HRP 57–60 for details of the Criddle mission.

125. USNA SDCF 684a.85322/3-2155.

126. Brecher, *Decisions in Israel's Foreign Policy*, 199 and HRP, 61–68.

127. HRP, 71 (22–23 Feb. 1955), also Brecher, *Decisions in Israel's Foreign Policy*, 200–202.

128. "The Jordan Valley Plan," 14–16.

129. FRUS 1955, 65–66 and HRP, 68–69 (19 Feb. 1955).

130. For negotiations leading up to memo see HRP, 73–78, and for memo text see HRP, 78–83. Israel pressed Johnston to make the memo binding, but Johnston balked. Johnston indicated that he was "unwilling to make 'further demands' on Israel beyond the position set forth in the memorandum of July 5." But he also reaffirmed that he would not state in writing or otherwise that he had reached a "common understanding with Israel" (HRP, 85, 23–26 Aug. 1955). In other words, he wanted to aid the pro-agreement faction of the Israeli government as well as maintain a degree of flexibility, which would have been lost. Israel wanted, for example, the 40 mcm from the Yarmouk and Johnston, at that point, was unwilling to commit in writing. The prime minister asked for "satisfactory adjustments" in the policy.

131. HRP, 87 (29 Aug. 1955).

132. HRP, 94 (7 Oct. 1955) and HRP, 89–93.

133. USNA SDCF 684a.85322/10-1555 and HRP, 94 (11 Oct. 1955).

134. By February 1956, Johnston conveyed to President Eisenhower that the technical aspects of his water plan were accepted by Israel and by the Arabs. However, the Arab states still had unresolved political issues (HRP, 102 (10 Feb. 1956)). That same month, the State Department instructed its embassies in Cairo, Amman, Damascus, and Tel Aviv to urge their respective governments to accept the Johnston Plan. Johnston wrote a letter to Nasser asking him to help move the Arab countries toward a positive final decision on the plan (HRP, 103–104 (23 Feb. 1956)). In fact, Lebanese President Chamoun indicated that Syria was the primary opponent of the plan and that "only Egypt could influence Syria" (HRP, 104 (27 Feb. 1956)). The United States, Britain, and the United Nations discussed using the incentive of giving international permission to Israel to resume work on B'not Yacov as a means to "sell" a positive decision on the Johnston Plan to the Arabs (HRP, 104 (10 March 1956) and 106 (17 May 1956)). Nasser made clear to the United States that Arab governments would not accept the Johnston Plan because of Israeli threats to resume the B'not Yacov project (HRP, 104 (27 Feb. 1956)). And, in the end, Dulles urged Israel not to resume work at B'not Yacov (HRP, 105 (28 March 1956)).

135. HRP, 100 (26 Oct. 1955). The Johnston Plan was also known as the Unified Plan, the Revised Unified Plan, and the Jordan Valley Plan. Nasser promised Johnston that the Arab League Council would meet again soon to discuss the Plan. (*Foreign Relations of the United States 1955–1957: Arab-Israeli Dispute January 1–July 26, 1956* vol. 15 (Washington, DC: US Government Printing Office, 1989) [Hereafter FRUS 1956], 162). The Arab League met in Cairo, mid-March 1956, and discussed the Johnston Plan, but again adjourned its meeting without taking any action.

136. For comparison of allocations of Jordan Valley Regional Water Plans: 1953–1955, see Brecher, *Decisions in Israel's Foreign Policy*, 204.

137. FRUS 1955, 364.

138. Barnes, "$200 Million For What?" 26.

139. FRUS 1955, 521; also see 568 and 364.

140. FRUS 1952–1954, 1571.

141. FRUS 1955, 54.

142. FRUS 1952–1954, 1382; also see Hadaddin, *Diplomacy on the Jordan*, 49–50.

143. FRUS 1952–1954, 1383.

144. Eisenhower Library, White House Office, USA NSA Box 5 NSC Series, Policy Papers subseries NSC 155/1–Near East (1) "Progress Report," 6; Alteras, *Eisenhower and Israel*, 121.

145. FRUS 1956, 360–361 and 429–430 and HRP, 105 (14 March 1956) and 94 (7 Oct. 1955). Lebanese Foreign Minister Lahoud also recommended two separate plans done quietly under the broad concept of the Johnston Plan (FRUS 1956, 286, and 710–713 and HRP, 106 (30 May 1956)); FRUS 1956, 169.

146. FRUS 1956, 183.

147. This position goes back to the Tripartite Declaration of May 1950 (see Sachar, *History of Israel*, 458).

148. Eisenhower Library, Dulles Papers, box 3, 14 Feb. 1955. Also see Shimon Shamir, "The Collapse of Project Alpha," in Roger Louis and William Roger Owen, eds., *Suez 1956* (Oxford: Clarendon Press, 1989). Neil Caplan, *Futile Diplomacy*, vol. I (Totowa, NJ: Frank Cass, 1983).

149. FRUS 1955, 38–42. No earlier documents concerning discussion with Johnston on the Alpha project were found at the United States National Archives.

150. FRUS 1955, 70.

151. FRUS 1955, 251–253.

152. HRP, 83 (11 July 1955).

153. FRUS 1955, 284–285, nt. 2.

154. HRP, 83 (11 July 1955).

155. HRP, 86 (26 Aug. 1955).

156. Eisenhower Library, US Department of State Press Release No. 517, 2.

157. Alteras, *Eisenhower and Israel*, 165–171.

158. FRUS 1956, 20; FRUS 1955, 204–205.

159. USNA "Subject: The United States Position with Respect to the Unified Plan," 29 March 1965, POL 33-1 Jordan River, 1.

160. "Joint Communiqué," 13 Oct. 1955; Johnston Files, box 2 file 27.

161. "The Jordan Valley Plan," 6–7.

162. "The Jordan Valley Plan," 10; "US-Arab Memorandum of Understanding," 11 Oct. 1955, Johnston files box 3, file 29, 1.

163. "The Jordan Valley Plan," 10.

164. "US-Arab Memorandum of Understanding," 2.

165. "US-Arab Memorandum of Understanding," 5–6.

166. HRP, 81–82 (5 July 1955) and Israel-US "Draft Memorandum of Understanding," 5 July 1955, Johnston files, box 3, file 30, 6.

167. "US-Arab Memorandum of Understanding," 6. The salt level does not exceed 2,500 parts per million of chlorine.

168. If Lake Tiberias were to be used as storage, the watermaster would deliver Jordan's share, in accordance with the "storage" section of the plan.

169. "US-Arab Memorandum of Understanding," 7–8.

170. Security refers to riparians not being dependent on Israel for Lake Tiberias water supply.

171. HRP, 82 (5 July 1955) and Israel-US "Draft Memorandum of Understanding," 7.

172. "US-Arab Memorandum of Understanding," 5; similar language in US-Israel "Draft Memorandum of Understanding," 3.

173. Israel-US "Draft Memorandum of Understanding," 7; "US-Arab Memorandum of Understanding," 6.

174. "US-Arab Memorandum of Understanding," 3; however, the Israel memo only states "from a list prepared by an agreed body," 4.

175. "US-Arab Memorandum of Understanding," 3.

176. "The Jordan Valley Plan," 19.

177. Nadav Safran, *Israel: The Embattled Ally* (Cambridge: Harvard University Press, 1981), 334.

178. Safran, *Israel: The Embattled Ally*, 225–226.

179. See Elie Kedourie, *Democracy and Arab Political Culture* (Washington, DC: Washington Institute for Near East Policy, 1992) and Shalev, *Israel-Syria Armistice Regime 1949–1955*, 15 and 91–92.

180. See, for example, George Lenczowski, The Middle East in World Affairs, 4th ed. (Ithaca: Cornell University Press, 1980).

181. Shalev, *Israel-Syria Armistice Regime 1949–1955*, 15 and 93–94.

182. HRP, 58 (5 Nov. 1954).

183. Safran, *Israel: The Embattled Ally*, 225.

184. Safran, *Israel: The Embattled Ally*, 334.

185. Peter Haas, "Introduction: Epistemic Communities and International Policy Coordination," *International Organization* 46:1 (Winter 1992), 1–35.

186. Peter Evans, Harold Jacobson, and Robert Putnam, eds., *Double-Edged Diplomacy: International Bargaining and Domestic Politics* (Berkeley: University of California Press, 1993), especially the "Introduction" by Andrew Moravcsik, 3–42.

187. HRP, 93 (7 Oct. 1955).

188. Shalev, *Israel-Syria Armistice Regime 1949–1955*, 51.

189. Shalev, *Israel-Syria Armistice Regime 1949–1955*, 69.

190. Shalev, *Israel-Syria Armistice Regime 1949–1955*, 81–82.

191. James Fearon, "Counterfactuals and Hypothesis Testing in Political Science," *World Politics* 43:2 (January 1991), 169–195.

192. In Paris, from September 13 to November 19, 1951, the Palestine Conciliation Commission held a conference with the objective of achieving "a political settlement between Israel and its Arab neighbors." The conference failed (HRP, 22).

193. "The US Position with Respect to the Unified Plan," USNA, POL-33-1, Jordan River file 29 March 1965, 2.

194. FRUS 1956, 24–25, 90, 178, and 400–401.

195. FRUS 1956, 401–402.

196. FRUS 1955, 586–587 and 567–568.

CHAPTER 3: WATER DEVELOPMENT AND CONFLICT, 1957–1967

1. "The Jordan Valley Water Question 1919–1984," Historical Research Project No. 1403 US State Department, Bureau of Public Affairs, Office of the Historian (August 1984) [hereafter HRP], 108 (10 April–5 May 1957). Also HRP, 107–108.

2. HRP, 108–109. By February 1958, the State Department approved $8.56 million for the construction of the East Ghor Canal system (HRP, 112 (1 Feb. 1958)). During May 1960, the United States gave $1.525 million to Jordan to complete the present phase of the project (HRP, 129 (28 May 1958)). Also HRP, 123. The United States also agreed to provide military assistance to Jordan. HRP, 108 (25, 27, and 29 June 1957).

3. Ian Bickerton and Carla L. Klausner, *A Concise History of the Arab-Israeli Conflict* (Englewood Cliffs, NJ: Prentice-Hall, 1991), 143.

4. *Foreign Relations of the United States 1955–1957: The Arab Israeli Dispute 1957,* vol. 17 (Washington, DC: US Government Printing Office, 1990), [hereafter FRUS 1957], 742 and 751, and State Department Central Files [hereafter SDCF] 320.51/7–257. *Foreign Relations of the United States 1961–1963: Near East 1961–1962,* vol. 17 (Washington, DC: US Government Printing Office, 1994), [hereafter FRUS 1961–1962], 53. In New York, Johnston met with Arab leaders who told him they favored a "piecemeal" approach to the Jordan water issue so as not to inflame the region (HRP, 124 (13 Oct. 1959)).

5. FRUS 1957, 751.

6. By 1959, Eric Johnston was an outspoken proponent for US assistance to Jordan for building the Maqarin Dam. In the early 1960s, Johnston quietly met with Arab leaders and discussed aspects of his water-sharing plan, but, after 1955, he did not return to the region in an official capacity to mediate (*Foreign Relations of the United States 1958–1960: Arab-Israeli Dispute; United Arab Republic; North Africa,* vol. 13 (Washington, DC: US Government Printing Office, 1992). [Hereafter FRUS 1958–1960, vol. 13], 161–162.

7. By 1962, the United States began an initiative to resolve the Palestinian refugee question through the Joseph Johnson mission. In the end, this mission also was not successful, see *Foreign Relations of the United States 1961–1963: Near East 1962–1963,* vol. 18 (Washington, DC: US Government Printing Office, 1995). (Hereafter FRUS 1962–1963).

8. *Foreign Relations of the United States 1958–1960: Near East Region; Iraq; Iran; Arabian Peninsula,* vol. 12 (Washington, DC: US Government Printing Office, 1993) [hereafter FRUS 1958–1960, vol. 12]. Also known as NSC 5801, #40 (24 January 1958), 28. Emphasis added.

9. FRUS 1958–1960, vol. 13, 35, President Eisenhower initialed a 28 March 1958 memorandum approving this policy; see, Eisenhower Library, Whitman file, Administration series, box 11, Cutler, General Robert L., 1958, 3. It should be added that the United States, in the end, followed a recommendation proposed two years earlier by Nasser and other Arab leaders; see chapter 2.

10. FRUS 1958–1960, vol. 13, 255–256.

11. FRUS 1957, 750.

12. FRUS 1961–1962, 15–17 and 521.

13. Many US policymakers believed that the Arab League had blocked the Johnston Plan for political reasons and that Israel's water use still allowed Jordan to irrigate much of the Jordan Valley. For the United States, it was illogical to expect Israel to halt its water development program merely because the Arab states could not reach a political agreement among themselves (FRUS 1961–1962, 15–17).

14. United States National Archives [USNA] "Jordan Water," 6 December 1963, p. 1, POL 33–1 Isr-Jordan also HRP, 143 (6 Dec. 1963).

15. FRUS 1962–1963, vol. 18, 80.

16. Marjorie M. Whiteman, *Digest of International Law*, vol. 3 (Washington, DC: Department of State, 1964), 1018.

17. For example, correspondence from Ben-Gurion to Kennedy [HRP, 134 (24 June 1962)].

18. HRP, 114 (4 March 1958) and 121 (28 Jan. 1959). Also, in 1956, Israel and the United States were discussing a $75 million Export-Import Bank loan to develop Israel's water sources (HRP, 105–106 (March–April 1956)). By January 1958, officials at State were arguing that a bank loan "would not be politically wise" at that time (HRP, 110 (3 Jan. 1958)). In the end, the State Department deferred action on the loan request (HRP, 110 (6 Jan. 1958)). The United States had also unsuccessfully tried to link the Arab refugee issue to aid for water development (HRP, 112 (28 Jan. 1958)).

19. HRP, 111 (8 Jan. 1958) and 113 (27 Feb. 1958).

20. HRP, 113 (24 Feb. 1958).

21. HRP, 113 (25 Feb. 1958).

22. HRP, 121 (30 Dec. 1958).

23. USNA "East Ghor Development scheme" p. 1, Johnston files, box 5, file 47 and HRP, 130 (7 Aug. 1960). Also see the US-Jordan agreement on American funding for the canal project, 28 May 1960. Design of the East Ghor Canal had begun by Jordan in 1957. It was intended as the first section of a much more ambitious plan known as the Greater Yarmouk Project. Thomas Naff and Ruth Matson, eds., *Water in the Middle East: Conflict or Cooperation?* (Boulder: Westview Press, 1984), 43.

24. The State Department's response was that America was providing $80 million in assistance to Israel in 1958 that included the $24.2 million Export-Import Bank loan for developing Israel's water resources outside the Jordan Valley (FRUS 1958–1960, vol. 13, 35).

25. Meron Medzini, ed., *Israel's Foreign Relations: Selected Documents 1947–1974* (Jerusalem: Ministry for Foreign Affairs, 1976), 471.

26. SDCF 684a.85322/4–1062. Also Water Planning for Israel *Yarkon-Negev Project: Detailed Report* (Tel Aviv, 1956). This scheme was based on a ten-year plan that evolved from the 1953 seven-year plan. Michael Brecher, *Decisions in Israel's Foreign Policy* (New Haven: Yale University Press, 1975), 209–210.

27. HRP, 121 (4 Mar. 1959).

28. Brecher, *Decisions in Israel's Foreign Policy*, 208.

29. Brecher, *Decisions in Israel's Foreign Policy*, 208–209 and HRP, 122 (9 March 1959).

30. More recently, in 1992, Israel was using 12 percent of its electricity to pump water and Jordan was using 20 percent. Stephen Lonergan and David Brooks, *Watershed: The Role of Water in the Israel-Palestinian Conflict* (Ottawa: International Development Research Centre, 1994), 69.

31. SDCF 684a.85322/6-1462 also HRP, 135 (31 Aug 1962).

32. Prior to this loan, the United States lent Israel approximately $45 million for water development. Most of this was used for projects not related to the National Water Carrier project (SDCF 684a.85322/6–1462).

33. USNA, "Johnston Plan Chronology," Johnston files, box 3, file 36 (circa 1960).

34. HRP, 127 (28 Dec, 1959).

35. For a short biography, see "Death: Wayne D. Criddle" *Desert News* Archives, Dec. 4, 1996, B4.

36. For example, HRP, 162 (22 Sept. 1964) and 147 (7–9 Jan. 1964) and FRUS 1962–1963, vol. 18, 767.

37. Israel, along with the United States, wanted to address Jordan's existing water problems, presumably because an unfairly treated Jordan might give Arab critics of Israel's water program strong grounds in international law that the Jordan River water was being unequally distributed and provide strength for the argument that the Israeli project should be suspended.

38. USNA "Criddle Visit" 17 July 1963, POL 33–1 Isr-Jor., 4.

39. *Foreign Relations of the United States 1964–1968:* vol. 18 *Arab-Israeli Dispute, 1964–1967* (Washington, DC: US Government Printing Office, 2000), [hereafter FRUS 1964–1967], 27 nt. 5. HRP, 147–148 (7–9 Jan. 1964); also HRP, 156 (23 June 1964).

40. HRP, 153 (3,7, and 19 March 1964) and HRP, v.

41. HRP, 154 (21 April 1964).

42. HRP, 59 (10 Nov. 1954).

43. HRP, 59–60 (ca. 14 Dec. 1954). Criddle noted that the Israel water claim of 2.3 cms "is probably based on the fact that a large percentage of the area is devoted to fish culture and to raising bananas," both of which required considerable water (HRP, 59 (10 Nov. 1954)). Criddle explained that water requirements for Arab lands were much lower than what the Israelis were computing for the Yarmouk Triangle.

44. "Criddle Visit," 1. "Jordan Waters" 13 May 1963, POL-33-1 Isr-Syr. This is equivalent to about 2 cms during the five summer months. Jordan followed this secret cooperative arrangement for almost thirty-five years ("Criddle Visit"). Also see HRP, 115 (13–14 March 1958). During this period, Israel was still arguing for 40 mcm, which is 2.5 cms or higher (HRP, 116 (2 Apr. 1958) and 115 (27 March 1958)).

45. "Criddle Visit," 4; "Jordan Waters" 13 May 1963, POL 33-1 Isr-Syr.

46. "Criddle Visit" and 17 July 1963 POL 33-1 ISR-JOR [cover aerogram].

47. HRP, v.

48. HRP, 136 (17 Jan. 1963).

49. HRP, 142 (30 Sept. 1963).

50. HRP, 136 (20 March 1963).

51. HRP, 163 (25 Sept. 1964). HRP, 116 (27 March 1958) also see HRP, 162–163 (22–25 Sept. 1964). "Criddle Visit," 3–4.

52. HRP, 164 (5, 6, and 12 Oct. 1964).

53. FRUS 1964–1967, 92.

54. FRUS 1958–1960, 206 and 250.

55. SDCF 684a.85322/8–362. The seven-man MAC group consisted of two Jordanian officials, two Israeli army officers, a representative of the Israeli water planning authority, and two UNTSO representatives. During the summer season this group inspected the weir (SDCF 684a.85322/9-2862). Also see HRP, 135 (3, 13–14 Sept. and 6 Nov. 1962).

56. SDCF 684a.85322/11-1562 also HRP, 134 (1 Aug. 1962) and 135 (17 Sept. 1962).

57. USNA, "Jordan Water: Yarmouk Flow," 19 June 1965, POL 33-1 Jordan River, 3.

58. USNA, "Jordan Water: Israel: Request for Jordanian Assurances," 11 Dec. 1965, POL 33-1 Jordan River, 1–2.

59. USNA, "Jordan Waters: Yarmouk Flow," 11 June 1965, POL 33-1 Jordan River.

60. FRUS 1961–1962, 30.

61. Aharon Klieman, *Statecraft in the Dark: Israel's Practice of Quiet Diplomacy* (Boulder: Westview Press, 1988), 98.

62. King Hussein told US diplomats that he had been meeting with Israeli leaders between 1963 and 1966 (FRUS 1964–1967, 713).

63. HRP, 155 (10 June 1964).

64. HRP, 156–7 (3 July 1964).

65. HRP, 159 (18 July 1964).

66. HRP, v.

67. HRP, 160 (10 Aug. 1964) also (24 and 29 July 1964) and 161 (2 Sept. 1964). FRUS 1964–1967, 109–110.

68. HRP, 161 (2 Sept. 1964).

69. USNA, "Jordan Water: Comments on Eshkol's 'Warning' to King Hussein," 14 May 1965, POL 33-1 Jordan River.

70. USNA, "Jordan Water: Comments on Eshkol's 'Warning' to King Hussein," 14 May 1965, POL 33-1 Jordan River.

71. HRP, 179 (15 June 1965). Jordan was upset at Israel's dumping the saline springs in the lower Jordan. That might have been another reason why Israel did not protest more vigorously earlier.

72. USNA, "US Position if Jordan Cuts Off Yarmuk," 26 May 1965, POL 33-1 Isr-Jor also HRP, 177–178 (2 June 1965).

73. Yossi Melman and Dan Raviv, *Behind the Uprising: Israelis, Jordanians and Palestinians* (New York: Greenwood Press, 1989), 75–76.

74. USNA, "Jordan Water: Yarmuk Water for Adasiyah Triangle—II," 28 January 1965, POL 33-1 Jordan River, 2. USNA "Jordan Water: Review of Current Status of Arab Activities," 20 Oct. 1966, POL 33-1 Jordan River, 4.

75. USNA, "Jordan Water: Yarmuk Water for Adasiyah Triangle—II," 28 Jan. 1965, POL 33-1 Jordan River, 2.

76. HRP, 133 (10 March 1962). Also see HRP, 129 (18 March 1960) and 131 (23 May 1961).

77. Whiteman, *Digest of International Law*, 1019. Israeli intelligence warned that the Syrians had formed a committee to divert water from Israel (HRP, 126 (8 Dec. 1959)). For details of the Arab diversion plan, see Munther Haddadin, *Diplomacy on the Jordan* (Boston: Kluwer, 2002), 167–173 and Moshe Shemesh, "Prelude to the Six-Day War: The Arab-Israeli Struggle Over Water Resources," *Israel Studies* 9:3 (Fall 2004), 1–45.

78. HRP, 126 (10 Dec. 1959).

79. HRP, 149 (13–17 Jan. 1964) and 161 (5–11 Sept. 1964).

80. HRP, 144 (12 Dec. 1963).

81. Melman and Raviv, *Behind the Uprising*, 72.

82. Naff and Matson, *Water in the Middle East*, 44.

83. FRUS 1958–1960, vol. 13, 255 and 258–259.

84. FRUS 1961–1962, 16. Also see chapter 2.

85. FRUS 1962–1963, vol. 18, 771 and HRP, 103 (20 Feb. 1956).

86. HRP, 103 (20 Feb. 1956).

87. FRUS 1961–1962, 502.

88. FRUS 1964–1967, 92–3.

89. Whiteman, *Digest of International Law*, 1019. During this period, there was Arab concern over the US decision in 1962 to supply Israel with Hawk missiles, the first major weapon system provided to Israel by the United States. Another issue of concern was Israel's nuclear reactor at Dimona (FRUS 1961-1962). Also see Warren Bass, *Support Any Friend: Kennedy's Middle East and the Making of the US-Israel Alliance* (New York: Oxford University Press, 2003).

90. HRP, 145–146 (2 Jan. 1964).

91. USNA, "Jordan Waters," 20 Dec. 1963, POL 33–1 Jordan Waters, 1–2.

92. FRUS 1961–1962, 490–493 and HRP, 139 (22 May 1963).

93. Nadav Safran, *Israel: The Embattled Ally* (Cambridge: Belknap Press, 1981), 386–387.

94. Fred Lawson, *Why Syria Goes to War* (Ithaca: Cornell University Press, 1996), 35.

95. HRP, 134 (24 June 1962).

96. "The Arab Plan to Divert the Headwaters of the River Jordan," Topics no. 14 (Jerusalem: Ministry for Foreign Affairs, Information Department, April 1965).

97. "The Arab Plan to Divert the Headwaters of the River Jordan," 7.

98. "The Arab Plan to Divert the Headwaters of the River Jordan," 7.

99. "The Arab Plan to Divert the Headwaters of the River Jordan," 7.

100. HRP, 150 (20 Jan. 1964).

101. Brecher, *Decisions in Israel's Foreign Policy*, 182; also Terence Prittie, *Eshkol: The Man and the Nation* (New York: Pitman, 1969).

102. HRP, 164 (5 Nov. 1964).

103. HRP, 164 (5 Nov. 1964). This was also true for the British and French, see Moshe Gat, *Britain and the Conflict in the Middle East, 1964–1967: The Coming of the Six-Day War* (Westport, CT: Praeger, 2003).

104. FRUS 1962–1963, vol. 18, 731.

105. FRUS 1962–1963, vol. 18, 732–733.

106. FRUS 1961–1962, 522.

107. HRP, 132 (2 Feb. and 26 Aug 1962).

108. HRP, 144 (12 Dec. 1963) and 143 (30 Oct. 1963).

109. FRUS 1962–1963, vol. 18, 765.

110. FRUS 1962–1963, 767; USNA, "Meeting with Israeli Ambassador," 26 December [1963] POL 33-1 Jordan River; USNA "Jordan Waters: our commitment to support Israel," 24 March 1965 POL 33-1 Jordan River.

111. USNA, "Jordan Waters: Our Commitment to Support Israel," and HRP, 146 (7 Jan. 1964). Also FRUS 1964–1967, 1–2.

112. Mordechi Gazit, *President Kennedy's Policy Toward the Arab States and Israel: Analysis and Documents* (Tel Aviv: Shiloah Center, Tel Aviv University, 1983), 48 and 95–96 and HRP, 134 (13 June 1962).

113. USNA "Jordan Waters: our commitment to support Israel," 1–2, and *Congressional Record*, 8 July 1964, 15,596.

114. USNA, "Recommended Demarche to Israeli Ambassador on Jordan Waters," 9 Feb. 1965, POL 33–1 Jordan River.

115. USNA, "Talking Points" circa 1965, POL 33-1 Jordan River, 2.

116. *FRUS 1964–1967*, 284.

117. *FRUS 1964–1967*, 485 also see 459 and 132. The United States was also concerned that the water dispute might jeopardize its oil interests (*FRUS 1964–1967*, 23).

118. USNA "Jordan Waters: Summary of Recent Meetings with Israel," 1 April 1965, POL 33–1 Jordan River.

119. Stephen Walt, *The Origins of Alliances* (Ithaca: Cornell University Press, 1987), 94. By 1966, these US efforts to improve relations with Egypt ended (Walt, *Origins of Alliances*, 97). As previously noted, during the Kennedy administration, the United States also committed itself to protecting Israel's security and sold military equipment to Israel to counter Soviet aid to Arab states.

120. HRP, 137 (26 April 1963).

121. FRUS 1964–1967, 335.

122. FRUS 1964–1967, 383–384 and 347.

123. HRP, 170 (5 Feb. 1965). USNA "Jordan Waters: Our Commitment to Support Israel."

124. HRP, 168 (21 Jan. 1965) and 166 (1 Jan. 1965).

125. HRP, 168 (21 Jan. 1965).

126. HRP, 169 (1 and 5 Feb. 1965). Lebanon indicated to the US that it would "go very slow" in the construction of the diversion project [HRP, 178 (11 June 1965)].

127. HRP, 169 (4 Feb. 1965).

128. HRP, 170 (10 and 11 Feb. 1965).

129. HRP, 170 (12 Feb. 1965). FRUS 1964–1967, 325.

130. Harriman was in the region from Feb. 25 to April 3, 1965 (HRP, 171). USNA "Referral of Jordan Waters Question to United Nations" 3 April 1965, POL 33-1 Jor.

131. HRP, 172 (1 and 12 March 1965).

132. HRP, 173 (15 March 1965).

133. HRP, 173–174 (17 and 26 March 1965) and Shemesh, "Prelude to the Six-Day War," 26–33.

134. HRP, 176 (7 April 1965).

135. HRP, 176 (8, 9, and 12 April 1965).

136. HRP, 177 (13 May 1965).

137. USNA, "Israeli Concerns over Lebanese Canal Construction," 14 July 1965, POL 33-1 Jordan River, 5.

138. USNA, "Jordan Waters: Lebanese Diversion Project," 23 July 1965, POL 33-1 Jordan River, 1–2.

139. USNA, [Government of Israel is] Relatively Calm on Water Diversion," 25 June 1966, POL 33-1 Jordan River.

140. HRP, 195 (14 July 1966) and Shemesh, "Prelude to the Six-Day War," 26–33.

141. HRP, 196 (25 and 26 July 1966).

142. HRP, 195 (16 July 1966).

143. HRP, 195–196 (16 and 17 July 1966).

144. HRP, 198 (9 Jan. 1967).

145. HRP, 184 (3 Sept. 1965).

146. HRP, 185 (4 Nov. 1965).

147. HRP, 185–186 (17 Nov. 1965).

148. HRP, 192 (20 April 1966).

149. HRP, 198 (3 Jan. 1967).

150. HRP, 187 (4–11 Jan. 1965).

151. Lawson, *Why Syria Goes to War*, 51 and FRUS 1962–1963, 763.

152. Richard Parker, *The Politics of Miscalculation in the Middle East* (Bloomington: Indiana University Press, 1993), 25.

153. Haddadin, *Diplomacy on the Jordan*, 197–198.

154. For US documents and analysis of the 1967 Arab-Israel War, see Michael Oren, *Six Days of War: June 1967 and the Making of the Modern Middle East* (New York: Oxford University Press, 2002) and *Foreign Relations of the United States 1964–1968: The Arab-Israeli Crisis and War*, vol. 16 (Washington, DC: US Government Printing Office, 2004).

155. Paul Simon, *Tapped Out* (New York: Welcome Rain, 1998), 49–50.

156. Naff and Matson, eds., *Water in the Middle East*, 44. Also see Safran, *Israel: The Embattled Ally*, 386, and Aryeh Shalev, *Israel and Syria: Peace and Security on the Golan* (Tel Aviv: Jaffee Center for Strategic Studies, 1994), 49.

157. Aaron Wolf, "'Water Wars' and Water Reality: Conflict and Cooperation Along International Waterways," in S. C. Lonergan, ed., *Environmental Change, Adaptation, and Security* (Boston: Kluwer,1999), 254.

158. Norman Myers, *Ultimate Security: The Environmental Basis of Political Stability* (New York: Norton, 1993) as cited by Wolf in "'Water Wars' and Water Reality," 254.

159. Safran, *Israel: The Embattled Ally*, 386.

160. Joseph Nye, *Understanding International Conflicts: An Introduction to Theory and History*, 3rd ed. (New York: Longman, 2000), 71.

161. Kenneth Waltz, *Theory of International Politics* (New York: McGraw-Hill, 1979).

CHAPTER 4: THE YARMOUK, 1967–1994

1. The three tributaries are the Dan, which was already within pre–1967 Israel, the Banias, whose headwaters are part of the captured Golan Heights, and the Hasbani,

which rises in southeastern Lebanon, close to the Israeli border. Israel gained control of the Syrian side of the Mukheibeh Dam site. "The Jordan Valley Water Question 1919–1984," Historical Research Project No. 1403 US State Department, Bureau of Public Affairs, Office of the Historian (August 1984) [hereafter HRP], vi and 201 (31 July 1967 and 14 Aug 1967). Before 1967, the north bank of the Yarmouk, opposite the canal intake, was part of the demilitarized zone, and controlled by Syria.

2. In 1987, the East Ghor Canal was renamed the King Abdullah Canal.

3. HRP, vi, 202 (26 Oct. 1967), and 203 (7–10 Nov. 1967). During this period Lebanon also cancelled its Meifdoun Dam project.

4. "Briefing to Israel Team" (photocopy) document obtained through a Freedom of Information Act petition [hereafter FOIA], July 1990, 4.

5. See, for example, Laurie Brand, *Jordan's Inter-Arab Relations: The Political Economy of Alliance Making* (New York: Columbia University Press, 1994).

6. Specific security arrangements for the Golan area, which were negotiated after the 1973 Arab-Israeli War, were adhered to by both Syria and Israel (Moshe Ma'oz, *Asad: The Sphinx of Damascus: A political biography* (New York: Weidenfeld & Nicholson, 1988), 90–97.

7. Between December 1967 and August 1968 Israel considered and then dropped a Yarmouk-Tiberias Canal project. Even with its military victories, Israel was reluctant to challenge the United States and its understanding of the Johnston Plan (HRP, 206 (17 Aug. 1968)).

8. Yossi Melman and Dan Raviv, *Behind the Uprising: Israelis, Jordanians, and Palestinians* (New York: Greenwood Press, 1989), 93–96 and Aharon Klieman, *Statecraft in the Dark: Israel's Practice of Quiet Diplomacy* (Boulder: Westview Press, 1988), 99–101.

9. Even after West Bank control passed from Jordan to Israel, Amman continued to pay most West Bank civil servants' salaries. West Bank schools continued to use Jordanian curricula and textbooks. Furthermore, Israel and Jordan attempted to work out arrangements for West Bank agriculture, banking, passport control, tourism, land registry, hospital, and court operations, electricity gridding, and administration of the bridges across the Jordan. See Adam Garfinkle, *Israel and Jordan in the Shadow of War* (New York: St. Martin's Press, 1992) and Yehuda Lukacs, *Israel, Jordan, and the Peace Process* (Syracuse: Syracuse University Press, 1997).

10. Ian Lustick, "Israel and Jordan: The Implications of an Adversarial Partnership," *Policy Papers in International Affairs*, no. 6 (Berkeley: Institute of International Studies, University of California, 1978), 7.

11. HRP, 203 (22 Dec. 1967); 205 (16 May 1968) and 206 (7 Aug. 1968).

12. *Fedayeen* mean those who are willing to sacrifice themselves for their cause's sake (Nadav Safran, *Israel: The Embattled Ally* (Cambridge: Belknap Press, 1981), 266).

13. Rami Khouri, *The Jordan Valley: Life and Society Below Sea Level* (London: Longman, 1981), 102.

14. Khouri, *The Jordan Valley*, 99.

15. HRP, 204–208. Israel had also damaged the canal during the 1967 Arab-Israeli War.

16. HRP, 204 (21 March 1968).

17. Thomas Naff and Ruth Matson, eds., *Water and the Middle East: Conflict or Cooperation?* (Boulder: Westview Press, 1984), 45, and Khouri, *The Jordan Valley: Life and Society Below Sea Level*, 101.

18. "Terrorists Blast Hydro Plant—in Jordan," *Jerusalem Post*, 12 Sept. 1969; Naff and Matson, *Water in the Middle East*, 45. Also Sara Reguer, "Rutenberg and the Jordan River: A Revolution in Hydroelectricity," *Middle East Studies* 31:4 (Oct. 1995), 691–729; Tirza Yuval, "Power Politics," *Eretz Magazine*, vol. 40 (May–June 1995), 19–26.

19. "Terrorists Blast Hydro Plant—in Jordan," *Jerusalem Post*, 19 Sept. 1969.

20. HRP, 207 (12 Aug. 1969).

21. HRP, 207–208 (20 Aug. 1969) and 208 (3 Sept. 1969).

22. Naff and Matson, *Water in the Middle East*, 45.

23. As a result of the Jordanian civil war, Arab financial assistance from Saudi Arabia, Libya, Iraq, and other Arab states was greatly reduced or altogether cut off to Jordan. See, for example, William Quandt, *Decade of Decision: American Policy Toward the Arab-Israeli Conflict, 1967–1976* (Berkeley: University of California Press, 1977), 110–119; Adam Garfinkle, "US Decision Making in the Jordan Crisis: Correcting the Record," *Political Science Quarterly* 100:1 (Spring 1985), 117–138; and Henry Kissinger, *White House Years* (Boston: Little, Brown, 1979), 594–631.

24. Khouri, *The Jordan Valley*, 9–11.

25. Daniel Pipes, "The Unacknowledged Partnership," *The National Interest* (Winter 1987–1988), 98.

26. Pipes, "The Unacknowledged Partnership," 97.

27. Jordan Valley Commission, *Rehabilitation and Development Plan of the Jordan Valley (East Bank) 1973–1975* (Amman: October 1972).

28. Khouri, *The Jordan Valley*, 112 and Naff and Matson, *Water in the Middle East*, 50–51. Also, Munther Haddadin, *Diplomacy on the Jordan: International Conflict and Negotiated Resolution* (Boston: Kluwer, 2002), 218–219.

29. Harza Overseas Engineering Company, *Jordan Valley Irrigation Project, Stage II Project Overview* (Chicago: Harza, September 1979). As discussed in chapter 2, a Yarmouk dam as part of a larger Jordanian river development dates back to the 1930s. The Maqarin location dates back to 1952 and is part of the Johnston Plan.

30. Khattan Salman, "Jordan Remains Under-Supplied by Region's Water Sources," *Jordan Times*, 29 July 1995.

31. Haddadin, *Diplomacy on the Jordan*, 224.

32. For description of pipeline system, see "Visit to Yarmouk Triangle Water System" (Tel Aviv 4710) 28 March 1988.

33. Joseph C. Wheeler, USAID testimony, Foreign Assistance Legislation for FY 1981 (Part 3), "FY 81 Foreign Assistance Requests for Europe and the Middle East." House Foreign Affairs Committee (CIS no. 80–H381–63) [96th Congress, second session, Jan./Feb./March 1980], "Hearing before the Subcommittee on Foreign Affairs," House of Representatives (Washington, DC: US Government Printing Office, 1980), [hereafter cited as US Congress 1980], 136 and xix. Also see HRP, 213 (23 Jan. 1975) and HRP, 214–215 (1 July 1975).

34. Joseph C. Wheeler, USAID testimony, Foreign Assistance Legislation for FY 1979 (Part 5), [95th Congress, second session, Feb./March 1978], House Committee on International Relations (Washington, DC: US Government Printing Office, 1978), [hereafter cited as US Congress 1978], 100; US Congress 1980, 136; Selig Taubenblatt, "The Jordan River Basin Water Dilemma: A Challenge for the 1990's" in Joyce Starr and Daniel Stroll, eds., *The Politics of Scarcity: Water in the Middle East* (Boulder: Westview Press, 1988), 48.

35. Theodore Lustig, "The Maqarin Dam Project Riparian Rights Issues: 1976 to 1980," (photocopy) FOIA November 1980, 8. Lustig was Director of Project Development, Bureau for Near East, USAID.

36. Lustig, "The Maqarin Dam Project Riparian Rights Issues," 6.

37. Safran, *Israel: The Embattled Ally*, 521–534.

38. Moshe Ma'oz, "Jordan in Asad's Greater Syria Strategy," in Joseph Nevo and Ilan Pappé, eds., *Jordan in the Middle East: Making of a Pivotal State, 1948–1988* (Essex, UK: Frank Cass and Co., 1994), 98–99.

39. HRP, 221 (1 June 1977).

40. Jordan legally adopted it, but it did not go through the constitutional procedures in Syria. Salman, "Jordan Remains Under-Supplied by Region's Water Sources."

41. US Congress 1980, xix.

42. Joseph C. Wheeler, USAID testimony, Foreign Assistance Legislation for FY 1980–1981 (Part 3), [96th Congress, first session, Feb./March 1979], "House Foreign Affairs Committee Hearing" (CIS no: 79-H381-10)(Washington, DC: US Government Printing Office, 1979) [hereafter cited as US Congress 1979], 271.

43. HRP, 226–227 (25 April–15 May 1978).

44. US Congress 1980, 145. HRP, 238 (10–12 Oct. 1979). Also Haddadin, *Diplomacy on the Jordan*, 230–231.

45. HRP, 226 (8–11 April 1978).

46. US Congress 1979, 275.

47. Lustig, "The Maqarin Dam Project Riparian Rights Issues," 4.

48. Lustig, "The Maqarin Dam Project Riparian Rights Issues," 3.

49. "Legal Questions Arising Out of the Construction of a Dam at Maqarin on the Yarmouk River," a report by a Working Group of the American Society of International Law, 31 July 1977, 74 as cited in Lustig, "The Maqarin Dam Project Riparian Rights Issues," 5. The report is referred to as the Baxter Report after its principle author, R. R. Baxter, who had been a Harvard Law School professor and International Court of Justice judge.

50. HRP, 216 (11 Oct. 1976). Also, "Maquarin Dam Project" (SDC State 86713) 23 Nov. 1976.

51. HRP, 216 (19 Nov. 1976). Also, see Miriam Lowi, *Water and Power* (New York: Cambridge University Press, 1993), 174–175.

52. HRP, 217.

53. HRP, 217 (2 Feb. 1977) and (28 Nov. 1976) and (2 Feb. 1977).

54. As discussed in chapter 2, Israel claimed as valid a concession granted to the Palestine Electric Company in 1926 giving it rights to use the Yarmouk for power generation.

55. Related to this issue, during negotiations there was discussion of the Mediterranean-Dead Sea canal to address the issue of a shrinking Dead Sea because of reduced flow from the Jordan River (Lustig, "The Maqarin Dam Project Riparian Rights Issues," 22).

56. HRP, 218 (6 Feb. 1977).

57. HRP, 214 (22 April 1975).

58. HRP, 224 (15 Nov. 1977).

59. HRP, 218 (12–13 Feb. 1977) and (28 Feb. 1977).

60. HRP, 219 (22 March 1977).

61. Lustig, "The Maqarin Dam Project Riparian Rights Issues," 13–15.

62. HRP, 219 (25–26 April 1977). 63. HRP, 220 (26 May 1977).

64. HRP, 219 (25 May 1977) and 224 (11 Nov. 1977). one cms = .0864 mcm at 24 hours; 2.6 mcm a month; 31.2 a year. The East Ghor Canal flow capacity was 20 cms in 1990 ("trip II Jordan 11/11–17" (photocopy) FOIA).

65. J. B. Schwartz, "Allocations of Yarmouk River to Israel" (photocopy) FOIA—Draft 28 June 1983, 15. Also see HRP, 251 (10 Nov. 1983).

66. HRP, 224 (12 Nov. 1977).

67. HRP, 225 (7 Dec. 1977).

68. US Congress 1980, 142–143; "US Team Talks to Israel, Jordan about Yarmok River," *Jerusalem Post*, 20 December 1979. "Parting of the Jordan Likely to Cause Waves," *Jerusalem Post*, 22 Feb. 1980.

69. HRP, 241 (12 and 14 May 1980).

70. Interview by author with Yacov Vardi, former senior secret water talks negotiator and consultant to Israeli government on Yarmouk River and retired senior vice president, Tahal official, 22 Dec. 1995, Tel Aviv; "US Envoy Habib Relaying Yarmouk Water 'Bargaining,'" *Jerusalem Post*, 13 May 1980.

71. State Department Report, "Report of Habib Mission on Maqarin Dam/Yarmouk River Water Rights," [hereafter Habib Report] FOIA, 27 May 1980, 1.

72. The allocation of 25 mcm for Yarmouk Triangle was accepted by Israel if the other issues of the Habib mission were resolved, which they were not. Even so, after the Habib mission there was little debate about 25 versus 40 Johnston Plan interpretation of Israel's Yarmouk allocation. Habib Report, 3 and L. P. Bloomfield, "Unity Dam Mediation: U.S.–Sponsored Meeting of Israeli and Jordanian Technical Experts Chicago, Illinois, December 6–8, 1989," FOIA (photocopy), 21. Garfinkle, *Israel and Jordan in the Shadow of War*, 165.

73. "Maqarin Dam: Habib Mission" (SDC Amman 2995), FOIA, 6 May 1980.

74. Similar to earlier Israel-Jordan agreements, the Jordanians were prepared to enter into an agreement with the United States with the understanding that Israel would enter into a parallel agreement (Lustig, "The Maqarin Dam Project Riparian Rights Issues, 17).

75. HRP, 241 (12 May 1980).

76. Habib Report, 1. With Habib, Israel argued that West Bank Palestinians were entitled to 140 mcm from the Yarmouk. This quantity was based on a pre–1967 Yugoslavian feasibility study for a Jordanian Yarmouk Dam. The Israelis emphasized that the quantity is still subject to negotiations (Habib Report, 4–5). According to the Baxter Report, "there is no clear law on the obligation of Jordan with respect to the West Bank, as the law stands at present" and that "only one thing may be said with conviction—that there is no requirement of international law that an allocation of water be set aside for a political entity that has not yet but might later come into existence" (Chapter V as cited in Lustig, "The Maqarin Dam Project Riparian Rights Issues," 37).

77. Interview by author with Yacov Vardi, former senior secret water talks negotiator and Tahal official, 22 Dec. 1995, Tel Aviv; "Parting of the Jordan Likely to Cause Waves," *Jerusalem Post*, 22 Feb. 1980.

78. "Israel and Jordan Negotiate Indirectly About a Dam," *New York Times*, 18 May 1980, 4.

79. Interviews by author with Munther Haddadin, former lead Jordanian secret talks negotiator and Jordan Valley Authority chairman, 26 Feb. 1996, Amman.

80. Interview by author with Selig Taubenblatt, former senior USAID official who mediated Maqarin Dam negotiations, 11 Oct. 1996, Washington, DC.

81. Habib Report, 3. Jordan established a "special commission" to review the West Bank issue (Habib Report, 10), but no further Habib negotiations took place. Also see HRP, 242 (15 May 1980).

82. Haddadin, *Diplomacy on the Jordan*, 232–233 and Lowi, *Water and Power*, 176. Also Patrick Seale, *Asad of Syria: The Struggle for the Middle East* (Berkeley: University of California Press, 1989), 320–334. By August 1979, Jordan believed Syria was using more water than was allotted to it under the Johnston Plan (90 mcm) and therefore concluded that a new agreement was needed to restrict further Syrian utilization.

83. Joseph C. Wheeler, USAID testimony, Foreign Assistance Legislation for FY 1982 (Part 3) [97th Congress, first session, Feb./March/April 1981], "House Committee on Foreign Affairs" (CIS no.: 81–H381–78) (Washington, DC: US Government Printing Office, 1981), [hereafter US Congress 1981], 47.

84. US Congress 1981, 77 and 47.

85. Lustig, "The Maqarin Dam Project Riparian Rights Issues," 1 and 8. USAID was actively engaged in the Maqarin Dam project since 1977 and spent $14 million ($5 million for the feasibility study and $9 million for initial work in 1980) on the aborted project (US Congress 1981).

86. "Maqarin Dam Riparian Issues—Meeting with Jordan Officials" (SDC Amman 7250) 5 Nov. 1980.

87. The name, Point 121, refers to the Israeli road exit to the site.

88. "Potential Breakthrough on Unity Dam" SD memo 1 April 1991.

89. "Yacov Vardi Discusses His Meeting with New JVA SECGEN Al Wishah" (SDC Tel Av 11462), 16 Aug 1990.

90. Interview by author with Yacov Vardi, former senior secret water talks negotiator and Tahal official, 22 December 1995, Tel Aviv. In 1977, there was on-site cooperation, but, after one meeting, it failed to continue because of cheating on the measuring rules. Interview by author with Noah Kinarti, former lead secret water talks negotiator, former secretary of Kibbutz Kinneret, former head, Kinneret Regional Water Authority, 17 November 1995, Tel Aviv.

91. HRP, 213. Hasan had requested Wadi Araba data.

92. "Israeli Farmers Complain About Damming of Yarmouk," *Jerusalem Post*, 1 Aug. 1976.

93. Interviews by author with Thomas Pickering, former US ambassador to Jordan, 6 March 1997, Washington, DC; Yacov Vardi, senior secret water talks negotiator and Tahal official, 22 Dec. 1995, Tel Aviv.

94. Haddadin, *Diplomacy on the Jordan*, 238.

95. Haddadin, *Diplomacy on the Jordan*, 214.

96. Haddadin, *Diplomacy on the Jordan*, 242.

97. HRP, 230 (21 and 27 June 1979) and 230–231 (10 July 1979).

98. HRP, 231 (12 July 1979).

99. Schwartz, "Allocation of Yarmouk River to Israel," 17.

100. HRP, 231 (12 July 1979).

101. HRP, 232 (13 July 1979).

102. HRP, 231 (12 July 1979).

103. HRP, 233 (15 July 1979).

104. "Criddle claimed to have discussed 2.3 cms with the Jordanians in 1964 in the context of the East Ghor Canal" (HRP, 234–235 (17 July 1979)).

105. Haddadin, *Diplomacy on the Jordan*, 243.

106. Haddadin, *Diplomacy on the Jordan*, 267 nt. 287. For an extensive discussion of the 2.3 cms issue, see Schwartz, "Allocations of Yarmouk River to Israel."

107. HRP, 231 (16 July 1979).

108. Interview by author with Munther Haddadin, former lead Jordanian secret talks negotiator and Jordan Valley Authority chairman, 26 Feb. 1996, Amman.

109. "Yarmouk Water Dispute" (SDC State 184537) FOIA, 18 July 1979, 2.

110. Interview by author with Noah Kinarti, former lead secret water talks negotiator and chief Jordan Valley Water Association official, 17 Nov. 1995, Tel Aviv.

111. Haddadin, *Diplomacy on the Jordan*, 245.

112. Interview by author with Noah Kinarti, former lead secret water talks negotiator and chief Jordan Valley Water Association official, 17 Nov. 1995, Tel Aviv. Interview by author with Munther Haddadin, former lead Jordanian secret talks negotiator and Jordan Valley Authority chairman, 26 Feb. 1996, Amman.

113. HRP, 230–237 and Haddadin, *Diplomacy on the Jordan*, 243–251.

114. HRP, 223 (18 Oct. 1977).

115. See other discussions of the Jordan-Israel Yarmouk cooperation, for example, Naff and Matson, *Water in the Middle East*, 52; Jonathan Randel, "Lower Key Talks Bring Opposing Sides Together," *Guardian Weekly*, 24 May 1992; Adam Garfinkle, *Deep and Wide: Water, War and Negotiation in the Jordan Basin, 1916–1996* (Manuscript, 22 April 1993), 293–294.

116. HRP, vii.

117. The precedent was a similar event in July 1964 (see chapter 3) when the United States told Jordan it must allow Israel an average rate of 2.3 cms for the summer until Israel received 25 mcm. Jordan did not reply to the United States in writing but did increase the flow to Israel which the United States saw as evidence of acceptance of the 2.3 cms formula (HRP, 231 (13 July 1979)). Jordan asked the United States for documents because the records of the Jordanian water bureaucracy were in poor condition. Many critical documents were nowhere to be found, and Jordanian officials had to "play it by ear." (Haddadin, *Diplomacy on the Jordan*, 241).

118. HRP, 234 (17 July 1979).

119. Schwartz, "Allocations of Yarmouk River to Israel," 7 and 18–20.

120. Also "Regional Water Issue" (SDC State 111273) FOIA, 11 May 1983, 1.

121. HRP, 234 (17 July 1979).

122. HRP, 234 (16 July 1979).

123. HRP, 235 (18 July 1979) and 234 (17 July 1979).

124. HRP, 236 (20 July 1979) and 236 (23 July 1979).

125. "Yarmouk Water Dispute" (SDC Tel Aviv 15617) 20 July 1979 and "Yarmouk Water Dispute" (SDC Tel Aviv 15617, b) 21 July 1979, 2.

126. "July 25 Conversations with GOJ on Yarmouk Water Dispute" (SDC Amman 4686) FOIA, 25 July 1979,1 and HRP, 236 (25 July 1979).

127. HRP, 236 (27 July 1979).

128. HRP, 236 (30 July 1979).

129. "Review of Latest Developments on Yarmouk Water Dispute" (SDC Amman 4979) FOIA, 9 Aug. 1979 and HRP, 237 (9 Aug. 1979).

130. Interviews by author with Noah Kinarti, former lead secret water talks negotiator and chief Jordan Valley Water Association official, 17 November 1995, Tel Aviv; and with Arik Belkin, Jordan Valley Water Association chairman and former secret water negotiator, 23 Nov. 1995, Yarmouk Triangle.

131. Interview by author with Noah Kinarti, former lead secret water talks negotiator and chief Jordan Valley Water Association official, 17 Nov. 1995, Tel Aviv.

132. HRP, 237 (14–16 Sept. 1979).

133. HRP, 238 (17–18 Sept. 1979).

134. HRP, 245–6 (Nov. 1980–Dec. 1981).

135. Interview by author with Yacov Vardi, former senior secret water talks negotiator and Tahal official, 22 Dec. 1995, Tel Aviv.

136. Interview by author with Munther Haddadin, former lead Jordanian secret talks negotiator and Jordan Valley Authority chairman, 26 Feb. 1996, Amman.

137. HRP, 246–248 (Jan.–April 1983).

138. Interviews by author with Munther Haddadin, former lead Jordanian secret talks negotiator and Jordan Valley Authority Chairman, 26 Feb. 1996, Amman; and with Arik Belkin, Jordan Valley Water Association chairman and former secret water negotiator November 23, 1995, Yarmouk Triangle.

139. Interviews by author with Eli Rosenthal, senior hydrologist, Israeli Hydrological Service and former senior secret water talks negotiator, 20 May 1993, Washington, DC; and with Yacov Vardi, former senior secret water talks negotiator and Tahal official, 22 Dec. 1995, Tel Aviv. Munther Haddadin, former lead Jordanian secret talks negotiator and Jordan Valley Authority chairman, 26 Feb. 1996, Amman; and with Arik Belkin, Jordan Valley Water Association chairman and former secret water negotiator Nov. 23, 1995, Yarmouk Triangle.

140. The bridge was more convenient to both Amman and Jerusalem and was used when it was unnecessary to be in the field—i.e., for taking measurements. (Interview by author with Eli Rosenthal, agriculture ministry project director and former senior secret water talks negotiator, 14 Dec. 1995, Jerusalem).

141. Interview by author with Arik Belkin, Jordan Valley Water Association chairman and former secret water negotiator 23 Nov. 1995, Yarmouk Triangle.

142. Interview by author with Yacov Vardi, former senior secret water talks negotiator and Tahal official, 22 Dec. 1995, Tel Aviv.

143. Interview by author with Eli Rosenthal, agriculture ministry project director and former senior secret water talks negotiator, 14 Dec. 1995, Jerusalem.

144. Interviews by author with Yacov Vardi, senior secret water talks negotiator and Tahal official, 22 Dec. 1995, Tel Aviv; and with Arik Belkin, Jordan Valley Water Association chairman and former secret water negotiator, Nov. 23, 1995, Yarmouk Triangle and with Munther Haddadin, former lead Jordanian secret talks negotiator and Jordan Valley Authority chairman, 26 Feb. 1996, Amman.

145. Interviews by author with Noah Kinarti, former lead secret water talks negotiator and chief Jordan Valley Water Association official, 17 Nov. 1995, Tel Aviv; and with Munther Haddadin, former lead Jordanian secret talks negotiator and Jordan Valley Authority chairman, 26 Feb. 1996, Amman.

146. Israel had Lake Tiberias for storage, thus making loans possible. Jordan did not have such a reservoir.

147. "Yarmouk River: Jordan Needs Greater Flow for Next Two Weeks" (SDC Amman 7243), 4 June 1992. Interviews by author with Munther Haddadin, former lead Jordanian secret talks negotiator and Jordan Valley Authority chairman, 26 Feb. 1996, Amman; and with Arik Belkin, Jordan Valley Water Association chairman and former secret water negotiator, 23 Nov. 1995, Yarmouk Triangle; Interview by author with Eli Rosenthal, agriculture ministry project director and former senior secret water talks negotiator, 20 May 1993, Washington, DC.

148. Interview by author with Eli Rosenthal, agriculture ministry project director and former senior secret water talks negotiator, 20 May 1993, Washington, DC.

149. Interview by author with Arik Belkin, Jordan Valley Water Association chairman and former secret water negotiator, 24 Dec. 1995, Yarmouk Triangle.

150. Interviews by author with Yossi Ben Aharon, former director-general, prime minister's office, 25 April 1995, Jerusalem; and with Mohammed Bani Hani, former Jordan Valley authority secretary general and Jordanian water ministry senior official and former lead secret water talks negotiator, 28 Feb. 1996, Amman. Also see Haddadin, *Diplomacy on the Jordan,* 259.

151. Interviews by author with Yossi Ben Aharon, former director-general, prime minister's office, 25 April 1995, Jerusalem; and Yacov Vardi senior secret water talks negotiator and Tahal official, 22 Dec. 1995, Tel Aviv.

152. Interview by author with Yacov Vardi, former senior secret water talks negotiator and Tahal official, 22 Dec. 1995, Tel Aviv.

153. Interview by author with Eli Rosenthal, agriculture ministry project director and former senior secret water talks negotiator, 20 May 1993, Washington, DC.

154. Interview by author with Noah Kinarti, former lead secret water talks negotiator and chief Jordan Valley Water Association official, 17 Nov. 1995, Tel Aviv.

155. Interview by author with Munther Haddadin, former lead Jordanian secret talks negotiator and Jordan Valley Authority chairman, 26 Feb. 1996, Amman.

156. Interview by author with Arik Belkin, Jordan Valley Water Association chairman and former secret water negotiator, 23 Nov. 1995, Yarmouk Triangle.

157. "Israelis Go Public on Maqarin Negotiations" (US State Department Cable [hereafter SDC] Tel Aviv 25876), FOIA, 8 Dec. 1979. For example, during the Maqarin talks, earlier Israeli diplomats refused to confirm that the US team would be going to Jordan after meetings in Jerusalem. However, Israeli television had reported "that negotiations had been proceeding for some time with Jordan with the tacit consent of Syria." The Jordanian government quickly denied the Israel television report. A Jordanian government spokesman in Amman called the reports "untrue and groundless," adding that these were "fabricated" by the Israeli news media to hinder Jordan's effort to build the Maqarin Dam ("Israelis Go Public on Maqarin Negotiations" (US SDC Tel Aviv 25876), FOIA, 8 Dec. 1979, and "GOJ Denies Contact on the Maqarin" (SDC Amman 7743), FOIA, 10 Dec. 1979 "US Official to Help Bridge Yarmouk River," *Jerusalem Post*, 10 Dec. 1979). To say the least, Jordan, and, for that matter, the United States were concerned that any publicity on the negotiations with Israel could destroy the Maqarin Dam project.

158. Interview by author with Munther Haddadin, former lead Jordanian secret talks negotiator and Jordan Valley Authority chairman, 26 Feb. 1996, Amman.

159. "Regional Water Issues" (SDC Amman 9985), FOIA, 17 Nov. 1983, 2. Even in his more recent writings, Haddadin insists that "nothing but the transient water diversion arrangements and the sandbar issue were ever discussed between the two sides" (Haddadin, *Diplomacy on the Jordan*, 259*)*.

160. Interview by author with Munther Haddadin, former lead Jordanian secret talks negotiator and Jordan Valley Authority chairman, 26 Feb. 1996, Amman.

161. HRP, 253 (29 Feb. 1984–6 March 1984).

162. In 1984, Israel questioned the necessity of UN presence at the picnic table and subsequently Crown Prince Hasan accused Israel of "strong-arm tactics" and attempting to marginalize the UN MAC role and to force direct bilateral talks. "Regional Water Issues: February 14 Meeting—A Readout" (SDC Amman 1616), 16 Feb. 1984.

163. Interview by author with Arik Belkin, Jordan Valley Water Association chairman and former secret water negotiator, 23 Nov. 1995, Yarmouk Triangle.

164. Interviews by author with Thomas Pickering, former US ambassador to Jordan, 6 March 1997, Washington, DC; Yacov Vardi, senior secret water talks negotiator

and Tahal official, 22 Dec. 1995, Tel Aviv; and with Munther Haddadin, former lead Jordanian secret talks negotiator and Jordan Valley Authority Chairman, 26 Feb. 1996, Amman.

165. Interview by author with Yacov Vardi, former senior secret water talks negotiator and Tahal official, 22 Dec. 1995, Tel Aviv.

166. Interview by author with Munther Haddadin, former lead Jordanian secret talks negotiator and Jordan Valley Authority chairman, 26 Feb. 1996, Amman.

167. HRP, 253–254 (14 Feb. 1984 and 21 March 1984). Also "Regional Water Issues: Feb. 14 Meeting" (SDC Amman 1616), FOIA, 16 Feb. 1984.

168. HRP, 247–248 (22 April 1983).

169. HRP, 248 (5 May 1983).

170. HRP, 249 (15–16 May 1983).

171. HRP, 249 (23 May 1983).

172. "Regional Water Issues: Next Steps" (SDC Amman 1840), FOIA, 26 Feb. 1984.

173. "Regional Water Issues: Ambassador Meets with JVA President Haddadin" (SDC Amman 4423), FOIA, 9 May 1984.

174. "Regional Water Issues: Next Steps" (SDC Amman 1840), FOIA, 26 Feb. 1984.

175. "Regional Water Issues: Ambassador Meets with JVA President Haddadin" (SDC Amman 4423), FOIA, 9 May 1984.

176. "Sharing Yarmouk Water: Demarché to GOI and GOJ" (SDC State 156868), FOIA, 28 May 1984, 2.

177. "Regional Water Issues: Ambassador's June 5 meeting with Prime Minister Shamir" (SDC Tel Av 8373), 7 June 1984.

178. "Yarmouk Waters" (SDC Tel Av 8939), FOIA, 19 June 1984.

179. Haddadin, *Diplomacy on the Jordan*, 259–267, and interview by author with Munther Haddadin, former lead Jordanian secret talks negotiator and Jordan Valley Authority chairman, 26 Feb. 1996, Amman.

180. "Israel to Draw Full Allocation from Yarmouk," *Jerusalem Post*, 4 April 1984.

181. Interview by author with Munther Haddadin, former lead Jordanian secret talks negotiator and Jordan Valley Authority chairman, 26 Feb. 1996, Amman.

182. See, Garfinkle, *Israel and Jordan in the Shadow of War*, 111–114.

183. Interview by author with Munther Haddadin, former lead Jordanian secret talks negotiator and Jordan Valley Authority chairman, 26 Feb. 1996, Amman.

184. Interview by author with Munther Haddadin, former lead Jordanian secret talks negotiator and Jordan Valley Authority chairman, 26 Feb. 1996, Amman.

185. Melman and Raviv, *Behind the Uprising*, 184.

186. Map 4-2 shows Point 121 but does not convey all the details of the map that was originally attached to this document.

187. "Yarmouk" (photocopy) FOIA, 3 Oct. 1985. Subsequently, there was a great deal of disagreement between Israeli and Jordanians on point "e." This is discussed later ("Yarmouk Water" (SDC Amman 6735), FOIA, 5 July 1986, 3).

188. "Regional Water Issues—Israeli Readout on December 6 Meeting" (SDC Tel Av 17678), FOIA, 14 Dec. 1984. Also see, "[Y]armuk Water: Yitzhak Alster July 12 Meeting NEA" (SDC State 214723), FOIA, 21 July 1984 and "Regional Water: Readout of May 7 Meeting" (SDC Amman 4441), FOIA, 9 May 1985.

189. "Regional Water Issues—February 11 Meeting" (SDC Tel Av 3144), FOIA, 27 Feb. 1985.

190. "Regional Water Meeting of June 24—Jordanian Readout" (SDC State 199180), FOIA, 28 June 1985.

191. Interviews by author with Noah Kinarti, former lead secret water talks negotiator and chief Jordan Valley Water Association official, 17 Nov. 1995, Tel Aviv; and with Munther Haddadin, former lead Jordanian secret talks negotiator and Jordan Valley Authority chairman, 26 Feb. 1996, Amman.

192. Interview by author with Noah Kinarti, former lead secret water talks negotiator and chief Jordan Valley Water Association official, 17 Nov. 1995, Tel Aviv.

193. "Yarmouk Water Talks: Jordanian Readout on October 21 Meeting" (SDC Amman 10138), FOIA, 23 Oct. 1985.

194. According to Kinarti, the Israeli farmer in charge quickly removed the boulder from the area and had no plan to return it to the riverbed (interview by author with Noah Kinarti, former lead secret water talks negotiator and chief Jordan Valley Water Association official, 17 Nov. 1995, Tel Aviv).

195. "Yarmouk Water Meeting of May 22: Jordan Readout" (SDC Amman 5304), FOIA, 25 May 1986, 2.

196. "Yarmouk Water: Haddadin Views and Proposals" (SDC Amman 7262), FOIA, 20 July 1986.

197. "Regional Water Talks: Readout of June 23 Meeting" (SDC Amman 7456), FOIA, 28 June 1987.

198. "Yarmouk Water Discussions: Off Track for Now" (SDC Amman 11967), FOIA, 23 Nov. 1986.

199. The November 1986 unilateral Israeli dredging was more limited in scope ("No Linkage Between Yarmouk Dredging and Maqarin Dam Accord" (SDC Amman 11590), FOIA, 24 Sept. 1987.

200. "Israeli Action in Yarmouk Pool Area" (SDC E.O. 12356), FOIA, 13 Aug. 1987.

201. A month earlier, Bani Hani had unilaterally closed the King Abdullah Canal gate to increase flow to Israel ("Regional Water Talks: Readout of June 14 Meeting" (SDC Amman 7072), FOIA, 17 June 1987).

202. Beilin said the United States was not informed because Israel did not want to put it in the middle. ("Israeli Action in Yarmouk Pool Area" (SDC E.O. 12356), FOIA, 13 August 1987.)

203. Haddadin said that he resigned for "personal reasons" (Haddadin, *Diplomacy on the Jordan*, 280). He still indicated great reservations about the 1987 treaty with Syria.

204. "Yarmouk Water Talks: Jordanian Readout of June 12 Water Meeting" (SDC Amman 7227), FOIA, 15 June 1988. It can be assumed that since Haddadin was no longer in charge of the JVA, the "symbolic rock" issue was thus no longer an obstacle to a cooperative dredging, as it had been in the past.

205. Bloomfield, "Unity Dam Mediation," 13. Gauging took place upstream, downstream, and at the King Abdullah Canal intake. Also, gauging now took place during the winter ("Yarmouk Water Meetings: Jordanian Readout of March 17 Meeting (SDC AMMAN 3391), FOIA, 23 March 1989) and "Unity Dam and Water Sharing" (SDC Amman 9610), FOIA, 15 Aug. 1988.

206. "Yarmouk Water Talks: Jordanian Readout of June 12 Water Meeting" (SDC Amman 7227), FOIA, 15 June 1988.

207. "Yarmouk Water Meeting: Jordanian Readout of March 28 Meeting" (SDC Amman 3663), FOIA, 30 March 1989.

208. "May 22 Meeting with Eli Rosenthal on Yarmouk River/Unity Dam—GOI Provides More Data" (SDC Tel Av 7327), FOIA, 25 May 1989.

209. "Mohammad Bani Hani . . ." (SDC Amman 6619), FOIA, 11 June 1989.

210. Haddadin, *Diplomacy on the Jordan*, 244 note 279.

211. "Mohammad Bani Hani . . ." (SDC Amman 6619), FOIA, 11 June 1989.

212. "Readout of June 25 Meeting with Jordan Valley Authority (JVA) Secretary General, Mohammad Bani Hani," 2 July 1989 (SDC Amman 7610).

213. Bloomfield, "Unity Dam Mediation,"20.

214. "Readout of Joint/Israeli Meeting Re: Yarmouk River Flows of July 10, 1989" (SDC Amman 8187), FOIA, 16 July 1989.

215. For example "Sharing Summer Water–Meeting at the Picnic Table, May 17" (SDC Amman 6796), FOIA, 24 May 1990.

216. Bloomfield, "Unity Dam Mediation," 1 and 7.

217. Bloomfield, "Unity Dam Mediation," 16.

218. Bloomfield, "Unity Dam Mediation," 20.

219. Bloomfield, "Unity Dam Mediation," 20.

220. "Summer Armitage Team Visit" (SDC Amman 7654), FOIA, 13 June 1990. In the same cable, the US diplomat mentioned that there were widespread and persistent rumors that Bani Hani was involved in some illegal aspects of the scandal.

221. "Impact on Mediation of Bani Hani's Departure" (SDC Amman 8679), FOIA, 11 July 1990.

222. "Yarmouk Summer Water Dispute" (SDC Amman 8397), FOIA, 1 July 1990.

223. "Yaacov Vardi Discusses His Meeting with New JVA SECGEN Al Wishah" (SDC Tel Av 11462), FOIA, 16 Aug. 1990.

224. "Yarmouk Water Update" (SDC Tel Av 14679), FOIA, 8 Nov. 1991.

225. "Unity Dam/Yarmuk: March 13 Conversation with Senior Israeli Hydrologist, Dr. Eli Rosenthal" (SDC Tel Av 3171), 15 March 1991.

226. In excess of 200 mcm (HRP, 252 (29 Dec. 1983)).

227. HRP, 251 (16 Aug. 1983) and Haddadin, *Diplomacy on the Jordan*, 213 and 220.

228. Haddadin, *Diplomacy on the Jordan*, 241.

229. "Syria Causing Water Problems," *Jerusalem Post*, 19 Aug. 1987, and "39 Years Later, US Backed 'Unity Dam' Holds No Water, Little Hope," *Washington Post*, 14 May 1992.

230. This plan was described in the Syrian newspaper *A Thawa* in May 1984 ("Israeli Views on Syrian Usage of Yarmouk River" (SDC Tel Av 5022), FOIA, 10 April 1987 and "Israeli Views on Syrian Usage of Yarmouk River" (SDC State 127276), FOIA, 28 April 1987). Another issue that did not receive much attention was Syrian impact on water quality. According to US sources the Syrians were using DDT and other dangerous chemicals ("Trip II Jordan 11/11–17," FOIA (photocopy)).

231. "Former Prime Minister Rifa'i on Unity Dam" FOIA, SD memo, 12 Dec. 1989. In June 1987, JVA Head Haddadin told the US ambassador to Jordan that "Asad expected Jordan to handle any downstream sharing with Israel on the basis of the Johnston Plan. Syria expected Jordan to handle such sharing so quietly it did not become an issue in international financing discussions, so Syria did not have to deal with it." (SDC (Amman 7487), FOIA 28 June 1987).

232. Haddadin, *Diplomacy on the Jordan*, 272–281.

233. Unity Dam Treaty Article 6 (Unity Dam Treaty Text in Garfinkle, *Israel and Jordan in the Shadow of War*, 207–213); also see *Al Wehdah Dam Project* (Amman: Ministry of Water and Irrigation and Jordan Valley Authority, circa 1988).

234. Lowi, *Water and Power*, 180.

235. Unity Dam Treaty, Article 7.

236. Garfinkle, *Israel and Jordan in the Shadow of War*, 165. The treaty does not give specific allocation numbers. However, article 7 does restrict Syria from using "water which springs upstream of the dam and below the 250 meter contour."

237. Unity Dam Treaty, Article 3.

238. Interview by author with Munther Haddadin, former lead Jordanian secret talks negotiator and Jordan Valley Authority chairman, 26 Feb. 1996, Amman; "Syria Causing Water Problems," *Jerusalem Post*, 19 Aug. 1987.

239. Alistair Lyon "Jordan Pins Irrigation Hopes on Long-Postponed 'Unity Dam'." *Reuter Library Report*, 29 Sept. 1987. The minister also said the water from the dam would allow reclamation of at least 100,000 hectares (250,000 acres) of land. Jordan already cultivated 350,000 hectares (865,000 acres) in the Jordan Valley. The Jordanian agriculture minister explained that they wanted "to raise the total to 500,000 hectares (1.24 million acres)" (Lyon, "Jordan Pins Irrigation Hopes on Long-Postponed 'Unity Dam'."). Mohammad Bani Hani subsequently became Jordan's lead negotiator and head of the JVA.

240. "Jordan Seeks Financial Help for Dam Project," *Reuter Library Report*, 10 Oct. 1988.

241. "Position of the World Bank" (photocopy), FOIA, circa. 1989.

242. "Position of Bilateral Donor Organizations" (photocopy), FOIA, March 1989 and "Donors Meeting-Unity Dam October 10 to 12, 1988: Amman Jordan" (SDC Amman 12155), 16 Oct. 1988.

243. *World Bank Operational Manuals*, "Operational Directive 7:50: Projects on International Waterways," 18 Sept. 1989.

244. Bloomfield, "Unity Dam Mediation," 6.

245. "Yarmuk River Project" (Telex from Bank of Israel to World Bank) (photocopy), FOIA, 2 Jan. 1990.

246. "Syrian Views on Water Resources Issues, Including Maqarin Dam" (SDC Damasc 3495), FOIA, 13 June 1989.

247. "Technical Talks Under Jordanian-Syrian Joint Commission for Unity Dam" (photocopy), FOIA (circa Dec. 1989). Also "Meeting No. 4 the Jordanian-Syrian Yarmouk Joint Committee" (SDC Amman 3666), FOIA, 19 March 1990.

248. "Report on the Meeting of the Jordanian-Syrian Technical Committee . . ." (SDC Amman 12638), FOIA, 12 Oct. 1989.

249. "Briefing to Israeli Team" (photocopy), FOIA, July 1990, 1–8.

250. Garfinkle, *Israel and Jordan in the Shadow of War*, 168.

251. "Approach to Israeli Foreign Minister Arens on the Unity Dam," SD Action Memo, FOIA, 2 March 1989, 1 and (SDC Amman 7497) 1988 as cited in "Soviet Capabilities to Assist Jordanians in Construction of Unity Dam" (photocopy), FOIA, March 1989.

252. "Yarmuk Water Negotiations" SD Action Memo, 17 July 1989, 3.

253. US-Syrian relations were poor and thus US Yarmouk mediation excluded Syria.

254. This cancellation occurred in 1991. Israel demanded that "a diversion weir will be jointly designed, constructed, and operated by Israel and Jordan." Jordan rejected "formal joint management and operations ("Trip II Jordan 11/11-17," FOIA (photocopy). Israel still wanted greater voice in the operations of the dam and the Adasiya weir. A senior Israeli government official was quoted as saying that "we are in favor of

the dam being built and of effective exploitation of water in the region, but the Jorda-nians must relinquish their claim to total control over the water supply as a matter of principle" (Isabel Kershner, "Talking Water," *Jerusalem Report*, 25 Oct. 1990, 45).

255. "US Diplomatic Note to Jordan" (photocopy), FOIA, cira 1990.

256. Israel's 1990 Yarmouk to Lake Tiberias pumping capacity was 21.5 mcm per month and the Rutenberg's pool capacity was 5 mcm ("Trip II Jordan 11/11–17," FOIA (photocopy).

257. (SDC Tel Av 9587) as cited in "Trip II 11/11–17.

258. "Approach to Israeli Foreign Minister Arens on the Unity Dam" SD Action Memo, FOIA, 2 March 1989, 2.

259. "Approach to Israeli Foreign Minister Arens on the Unity Dam," SD Action Memo, FOIA, 2 March 1989, 2.

260. Garfinkle, *Deep and Wide*, 322.

261. "Second Trip to Jordan for Yarmouk Water Talks" (SD Doc 6146L), FOIA, 21 Nov. 1989, 2. Jordan government elites believed the reason the Islamic groups made such a strong show was because of "a combination of economic austerity, widespread irritation over official corruption, low voter turnout and the fact that the Islamic candi-dates constituted the only organized political force in the country" ("Second Trip to Jor-dan for Yarmouk Water Talks" (SD Doc 6146L), FOIA 21 Nov. 1989, 2).

262. Correspondence: Armitage to Secretary of State (photocopy), FOIA, 11 April 1990.

263. "Political and Meteorological climate in Israel" (SDC Tel Av 1803), FOIA, 6 Feb. 1990.

264. Correspondence: Armitage to Secretary of State (photocopy), FOIA, 20 Feb. 1990.

265. (SDC Tel Av 6622), FOIA, 9 May 1989 as cited in "Trip II 11/11–17."

266. "Yacov Vardi Discusses his meeting with New JVA SECGEN Al Wishah" (SDC Tel Av 11462), 16 Aug. 1990.

267. Dale Copeland, "Economic Interdependence and War: A Theory of Trade Expectations," *International Security* 20:4 (spring 1996), 5–41.

268. Kenneth Oye, "Explaining Cooperation Under Anarchy" in Kenneth Oye, ed., *Cooperation Under Anarchy* (Princeton: Princeton University Press, 1986), 18–20.

269. Robert O. Keohane and Joseph S. Nye, *Power and Interdependence*, 3rd ed. (New York: Longman, 2001).

270. Interviews by author with Noah Kinarti, former lead secret water talks nego-tiator and chief Jordan Valley Water Association official, 17 Nov. 1995, Tel Aviv; and with Munther Haddadin, former lead Jordanian secret talks negotiator and Jordan Val-ley Authority chairman, 26 Feb. 1996, Amman.

271. Interview by author with Yacov Vardi, former senior secret water talks negotiator and Tahal official, 22 Dec. 1995, Tel Aviv.

272. Interview by author with Munther Haddadin, former lead Jordanian secret talks negotiator and Jordan Valley Authority chairman, 26 Feb. 1996, Amman.

273. "Yarmuk Water Negotiations," SD Action Memo, FOIA, 17 July 1989, 1.

CHAPTER 5: THE WEST BANK AND GAZA, 1948–1992

1. For books that focus on the West Bank and Gaza, see Alwyn Rouyer, *Turning Water into Politics* (New York: St. Martin's, 2000); Julie Trottier, *Hydropolitics in the West Bank and Gaza Strip* (Jerusalem: PASSIA, 1999); Fadia Daibes, ed., *Water in Palestine: Problems—Politics—Prospects* (Jerusalem: PASSIA, 2003); Sharif Elmusa, *Water Conflict: Economics, Politics, Law and Palestinian-Israeli Water Resources* (Washington, DC: Institute for Palestine Studies, 1997); and Jan Selby, *Water Power and Politics in the Middle East: The Other Israeli-Palestinian Conflict* (London: I. B. Tauris, 2003).

2. This area is also known as Judea and Samaria, the Administered Territories, and the Occupied Palestinian Territories. No political intent is implied by the term West Bank.

3. This figure is based on Israel's total consumption of 1,400 mcm and use of West Bank water. Israel's other main water resources are the Lake of Tiberias and the coastal aquifer.

4. Based on Arab West Bank consumption of 120 mcm. About 15 mcm comes from other sources, including the National Water Carrier, local cisterns, and surface water.

5. Howard Sachar, *A History of Israel* (New York: Knopf, 1976), 673–677. For discussion of Labor's territorial compromise policy, see Mark Tessler, *A History of the Israeli-Palestinian Conflict* (Bloomington: Indiana University Press, 1994), 487, 500, 520–521, and 540.

6. Joseph Alpher, *Settlements and Borders* (Tel Aviv: Tel Aviv University, Jaffee Center for Strategic Studies, 1994), 12–13. Local-tactical defense includes securing Jerusalem as well as protecting Ben-Gurion Airport and the isolation/fragmentation of Arab municipal concentrations.

7. Alpher, *Settlements and Borders*, 24.

8. Interview by author with Abdul al-Rahman Tamimi, Palestian Hydrology Group, Jerusalem, 14 Feb. 1996. For discussion of Palestinian grievances, see Joost Hiltermann, *Behind the Intifada: Labor and Women's Movements in the Occupied Territories* (Princeton: Princeton University Press, 1991), 37 and 211–212; Zachary Lockman and Joel Beinin, eds., *Intifada: The Palestinian Uprising Against Israeli Occupation* (Boston: South End Press, 1989), 134; Elmusa, *Water Conflict*, 144; Selby, *Water Power and Politics in the Middle East*, 30, 90–91, and 161.

9. *Atlas of Israel*, 3rd ed. (Tel Aviv: Survey of Israel, 1985), sheets 1–5.

10. The eastern slope's annual precipitation drops sharply from 600 to 150 mm per year.

11. *Atlas of Israel*, sheet 12.

12. Prior to the increased agricultural development in the 1950s, groundwater spontaneously flowed out through springs. However, with increased consumption and a subsequent drop in the water table, water today must be pumped. J. Schwarz "Water Resources in Judea, Samaria, and Gaza Strip" in Daniel Elazar, ed., *Judea, Samaria, and Gaza: Views on the Present and the Future* (Washington, DC: American Enterprise Institute for Public Policy Research, 1982), 89.

13. Measurements are based on map compiled by Water Commissioner Shmuel Cantor for Prime Minister Menachem Begin in 1977 (photocopy) (Hebrew) [hereafter Begin Map]. In the course of the past fifty years, these numbers have fluctuated somewhat.

14. The western aquifers area spreads over 1,800 square kilometers, of which 1,400 sq. km lie within the West Bank (recharge area) and 400 within Israel (storage area). The storage area of the aquifer is almost entirely within Israel. The recharge and storage area of the northeastern basin is over 700 sq. km, of which 650 sq. km are located within the West Bank. Only 50 sq. km are located within Israel. However, most of the water emerging from springs is pumped through wells located in Israel (Eyal Benvenisti and Haim Gvirtzman, "Harnessing International Law to Determine Israeli-Palestinian Water Rights: The Mountain Aquifer," *Natural Resources Journal* vol. 33 (Summer 1993), 555–556).

15. Schwarz, "Water Resources in Judea, Samaria and Gaza Strip," 93–95.

16. Yohanan Boneh and Uri Baida, "Water Resources and Its Utilization in Judea and Samaria," *Judea and Samaria (Yehuda Veshomron)*, A. Shmueli, D. Grossman, and K. Zeevi, eds. (Tel Aviv: Bar Ilan University, 1977) [Hebrew], 34–47.

17. Boneh and Baida, "Water Resources and its Utilization in Judea and Samaria," 42–44.

18. The western slope's agriculture was irrigated fields of vegetable crops; the mountain ridge consisted of non-irrigated fruit trees, while the Jordan Valley was suitable for irrigated vegetables and fruit trees. David Kahan, *Agriculture and Water in the West Bank and Gaza* (Jerusalem: The West Bank Data Project, 1983), 6; *The Middle East and North Africa: 1966–1967*, 13th ed. (London: Europa Publications, 1966), 360–361.

19. Kahan, *Agriculture and Water in the West Bank and Gaza*, 6–7.

20. Prior to the 1967 War, Jordan had an agreement with the World Bank under which Jordan would receive a $3.5 million loan for Jerusalem-Ramallah drinking water pipeline projects. These projects were not completed by 1967 (Jerusalem Water Understanding "Introduction" www.jwu.org/about/intro.html). Also see Yousef Nasser, "Palestinian Water Needs and Rights in the Context of Past and Future Development"

in Fadia Daibes, ed., *Water in Palestine*, 93–97. Interview by author with Joshua Schwarz, Tahal water engineer, Tel Aviv, 10 May 1996; Ze'ev Schiff, *Security for Peace: Israel's Minimal Security Requirements in Negotiations with the Palestinians* (Washington, DC: Washington Institute for Near East Policy, 1989), 21.

21. Yeruham Cohen, *Tachnut Allon* [The Allon Plan] (Tel Aviv: Hakibbutz Hameuhad, 1972) (Hebrew). The settlements referred to are Jewish communities beyond the Green Line. For this work's purposes, the new neighborhoods built in Eastern Jerusalem since 1967 that fall within the capital's municipal boundaries are not referred to as settlements.

22. Aryeh Shalev, *The West Bank: Line of Defense* (New York: Praeger, 1985), 125–128 and Alpher, *Settlements and Borders*, 8–9; Howard Sachar, *A History of Israel* (New York: Knopf, 1974), 680. Settlements were also built as buffers between Gaza and Egypt.

23. Alpher, *Settlements and Borders*, 9; this was also known as the "Double Column Plan."

24. State of Israel Ministry of Defense, Coordinator of Government Operations in Judea and Samaria and Gaza District, *An Eighteen Year Survey (1967–1985)* (Tel Aviv: Ministry of Defense, 1986), 73.

25. See Marcia Drezon-Tepler, "Contested Waters and the Prospects for Arab-Israeli Peace," *Middle East Studies*, 30:2 (April 1994), 290–295 and David Wishart, "An Economic Approach to Understanding Jordan Valley Water Disputes," *Middle East Review* 21: 4 (Summer 1989), 47–51.

26. State of Israel Ministry of Defense, *An Eighteen Year Survey (1967–1985)*, 75.

27. Meron Benvenisti, *The West Bank Data Project: A Survey of Israel's Policies* (Washington, DC: American Enterprise Institute for Public Policy Research and West Bank Data Base Project, 1984), 14; Jeffrey Dillman, "Water Rights in the Occupied Territories," *Journal of Palestine Studies* 19:1 (Autumn 1989), 56. Also see Miriam Lowi, "Bridging the Divide: Transboundary Resource Disputes and the Case of the West Bank Water" *International Security* 18:1 (Summer 1993), 113–138 and Uri Davis, Antonia Maks, and John Richardson, "Israel's Water Policies," *Journal of Palestine Studies* 9:2 (Winter 1980), 3–31.

28. State of Israel Ministry of Defense, *An Eighteen Year Survey (1967–1985)*, 77.

29. Natasha Beschorner, "Water and Instability in the Middle East," *Adelphi Paper 273* (London: Brassey's, Winter 1992/93), 13.

30. See "open bridges" policy in Moshe Dayan, *Story of My Life* (New York: William Morrow, 1976), 385–455. Also see Nadav Safran, *Israel: The Embattled Ally* (Cambridge: Belknap Press, 1981), 268–269, Hiltermann, *Behind the Intifada*, 19, and Salim Tamari, "What the Uprising Means," in Lockman and Beinin, eds. *Intifada*, 127.

31. State of Israel Ministry of Defense, *An Eighteen Year Survey*, 73–79; Kahan, *Agriculture and Water in the West Bank and Gaza*, 15.

32. Kahan, *Agriculture and Water in the West Bank and Gaza*, 25–26.

33. State of Israel Ministry of Defense, *An Eighteen Year Survey (1967–1985)*, 73.

34. See Boneh and Baida, *Water Resources and its Utilization in Judea and Samaria*; State of Israel Ministry of Defense, *An Eighteen Year Survey (1967–1985)*, 27.

35. State of Israel Ministry of Defense, *An Eighteen Year Survey (1967–1985)*, 27; some 4,255 tractors were in use in 1985, as compared with 460 in 1968.

36. [Israeli] Central Bureau of Statistics, *Statistical Abstract of Israel*, no. 32 (1981), 734. Survey, 27; Kahan, *Agriculture and Water in the West Bank and Gaza*, 34 and 37; Meron Benvenisti, *The West Bank Handbook: A Political Lexicon* (Jerusalem: Jerusalem Post, 1986), 1–3.

37. Kahan, *Agriculture and Water in the West Bank and Gaza*, 31–58.

38. Alpher, *Settlements and Borders*, 10.

39. Meron Benvenisti and Shlomo Khayat, *The West Bank and Gaza Atlas* (Jerusalem: The West Bank Data Base Project, 1988), 32.

40. Azmy Bishara, "The Uprising's Impact on Israel" in Lockman and Joel Beinin, eds., *Intifada*, 219.

41. Alpher, *Settlements and Borders*, 10.

42. See Ian Lustick, *For the Land and the Lord; Jewish Fundamentalism in Israel* (New York: Council on Foreign Relations, 1988); Ehud Sprinzak, *The Ascendance of Israel's Radical Right* (New York: Oxford University Press, 1991); and Jeffrey Goldberg, "Among the Settlers: Will They Destroy Israel?" *New Yorker* 31 May 2004, 46–69.

43. See Sharon, *Haaretz*, 7 May 1993, 3 (Hebrew); Shalev, *The West Bank*, 128–130; Alpher, *Settlements and Borders*, 11.

44. Benvenisti and Khayat, *The West Bank and Gaza Atlas*, 65.

45. David Newman, "Colonia in Suburbia: Reflections on 25 Years of Jewish Settlement in the West Bank," Israeli-Palestinian Peace Research Project, Working Paper Series 18 (Jerusalem: Harry S Truman Research Institute for the Advancement of Peace, Winter 1991/92); Howard Sachar, *A History of Israel*, Vol. II (New York: Oxford University Press, 1987), 153–156.

46. *The Israel Statistical Yearbook* sets the number of settlements in 1992 at 1,120 settlements with a 104,800 settler population in the West Bank. Gaza settlements number was 14 with 4,300 settlers.

47. See, for example Ze'ev Schiff and Ehud Ya'ari, *Intifada* (New York: Touchstone, 1991), 79–100.

48. Tamari, "What the Uprising Means," in Lockman and Beinin, eds., *Intifada*, 127–128.

49. Sharif S. Elmusa, "The Water Issue and the Palestinian-Israeli Conflict" (Washington, DC: The Center for Policy Analysis on Palestine, 1993), 2–3. Schiff and Ya'ari, *Intifada*, 97; Davis, Maks, and Richardson, "Israel's Water Policies," 13.

50. Schiff and Ya'ari, *Intifada*, 97.

51. Beschorner, "Water and Instability in the Middle East," 14; interview by author with Jad Isaac, Research Institute Analyst, Bethlehem, 13 May 1996; United Nations, Committee on the Exercise of Inalienable Rights of the Palestinian People, "Israel's Policy on the West Bank Water Resources" (New York: United Nations, 1980), 13–15.

52. Schiff and Ya'ari, *Intifada*, 97. For legal discussion of "current policies [that] have led to unilateral, exclusive and discriminatory pattern of water resource distribution between Palestinian population of the West Bank" see Palestinian Hydrology Group et al., *Legal Status of West Bank Groundwater Resources* (case document submitted to International Water Tribunal II, Amsterdam, 1991).

53. Jad Isaac et al. "A Study of Palestinian Water Supply and Demand," *Symposium on Water Capacity in Palestine* (Sept. 1995), table 4. Between 1981 and 1984, eight legal wells were successfully drilled in the Tulkarm district for drinking. Embassy of Israel, "Background: Water, Israel and the Middle East," *Background Paper* (Washington, DC: Embassy of Israel, 1991), 5–6.

54. *Background Paper*, 5–6.

55. The comptroller reports that Jewish settlers pay Mekorot only 15 agorot per cubic meter for agricultural supplies while Arab farmers pay the Civil Administration almost five times that amount (70 agorot per cm) for Mekorot supplied water. Local Arab authorities charge between NIS (new Israeli shekel) 1 to 1.60 per cm for domestic use by Palestinians while Mekorot charges settlers only 23 agorot. ("Territories Water Supply Drying Up with Overuse," *Jerusalem Post* 2 July 1987). Also Kahan, *Agriculture and Water in the West Bank and Gaza*, 114.

56. Miriam Lowi, *Water and Power* (New York: Cambridge University Press, 1993), 186–191.

57. Benvenisti, *The West Bank Handbook*, 1–3.

58. Hiltermann, *Behind the Intifada*, 18–20, and Geoffrey Aronson, *Israel, Palestinians and the Intifada: Creating Facts on the West Bank* (London: Kegan, 1990), 315.

59. "A Dwindling Natural Resource," *Washington Post*, 13 May 1992, A29.

60. Task Force of the Water Resources Action Program (WRAP)—Palestine, *Palestinian Water Resources* (Gaza Strip: WRAP, 1994), 6.

61. Interview by author with Abdul al-Rahman Tamimi, Palestian Hydrology Group, Jerusalem, 14 Feb. 1996. Water Resources Action Program Task Force, *Palestinian Water Resources*, 6–7. Isam Shawwa "The Water Situation in the Gaza Strip," in Gershon Baskin, ed., *Water: Conflict or Cooperation* (Jerusalem: Israel/Palestine Center for Research and Information, 1993), 23–36.

62. Interview by author with Shaul Arloseroff, former water commissioner, Tel Aviv, July 1995.

63. Sharif Elmusa, "Dividing The Common Palestinian-Israeli Waters: An International Water Law Approach," *Journal of Palestine Studies* 22:3 (Spring 1993), 61;

also see Sara Roy, *Gaza Strip Survey* (Jerusalem: West Bank Data Base Project, 1987). The settler population living in Gaza (1988/89) used 2 mcm, or 3 percent, of the total groundwater while the Arab population consumed 92 mcm, or 97 percent.

64. Excerpts in this section were taken from Jeffrey Sosland, "Understanding Environmental Security: Water Scarcity, the 1980s' Palestinian Uprising, and Implications for Peace" in Tami Amanda Jacoby and Brent Sasley, eds., *Redefining Security in the Middle East* (New York: University of Manchester Press, 2002), 116–123.

65. Comptroller, *Annual and Special Reports*, 63.

66. Comptroller, *Annual and Special Reports*, 49.

67. Comptroller, *Annual and Special Reports*, 39.

68. Comptroller, *Annual and Special Reports*, 43.

69. "Territories Water Supply Drying Up with Overuse," *Jerusalem Post*, 2 July 1987.

70. Elaine Ruth Fletcher, "Fouling Their Own Waters" *Jerusalem Report*, 1 Aug. 1991.

71. Interview by author with Abdul al-Rahman Tamimi, Palestinian Hydrology Group, Jerusalem, 14 Feb. 1996. Dror Avisar, an Israel Union for Environmental Defense hydrologist also found similar signs of pollution in his ongoing study of the western aquifer. See Fayez Freijat, "Impact of Jewish Settlements on Palestinian Water Resources," in Daibes, ed., *Water in Palestine*, 153–180.

72. Comptroller, *Annual and Special Reports*, 37.

73. *Israel Yearbook and Almanac 1991/1992*, vol. 46 (Jerusalem: IBRT Translations, 1992), 107.

74. Aaron Wolf, *Hydropolitics Along the Jordan River* (New York: United Nations University Press, 1995), 234. See *Hydropolitics Along the Jordan River*, 233–239 for entire text of advertisement and for the Ministry of Agriculture position paper expanding on the arguments made in the ad and defending the ministry's use of funds for the ad.

75. Today, the Jordan Valley settlement program is considered an economic failure. The Jewish population is no more than 5,000 (www.btselem.org). These settlements have been highly dependent on government grants and consume a large portion of the eastern aquifer's water for agriculture (Alpher, *Settlements and Borders*, 10). The Jordan Valley settlements were established to create a defensible border zone that would be retained in a deal that returned the heavily Arab-populated mountain ridge areas to Jordan sovereignty. These isolated settlements were to delay an enemy attack from the east while Israel mobilized, but in the age of modern armored warfare, their effectiveness is questionable.

76. To drill for water, the coastal plain is 60 meters deep, the western foothills are 150–200 meters deep, and the mountain ridge is 700 meters deep. Wolf, *Hydropolitics Along the Jordan River*, 79, and map 29.

77. The outline of possible withdrawal lines from the Golan Heights is discussed in the next chapter.

78. Ze'ev Schiff, "First Light on a Shelved Report," *Haaretz*, Oct. 1993 (Hebrew). The report was authored by Joshua Schwarz and Aharon Zohar and titled "The Water Problem in the Context of Israel-Arab Agreements" (Hebrew), which had a limited distribution before it was classified. Author interviewed both Schwarz and Zohar.

79. See Alpher, map 8. According to Schiff, the classified report says that the border to protect the western aquifer "runs through Mei-Ami near Um el Fahm to Dir Sharf, to Jinsfut to Beit Liqia, Tsurif and Idna. Another critical line—in Northeastern Samaria—concerns the northeastern basins. It runs from Bardala and Zababa to Jenin. The critical line, the Jerusalem-Bethlehem area runs as follows: Bidu, Ein Fada, Abu Dis, Herodian, Bait Fajr, and Har Gilo." This is to protect part of the eastern basin (*Haaretz*, 8 October 1993).

80. Peter Gleick, "Water and Conflict: Fresh Water Resources and International Security," *International Security* 18:1 (Summer 1993), 106–107.

81. State Comptroller of Israel, "Management of Water Resources in Israel (Special Report, December 1990)," in *Annual and Special Reports: Selected Chapters* (Jerusalem: State Comptroller, 1992), 42.

82. See Robert Axelrod, *Evolution of Cooperation* (New York: Basic Books, 1984); Robert Keohane, "Reciprocity in International Relations," *International Organization* 40:1 (Winter 1986), 1–27.

83. Ze'ev Schiff, "Israel's Water Security Lines," The Washington Institute's *Policywatch*, no. 75, 4 Nov. 1993.

84. Lowi, "Bridge the Divide," 125. Lowi argues that it is extremely difficult for Israel to relinquish its control of the West Bank because of concerns for its water security.

CHAPTER 6: THE 1990S MADRID PEACE PROCESS AND AFTER, 1991–2006

1. See Israel Foreign Ministry Web site: www.israel.org/peace/madrid.html.

2. www.israel.org/peace/madrid.html.

3. www.israel.org/peace/madrid.html.

4. See David Makovsky, *Making Peace with the PLO: The Rabin Government's Road to the Oslo Accord* (Boulder: Westview Press, 1996).

5. An agreement was also initialed for Israeli redeployment from the city of Hebron in January 1997 between the Palestinian Authority and the newly elected Likud government. (See www.israel-mfa.gov.il/mfa/go.asp?MFAH00ql0.)

6. "Impasse Over Water," *Jerusalem Post*, 18 July 1995, 6.

7. See chapter 5.

8. "PA will not be Allowed to Divert Water from Israel's Aquifers," *Jerusalem Post*, 11 July 1995.

9. "Water; This is the Whole Story," *Yediot Achronot*, 24 July 1995, b7 (Hebrew).

10. "Peres, Arafat Come Closer to Deal on Water," *Jerusalem Post*, 20 July 1995, 1.

11. "Whose Water?" *The Economist*, 5 Aug. 1995, 40–41.

12. Interview by author with Noah Kinarti, senior Israeli water talks negotiator, 17 Nov. 1995, Tel Aviv; also see Zeev Schiff, "Again Forgetting the Water," *Haaretz*, 11 July 1995, b1 (Hebrew). Between 1994 and 1999, 1,500 illegal wells have been dug by Palestinians. Alwyn Rouyer, *Turning Water into Politics* (New York: St. Martin's, 2000), 214.

13. "Tzur on Water Accord, Supervision," *Qol Yisrael*, 24 Aug. 1995, [FBIS-NES–95-165, 25 Aug. 1995, 17].

14. "Water Dispute: No Immediate Solution on Tap," *Jerusalem Post*, 21 July 1995, 11.

15. "PLO Seals Partial West Bank Deal," *Reuters*, 11 Aug. 1995.

16. "Israelis Search for Solution to Water Shortage in Hebron," *Associated Press*, 20 Aug. 1995; "Israeli Cabinet Tackles Hebron Water Shortages," *Reuters*, 20 Aug. 1995; "TV Reports Prompts Cabinet to Discuss Water Supply in Areas," *Jerusalem Post*, 20 Aug. 1995, 1.

17. Interview by author with Jad Isaac, senior Palestinian water analyst, 23 July 1995, Bethlehem.

18. Interview by author with Jad Isaac, senior Palestinian water analyst, 23 July 1995, Bethlehem.

19. "Israel, PLO End Talks on Water Rights in Deadlock," *Reuters*, 3 Aug. 1995.

20. Uri Savir, *The Process* (New York: Random House, 1998), 213.

21. Savir, *The Process*, 213.

22. Savir, *The Process*, 214.

23. As discussed later, Israel had already made a similar concession two years earlier, during the May 1993 multilateral talks on water in Norway. The Israeli representative, Avraham Katz-Oz, agreed to use the term "water rights," and Prime Minister Rabin did not rescind the policy. "Water Dispute Deferred," *Haaretz*, 8 Sept. 1995, 1 (Hebrew). To better understand Israeli bureaucratic water politics and how this policy was reached, see "Divided Waters" *Jerusalem Post Magazine*, 1 Sept. 1995, 8–11. Interview by author with Noah Kinarti, senior Israeli water talks negotiator, 17 Nov. 1995, Tel Aviv.

24. "Tzur on Water Accord, Supervision," *Qol Yisrael*, 24 Aug. 1995 [FBIS-NES-95-165, 25 Aug. 1995, 17].

25. "Official on 'Breakthrough' Accord,'" *MBC Television*, 24 Aug. 1995 [FBIS-NES-95-165, 25 Aug. 1995, 18].

26. Sharif S. Elmusa estimates that the Palestinians are entitled to 209 mcmy from the Yarmouk, Jordan, and side wadis (Sharif S. Elmusa, "The Jordan-Israel Water Agreement: A Model or Exception?" *Journal of Palestine Studies* 24:3 (Spring 1995), 70–71). As discussed in chapter 4, 150 mcmy is an allocation historically associated with the Johnston Plan's West Ghor Canal. The greatest obstacle to applying the Johnston Plan to the Israeli-Palestinian negotiations is that the plan did not include groundwater allocations, the primary issue of dispute.

27. Walid Sabbath and Jad Isaac, "Toward a Palestinian Water Policy." See, www.arij.org, 26 July 1995, 6–7. The Jordan Rift Valley is a contentious aspect of the overall negotiations because, for Israel, it has been seen as an important buffer zone for military attack from the East. Zeev Schiff, "Jordan Valley Is the Kinneret," OP-ED *Haaretz*, English Internet edition, 3 July 2000; "Israel May be Giving PA Rights to Water," *Haaretz*, 3 July 2000; and "Jordan Valley Settlers Fear Abandonment," *Jerusalem Post*, Internet edition, 3 July 2000.

28. "Water; This is the Whole Story" *Yediot Achronot*, 24 July 1995, b7 (Hebrew). Also see, Karen Assaf et al., *A Proposal for the Development of a Regional Water Master Plan* (Jerusalem: Israel/Palestine Center for Research and Information, 1993). Fadia Daibes, "Water-Related Politics and Their Legal Aspects—A Progressive Approach for Solving the Water Conflict," Fadia Daibes, ed., *Water in Palestine: Problems—Politics—Prospects* (Jerusalem: PASSIA, 2003), 5–56.

29. Oslo II, annex III, appendix I, article 40, and schedules 8 to 10. For text of agreement, see Web site: www.israel.org/peace/interim.html.

30. Oslo II, article 40, 3.e.

31. Oslo II, article 40, 6.

32. Oslo II, article 40, 7.b.6.

33. Savir, *The Process*, 214.

34. Oslo II, article 40, 13 and 14.

35. Oslo II, Schedule 9,4.

36. Oslo II, Schedule 9,5.a.

37. Oslo II, Schedule 9,5.e.

38. Rouyer, *Turning Water into Politics*, 227.

39. Rouyer, *Turning Water into Politics*, 235.

40. "Illegal PA Water Drilling in Jenin Protested," *Qol Yisrael*, 21 Dec. 1995 [FBIS-NES-95-245, 21 Dec. 1995, 26].

41. Rouyer, *Turning Water into Politics*, 213–214 and 223, and Jan Selby, *Water Power and Politics in the Middle East: The Other Israeli-Palestinian Conflict* (London: I. B. Tauris, 2003), 113.

42. "US Gives Arafat $11 Million for Waste Water Project," *Reuters*, 27 July 1995.

43. Interview by author with Kinarti, senior Israeli water talks negotiator, 17 Nov. 1995, Tel Aviv; "Unsilent Partner: The US Takes an Active Role on Water," *Jerusalem Post*, 8 Sept. 1995.

44. Clyde Mark, "Palestinians and Middle East Peace: Issues for the United States," Congressional Research Service (CRS) Issue Brief for Congress (Order Code IB92052) updated 1 Oct. 2001, 4.

45. See US AID Web site: www.usaid.gov/wbg/program_water.htm.

46. See, for example, "Netanyahu Looks Beyond Hebron Talks," *Wall Street Journal*, 13 Jan. 1997, A14; "Why Can't Jews Live Anywhere They Like?," *Los Angeles Times*, 2 Dec. 1996.

47. Israeli control of Jerusalem, the Etzion bloc, areas along the Green Line, and roads are all part of the plan. Netanyahu dubbed the plan Allon plus, but it more closely resembles the Sharon Plan, which were all discussed in chapter 5.

48. According to Sharon, Palestinians consume 35 cm/person and Israelis consume 100 cm per person.

49. "Sharon Suggests Taking Over Water Sources in West Bank," *AP Worldstream*, 21 May 1997.

50. "Sharon Denies Holding Up US Drilling Project," *Jerusalem Post*, 22 May 1997.

51. "Palestinian Farmers 'Stealing' Water from Israeli Water Company—Israel TV," *BBC Worldwide Monitoring* 9 July 2002, and Selby, *Water Power and Politics in the Middle East*, 163–164.

52. Selby, *Water Power and Politics in the Middle East*, 115, and Marwan Haddad, "Future Water Institutions in Palestine," in Daibes, ed., *Water in Palestine*, 140.

53. "Palestinian Official says Israel Disrupting Water Projects," *Wafa* from *BBC Worldwide Monitoring*, 17 Feb. 2001. According to the *Jerusalem Report*, of the fifteen West Bank projects, nine are now frozen. Most of these projects were designed to protect the mountain aquifer from sewage pollution and other groundwater contamination ("Tainted Waters," 15 May 2006, 20).

54. "Water Could Dry Up Peace Process," *The Gazette* (Montreal), 20 Aug. 1998, B4.

55. "Water Could Dry Up Peace Process," *The Gazette* (Montreal), 20 Aug. 1998, B4.

56. "Water Demand Great in Mideast; Drought Aggravates West Bank Dispute," *Baltimore Sun*, 19 July 1999, 1A.

57. "Experts Urge Water Cooperation," *Jerusalem Post*, 3 March 1999, 4. Also see Alwyn Rouyer, "Basic Needs vs. Swimming Pools: Water Inequality and the Palestinian-Israeli Conflict," *Middle East Report* 227 (Summer 2003), 2–7.

58. Michael Hirsh, "The Lost Peace Plan," *Newsweek Internet* (2000). Also, "Dusting Off the Beilin-Abu Mazen Draft Accord," *Haaretz*, Internet edition, 10 July 2000. For text of Beilin-Abu Mazen Draft Accord see www.tiph.org/Documents/Beilin-AbuMazen.asp.

59. See www.mfa.gov.il. Also see Hussein Agha and Robert Malley, "Camp David: Tragedy of Errors," *The New York Review of Books*, 9 Aug. 2001, and Jeremy Pressman, "Visions in Collision: What Happened at Camp David and Taba?" *International Security* 28:2 (Fall 2003), 5–43. Dennis Ross, *The Missing Peace: The Inside Story of the Fight for Middle East Peace* (New York: FSG, 2004).

60. Carol Migdalovitz, "The Middle East Peace Talks" CRS Issue Brief for Congress (order code IB91137) updated 11 Oct. 2001, 2–3.

61. "Yitzhar Water Pipes Vandalized Again," *Jerusalem Post*, Internet edition, 9 Jan. 2001.

62. "Joint Israel-Palestinian Call to Protect Water Supply," www.mfa.gov.il, 1 Feb. 2001.

63. Zeev Schiff, "Unlikely Cooperation," *Haaretz*, 13 Feb. 2001.

64. Zeev Schiff, "Unlikely Cooperation," *Haaretz*, 13 Feb. 2001. The "Sharm El-Sheikh Fact-finding Committee Report" ["Mitchell Report"] also gives numerous confidence building measures: www.state.gov and www.tiph.org.

65. "Israel, Palestinians Cooperate on Water," *Jewish Telegraphic Agency*, 5 March 2003.

66. David M. Satterfield, statement of Deputy Assistant Secretary, Bureau of Near East Affairs, US Department of State, "Water Scarcity in the Middle East: Regional Cooperation as a Mechanism Toward Peace." House International Relations Committee (serial no. 108–118) [108th Congress, second session, 5 May 2004], (Washington, DC: US Government Printing Office, 2004) [hereafter cited as US Congress 2004], 23, and Selby, *Water Power and Politics in the Middle East*, 117 and 187.

67. See www.bitterlemons.org "Water," 16 August 2004 (edition 30), Ghassan Khatib, "Water and International Law," Yossi Alpher, "Things Could Get Worse," Abdel Rahman Tammi, "Water Wall," and Gidon Bromberg, "A Missed Opportunity to Rebuild Trust," Selby, *Water Power and Politics in the Middle East*, and US Congress 2004. "PA Expert Warns Against Separation Fence Impact on Future Water Negotiations," *Global News Wire*, 23 Dec. 2002. Zecharya Tagar, Tamar Keinan, Gidon Bromberg of Friends of the Earth Middle East, "A Sleeping Time Bomb: Pollution of the Mountain Aquifer by Sewage," Israel/Palestine Center for Research and Information, "Water for Life in the Middle East" 2nd Israeli-Palestinian-International Conference (Turkey, Oct. 2004). Zeev Schiff, "A Threat to the West Bank Pullout," *Haaretz*, 26 Nov. 2004.

68. For extensive discussions of these talks, see Haddadin, *Diplomacy on the Jordan* (Boston: Kluwer, 2002) 331–349.

69. There was also a Trilateral Israel-Jordan-US Economic Committee, which was established in Oct. 1993 and discussed specific issues, such as Jordan Rift Valley

cooperative projects, trade, and banking. The outcomes of these talks were incorporated into the peace treaty and some talks continued afterward. See Haddadin, *Diplomacy on the Jordan*, 349–353.

70. The annexes included water issues, boundary demarcation, police cooperation, environmental issues, and mutual border crossings.

71. See Robert Satloff, "The Jordan-Israel Peace Treaty: A Remarkable Document," *Middle East Quarterly* (March 1995), 47–51. For a more pessimistic analysis, see Elmusa, "The Jordan-Israel Water Agreement: A Model or Exception?," 63–73.

72. Haddadin, *Diplomacy on the Jordan*, 356–358.

73. Brent Sasley, "Changes and Continuities in Jordanian Foreign Policy," *Middle East Review of International Affairs (MERIA) Journal* 6:1 (March 2002), 5.

74. Israeli officials say Prime Minister Rabin overrode his water negotiators and was willing to offer Jordan up to 100 mcm of water to overcome King Hussein's hesitation to sign a peace treaty with Israel. The 4 mcm "gift," according to the Israeli press, was valued at approximately $70,000 and represented a little less than 1 percent of Jordan's yearly water usage (*Yediot Ahronot*, 8 Aug. 1994 (Hebrew)).

75. "Address by Prime Minister Yitzhak Rabin to the Knesset: 25 Oct. 1994," in State of Israel, *Peace between the State of Israel and the Hashemite Kingdom of Jordan* (Jerusalem: Ministry of Foreign Affairs, 1994), 42.

76. The other Jordanian negotiating positions were the amending of the "1987 Agreement with Syria to utilize the Yarmouk waters; adoption of the Mukheiba site in lieu of the Maqarin site for the construction of a dam with suitable storage capacity; doing away with whatever results came out of the Armitage intermediary efforts in connection with the Unity Dam; and discussing the rights of the West Bank and the Palestinians in the Jordanian Basin" (Haddadin, *Diplomacy on the Jordan*, 332). Haddadin was opposed to the Armitage talks resuming from where they had left off (Haddadin, *Diplomacy on the Jordan*, 296–297).

77. Haddadin, *Diplomacy on the Jordan*, 364, n. 331.

78. Haddadin, *Diplomacy on the Jordan*, 395.

79. Haddadin, *Diplomacy on the Jordan*, 400.

80. "Jordan Insists on Securing Water Rights in Peace Talks," *Jordan Times*, 3 Jan. 1994.

81. "Treaty of Peace Between the State of Israel and The Hashemite Kingdom of Jordan," Journal of Palestine Studies 2:23 (Winter 1995), 133–139 [hereafter Jordan-Israel Treaty], Annex II, Article 6, Para. 1.

82. Jordan-Israel Treaty, Annex II, Article 1, Para. 1.

83. See chapter 2.

84. Israel will transfer 10 mcm of Lake Tiberias water until the desalination plant is operational.

85. "Jordan Agrees to Additional Water Drills on its Territory for Israel," *Haaretz*, Internet edition, 9 June 1997.

86. Interview by author with Kinarti, senior Israeli water talks negotiator, 17 Nov. 1995, Tel Aviv. For a Jordanian version of the treaty negotiations, see Haddadin, *Diplomacy on the Jordan*, 385–392.

87. Frederic C. Hof, "The Yarmouk and Jordan Rivers in the Israel-Jordan Peace Treaty," *Middle East Policy* 3:4 (April 1995), 55. Also see Ali Ghezawi, "The Impact of the Middle East Peace on the Region's Water Resources and Agricultural Production" (photocopy), Feb. 1995; "Negotiator on Water Accord; Allocations Detailed," *Jordan Times* 20–21 Oct., 1994, 1–2 [FBIS-NES-94-204 21 Oct. 1994, 6].

88. "Officials View Water Section of Treaty with Jordan," *Davar*, 27 Dec. 1994, 7 [FBIS-NES-94-249, 28 Dec. 1994, 33].

89. Haddadin, *Diplomacy on the Jordan*, 384.

90. "King Inaugurates Pipeline Bringing Tiberias Water," *Jordan Times*, 27 June 1995; "King Hussein Inaugurates Jordan-Israel Pipeline," *DPA*, 26 June 1995. The pipeline has a capacity of five mcm a month, which will be pumped to the King Abdullah Canal. "Agriculture and Water" in *Maariv Business Supplement*, 25 July 1995.

91. Government of Israel, *Programs for Regional Cooperation: 1997* (Nov. 1996). This report was compiled for the Cairo Economic Conference.

92. Jordan-Israel Treaty, Annex II, Article 2, Para. 2.

93. Hof, "The Yarmouk and Jordan Rivers in the Israel-Jordan Peace Treaty," 53–54.

94. Author's e-mail correspondence with Zafer Alem, JVA secretary general, 12 Sept. 2005.

95. Jordan-Israel Treaty, Annex II, Article 2, Para. 1.

96. Government of Israel, *Programs for Regional Cooperation: 1997* (Nov. 1996); Government of Israel, *Partnership in Development 1998* (Nov. 1997), 16. Text also available on the Internet: www.israel.org/peace/projects/jrv2.html.

97. "Israel's Sharon in Jordan to Kick Off Dam Construction," *Agence France-Presse* (AFP), 26 Oct. 1998.

98. "Israel to Build Dam on Disputed Land Claimed by Syria," *New York Times*, 26 Aug. 1997, A3. Haddadin, *Diplomacy on the Jordan*, 414 and 427–439. "Israel's Sharon in Jordan to Kick Off Dam Construction," AFP 26 Oct. 1998.

99. Jordan-Israel Treaty, Annex II, Article 1. Para. 3.

100. *Haaretz*, 13 April 1997 (Hebrew).

101. Elmusa, "The Jordan-Israel Water Agreement," 67–68.

102. Fifty mcm is the quantity of municipal and industrial water to have been supplied by the Unity dam. (Hof, "The Yarmouk and Jordan Rivers in the Israel-Jordan Peace Treaty," 54–55).

103. "Ambassador: Jordan Disappointed About Peace Treaty Implementation" Xinhua News Agency, 11 Sept. 1996.

104. "Most Jordanians Would Annul Treaty with Israel—Opinion Poll," *DPA,* 22 Oct. 1996.

105. "Israel Praises Jordan on 11th Anniversary of Peace Deal Signing, but Islamists Condemn the Accord," *AP,* 25 Oct. 2005, and "Angry Jordanians Protest on 10th Anniversary of Israel Accord," *Jerusalem Post,* 27 Oct. 2004. For further explanation of Jordanian frustration with peace process, see Haddadin, *Diplomacy on the Jordan,* 415–417, and Paul Scham and Russell Lucas, "'Normalization' and 'Anti-Normalization' in Jordan: the Public Debate," *Middle East Review of International Affairs (MERIA) Journal* 5:3 (Sept. 2001).

106. "Israel, Jordan Reach Interim Water Accord," *Reuters,* 23 May 1997. Also see "Jordan's Crown Prince Snubs Israel over Water Row," *Reuters,* 6 May 1997; "Jordan: This is a crisis; Netanyahu: Only a mini-crisis," *Yediot Achronot,* 7 May 1997, 6–7 (Hebrew); "The Water Crisis Is Finished," *Yediot Achronot,* 11 May 1997, 4 (Hebrew); "Netanyahu Held Secret Talks with King Hussein to Resolve Water Dispute," AFP, 9 May 1997 and Haddadin, *Diplomacy on the Jordan,* chapter 12.

107. Frederic Hof, "Jordan's Water Diplomacy," *Journal of Commerce,* 18 June 1997, 6A. Haddadin, *Diplomacy on the Jordan,* 426.

108. "King Hussein Thanks Israel for Water," *DPA,* 27 May 1997. Also, see Hof, "Jordan's Water Diplomacy."

109. Twenty mcm of saline water from springs in the north of Lake Tiberias and 30 mcm from springs in Gilboa. The cost of supplying Jordan with the additional 50 mcm will be divided between Israel and Jordan ("Israel to Divert 50 Million Cubic Meters of Water to Jordan," *Haaretz,* Internet edition, 25 May 1997). For detailed description, see Israel, *Partnership in Development 1998,* 11–16. For Israeli analysis of agreement, see Zeev Schiff, "A Difficult Promise to Keep," *Haaretz,* 27 Aug. 1997.

110. "Jordan Agrees to Additional Water Drills on its Territory for Israel," *Haaretz,* Internet edition, 9 June 1997.

111. "Jordan Water and Irrigation Minister: No Plan to Use Kinneret as Jordanian Reservoir," *Jerusalem Post,* 6 April 1998, 3. Haddadin, *Diplomacy on the Jordan,* 417–439.

112. See Zeev Schiff, "They Are Forgetting the Golan's Water," *Haaretz,* 7 June 1995, b1 (Hebrew) and Jordan-Israel Treaty, Annex II, Article 1, 2a and d. In 1997, Jordan requested to store additional water in Lake Tiberias, which Israeli negotiators initially accepted, but subsequently rejected (*Jerusalem Report,* 12 June 1997 and Haddadin, *Diplomacy on the Jordan,* 438).

113. "Contaminated Drinking Water Scandal Sinks Jordanian Cabinet," *The Guardian* (London), 20 Aug. 1998, 10. For Haddadin's explanation of the episode, see Haddadin, *Diplomacy on the Jordan,* 439–443.

114. "Jordan Angered by Israel's Announcement of Cut in Water Supply," *AFP,* 15 March 1999, and "Emergency Water Cutbacks Ordered," *Jerusalem Post,* 12 April 1999, 4.

115. "Precede Jerusalem: Jordan Objects to Cut in Water Supplies from Israel," *AP Worldstream*, 15 March 1999.

116. "Jordan Rejects Israel's Request to Reduce Water Transfer," *Jerusalem Post*, 15 March 1999, 2.

117. "Jordan's Parliament Slams Israel for Cutting Water Rights," *AFP,* 17 March 1999.

118. "Israel Agrees to New Water Distribution Terms with Jordan," *AP Worldstream*, 17 Aug. 1999, and "Israel Scratches Plan to Cut 50 Percent Water Supply to Jordan," *AP Worldstream*, 21 April 1999.

119. "Jordan: Minister Says Water Among Issues Discussed with Turkey," *Al-Ra'y*, 21 May 1996, 1, 16 [FBIS-NES-96-099, 21 May 1996, 31].

120. "Jordan Looking to Other Water Resources Despite Israeli Pact," *DPA*, 20 May 1996. "Peres, Hassan Decide on Water Resources Plan," *Qol Yisrael*, 13 March 1995 [FBIS-NES-95-049, 14 March 1995, 41]; "Further on Talks," *Jordan Times*, 13 March 1995, 1, 3 [FBIS-NES-95-048, 41].

121. "Jordan Minister Off to Bonn on Mideast Water Plans," *Reuters*, 30 Jan. 1996; "Kohl Hopes Meeting with Rabin, Hussein will Help Mideast Peace," Deutsche Presse-Agentur *(DPA)*, 5 June 1995.

122. "Rabin Holds First Talks with Japanese Premier," *Reuters*, 12 Dec. 1994.

123. "Israel: Netanyahu Urges Implementation of Agreement with Jordan," *Haaretz*, 2 Aug. 1996, A1, A12. [FBIS-NES-96-150, 2 Aug. 1996, 26].

124. "Israel, Jordan Seek Japan's Support for Water Projects," *Japan Economic Newswire*, 25 Aug. 1997.

125. "Jordan Looking to other Water Resources Despite Israeli Pact," *DPA*, 20 May 1996, and "Jordan: Concern as Yarmouk Flow Drops to Critical Level" *Global News Wire*, 14 June 2005, and Arnon Soffer, "Geopolitical Aspects of Water Supply in the Levant Area," Israel/Palestine Center for Research and Information, "Water for Life in the Middle East," 2nd Israeli-Palestinian-International Conference (Turkey, October 2004).

126. See David Horovitz with Ehud Ya'ari, "Syria Looks on in Anger," *Jerusalem Report*, 17 Nov. 1994, 10; Syrian Arab News Agency, 18 Oct. 1994, as cited in Satloff, "The Jordan-Israel Peace Treaty: A Remarkable Document," 50.

127. "Jordan's King Travels to Syria for Talks," *Washington Post*, 4 Aug. 1996, A32. Press accounts state that Jordanian diplomats demanded that Syria implement the 1987 Maqarin Dam water-sharing provisions, in particular, Syria's Yarmouk water utilization. "Jordan: Syria Pledges to Prevent 'Infiltrations' into Jordan," *Al-Sharq Al-Awsat*, 5 Aug. 1996, 1 [FBIS-NES 96–151, 5 Aug. 1996, 42].

128. "Eitan Blasts Yarmouk Dam Proposal," *Jerusalem Post*, 23 Aug. 1996; "Jordan Rebuffs Israeli Criticism of Plan for Dam with Syria," Arab Press Services, 23 Aug. 1996.

129. "Ben-Meir: Yarmouk Dam Won't Harm Israel's Water Supply," 21 May 1998, 3.

130. Jordan-Israel Treaty, Annex II, Article 5, Para.1.

131. Jordan's Ministry of Water and Irrigation "Al-Wihdeh Dam," www.mwi.gov.jo. "Gov't Denies Crisis with Syria over Water," *Jordan Times*, 17 Oct. 2006 and "Syrian Source 'Astonished' by Jordanian Remarks on Water Resources," *BBC Worldwide Monitoring*, 28 Sept. 2006.

132. "Abdullah II meets with Assad in 'Spirit of Brotherhood.' Jordan Reports Israel Will Not Reduce Water Allocation," *Jerusalem Post*, 22 April 1999, 2.

133. "Syria Starting to Pump Water to Jordan," *DPA*, 14 July 2001, and "Bashar Offers Drought Stricken Jordan Precious Supply of Water," *AFP*, 19 July 2000. Syria was publicly critical of Israel's proposal to cut its supply to Jordan ("Israel Wants to Hurt Jordan: Syria," *AFP*, 17 March 1999).

134. "Jordan: King, Syrian President Launch Construction of Wihdeh Dam," *Global News Wire*, 10 Feb. 2004; "Jordan King, Syria President Launch Long Awaited Dam Project," *AFP*, 9 Feb. 2004; and "Jordanian, Syrian Leaders' Ceremony for Al-Wahdah Dam Project Postponed," *Global News Wire—BBC*, 20 Nov. 2003. In 2005, Syria and Jordan signed a water memorandum of understanding to increase their water-sharing cooperation ("Ministry of Water, Its Syrian Counterpart Sign Memorandum of Understanding," *Jordan News Agency-UPI*, 2 March 2005). Even so, tensions over Syrian use of Yarmouk water still exist ("Jordan: Concern as Yarmouk Flow Drops to Critical Level," *Global News Wire*, 14 June 2005).

135. "Jordan Receives Funds for Building Wehdah Dam," *AP Worldstream*, 30 Dec. 1999. Jordan's Ministry of Water and Irrigation, "Al-Wihdeh Dam," www.mwi.gov.jo.

136. "Jordan Seeks Cooperation with Israel to Save Dead Sea," *AP Worldstream*, 22 July 2002, and "For Dead Sea, A Slow and Seemingly Inexorable Death," *Washington Post*, 19 May 2005, A01.

137. "Israel, Jordan Discussing Akaba-Dead Sea Pipeline," *DPA*, 17 July 2002.

138. "Israelis and Jordanians Cast Accord upon the Dead Sea's Waters," *New York Times*, 2 Sept. 2002, A9.

139. "Israel, Jordan Announce Projects to Save Dead Sea," *Jerusalem Post*, 2 Sept. 2002.

140. "Peace Canal Deal for Thirsty Middle East," *The Guardian* (London), 9 May 2005, 18.

141. Hof, "The Yarmouk and Jordan Rivers in the Israel-Jordan Peace Treaty," 55–56. See "Jordanian-Israeli Water Committee Meets in Tiberias," *Amman Radio Jordan Network*, 11 Jan. 1995 [FBIS-NES–95–008, 12 Jan. 1995, 35].

142. Jordan-Israel Treaty, Annex II, Article 7.

143. Interview by author with Eli Rosenthal, Israeli water talks negotiator, 14 Dec. 1995, Jerusalem; "Jordan to allow Israel to drill well on returned land in Arava

desert," *BBC Summary of World Broadcasts*, 22 Dec. 1995. According to Munther Haddadin, as of 2006, Jordan and Israel still need to finalize construction plans for a desalination plant which will supply Jordan with 60 mcmy and "clarification of the concessions of 20 mcm from the Yarmouk to Israel and from Lake [Tiberias] to Jordan," Munther Haddadin, ed., *Water Resources in Jordan* (Washing, DC, RFF, 2006), 258.

144. For overview of Syrian-Israeli relations, see Moshe Ma'oz, "Syria, Israel and the Peace Process" in Barry Rubin, Joseph Ginat, and Moshe Ma'oz, eds., *From War to Peace: Arab-Israeli Relations, 1973–1993* (New York: New York University Press, 1994), 157–181.

145. "Statement to the Knesset by Prime Minister Ehud Barak on the Renewal of Israel-Syria Negotiations," Jerusalem, 13 Dec. 1999 (www.mfa.gov.il/mfa/go.asp? MFAH0gb50).

146. This was a key sticking point for both sides. The Syrians contended that Rabin committed to withdrawing to the 4 June 1967 border. Israeli officials such as Netanyahu challenged this position.

147. "Interview: Fresh Light on the Syrian-Israeli Peace Negotiations." An interview with Ambassador Walid al-Moualem, *Journal of Palestine Studies*, 26:2 (Winter 1997), 85. Also see for Syrian position: "Turkey: Syrian Envoy Discusses Water, Regional Peace," *Zaman*, 15 April 1996, 4 [FBIS-WEU-96-078, 22 April 1996, 39].

148. See Moshe Brawer, "Boundaries of Peace," *Israel Affairs* 1:1 (Autumn 1994), 41–63; Amos Harel, "The Portrait of a 'Line,'" *Haaretz*, 19 Dec. 1995, B3; Yonatan Ben-Nahum, "The Border That Has Not Stopped Moving," *Davar Rishon*, 19 Dec. 1995, 2–3; Frederic C. Hof, *Line of Battle, Border of Peace? The Line of June 4, 1967* (Washington, DC: Middle East Insight, 1999).

149. "Rabin: Water 'Greatest Danger' in Syria Talks," *Maariv*, 19 July 1995, 14 [FBIS-NES-95-138, 19 July 1995, 35].

150. "Peres: Water Rights on Golan Key to Peace Treaty with Syria," *Jewish Telegraph Agency (JTA)*, 14 Feb. 1996, 2.

151. Schiff, "They Are Forgetting the Golan's Water."

152. "The Border Line and the Water Line," *Davar Rishon*, 30 Jan. 1996, 7; Ambassador Itamar Rabinovich, "Israel-Syria Peace Talks: an Update," The Washington Institute's *Peacewatch* no. 80 (22 Jan. 1996).

153. See "Israel-Syria Negotiations," www.Israel-mfa.gov.il/peace/syria.html.

154. Rabinovich, "Israel-Syria Peace Talks: an Update,"*Peacewatch*.

155. For more detailed discussion of the Israel-Syrian negotiations, see Raymond Hinnebusch, "Does Syria Want Peace? Syrian Policy in the Syrian-Israeli Peace Negotiations," *Journal of Palestine Studies* 26:1 (Autumn 1996), 51–55.

156. Itamar Rabinovich, *The Brink of Peace: The Israeli-Syrian Negotiations* (Princeton: Princeton University Press, 1998), 219, and "Politics of Water Stalls Peace Process," *Baltimore Sun*, 8 Dec. 1999, 1A.

157. "Barak: Assad Not Ready for Peace," *Jerusalem Post*, Internet edition, 28 March 2000, and "Syria Puts Talks on Hold," *Jerusalem Post*, Internet edition, 18 Jan. 2000.

158. "Peace Walks on Water," Economist.com, 30 Sept. 2000, and Jerome Slater, "Lost Opportunities for Peace in the Arab-Israeli Conflict: Israel and Syria, 1948–2001," *International Security* 27:1 (Summer 2002), 79–106.

159. "Israel Will Give Up the Heights But Not the Depths," *Scripps Howard News Service*, 7 April 2000.

160. "Sea of Galilee Will Remain Under Israeli Sovereignty," communicated by Foreign Ministry spokesman, 10 April 2000, www.mfa.gov.il.

161. Bill Clinton, *My Life* (New York: Knopf, 2004), 903, and "Barak: Assad Not Ready for Peace," *Jerusalem Post*, Internet edition, 28 March 2000.

162. "Syria Press Blasts Israel," *DPA*, 13 April 2000.

163. "US Document: A Framework for Peace between Israel and Syria: The Draft Peace Treaty Presented by the Clinton Administration to Jerusalem and Damascus," *Haaretz*, 13 Jan. 2000.

164. Yossi Beilin, *The Path to Geneva: The Quest for a Permanent Agreement*, 1996–2004 (New York: RDV Books, 2004), 119–120.

165. Dan River 250 mcm, Banias 120 mcm, and Hasbani 120 mcm.

166. Another 5 mcmy are pumped from the Alonei Habashan settlement area. See Golan Residents Committee Web site for additional water data and maps (www.golan.org.il/water.html).

167. "US: Water Dispute between Israel and Syria: Pragmatic Solutions Can be Found," *Haaretz*, 19 Jan. 1996, 1 (Hebrew); also FBIS-NES-96-013, 19 Jan. 1996, 38.

168. "The Water Crisis," *Jerusalem Post*, 6 Feb. 2004, 8. Also see "Golan Sewage Joins Flow into Kinneret," *Jerusalem Post*, 12 Feb. 2003.

169. "Syria: Water Crisis in Capital," *New York Times*, 28 June 2001, A6.

170. "Drought-Hit Syria Battles Water Shortages," *AFP*, 26 July 2001, and "Syria: Water Crisis in Capital," *New York Times*, 28 June 2001.

171. Abdullah Droubi, "Quality of Water in Syria" (photocopy).

172. "Battle Lines Drawn for Euphrates," *Middle East Economic Digest*, 13 Oct. 1989, 5.

173. "Syrian Programmes to Save Water, Environment," *Reuters*, 23 Oct. 1996.

174. "Syria: Signing of Agreements with Germany for Financial Aid," *Global News Wire*, 23 May 2004, and "Japan Extends 7 Million Dollars of Aid to Syria for Water Project," *DPA*, 28 March 2005.

175. See "US: Water Dispute between Israel and Syria: Pragmatic Solutions Can be Found," *Haaretz*, 19 Jan. 1996, 1 (Hebrew). "The Turkish Aspect," *Haaretz*, 7 Feb. 1996, B1 (Hebrew), and Robert Olson, "Turkey-Syria Relations Since the Gulf War:

Kurds and Water," *Middle East Policy* 5:2 (May 1997), 168–189. Prior to the capture of the leader of the PKK, Abdullah Ocalan, a top Israeli source told one newspaper that "ultimately, what will be needed is a comprehensive solution. The Syrians will commit to cease terrorist activities [with the Kurdish separatist group, the PKK], and then they will get water from Turkey." ("US: Water dispute between Israel and Syria Pragmatic Solutions Can be Found," *Haaretz*. George Gruen, "Turkey's Regional Role in the Aftermath of Sept. 11, 2001," *American Foreign Policy Interests* 24:1 (2002) 3–29.

176. "US Hopeful Israel, Syria Can Reach Water Arrangement," *Jerusalem Post*, 8 Feb. 1996, 2.

177. Zeev Schiff, "First Light on a Shelved Report," *Haaretz*, 8 Oct. 1993, 2 (Hebrew). The report was authored by Joshua Schwartz and Aharon Zohar and titled "The Water Problem in the Context of Israel-Arab Agreements" (Hebrew); it had a limited distribution before it was classified secret. See chapter 5. Other proposals for Israeli-Syrian water problems, see Fred Hof, "The Water Dimension of Golan Heights Negotiations," *Middle East Policy* 5:2 (May 1997), 129–141.

178. Schiff, "First Light on a Shelved Report."

179. Schiff, "First Light on a Shelved Report."

180. "Zeev Schiff "Full Asking Price for Peace Aid: $65 Billion," *Haaretz*, 7 Jan. 2000.

181. In fact, this was part of a speculated solution, see "Israel and Syria Agree on Two Key Issues: Radio," *AFP*, 26 March 2000.

182. "Turkey Reportedly Rules out Concessions on Water Issue to Aid Israel-Syria Talks," *BBC Summary of World Broadcasts*, 6 Jan. 2000.

183. See Israel Ministry of Foreign Affairs Web site, www.Israel.org/peace/lebanon.html.

184. See, for example, Arnon Soffer, "The Litani River: Fact and Fiction," *Middle Eastern Studies* 30: 4 (Oct. 1994), 963–974.

185. "Lebanon's Proposed Water Station Pumps Up the Tension," *Haaretz*, Internet edition, 15 March 2001.

186. "US Ambassador to Lebanon Rejects 'Israeli Threats' over Water Diversion," *AFP*, 17 March 2001.

187. "Water Wars," *Mideast Mirror*, 11 Sept. 2002, and "Israel, US Seek to Defuse Tension From Lebanese Water Use Scheme," *JTA*, 17 Sept. 2002, and Flynt Leverett, *Inheriting Syria* (Washington, DC: Brookings, 2005), 26, n.27.

188. "Lebanon Scorns US mediation Efforts over Wazzani," *Jerusalem Post*, Internet edition, 18 Sept. 2002, and "Lebanon Says It Will Take 'Every Drop of Its Share' of Disputed River," *AFP*, 21 Sept. 2002. The *Jerusalem Post* notes that more than a year after Israel's withdrawal from southern Lebanon, it continued to supply water to fifteen villages. These Lebanese villages had not yet been reconnected to Lebanon's national water network ("United Nations Checks Israel's Complaint over Lebanese Water Pumping," *Jerusalem Post*, 30 July 2001, 2).

189. Joel Peters, *Pathways to Peace: The Multilateral Arab-Israeli Peace Talks* (London: Royal Institute of International Affairs, 1996), 6–7.

190. "Remarks by Secretary of State James A. Baker III before the Organizational Meeting for Multilateral Negotiations on the Middle East, House of Unions, 28 Jan. 1992 (www.israel.org/mfa/go.asp?MFAH0cos0).

191. Satterfield, US Congress 2004, 26 and www.israel.org/mfa/go.asp? MFAH0cos0.

192. For overview of the multilateral negotiations, see Peters, *Pathways to Peace*, and Dalia Dassa Kaye, *Beyond the Handshake: Multilateral Cooperation in the Arab-Israel Peace Process, 1991–1996* (New York: Columbia University Press, 2001), and "Madrid's Forgotten Forum: The Middle East Multilaterals," *The Washington Quarterly* 20:1 (Winter 1997), 167–186. For a focus on water negotiations, see Aaron Wolf, "International Water Dispute Resolution: The Middle East Multilateral Working Group on Water Resources," *Water International* 20 (1995), 141–150.

193. See multilateral working group on water resources press statement of the gavel holder, www.state.gov/www/regions/nea/ppmwg1.html.

194. The Moscow meeting was the organizing meeting for all multilateral groups. Round 1, January 28–29, 1992, Moscow, Russia; Round 2, May 14–15, 1992, Vienna, Austria; Round 3, September 16–17, 1992, Washington, DC; Round 4, April 27–29, 1993, Geneva, Switzerland; Round 5, October 26–28, 1993, Beijing China; Round 6, April 17–19, 1994 Muscat, Oman; Round 7, November 7–9, 1994, Athens, Greece; Round 8, June 18–22, 1995, Amman, Jordan; and Round 9, May 16, 1996, Hammamet, Tunisia.

195. "From Contention to Cooperation," 7.

196. "Gavelholder's Summary: Working Group on Water Resources," Amman, Jordan, 18–22 June 1995 (photocopy), 3.

197. See "Syria's al Allaf on Multilaterals," FBIS MEA, 10 May 1993, 5.[FBIS-NES-93-088]; "Foreign Minister Stresses Lebanon's Reservations on Attending Multilateral Talks," *Xinhua News Agency*, 9 June 1995.

198. "Palestinian Working Paper on Water," *Algiers Voice of Palestine*, 17 Sept. 1992 [FBIS-NES–92–183] 21 Sept. 1992, 6.

199. "Israeli Paper on 'Sharp Differences at Talks,'" [FBIS-NES–92–096] 18 May 1992, 2. Prior to the Oslo breakthrough, the multilateral and bilateral negotiations were almost stagnant. See Shimon Peres, *The New Middle East* (New York: Henry Holt, 1993), 10–15.

200. "Israeli-Palestinian Row Halts Mideast Water Talks," *Reuters*, 29 April 1993.

201. Peters, *Pathways to Peace*, 17–18; "Katz-Oz 'Not Disappointed' by Water Talks," *Jerusalem Post*, 4 May 1993.

202. "Mideast Water Conference Ends after Jordan Protest," *Reuters*, 19 April 1994.

203. "Bridge over Troubled Water," *Jerusalem Report*, 13 Feb. 1992, 14.

204. "Blueprint for an Idyllic Future," *Jerusalem Report*, 10 March 1994, 18. Also see "Divided Water," *Jerusalem Post*.

205. See "Divided Water," *Jerusalem Post*.

206. "Gavelholder's Thoughts on Water Future" (photocopy), Amman, Jordan, 18–22 June 1995, 1.

207. "From Contention to Cooperation," 8.

208. Satterfield, US Congress 2004, 26.

209. "From Contention to Cooperation," 5 and 9.

210. "Report: Middle East Water Data Banks Plan" (photocopy) 1; Middle East Water Data Banks Implementation Plan: Executive Action Team Terms of Reference: Jan. 24, 1995" (photocopy). "From Contention to Cooperation," 10. This has been one of the most successful projects. In 1998, the core parties began meeting among themselves in an addition to semiannual EXACT meetings (exact-me.org/). Jan Selby, *Water Power and Politics in the Middle East: The Other Israeli-Palestinian Conflict* (London: I. B. Tauris, 2003), 111.

211. Satterfield, US Congress 2004, 26.

212. "Draft Terms of Reference: Maximizing of Revenues through Intensive Agriculture Under Varying Water Quality Conditions in *Gaza*" (photocopy), Amman, Jordan, 18–22 June 1995, 2, and "From Contention to Cooperation," 11.

213. James Kunder, deputy assistant administrator, Bureau for Asia and the Near East, US AID, "Water Scarcity in the Middle East: Regional Cooperation as a Mechanism Toward Peace." House International Relations Committee (serial no. 108–118) [108th Congress, second session, 5 May 2004], (Washington, DC: US Government Printing Office, 2004), 32.

214. "From Contention to Cooperation," 11 and Satterfield, US Congress 2004, 26–7.

215. "Gavelholder's Thoughts on Water Future" (photocopy), 2.

216. See Rouyer, *Turning Water into Politics*, chapter 8; also see Israel/Palestine Center for Research and Information, "Water for Life in the Middle East" 2nd Israeli-Palestinian-International Conference (Turkey, October 2004), ipcri.org/.

217. See Franklin Fisher et al., *Liquid Assets* (Washington, DC: RFF Press, 2005).

218. Rouyer, *Turning Water into Politics*, chapter 8.

219. "Regional Study on Water Supply and Demand Management: Sponsored by the Federal Republic of Germany," Multilateral Working Group on Water Resources (photocopy), Amman, Jordan, 18–22 June 1995, 1.

220. "From Contention to Cooperation," 12.

221. For background on "peace pipeline" politics, see Joyce Starr, *Covenant over Middle Eastern Waters: Key to World Survival* (New York: Henry Holt, 1995).

222. Government of Israel, *Development Options for Cooperation: The Middle East/East Mediterranean Region: 1996* (Aug. 1995), 4–37.

223. "Experts Cool to Massive Mideast Water Pipe Idea," *Reuters*, 19 April 1994. See Stephen Lonergan and David Brooks, *Watershed: The Role of Fresh Water in the Israeli-Palestinian Conflict* (Ottawa: International Development Research Centre, 1994), 251–269.

224. "Israel Buys Turkish Water in $1 Billion, 20-Year Deal," *Washington Times*, 9 Aug. 2002, A13, and "Turkey-Israel Water Shipment Deal Said Cancelled," *BBC Monitoring*, 7 April 2006.

225. Satterfield, US Congress 2004, 27–28, and Uri Shamir, Director of the GWIRI, Faculty of Civil Engineering, Lawrence and Marie Feldman Chair in Engineering, Stephen and Nancy Grand Water Research Institute, "Water Scarcity in the Middle East: Regional Cooperation as a Mechanism Toward Peace," House International Relations Committee (serial no. 108–118) [108th Congress, second session, 5 May 2004], (Washington, DC: US Government Printing Office, 2004), 94–96.

226. "Gavelholder's Thoughts on Water Future" (photocopy), 3.

227. See www.medrc.org and Satterfield, US Congress 2004, 27.

228. "'Water Factory' Aims to Filter Tensions," BBC News, 7 Sept. 2004, and "The Water Crisis," *Jerusalem Post*, 6 Feb. 2004, 8. Also see Shamir, US Congress 2004, 93–96.

229. "New Israeli Desalination Plant May Defuse Mideast Water Crisis," *JTA*, 12 Oct. 2005.

230. See US AID Web site: www.usaid.gov/wbg/program_water.htm.

231. "Gavelholder's Thoughts on Water Future" (photocopy), 4.

232. "Jordanian Official: Israel, Jordan, Palestinian Water Accord Is Meaningless," *Jerusalem Post*, 15 Feb. 1996, 3. Riyad al-Khoudary, chief Palestinian representative to the water working group voiced similar complaints about the agreement (Rouyer, *Turning Water into Politics*, 240–241).

233. "From Contention to Cooperation," 14–15. The Norwegians financed a study on water laws and institutions and initiated a "Water Atlas" project, which is a database of historic, scientific, technical, legal, and economic literature ("From Contention to Cooperation," 14). This work is intended to assist in the creation of a regional institution.

234. "Gavelholder's Thoughts on Water Future" (photocopy), 3.

235. "Gavelholder's Thoughts on Water Future" (photocopy), 6.

236. Satterfield, US Congress 2004, 27.

Chapter 7: Conclusion

1. Miriam Lowi, *Water and Power* (New York: Cambridge University Press, 1993), 10.

2. These are results similar to Stephen Walt's, *The Origins of Alliances* (Ithaca: Cornell University Press, 1990).

3. For extensive discussion of the impact of foreign assistance to the Middle East see Walt, *The Origins of Alliances*, 218–242.

4. Dennis Ross, *The Missing Peace: The Inside Story of the Fight for Middle East Peace* (New York: FSG, 2004), 771.

5. Ross, *The Missing Peace*, 772.

Selected Bibliography

Allan, J. A., ed. *Water, Peace, and the Middle East*. New York: Taurus, 1996.

Allan, Tony. *The Middle East Water Question: Hydropolitics and the Global Economy*. London: I. B. Tauris, 2002.

Alpher, Joseph. *Settlements and Borders*. Tel Aviv: Tel Aviv University, Jaffee Center for Strategic Studies, 1994.

Alteras, Isaac. *Eisenhower and Israel: US-Israel Relations, 1953–1960*. Gainesville: University Press of Florida, 1993.

Amery, Hussein, and Aaron Wolf, eds. *Water in the Middle East: A Geography of Peace*. Austin: University of Texas Press, 2000.

Aronson, Geoffrey. *Israel, Palestinians, and the Intifada: Creating Facts on the West Bank*. New York: Kegan Paul International, 1990.

Arreguin-Toft, Ivan. "How the Weak Win Wars: A Theory of Asymmetric Conflict." *International Security* 26:1 (2001): 93–128.

Assaf, Karen et al. *A Proposal for the Development of a Regional Water Master Plan*. Jerusalem: Israel/Palestine Center for Research and Information, 1993.

Axelrod, Robert, and Robert Keohane. "Achieving Cooperation Under Anarchy: Strategies and Institutions." In *Cooperation Under Anarchy*, edited by Kenneth Oye, ed. Princeton: Princeton University Press, 1986.

Baechler, Gunther. "Why Environmental Transformation Causes Violence: A Synthesis." *The Woodrow Wilson Center Environmental Change and Security Project Report* 4 (1998): 30–31.

Baida, Uri, and Yohanan Boneh, "Water Resources and Its Utilization in Judea and Samaria" *Judea and Sameria (Yehuda Veshomron)*, A. Shmueli, D. Grossman, and K. Zeevi, eds. (Tel Aviv: Bar Ilan University, 1977) [Hebrew], 34–47.

Beilin, Yossi. *The Path to Geneva: The Quest for A Permanent Agreement, 1996–2004*. New York: RDV Books, 2004.

Beinin, Joel, and Zachary Lockman, eds. *Intifada: The Palestinian Uprising Against Israeli Occupation*. Boston: South End Press, 1989.

Benvenisti, Eyal, and Haim Gvirtzman. "Harnessing International Law to Determine Israeli-Palestinian Water Rights: The Mountain Aquifer." *Natural Resources Journal* 33 (1993), 543–567.

Benvenisti, Meron. *The West Bank Data Project: A Survey of Israel's Policies.* Washington, DC: American Enterprise Institute for Public Policy Research and West Bank Data Base Project, 1984.

Beschorner, Natasha. "Water and Instability in the Middle East." *Adelphi Paper 273.* London: Brassey's (Winter 1992/93).

Bickerton, Ian, and Carla Klausner. *A Concise History of the Arab-Israeli Conflict.* Upper Saddle River, NJ: Prentice Hall, 1998 and 1991.

Brand, Laurie. *Jordan's Inter-Arab Relations: The Political Economy of Alliance Making.* New York: Columbia University Press, 1994.

Brecher, Michael. *Decisions in Israel's Foreign Policy.* New Haven: Yale University Press, 1975.

Brecher, Michael. "International Crises and Protracted Conflicts." *International Interactions* 11:3–4 (1984): 237–297.

Brooks, David, and Stephen Lonergan. *Watershed: The Role of Fresh Water in the Israeil-Palestinian Conflict.* Ottawa: International Development Research Centre, 1994.

Brynen, Rex, ed. *Echoes of the Intifada: Regional Repercussions of the Palestinian-Israeli Conflict.* Boulder: Westview Press, 1991.

Bulloch, John, and Adel Darwish. *Water Wars: Coming Conflict in the Middle East.* London: Victor Goallzncz, 1993.

Charles T. Main, Inc. *The Unified Development of the Water Resources of the Jordan Valley Region.* Boston: Charles T. Main, 1953.

Conca, Ken. *Governing Water: Contentious Transnational Politics and Global Institution Building.* Cambridge: MIT Press, 2006.

Cooley, John. "The War Over Water." *Foreign Policy* 54 (1984): 3–26.

Copeland, Dale. "Economic Interdependence and War: A Theory of Trade Expectations." *International Security* 20: 4 (1996): 5–41.

Daibes, Fadia, ed. *Water in Palestine: Problems—Politics—Prospects. Jerusalem: PASSIA,* 2003.

Davis, Uri, Antonia Maks, and John Richardson. "Israel's Water Policies." *Journal of Palestine Studies* 9:2 (1980). 3–31.

Deudney, Daniel. "The Case Against Linking Environmental Degradation and National Security." *Millennium* 19:3 (Winter 1990): 461–476.

Dillman, Jeffrey. "Water Rights in the Occupied Territories." *Journal of Palestine Studies* 19:1 (1989): 46–71.

Dolatyar, Mostafa, and Tim S. Gray. *Water Politics in the Middle East: A Context for Conflict or Co-operation?* London: Macmillan, 2000.

Elhance, Arun. *Hydro-Politics in the 3rd World*. Washington, DC: US Institute of Peace Press, 1999.

Elmusa, Sharif. "Dividing The Common Palestinian-Israeli Waters: An International Water Law Approach." *Journal of Palestine Studies* 22:3 (1993): 57–77.

Elmusa, Sharif S. "The Water Issue and the Palestinian-Israeli Conflict." Washington, DC: The Center for Policy Analysis on Palestine, 1993.

Elmusa, Sharif S. "The Jordan-Israel Water Agreement: A Model or Exception?" *Journal of Palestine Studies* 24:3 (1995): 63–73.

Farsoun, Samih K., and Christina E. Zacharia. *Palestine and the Palestinians*. Boulder: Westview Press, 1997.

Feitelson, Eran, and Marwan Haddad. "Joint Management of Shared Aquifers." (Workshops 1–3). Jerusalem: Harry S Truman Institute and Palestine Consultancy Group, 1994–1996.

Fisher, Franklin et al. *Liquid Assets: An Economic Approach for Water Management and Conflict Resolution in the Middle and Beyond*. Washington, DC: Resources for the Future, 2005.

Garfinkle, Adam. *Israel and Jordan in the Shadow of War*. New York: St. Martin's Press, 1992.

Garfinkle, Adam. *Deep and Wide: Water, War and Negotiation in the Jordan Basin, 1916–1996*. (Manuscript, 22 April 1993).

Garfinkle, Adam. "Hung Out to Dry or All Wet? Water in the Jordan Valley." *Orbis* 39:1 (1995): 134–138.

Ghobshy, Omar Z. *The Development of the Jordan River*. New York: Arab Information Center, 1961.

Gleditsch, Nils Petter. "Armed Conflict and the Environment." In Paul Diehl and Gleditsch, *Environmental Conflict*. Boulder: Westview Press, 2001.

Gleick, Peter. "Water and Conflict: Fresh Water Resources and International Security," *International Security* 18:1 (1993), 79–112.

Gleick, Peter, ed. *Water in Crisis: A Guide to the World's Fresh Water Resources*. New York: Oxford University Press, 1993.

Gleick, Peter. *The World's Water: 1998–1999*. Washington, DC: Island Press, 1998.

Gleick, Peter. *The World's Water: 2000–2001*. Washington, DC: Island Press, 2000.

Gleick, Peter. *The World's Water: 2002–2003*. Washington, DC: Island Press, 2002

Gruen, George. "Turkey's Regional Role in the Aftermath of Sept. 11, 2001." *American Foreign Policy Interests* 24:1 (2002): 3–29.

Gubser, Peter. *Jordan: Crossroads of the Middle Eastern Events*. Boulder: Westview Press, 1983.

Haas, Peter. *Saving the Mediterranean*. New York: Columbia University Press, 1990.

Haddadin, Munther. *Diplomacy on the Jordan: International Conflict and Negotiated Resolution.* Boston: Kluwer, 2002.

Hillel, Daniel. *Rivers of Eden: The Struggle for Water and the Quest for Peace in the Middle East.* New York: Oxford University Press, 1994.

Hiltermann, Joost R. *Behind the Intifada: Labor and Women's Movement in the Occupied Territories.* Princeton: Princeton University Press, 1991.

Hinnebusch, Raymond. "Does Syria Want Peace? Syrian Policy in the Syrian-Israeli Peace Negotiations." *Journal of Palestine Studies* 26:1 (1996), 42–57.

Hof, Frederic C. "The Yarmouk and Jordan Rivers in the Israel-Jordan Peace Treaty." *Middle East Policy* 3:4 (1995), 47–56.

Hof, Frederic C. "Jordan's Water Diplomacy," *Journal of Commerce,* 18 June 1997, 6A.

Hof, Frederic C. "The Water Dimension of Golan Heights Negotiations." *Middle East Policy* 5:2 (1997), 129–141.

Hof, Frederic C. *Line of Battle, Border of Peace? The Line of June 4, 1967.* Washington, DC: Middle East Insight, 1999.

Homer-Dixon, Thomas. *Environment, Scarcity, and Violence.* Princeton: Princeton University Press, 2001.

Homer-Dixon, Thomas, and Jessica Blitt, eds., *Ecoviolence: Links among Environment, Population, and Security.* Lanham, MD: Rowman and Littlefield, 1999.

Homer-Dixon, Thomas. "On the Threshold: Environmental Changes as Causes of Acute Conflict." *International Security* 16:2 (1991): 76–116.

Isaac, Jad et al. "A Study of Palestinian Water Supply and Demand." *Symposium on Water Capacity in Palestine* (Sept. 1995).

Johnston, Eric. "My Mission to the Near East: Peacemaking on the Jordan." *New York Herald,* 14 Feb. 1954, 8–9.

"The Jordan Valley Water Question 1919–1984," Historical Research Project No. 1403, US State Department, Bureau of Public Affairs, Office of the Historian (August 1984).

Kahan, David. *Agriculture and Water in the West Bank and Gaza.* Jerusalem: The West Bank Data Project, 1983.

Kahl, Colin. "Population Growth, Environmental Degradation, and State-Sponsored Violence: The Case of Kenya, 1991–93." *International Security* 23:2 (1998): 80–119.

Kalpakian, Jack. *Identity, Conflict and Cooperation in International River Systems.* Burlington, VT: Ashgate, 2004.

Kaye, Dalia Dassa. "Madrid's Forgotten Forum: The Middle East Multilaterals." *The Washington Quarterly* 20:1 (1997), 167–186.

Kaye, Dalia Dassa. *Beyond the Handshake: Multilateral Cooperation in the Arab-Israel Peace Process, 1991–1996.* New York: Columbia University Press, 2001.

Keohane, Robert. *After Hegemony.* Princeton: Princeton University Press, 1984.

Keohane, Robert. "The Analysis of International Regimes: Towards a European-American Research Programme." In *Regime Theory and International Relations*, edited by Volker Rittberger. New York: Clarendon Press-Oxford, 1995.

Khouri, Rami. *The Jordan Valley: Life and Society Below Sea Level*. London: Longman, 1981.

Klieman, Aharon. *Statecraft in the Dark: Israel's Practice of Quiet Diplomacy*. Boulder: Westview Press, 1988.

Kliot, Nurit. *Water Resources and Conflict in the Middle East*. London: Routledge, 1994.

Krasner, Stephen. "Structural Causes and Regime Consequences: Regimes as Intervening Variables" in *International Regimes*, edited by Stephen Krasner. Ithaca: Cornell University Press, 1983.

Kratochwil, Friedrich. "Contract and Regimes: Do Issue Specificity and Variations of Formality Matter?" In *Regime Theory and International Relations*, edited by Volker Rittberger. New York: Clarendon Press-Oxford, 1995, 73–93.

Lawson, Fred. *Why Syria Goes to War*. Ithaca: Cornell University Press, 1996.

LeMarquand, David. *International Rivers: The Politics of Cooperation*. Vancouver: Westwater Research Centre, University of British Columbia, 1977.

Lieber, Robert. *Theory and World Politics*. Cambridge: Wintrop, 1972.

Lipson, Charles. "Why Are Some International Agreements Informal?" *International Organization* 45:4 (1991): 495–538.

Lowdermilk, Walter C. *Palestine: Land of Promise*. New York: Harper, 1944.

Lowi, Miriam. "Bridging the Divide: Transboundary Resource Disputes and the Case of West Bank Water." *International Security* 18:1 (1993). 113–138.

Lowi, Miriam. *Water and Power: The Politics of a Scarce Resource in the Jordan River Basin*. New York: Cambridge University Press, 1993 and 1995.

Lukacs, Yehuda. *Israel, Jordan, and the Peace Process*. Syracuse: Syracuse University Press, 1997.

Lustick, Ian. "Israel and Jordan: the Implications of an Adversarial Partnership." *Policy Papers in International Affairs*, no. 6. Berkeley: Institute of International Studies, University of California, 1978).

Makovsky, David. *Making Peace with the PLO: The Rabin Government's Road to the Oslo Accord*. Boulder: Westview Press, 1996.

Ma'oz, Moshe. *Asad: the Sphinx of Damascus: A Political Biography*. New York: Weidenfeld & Nicholson, 1988.

Ma'oz, Moshe. "Syria, Israel and the Peace Process." In *From War to Peace: Arab-Israeli Relations, 1973–1993*, edited by Barry Rubin, Joseph Ginat, and Moshe Ma'oz. New York: New York University Press, 1994.

Matson, Ruth, and Thomas Naff, eds. *Water in the Middle East: Conflict or Cooperation?* Boulder: Westview Press, 1984.

Medzini, Meron, ed. *Israel's Foreign Relations: Selected Documents 1947–1974.* Jerusalem: Ministry for Foreign Affairs, 1976.

Melman, Yossi, and Dan Raviv. *Behind the Uprising: Israelis, Jordanians, and Palestinians.* New York: Greenwood Press, 1989.

Moravcsik, Andrew. *The Choice for Europe.* Ithaca: Cornell University Press, 1998.

Moravcsik, Andrew. "Taking Preferences Seriously: A Liberal Theory of International Politics." In *Theory and Structure in International Political Economy*, edited by Charles Lipson and Benjamin Cohen, 33–44. Cambridge: MIT Press, 1999.

Morgenthau, Hans. *Politics Among Nations*, 6th ed. New York: McGraw-Hill, 1985.

Morris, Benny. *The Birth of the Palestinian Refugee Problem, 1947–1949.* Cambridge: Cambridge University Press, 1987.

Neff, Donald. "Israel-Syria: Conflict at the Jordan River, 1949–1967." *Journal of Palestine Studies* 23:4 (1994), 26–40.

Nye, Joseph. *Understanding International Conflicts: An Introduction to Theory and History*, 3rd ed. New York: Longman, 2000.

Oren, Michael. *Six Days of War: June 1967 and the Making of the Modern Middle East.* New York: Oxford University Press, 2002.

Oye, Kenneth. "Explaining Cooperation Under Anarchy." In *Cooperation Under Anarchy*, edited by Kenneth Oye. Princeton: Princeton University Press, 1986.

Parker, Richard. *The Politics of Miscalculation in the Middle East.* Bloomington: Indiana University Press, 1993.

Peretz, Don. *Intifada: The Palestinian Uprising.* Boulder: Westview Press, 1990.

Peters, Joel. *Pathways to Peace: The Multilateral Arab-Israeli Peace Talks.* London: Royal Institute of International Affairs, 1996.

Postel, Sandra. *Last Oasis: Facing Water Scarcity.* New York: W.W. Norton, 1997.

Postel, Sandra L., and Aaron T. Wolf. "Dehydrating Conflict." *Foreign Policy* (September/October 2001), 60–67.

Pressman, Jeremy. "Visions in Collision: What Happened at Camp David and Taba?" *International Security* 28:2 (2003), 5–43.

Rabinovich, Itamar. *The Brink of Peace: The Israeli-Syrian Negotiations.* Princeton: Princeton University Press, 1998.

Rabinovich, Itamar. *The Road Not Taken: Early Arab-Israeli Negotiations.* New York: Oxford University Press, 1991.

Reguer, Sara. "Rutenberg and the Jordan River: A Revolution in Hydro-electricity." *Middle East Studies* 31:4 (1995), 691–729.

Ross, Dennis. *The Missing Peace: The Inside Story of the Fight for Middle East Peace.* New York: FSG, 2004.

Rouyer, Alwyn R. *Turning Water into Politics: The Water Issue in the Palestinian-Israeli Conflict.* New York: Saint Martin's Press, 2000.

Rouyer, Alwyn. "Basic Needs vs Swimming Pools: Water Inequality and the Palestinian-Israeli Conflict." *Middle East Report* 227 (2003), 2–7.

Roy, Sara. *Gaza Strip Survey.* Jerusalem: West Bank Data Base Project, 1987.

Safran, Nadav. *Israel: The Embattled Ally.* Cambridge: Harvard University Press, 1981.

Satloff, Robert. "The Jordan-Israel Peace Treaty: A Remarkable Document." *Middle East Quarterly* (March 1995), 47–51.

Savir, Uri. *The Process.* New York: Random House, 1998.

Schiff, Ze'ev, and Ehud Ya'ari. *Intifada.* New York: Touchstone, 1991.

Schwarz, J. "Water Resources in Judea, Samaria, and Gaza Strip." In *Judea, Samaria, and Gaza: Views on the Present and the Future,* edited by Daniel Elazar, 89–95. Washington, DC: American Enterprise Institute for Public Policy Research, 1982.

Seale, Patrick. *Asad of Syria: The Struggle for the Middle East.* Berkeley: University of California Press, 1989.

Selby, Jan. *Water, Power and Politics in the Middle East.* London: I. B. Tauris, 2003.

Shalev, Aryeh. *The West Bank: Line of Defense.* New York: Praeger, 1985.

Shalev, Aryeh. *The Intifada: Causes and Effects.* Boulder: Westview Press, 1991.

Shalev, Aryeh. *Israel-Syria Armistice Regime 1949–1955.* Boulder: Westview Press, 1993.

Shalev, Aryeh. *Israel and Syria: Peace and Security on the Golan.* Boulder: Westview Press, 1994.

Shawwa, Isam. "The Water Situation in the Gaza Strip," In Gershon Baskin, ed., *Water: Conflict or Cooperation* (Jerusalem: Israel/Palestine Center for Research and Information, 1993), 23–36.

Shemesh, Moshe. "Prelude to the Six-Day War: The Arab-Israeli Struggle Over Water Resources." *Israel Studies* 9:3 (2004), 1–45.

Slater, Jerome. "Lost Opportunities for Peace in the Arab-Israeli Conflict: Israel and Syria, 1948–2001." *International Security* 27:1 (2002), 79–106.

Soffer, Aron. *Rivers of Fire: The Conflict Over Water in the Middle East.* Lantham, MD: Rowman & Littlefield, 1999.

Sosland, Jeffrey. "The Domestic-International Confluence: The Challenge of Israel's Water Problems." In *Review Essays in Israel Studies,* edited by Laura Zittrain Eisenberg and Neil Caplan, 221–238. Albany: State University of New York Press, 2000.

Sosland, Jeffrey. "Understanding Environmental Security: Water Scarcity, the 1980s' Palestinian Uprising, and Implications for Peace." In *Redefining Security in the Middle East,* edited by Tami Amanda Jacoby and Brent Sasley, 105–127. New York: University of Manchester Press, 2002.

Starr, Joyce. "Water Wars." *Foreign Policy* 82 (1991): 17–36.

Starr, Joyce. *Covenant over Middle Eastern Waters: Key to World Survival.* New York: Henry Holt, 1995.

Stevens, Georgina. *Jordan River Partition.* Stanford: Hoover Institute, 1965.

Taubenblatt, Selig. "The Jordan River Basin Water Dilemma: A Challenge for the 1990's." In *The Politics of Scarcity: Water in the Middle East,* edited by Joyce Starr and Daniel Stroll. Boulder: Westview Press, 1988.

Tessler, Mark. *A History of the Israeli-Palestinian Conflict.* Bloomington: Indiana University Press, 1994.

Walt, Stephen. *The Origins of Alliances.* Ithaca: Cornell University Press, 1987 and 1990.

Waltz, Kenneth. *Theory of International Politics.* New York: McGraw-Hill, 1979.

Wishart, David. "An Economic Approach to Understanding Jordan Valley Water Disputes." *Middle East Review* 21:4 (1989), 45–53.

Wolf, Aaron. *Hydropolitics Along the Jordan River.* New York: United Nations University Press, 1995.

Wolf, Aaron. "Conflict and Cooperation Along International Waterways." *Water Policy* 1:8 (1998): 251–265.

Index

Abbas, Mohammed (or Abu Mazen), 171
> *See* also Beilin, Yossi

Abdullah, 32–33, 40, 56–57, 75

Abdullah II, 16, 180, 182

Adasiya, 28, 54, 68, 102, 105, 110, 117, 131, 177, 224n114, 251n254
> *See* also Point 121; Yarmouk forum

agriculture
> in Gaza, 152–153
> in Israel, 12, 25–26, 57, 70, 81, 146–147, 149, 152, 154–155, 163, 206
> in Jordan, 25, 99, 103, 177
> in multilaterals, 196
> in Palestinians, 167, 170, 173
> in Syria, 132
> in West Bank, 144, 146–147, 149, 152, 157, 163, 237n9, 254n18
> *See also* food security

Ala, Abu (Ahmad Quray), 165

Allon Plan, 147

Allon, Yigal, 104

Alon, Moshe, 104

Alpha plan, 47–49, 60, 205, 226n149

Anderson, Robert B., 48–49

Aoun, Michel, 108

Aqaba, 179

Arab diversion plan, 77–84

Arab-Israeli War
> of 1948, 25, 98, 186, 220n35

of 1956 (Suez), 32, 34, 49, 63, 65, 85
of 1967, 6, 17, 60, 64, 77–92, 93, 97, 120, 142

Arab-Israeli conflict, 203, 209, 211
> from 1948–1956, 32, 34–35, 37, 41, 46–49, 56, 59
> from 1956–1967, 63, 65, 78, 84, 89–90
> from 1967–2006, 93, 160

Arab League, 42, 44, 46, 49, 60, 61, 77, 79, 226n135, 229n13

Arafat, Yasser, 162–163, 171

Armitage, Richard, 134–136, 264n76

al-Asad, Bashar, 182

al-Asad, Hafez, 14, 99, 102–103, 108, 132, 140, 181–182, 185, 187, 250n231

Aswan Dam, 42, 47–49

Atallah, Isa, 171

Baath party, 14, 63, 76, 187

Baker, Alan, 130

Baker and Harza. *See* Harza

Baker, James, 134, 160, 191–192

Bani Hani, Mohammad, 17, 128–131, 133, 137, 248n201, 249n220, 251n239

Barak, Ehud, 171, 187–188

Baxter Report, 104, 240n49, 241n76

Begin, Menachem, 106–107, 155–156, 254n13

SUNY series in Global Politics
James N. Rosenau, editor

American Patriotism in a Global Society—Betty Jean Craige

The Political Discourse of Anarchy: A Disciplinary History of International Relations—Brian C. Schmidt

Power and Ideas: North-South Politics of Intellectual Property and Antitrust—Susan K. Sell

From Pirates to Drug Lords: The Post–Cold War Caribbean Security Environment—Michael C. Desch, Jorge I. Dominguez, and Andres Serbin (eds.)

Collective Conflict Management and Changing World Politics—Joseph Lepgold and Thomas G. Weiss (eds.)

Zones of Peace in the Third World: South America and West Africa in Comparative Perspective—Arie M. Kacowicz

Private Authority and International Affairs—A. Claire Cutler, Virginia Haufler, and Tony Porter (eds.)

Harmonizing Europe: Nation-States within the Common Market—Francesco G. Duina

Economic Interdependence in Ukrainian-Russian Relations—Paul J. D'Anieri

Leapfrogging Development? The Political Economy of Telecommunications Restructuring—J. P. Singh

States, Firms, and Power: Successful Sanctions in United States Foreign Policy—George e. Shambaugh

Approaches to Global Governance Theory—Martin Hewson and Timothy J. Sinclair (eds.)

After Authority: War, Peace, and Global Politics in the Twenty-First Century—Ronnie D. Lipschutz

Pondering Postinternationalism: A Paradigm for the Twenty-First Century?—Heidi H. Hobbs (ed.)

Globalization, Security, and the Nation State: Paradigms in Transition—Ersel Aydinli and James N. Rosenau (eds.)

Identity and Institutions: Conflict Reduction in Divided Societies—Neal G. Jesse and Kristen P. Williams

Globalizing Interests: Pressure Groups and Denationalization—Michael Zürn (ed., with assistance from Gregor Walter)

International Regimes for the Final Frontier—M. J. Peterson

Ozone Depletion and Climate Change: Constructing A Global Response—Matthew J. Hoffmann

States of Liberalization: Redefining the Public Sector in Integrated Europe—Mitchell P. Smith

Mediating Globalization: Domestic Institutions and Industrial Policies in the United States and Britain—Andrew P. Cortell

The Multi-Governance of Water: Four Case Studies—Matthias Finger, Ludivine Tamiotti, and Jeremy Allouche, eds.

Building Trust: Overcoming Suspicion in International Conflict—Aaron M. Hoffman

Global Capitalism, Democarcy, and Civil-Military Relations in Colombia—Williams Avilés

Complexity in World Politics: Concepts and Methods of a New Paradigm—Neil E. Harrison

Technology and International Transformation: The Railroad, the Atom Bomb, and the Politics of Technological Transformation—Geoffrey L. Herrera

The Perils and Promise of Global Transparency: Why the Information Revolution May Not Lead to Security, Democracy, or Peace—Kristin M. Lord

Well-Oiled Diplomacy: Strategic Manipulation and Russia's Energy Statecraft in Eurasia—Adam N. Stulberg

Global Liberalism and Political Order: Towards a New Grand Compromise?—Steven Bernstein and Louis W. Pauly, eds.

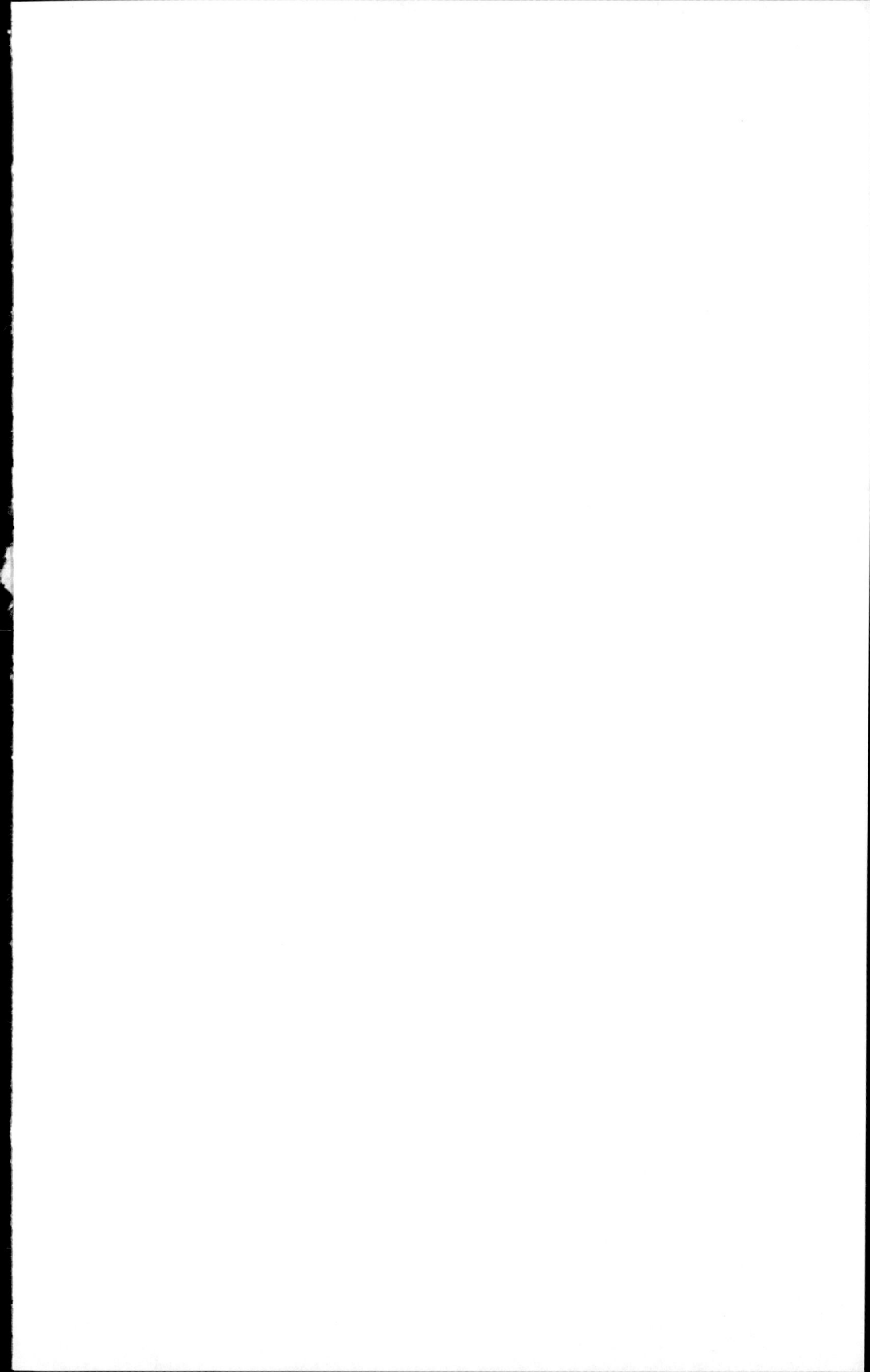

www.ingramcontent.com/pod-product-compliance
Lightning Source LLC
Chambersburg PA
CBHW030642270326
41929CB00007B/172